BLUE GUIDES

D1490489

Ivette

Please write in with your comments, suggestions and corrections for the next edition of the Blue Guide. Writers of the most helpful letters will be awarded a free Blue Guide of their choice.

BLUE GUIDE

PRAGUE

Jasper Tilbury

A&C Black • London
WW Norton • New York

Second edition 2004
Published by A&C Black Publishers Limited
37 Soho Square, London W1D 3QZ

© Jasper Tilbury 2004

First edition 1999, by Michael Jacobs

Maps and plans drawn by The Mapping Company Ltd and Robert Smith © A&C Black
Illustrations © Jim Urquhart
'Blue Guides' is a registered trade mark

A CIP catalogue record of this book is available from the British Library

ISBN 0–7136–6780–X

Published in the United States of America by
WW Norton and Company, Inc
500 Fifth Avenue, New York, NY 10110

Published simultaneously in Canada by
Penguin Books Canada Limited
10 Alcorn Avenue, Toronto, Ontario M4V 3B2

ISBN 0–393–32587–3 USA

The author and the publishers have done their best to ensure the accuracy of all the information in Blue Guide Prague; however, they can accept no responsibility for any loss, injury
or inconvenience sustained by any traveller as a result of information or advice contained
in the guide.

Jasper Tilbury graduated in modern history from the University of St Andrews. He spent
the 1990s in Central Europe, and is the author of Blue Guide Kraków and Blue Guide
Poland. He currently lives in London, where he works as a writer, editor and translator.

Cover pictures. Top: sculptural detail in Wenceslas Square. Bottom: on the Charles Bridge at
dawn, looking east towards Staré Město. Both pictures are the copyright © of Joe Cornish.
Frontispiece: Prague from the riverside by Jim Urquhart.

A&C Black uses paper produced with elemental chlorine-free pulp, harvested from managed
sustainable forests.

Printed and bound in Israel by M.G.I. Print.

Contents

Maps and plans

Introduction

Prague, capital of the Czech Republic, straddles the Vltava River, its western half spread over wooded hills rising up to the 'Hrad', or castle, which dominates the city's skyline. To the east, across the famous Charles Bridge, extends the Old Town, one of the five historic townships, whose focal point is the medieval Old Town Square. Unlike so many Central European cities, Prague was spared destruction during the Second World War, and its perfectly-preserved centre at times seems more akin to a giant, fantastical film set than a real place inhabited by real people. It is a city of undeniable and haunting beauty, one that has been a constant source of inspiration to the many great writers and artists to have lived here. Looking down over the red rooftops and Gothic spires from the top of Petřín Hill, Milan Kundera was even moved to call it 'the most beautiful city in the world'.

The dramatic opening up of Prague after the fall of Communism in 1989 has helped to emphasise that this city has a cultural complexity virtually unrivalled for a place of its size. Widespread restoration, the renewal of grand turn-of-the-last-century hotels and cafés, and promotional campaigns stressing Prague's links with Mozart and Mucha may have somewhat cheapened its appeal, but they have shown as well how this city, so rich in medieval and Renaissance monuments, is a place that has contributed enormously to the flowering of the Baroque, Rococo and Art Nouveau.

'Tourist Prague' is essentially limited to the old coronation route used by Bohemian monarchs that leads up from the Old Town to the castle, and which is today lined with over-restored buildings with an artificial, dolls-house appearance. Yet there is much more to Prague than this, and visitors who wish to get a truer flavour of the city will need to venture beyond the over-prettified tourist areas. The suburb of Holešovice, for instance, is home to the Trade Fair Palace, the city's best modern-art gallery, which has done much to highlight both the sheer originality of Czech art between the wars and the stunning beauty of Functionalist architecture in its pioneering phase.

From the tourist's point of view, the changes since 1989 cannot be said to have been entirely beneficial. The great improvements in standards of food and accommodation have to be set against the transformation of much of Central Prague into a congested Disneyland, with long queues preventing easy access to the Charles Bridge and other important sites. Some visitors might be shocked by the way in which charming streets like Karlova have been turned into a mass of souvenir shops, exchange offices and neon-lit fast-food establishments; others, perhaps recalling the earthy and atmospheric beer-halls so evocatively described by the writer Bohumil Hrabal, will surely be dismayed to find many of them transformed into crude and soulless tourist traps.

Yet no amount of commercialisation will ever fully nullify Prague's magical appeal. It remains one of Europe's most captivating cities, and no doubt will continue to inspire superlatives and effusive prose for years to come. Czech culture has, over the centuries, begotten names with which every Anglo-Saxon visitor will be familiar—from Kafka and Havel to 'good king Wenceslas' and Budweiser beer—but Czech cultural history remains essentially unknown outside the country. The aim of this Guide is to go some way towards bridging that gap; to instil a greater knowledge of, and enthusiasm for, Czech art, architecture, literature and music among a Western readership.

Acknowledgements

Several people were directly involved in the publication of this Guide. First and foremost, I wish to thank Gemma Davies and all the staff at A&C Black for their moral support and thorough editorial work. I am also indebted to the staff of the Małopolska School of Public Administration in Kraków, who, as is now customary, gave me free and unlimited use of their state-of-the-art office equipment during the writing of this book. A special word of gratitude is due to Michael Jacobs, author of the first edition, whose great insight and erudition prepared much of the groundwork and made my task that much easier. Many thanks also to Leila McAlister for providing me with several useful contacts, to Clare Wigfall for contributing her insider's knowledge on Prague art galleries, and to my fixer Tomáš Veselý for his indispensable assistance in all matters Czech. Last but not least, I wish to thank Olga Červinková, who was the perfect companion on many memorable evenings in the city.

In keeping with the new style of the Blue Guides, this second edition of Blue Guide Prague contains more practical information than before, including extensive hotel, restaurant, bar and café listings. The author has taken every effort to ensure that this information is accurate, but the pace of change in Prague inevitably means that some of it will already be outdated. Any comments or suggestions are most welcome.

How to use the Guide

The main text of this Guide is structured around eight self-contained walks. Four of these describe the historic centre of Prague, while a further four venture out into the city's suburbs. The final chapter covers some popular day excursions.

One confusing anomaly of the Czech Republic is the **dual numbering** of all buildings. In this Guide, the blue-and-white numbers are used.

Prices are given in euro (€) and/or Czech crowns (Kč)

Stars have been used in this Guide to denote places or buildings of special interest. Those prefixed by two stars are considered to be of particular importance.

Times follow the 24-hour clock, as is conventional in the Czech Republic.

Highlights

Prague is divided into ten postal districts, the sights of interest to tourists being mainly to be found in Praha 1, which extends on either side of the Vltava River and comprises the five historical townships of Staré Město (Old Town), Malá Strana (Little Quarter), Hradčany (Castle District), Nové Město (New Town) and the former Jewish enclave within Staré Město known as Josefov. Although this forms a relatively small area that is easily manageable on foot, the wealth of monuments to be seen within is such that at least one week is needed to begin to do it justice. Those with only two or three days to spare should devote their attention largely to the streets and monuments along the so-called Royal Route, notably the Powder Gate, Celetná Street, Old Town Square, Karlova Street, Charles Bridge, St Nicholas in the Little Quarter, Nerudova Street and Prague Castle; additional nearby sights that should certainly not be missed are the Jewish Museum in Josefov, the Týn Church, Municipal House, National Theatre, Loreto shrine, Strahov Monastery, gardens of Malá Strana, and the National Gallery's collections in the Šternberg Palace and Convent of St Agnes.

PRACTICAL INFORMATION

 ## Planning your trip

When to go

Prague's climate is typically continental, with warm summers and cold winters, and the best time to visit is either in spring or autumn. Spring can sometimes not show at all, but is the most attractive season when it does. Average temperatures in April are between 3 and 12°C and in May between 8 and 17°C. Summer, when the average temperature is between 12 and 23°C, sees Prague abandoned to tourists and very crowded; the air can be hot and humid, with thundery showers. Autumn is a close contender with spring for prettiness, with crisp air, clear skies and an average temperature in September and October between 5 and 17°C. Winter is long, cold and grey, and many shops and restaurants are shut, but the romance of Christmas helps break it up. When it snows, Prague is charming, but the smog from coal heating is often bad. Average winter temperatures are between -4 and 3°C.

National tourist boards

UK Czech Tourist Authority (www.tourist-offices.org.uk/Czech_Republic), Suite 29–31, 2nd Floor, Morley House, 320 Regent Street, London W1B 3BG, ☎ 020 7631 0427, 🖷 020 7631 0419 (open Mon–Fri 10.00–18.00). The Authority will send out free of charge tourist brochures on all regions in the Czech Republic, national accommodation details, road maps and advice for motorists, lists of campsites, listings of cultural events in Prague and other regions as well as information on tour operators and travel agents from the UK to the Czech Republic (send a stamped and self-addressed envelope).
Czech Centre London (www.czechcentre.org.uk), 13 Harley Street, London W1G 9QG, ☎ 020 7307 5180, 🖷 020 7323 3709 (open Tues–Fri 10.00–18.00). Affiliated to the Czech Ministry of Foreign Affairs, the Centre provides information to tourists and businesspeople and organises cultural events.
US Czech Center New York (www.czechcenter.com), 1109 Madison Avenue, New York, NY 10028, ☎ 212 288 0830, 🖷 212 288 0971 (open Tues–Wed, Fri 09.00–17.00, Thurs 09.00–19.00). The Centre has information on a variety of subjects.
Canada Czech Tourist Authority, P.O. Box 198, Exchange Tower, 2 First Canadian Place, 14th Floor, Toronto, Ontario M5X 1A6, ☎ 416 367 3432, 🖷 (416) 367 3492.

When planning your trip, the following **websites** have plenty of information on every aspect of life in Prague:
The Czech Tourism Pages, www.czech-tourism.com
The Czech Info Centre, www.muselik.com
Welcome to the Czech Republic, www.czech.cz

Tour operators

UK

Czechbook Agency (www.czechbook.com), Jopes Mill, Trebrownbridge, Cornwall PL14 3PX, ☎/🖷 01503 240 629. A family-run agency specialising in accommodation all over the Czech Republic, but not travel.

Czech and Slovak Tourist Centre (www.czechtravel.co.uk), 16 Frognal Parade, Finchley Road, London NW3 5HG, ☎ (020) 7794 3263, 🖷 020 7794 3265; free call: 0800 026 79432 (open Mon–Fri 10.00–18.00). A tour operator for the whole Czech Republic, with information on everything except timetables for trains, which change constantly. It can help you with many enquiries, whether it be printing opera tickets or organising your hen night.

Czech Travel Ltd (www.czechtravel.freeuk.com), 16 Albemarle Gardens, Braintree, Essex CM7 9UQ, ☎ 01376 560592/3, 🖷 01376 560593. Specialist in flights and accommodation.

Čedok Travel Ltd (www.cedok.co.uk), Suite 22–23, 5th Floor, Morley House, 314–322 Regent Street, London W1B 3BG, ☎ 020 7580 3778, 🖷 020 7580 3779. The former state travel agency, now privatised, offers package deals, flights, accommodation, car hire and much else.

Martin Randall Travel (www.martinrandall.com), Voysey House, Barley Mow Passage, Chiswick, London W4 4GF, ☎ 020 8742 3355, 🖷 020 8742 7766. Upmarket art and architecture tours.

US

Abercrombie & Kent (www.abercrombiekent.com), 1520 Kensington Road, Suite 212, Oak Brook, Illinois, 60523–2156, ☎ 630 954 2944, 🖷 630 954 3324. Deluxe tours.

Travcoa (www.travcoa.com), 2424 SE Bristol Street, Suite 310, Newport Beach, CA 92660, ☎ 949 476 2800, 🖷 949 476 2538. Worldwide luxury tours.

Maupintour (www.maupintour.com), 10650 W. Charleston Blvd, Summerlin, NV 89135, ☎ 800 255 4266, 🖷 702 260 3787. Escorted and independent Central European tours.

Passports and formalities

Entry regulations are set to change when the Czech Republic joins the European Union in May 2004, so it is best to visit the Czech Ministry of Foreign Affairs' website (www.mzv.cz) before you leave for up-to-date information. At the time of writing, visitors from the US, New Zealand, the EU and most other European countries do not need a visa to enter the Czech Republic but do need a valid passport with six months to spare by the end of the visit. Visas are required of Canadian and Australian citizens, and these must be arranged at a Czech Embassy outside the Czech Republic. Visas are no longer obtainable at border crossings.

British nationals can stay for up to 180 days; Americans, New Zealanders, Irish, and other EU nationals for up to 90 days; Australians and Canadians for up to 30 days. If you wish to stay longer than your visa or visa-free period allows, you can apply to the Foreigners' Police (*Cizinecká policie*) at Olšanská 2, Žižkov, Prague 3, ☎ 261 441 336, for an extension, but in practice these are very difficult to obtain. Many people avoid the issue by leaving the country for a few days. If you do this, make sure you get your passport stamped.

Technically you are meant to register with the local police within 30 days of arrival in Prague—hotels will do this for you—but many visitors do not bother.

Czech embassies abroad

Australia, 169 Military Road, Dover Heights 2030, Sydney, NSW, ☎ 02 9371 8887 (visas), ▤ 9371 9635.

Canada, 251 Cooper Street, Ottawa, Ontario, K2P 0G2, ☎ 613 562 3875, ▤ 613 562 3878.

Ireland, 57 Northumberland Road, Ballsbridge, Dublin 4, ☎ 01 668 1135, ▤ 01 668 1660.

New Zealand, 48 Hair Street, Wainuiomata, ☎ 04 939 1610, ▤ 04 564 9022.

UK, 26 Kensington Palace Gardens, London W8 4QY, ☎ 020 7243 1115, ▤ 020 7727 9654, visas 020 7243 7915.

US, 3900 Spring of Freedom St, NW, Washington DC 20008, ☎ 202 274 9100, ▤ 202 966 8540.

Foreign embassies in Prague

Australian Trade Commission and Honorary Consulate, Klimentská 10, Prague 1, ☎ 296 578 350, ▤ 296 578 352. Metro Náměstí Republiky. Open Mon–Fri 08.30–13.00 and 14.00–17.00.

British Embassy, Thunovská 14, Prague 1, ☎ 257 402 111, ▤ 257 402 296. Metro Malostranská. Open Mon–Fri 08.30–12.00.

Canadian Embassy, Muchova 6, Prague 6, ☎ 272 101 800, ▤ 272 101 890. Metro Hradčanská. Open 08.30–12.00 and 14.00–16.30.

Irish Embassy, Tržiště 13, Prague 1, ☎ 257 530 061. Metro Malostranská. Open Mon–Fri 09.00–12.30.

US Embassy, Tržiště 15, Prague 1, ☎ 257 530 663, ▤ 257 534 028. Metro Malostranská. Open Mon–Fri 09.00–12.00.

Customs

For the latest import and export limits on alcohol and tobacco, visit the Czech Ministry of Foreign Affairs' website (www.mzv.cz). To export an antique you need to obtain an official certificate from a recognised art gallery or museum (which may have already been arranged by the dealer). To find out if an object is an antique or not, contact the curator at the National Museum in Prague: ☎ 224 497 111. Visitors entering the country must be able to prove access to at least 6000Kč (€190); this rule is unlikely to be enforced unless you look very shabby. There are no restrictions on the import or export of Czech currency, but exported amounts in excess of 350,000Kč need to be declared at Customs. VAT refunds apply to items worth more than 2500Kč.

Currency and banks

Credit cards such as Visa, Mastercard and Amex are now widely accepted in hotels, restaurants and shops, and there are plenty of ATMs in the city centre if you need to withdraw cash on a debit card. Most banks will give cash advances on credit cards. If you intend to take travellers' cheques for extra security, **Thomas Cook** (Národní 28; ☎ 221 105 371) and **American Express** (Václavské náměstí 56; ☎ 222 800 111) are the best known. In case of loss or theft of a credit card, you should immediately stop the card by phoning your bank's emergency number. Visa and Mastercard holders can also call the Komerční Banka's emergency number: 224 248 110.

The Czech crown is fully convertible. Commission at banks (2%) is less than at the exchange bureaux (up to 6%), but the queues are longer and the opening times less flexible. It may be a good idea to change some money before you arrive to avoid delays at the airport exchange counter (open 24 hours), though there are ATMs at the airport as well.

Accommodation will take the largest chunk out of your money; otherwise everything is still cheap, though prices are creeping up. You should expect to spend about €45 a day. This assumes you want to eat well and are not roughing it. You can easily double this if splashing out.

The **Czech crown** (*koruna česká* or Kč) is made up of 100 *haléřů* (h). Coins come in 10h, 20h, 50h, 1Kč, 2Kč, 5Kč, 10Kč, 20Kč and 50Kč. Notes come in 20, 50, 100, 500, 1000, 2000 and 5000Kč denominations. There are about 45Kč to £1 sterling and 32Kč to €1 (January 2004).

Health and insurance

Healthcare in Prague is not quite up to Western standards, but is improving all the time. There are no major health risks in the Czech Republic and no vaccinations are needed. The tap water is safe to drink, but does not taste great; mineral water is easily obtained in shops, restaurants and hotels.

Pharmacies (*lékárna*) are open until about 18.00 on weekdays. Pharmacies that are open 24 hours a day are listed in Yellow Pages (*Zlaté stránky*) under 'Lékárny s nepřetržitou pohotovostní službou'. There are 24-hour pharmacies at Belgická 37, Prague 2, and Štefánikova 6, Prague 5.

Britain (but not the US) has a reciprocal agreement with the Czech Republic that entitles British citizens to free medical and dental care in case of accidents or emergencies. **24-hour emergency medical care** is provided at the Na Homolce hospital (www.homolka.cz), Roentgenova 2, Prague 5, ☎ 257 271 111. Most of the doctors speak English and/or German. For **dental emergencies**, ☎ 224 946 981. **Medical insurance** is a good idea wherever you have come from, as the costs are minimal compared to the potential benefits; when you do receive treatment, do not forget to ask for proof of any expenses.

There are several private clinics in Prague offering emergency and general healthcare services. One of the best is **Canadian Medical Care** (www.cmc.praha.cz), Veleslavínská 1, Prague 6, ☎ 235 360 133 (724 300 301 after hours). Open Mon, Wed, Fri 08.00–18.00, Tues, Thur 08.00–20.00.

Getting there

By air

The cheapest flights can be bought from specialist agents, but these allow little flexibility, and the same applies to charter flights. Fares always depend on the season—the high season is the summer and around Christmas and Easter, and weekend flights cost more than those in mid-week. The cheapest flights are Apex tickets, but must be booked 21 days before your departure, and you must spend at least seven days abroad. Super Apex tickets limit your stay to between 7 and 21 days. Most cheap fares require you to spend a Saturday in the Czech Republic. If you can't find a cheap direct flight, another option is to fly to Vienna or Berlin and continue your journey by train (approximately 5 hours).

From the UK
The flight time is approximately two hours.
British Airways (www.ba.com), ☎ 0870 850 9850, flies to Prague from London Heathrow at least once a day.
bmibaby (www.bmibaby.com), ☎ 0870 264 2229, has flights from Cardiff, East Midlands, Manchester and Teesside. Check the website for flight days and times.
Czech Airlines (www.czechairlines.com), ☎ 0870 444 3747, departs from London Heathrow, London Stansted, Manchester, Birmingham and Edinburgh.
easyJet (www.easyjet.com), ☎ 0871 750 0100 has regular flights from Stansted.
flybe (www2.flybe.com), bookings ☎ 0871 700 0535, general information ☎ 0906 209 0005 (calls cost £1 a minute), with flights from Southampton.
Jet2 (www.jet2.com), ☎ 0870 737 8282, flies from Leeds Bradford.

From Ireland
Czech Airlines (www.czechairlines.com), ☎ (1) 814 4626 operates direct flights from Dublin and Cork to Prague; these tend to be expensive so it may be better to travel via London.

From the USA and Canada
To those travelling from the US, all the major airlines offer plenty of flights from plenty of airports, but **Czech Airlines** (ČSA), ☎ (800) 223 2365 (www.czechairlines.com), is the only non-stop carrier from the States, departing from New York. All others make stopovers in Europe. Flights from New York take approximately 9 hours. ČSA also flies direct to Prague from Canada, ☎ (514) 844 4200, with daily flights from Montreal in the summer.

On arrival
Prague's airport, Ruzyně (☎ 220 113 314 for arrival and departure information), was built by BAA and is fairly modern. The airport is about 20km northwest of the centre of Prague, and is only served by buses, although some hotels will collect you if you book ahead. The **express airport bus** is quick and cheap; it goes to náměstí Republiky and Revoluční every half hour between 08.00 and 20.00. Čedaz, a private company, goes to náměstí Republiky and the Dejvická metro station (the last station on the green line A), and runs every hour from 05.00–22.00.

Three **local buses** go from outside the arrivals hall to metro stations every 20 minutes between 05.00 and 24.00. No. 179 goes to Metro Nové Butovice (yellow line B); No. 108 goes to Metro Hradčanská (green line A); No. 119 goes to Metro Dejvická (green line A). You can buy tickets from the ticket machines or information desk inside the arrivals hall.

Special airport **taxis** (Airport Cars)—usually white limousines—also operate a service. Normal taxis are not allowed to park at the airport. The airport taxi will cost about €12 (400Kč) if your hotel is in the centre of Prague, and about €18 (600Kč) if it is on the further side of town. The company operates a set-price system, so you are less likely to be ripped off.

By rail

From London's Waterloo Station the train journey takes approximately 22 hours, via the Eurostar to Brussels, then Cologne and Frankfurt. The train arrives at Hlavní nádraží, which is the city's main international railway station.

The cheapest Eurostar tickets require that you are away over a Saturday night. For the second part of the journey (Brussels–Prague) it is always worth getting at least a couchette, as this provides much greater comfort and adds only €20 to the total fare; sleepers are about three times more expensive.

Taking the train only pays if you are under 26 or over 60, as a standard ticket costs more than an Apex flight, although unlimited stopovers are allowed. Inter-Rail passes are valid in the Czech Republic and are a good option if you qualify.

Train tickets from the UK to Prague can be purchased from several agencies, including **European Rail** (www.europeanrail.com), ☎ (020) 7387 0444, and **Rail Europe** (www.raileurope.co.uk), ☎ (0870) 584 8848. **Eurostar** (www.eurostar.com), ☎ (020) 7922 6180, can only book your journey as far as Brussels.

On arrival

Prague's central station (Hlavní nádraží) is located on red line C of the metro and is 5 minutes' walk from Wenceslas Square. It has all the usual facilities, including an accommodation agency (AVE), bureau de change, left-luggage lockers, and a rail information office with English-speaking staff (☎ 224 224 200). The other international rail station in Prague is nádraží Holešovice, also on red line C. For train and bus timetables within the Czech Republic, visit www.idos.cz.

By coach

This is the cheapest way of getting to Prague, but also the most exhausting. **Eurolines** (www.eurolines.co.uk), ☎ (0870) 580 8080, a branch of National Express, departs from London's Victoria Coach Station almost every day and takes about 23 hours. The Czech-run **Kingscourt Express** (www.kce.cz), ☎ (020) 8673 7500, leaves on Tues, Wed, Sat and Sun at 19.00 and arrives in Prague 18 hours later. During the high season (June to September) there are six departures a week (every day except Mon). All coaches arrive at the Florenc station.

On arrival

Prague's main coach station is Florenc, a grim and dirty place with few facilities to speak of. It's on red line C and yellow line B of the metro.

By car

The drive from the UK to Prague takes at least 18 hours, without an overnight stop. Paris to Prague is 1078km (670 miles), Brussels to Prague is 925km (575 miles) and Geneva to Prague is 950km (590 miles). You may have to pay motorway tolls in certain European countries, and you must have an authorisation sticker to drive on motorways in the Czech Republic (see Driving, p 23). From Calais/Dunkirk, follow signs to Lille, Brussels, Cologne, Frankfurt and Nuremberg. You can enter the Czech Republic at the Waidhaus–Rozadov border crossing. The other border crossing is the Reitzanhain–Pohraniční, which you reach by following signs to Lille, Brussels, Cologne, Hessen via Erfurt and Chemnitz.

Where to stay

Finding a room used to be quite a challenge in Prague. Hotels were poor compared to those in the West—you could easily find yourself in a high-rise—and expensive. Service and accommodation have vastly improved now that entrepreneurs have finished their renovation schemes, and a law has been passed that prohibits charging foreigners more than locals. That said, accommodation is still over-priced and will be the most expensive part of your stay. Prague caters well to rich businesspeople and penniless backpackers, but visitors who fall between these two price categories may struggle to find suitable accommodation.

Hotels should always be booked ahead; most places are full months in advance between April and September. Most hotels now have websites and English-speaking staff, so you can easily book direct (see the listings below for addresses and telephone numbers) or, alternatively, through British- and US-based agencies before arrival (see Tour Operators, p 10).

Hotel charges

For a double room with breakfast in a top-end hotel or pension you should expect to pay upwards of €180 per night; the price for a similar room in a bottom-end hotel starts at around €70. Hotels tend to charge per room, not per person; however, some will offer discounts for single occupancy of double rooms, and virtually all will offer discounts to tour groups. If you are staying a while, say two weeks, you can get better deals; in off-season prices fall dramatically, so winter breaks may be an attractive option. For stays longer than a month, you might consider renting an apartment through a lettings agency such as **Golgot**, Pod stanicí 7, ☎ +420 271 961 582, 📠 +420 271 961 003 (www.golgot.cz/property).

Most hotels have bars and restaurants and breakfast is included in the price of the room; however, you should confirm this when making your reservation. Check-out time is usually 12.00, but you will normally be allowed to leave your luggage at reception if required. Telephone calls from hotels are expensive, and it is better to use a public card phone (available at kiosks and post offices). Many hotels have extra beds, which can be put into rooms so that children can be with their parents. Some hotels will charge for this, others not. For English-speaking babysitters, a reputable agency is **Tetty**, Muchova 11, ☎ +420 233 340 766 (www.tetty.cz).

Recommended hotels and pensions

The listed prices are for the cheapest double room with bathroom in high season. **Expensive**: over €180; **moderate**: €100–180; **inexpensive**: €70–100.

Staré Město and Josefov
Expensive
Apostolic Residence, Staroměstské náměstí 25, ☎ +420 221 632 222, 📠 +420 221 632 204 (www.prague-residence.cz). Charming Baroque building on the Old Town Square, with views of the Astronomical Clock (see p 98). Only one double room and two apartments, all filled with tasteful antique furniture. Booking essential. €190.

Casa Marcello, Řásnovka 783, ☎ +420 222 310 260, +420 222 311 230, ▤ +420 222 313 323 (www.casa-marcello.cz). Atmospheric hotel housed in a building of 13C origin once used as a dormitory by the nuns of the adjoining St Agnes Convent (see p 117). 32 rooms. €230.

Four Seasons, Veleslavínova 2a, ☎ +420 221 427 000, ▤ 420 221 426 000 (www.fourseasons.com). Luxury modern hotel nestled on the banks of the Vltava River. A combination of three historic buildings, with special suites available in the Baroque part. Impressive views of the Charles Bridge and Prague Castle from the hotel restaurant. 162 rooms. €280.

Josef, Rybná 20, ☎ +420 221 700 111, ▤ +420 221 700 999 (www.hoteljosef.com). Modern hotel designed by London-based architect Eva Jiřičná, winner of an AIA Excellence in Design Award 2003. Bright, airy and minimalist interiors. 110 rooms, most facing the summer garden. €247.

Paříž, U Obecního domu 1, ☎ +420 222 195 666, ▤ +420 224 225 475 (www.hotel-pariz.cz). Turn-of-the-last-century elegance reinterpreted for the modern age. Adjacent to Prague's most famous Art Nouveau building—the Municipal House (see p 88). 94 rooms. €320.

U Prince, Staroměstské náměstí 29, ☎ +420 224 213 807, ▤ +420 224 213 807 (www.hoteluprince.cz). A 12C building given a complete makeover in 2001. Spacious and beautifully furnished rooms whose ambience is marred only by the noise coming from the square. Seafood restaurant and roof terrace. 24 rooms. €193.

Moderate

Betlem Club, Betlémské náměstí 9, ☎ +420 222 221 574, ▤ +420 222 220 580 (www.betlemclub.cz). The 13C cellar bar is the most appealing interior feature of this tackily furnished if well-situated hotel. 21 rooms. €122.

Černý Slon, Týnská 1, ☎ +420 222 321 521, ▤ +420 222 310 351 (www.hotelcernyslon.cz). A UNESCO-listed Gothic building with views of the Týn Church (see p 94). Recently renovated to a high standard, with a cellar bar and restaurant offering fine Moravian wines. 16 rooms. €155.

Intercontinental, náměstí Curieových 43/5, ☎ +420 296 631 111, ▤ +420 224 811 216 (www.prague.intercontinental.com). Rightly described as a blight on the Prague skyline, and generally packed with tour groups, but with an unsurpassed location at the very centre of the city. Riverside views. 373 rooms. €159.

U Klenotníka, Rytířská 3, ☎ +420 224 211 699, ▤ +420 224 221 025 (www.uklenotnika.cz). Despite the awful décor, this medieval town house is unbeatable value for its central location. 11 rooms. €105.

Ungelt, Malá Štupartská 1, ☎ + 420 224 828 686, ▤ + 420 224 828 181 (www.ungelt.cz). Medieval building named after the courtyard on which it stands. Ten apartments sleeping up to four people. Booking essential. €160.

U Zlaté Studny, Karlova 3, ☎ +420 222 220 262, ▤ +420 222 220 262 (www.uzlatestudny.cz). This impressive Renaissance house situated on the 'Royal Route' retains some original painted wooden ceilings and a 16C Gothic cellar; the furnishings, though, are largely replicas. Only four suites and two doubles, so booking is essential. €150.

Inexpensive

Penzion Unitas, Bartolomějská 9, ☎ +420 224 221 802, ▤ +420 224 217 555 (www.unitas.cz). Cheap whitewashed cells with iron doors in a former convent once used for putting up detainees of the secret police, including Václav Havel (he stayed in the now much-sought-after Room P6). The premises are leased out by the Sisters of Mercy, who show little mercy to those who smoke, drink or stay up later than 1 o'clock at night. Higher-standard rooms are available on the ground floor and in the nearby Cloister Inn (Konviktská 14), which is run by the same management. €45.

U Krále Jiřího, Liliová 10, ☎ +420 222 220 925, 🖷 +420 224 248 797 (www.kinggeorge.cz). Basic but clean and excellently located bed and breakfast. 12 rooms. €97.

U Medvídků, Na Perštýně 7, ☎ +420 224 211 916, 🖷 +420 224 220 930 (www.umedvidku.cz). No-frills accommodation above a famous old beer hall of the same name (see p 35). Cheap, clean, central. All things considered, you could do a lot worse in the Old Town. 32 rooms. €94.

U Zlatého Stromu, Karlova 6, ☎ +420 222 220 441, 🖷 +420 222 220 441 (www.zlatystrom.cz). 21 miniscule rooms behind an attractive gabled façade on the 'Royal Route'. Basement disco. €85.

Malá Strana and Hradčany
Expensive

Best Western Kampa, Všehrdova 16, ☎ +420 257 404 444, 🖷 +420 257 404 333 (www.bestwestern-ce.com/kampa). Located in a quiet street just below Petřín Hill, the Kampa has been recently redecorated in medieval-armoury style, complete with swords and shields stuck on the walls and a 'Knight's Hall' restaurant with summer garden. 84 rooms. €181.

Pod Věží, Mostecká 2, ☎ +420 257 532 041, 🖷 +420 257 532 069 (www.podvezi.com). Soberly decorated bedrooms in a wonderfully situated Baroque palace overlooking the Charles Bridge. 12 rooms. €194.

U Páva, U Lužického seminára 32, ☎ +420 257 533 573, 🖷 +420 257 530 919 (www.romantichotels.cz/upava). A well-appointed and tastefully restored 17C palace in the northern half of Kampa Island. Some of the 27 rooms have outstanding views up to Prague Castle. €184.

U Raka, Černínská 10, ☎ +420 220 511 100, 🖷 +420 233 358 041 (www.romantikhotels.com). This tiny former pension in an 18C cottage-like building is located at the bottom of the quiet district of Nový Svět; it now forms part of the Romantik Hotels and Restaurants chain. 6 rooms, including one with an open fireplace and winter garden. €185.

U Tří Pštrosů, Dražického náměstí 12, ☎ +420 257 532 410, 🖷 +420 257 533 217 (www.utripstrosu.cz). Occupying a famous building at the foot of the Charles Bridge (see p 129), this was once Prague's most endearing hotel but is now slightly lack-lustre; at least the riverside views remain as enchanting as ever. 18 rooms with beamed ceilings and antique furnishings. €230.

U Zlaté Studně, U zlaté studně 4, ☎ +420 257 011 213, 🖷 +420 257 533 320 (www.zlatastudna.cz). A 16C house in a fairytale location, with spectacular views over the spires and rooftops of the Little Quarter. From the restaurant you can walk through beautiful terraced gardens all the way up to the Castle. 20 rooms. €258.

Waldstein, Valdštejnské náměstí 6, ☎ +420 251 556 457, 🖷 +420 251 555 156. Hidden away in a quiet corner of the square, the Waldstein boasts elegant apartments with original 17C painted ceilings situated around a pleasant courtyard. 10 rooms. €170.

Moderate

Dientzenhofer, Nosticova 2, ☎ +420 257 311 319, +420 257 316 830, 🖅 +420 257 320 888 (www.dientzenhofer.cz). Located in the southern half of Malá Strana, this simple and friendly pension is the birthplace of the architect Kilian Ignaz Dientzenhofer (see p 48). 9 rooms (most with wheelchair access). €115.

The Charles, Josefská 1, ☎ +420 257 531 380, 🖅 +420 257 532 910. Luxury hotel in an elegantly restored 17C building, intimate in atmosphere, and with some painted wooden-beam ceilings. 31 rooms. €140.

U Červeného Lva, Nerudova 41, ☎ +420 257 532 867, 🖅 +420 257 533 624 (www.hotelredlion.com). Gothic, Renaissance and Baroque are all in evidence in this Malá Strana townhouse, the birthplace of the painter Petr Brandl (see p 59). Several of the rooms have hand-painted wooden ceilings and original period furniture. Convenient for visiting the Castle and its environs. 8 rooms. €153.

U Karlova Mostu, Na Kampě 15, ☎ +420 257 531 430, +420 257 531 432, 🖅 +420 257 533 168 (www.nakampe15.cz). Converted from a medieval tavern, this large hotel on Kampa Island was reopened in 2003 following extensive flood damage. The ground floor accommodates a lively pub (see p 35) with a beer-garden. 28 rooms. €168.

U Kříže, Újezd 20, ☎ +420 257 312 451, 🖅 +420 257 312 452 (www.ukrize.com). Modern hotel on a busy street next to the Petrín Park. 22 rooms. €115.

Inexpensive

Dům U Velké Boty, Vlašská 30, ☎ +420 257 532 088, +420 257 534 209, +420 257 531 360, +420 257 533 234 (www.volweb.cz/rippl). Situated opposite the German Embassy, this discreetly stylish pension is run by a helpful and very friendly couple—Charlotta and Jan Rippl. 8 rooms. €95.

Nové Město

Expensive

Adria, Václavské náměstí 26, ☎ +420 221 081 111, +420 221 081 200, 🖅 +420 221 081 300 (www.hoteladria.cz) A restaurant dripping with stalactites is about the most imaginative feature of this otherwise unadventurously transformed late-18C building. However, it is comfortable, efficiently run, and rather less sleazy than the other hotels on Wenceslas Square. 87 rooms. €220.

Esplanade, Washingtonova 19, ☎ +420 224 501 111, 🖅 +420 224 229 306 (www.esplanade.cz). Despite major renovation carried out in recent years, the Esplanade retains the same marbled, chandeliered magnificence of the original 1920s' structure. Imposing yet friendly and intimate, this is in many ways the most appealing of Prague's luxury hotels, and is in easy reach of the Central Railway Station. The restaurant serves excellent French food in an Art Nouveau setting. 74 rooms. €218.

Hotel Élite, Ostrovní 32, ☎ +420 224 932 250, 🖅 +420 224 930 787 (www.hotelelite.cz). A small modern hotel housed in a 14C building with a pleasant open atrium. The popular 'Ultramarin' restaurant offers grilled Mediterranean cuisine on the ground floor, while its basement cocktail bar doubles as a Latino dance club. Top marks for friendly and efficient service. 77 rooms. €198.

Palace, Panská 12, ☎ +420 224 093 111, 🖅 +420 224 093 217

(www.palacehotel.cz). A grand turn-of-the-last-century establishment fully refurbished in 2000, with first class service and prices to match. Located approximately 200m from Wenceslas Square. 124 rooms. €260.

Radisson SAS Alcron, Štěpánská 40, ☎ +420 222 820 058, 📠 +420 222 820 120 (www.radissonsas.com/praguecs). A revamped 1930s' Art Deco building catering primarily to an international business clientele. Service and facilities of the highest standard are what one would expect from the Radisson chain, and the Alcron does not disappoint. Begin your evening with superb cocktails and live jazz at the BeBop bar, followed by a meal at the renowned seafood restaurant, voted 'Best Prague Restaurant' by the Gourmet Dining Guide 2002. 211 rooms. €210.

Moderate

Hotel Axa, Na poříčí 40, ☎ +420 224 816 332, 📠 +420 224 214 489 (www.hotelaxa.com). Occupying a Constructivist building of 1935, the Axa offers bland mid-range accommodation at prices that won't break the bank. The views at the back are best forgotten, while the front overlooks a busy tram route. 134 rooms. €118.

Grand Hotel Evropa, Václavské náměstí, ☎ +420 224 215 387, 📠 +420 224 224 544 (www.evropahotel.cz). Art Nouveau splendour gone somewhat to seed, this will appeal to those who prefer architecture and atmosphere over comfort and cheerfulness. Frosty service rules at the Evropa, but the price is a bargain for Wenceslas Square, and the famous café and 'Titanic' restaurant are not to be missed. 90 rooms. €125.

Hotel 16 u sv. Kateřiny, Kateřinská 16, ☎ +420 224 920 636, 📠 +420 224 920 626 (www.hotel16.cz). Small, family-run hotel located close to the University Botanical Gardens (see p 182). Friendly atmosphere. 14 rooms, some with garden views. €106.

Nad Zlatém Kříži, Jungmannovo náměstí 2, ☎ +420 224 219 501, 📠 +420 222 245 418 (www.goldencross.cz). Spacious if plainly furnished rooms at a very reasonable price considering the excellent central location. 8 rooms. €112.

Inexpensive

Salvator, Truhlářská 10, ☎ +420 222 312 234, 📠 +420 222 316 355 (www.salvator.cz). Central location close to the Municipal House (see p 88). 30 simply furnished but clean rooms, some with shared bathrooms, set around an inner courtyard. €96.

U Šuterů, Palackého 4, ☎ +420 224 948 235, 📠 +420 224 948 233 (www.usuteru.cz). Bargain-priced pension set in a fine 18C Baroque house with Gothic elements visible in the atmospheric restaurant and some of the rooms. About 100m from the metro and Wenceslas Square. €80.

Smíchov

Moderate

U Blaženky, U Blaženky 1, ☎ +420 251 564 532, 📠 +420 251 563 529 (www.ublazenky.cz). An imposing villa transformed into a hotel in the mid-1990s when it was returned to its former owners. Hilly location with views over Prague. 20 minutes by bus from the city centre. 13 rooms. €130.

Julián, Elišky Peškové 11, ☎ +420 257 311 150, 📠 +420 257 311 149 (www.julian.cz). Situated on the borders of Smíchov and Malá Strana, this friendly hotel offers rooms with en suite kitchenettes and a cosy downstairs lounge with an open fire. A brisk 15-minute walk from the Old Town Square. 32 rooms, all with wheelchair access. €122.

Vinohrady
Expensive
Hotel Le Palais, U Zvonařky 1, ☎ +420 234 634 111, 📠 +420 222 563 350 (www.palaishotel.cz). A sumptuous building redesigned in the late 19C by Luděk Marold (see p 210), whose frescoes can still be seen here. Period furnishings dominate the rooms, some of which have their own fireplace. The hotel is 5 minutes' walk from the metro and 15 minutes' from the top of Wenceslas Square. 72 rooms. €250.

Inexpensive
City, Belgická 10, ☎ +420 222 521 606, 📠 +420 222 522 386 (www.hotel-city.cz). Situated in the residential district of Vinohrady, this modern hotel/pension offers large clean rooms with basic amenities. 10 minutes' walk from Wenceslas Square. 19 rooms. €73.

Žižkov
Expensive
Arcotel Teatrino, Bořivojova 53, ☎ +420 221 422 111, 📠 +420 221 422 222 (www.arcotel.at). An Austrian-run hotel converted from a 19C theatre—the stage and balcony boxes are still visible in the restaurant. Reopened in 2000 after lengthy refurbishment, the Teatrino boasts original Art Nouveau features on the ground floor and modern bedrooms designed by architect Harald Schreiber on the upper floors. The hotel is situated in the heart of Žižkov, a former workers' district filled with bars and pubs of a distinctly local character. 73 rooms. €180.

Inexpensive
Tříska, Vinohradská 105, ☎ +420 222 727 313, +420 222 727 488, 📠 +420 222 723 562 (www.hotel-triska.cz). Situated on a busy street close to the Jiřího z Poděbrad metro station (green line), the Tříska scores high points for friendly service and price, but the ridiculously fussy décor is hard to bear. 51 rooms. €74.

Dejvice
Expensive
Crowne Plaza Hotel, Koukalova 15, ☎ +420 224 393 111, 📠 +420 296 537 849 (www.crowneplaza.cz). Formerly the Hotel International, this is one of a dying breed of grim Stalinist blocks, hailed in its time as triumphant fusion of Socialist Realism and Art Deco. Friezes, grandiose columns and marble fittings abound, but the joys of this retro experience hardly warrant the inflated prices. 5 minutes' walk from the Dejvická metro station (green line), 10 minutes' drive from the airport. 250 rooms. €280.

Břevnov
Inexpensive
Hotel Adalbert, Markétská 1, ☎ +420 220 406 170, 📠 +420 220 406 190 (www.intercatering.cz/adalbert.html). A newly modernised Baroque building that is actually part of the Břevnov Monastery (see p 199). The setting is appropriately peaceful and bucolic, yet only 20 minutes by tram from the centre of Prague. 23 clean, bright and decently furnished rooms, some with views over the beautiful surrounding parkland. €97.

Private rooms

Choosing private accommodation—a room in someone's house—is a good way of paying less and feeling more of a local, but be sure you are not stuck in the outskirts. Check which facilities you will have to share with the owners, and what your proximity to them will be. Breakfast, if available, is usually charged extra. It is probably best to stay one night and then decide if you want to stay longer. Private rooms can be booked through foreign-based tour operators (see p 10) or local accommodation agencies such as:

AVE (www.avetravel.cz), which has offices at the airport (Praha Ruzyně; ☎ +420 220 114 650, 📠 224 230 783; open daily 07.00–09.00), at both international railway stations: Hlavní nádraží (☎ +420 224 223 226, +420 224 223 521, 📠 +420 224 230 783; open daily 06.00–23.00), nádraží Holešovice (☎ +420 266 710 514, 📠 +420 224 230 783; open daily 07.00–20.30), and at other points around the city.

City of Prague Accommodation Service (www.apartmentforrent.cz), Haštalská 7 (☎ +420 224 813 022, +420 222 310 202, 📠 +420 222 316 640; open Mon–Fri 09.00–13.00 and 14.00–18.00).

Stop City (www.stopcity.com), Vinohradská 24 (☎ +420 222 521 233, +420 222 521 234, 📠 +420 222 521 252; open daily April–Oct 10.00–21.00, Nov–Mar 11.00–20.00).

Hostels and student dormitories

The choice of hostel accommodation in Prague is surprisingly good, with places usually available even in high season. You should expect to pay around €10 per night, and members of Hostelling International may get discounts. Facilities are very basic, with multi-person rooms and shared bathrooms, and curfews often apply. Some hostels are open all year round, others in summer only. Cheap summer accommodation is also provided by the Charles University, which lets out its student dormitories to visitors. Again, facilities are basic, though standards have improved in recent years.

Charles University Dormitories, Voršilská 1 (☎ +420 224 913 692; open Mon–Thur 09.00–13.00, Fri 13.00–16.00). This is the central office, which will arrange accommodation for you in a dorm.

Travellers' Hostel (www.travellers.cz), Dlouhá 33 (☎ +420 224 826 662, 📠 +420 224 826 665). Internet access. No curfew. Next to the Roxy dance club (see p 34).

The Clown and Bard (www.clownandbard.com), Bořivojova 102, (☎ +420 222 716 453). No curfew. Above a lively bar of the same name.

Getting around

Maps

Maps in English are readily available from tourist offices, bookshops and hotels. A Prague city map (*plán města*) is definitely worth buying as it will provide additional information not covered in this Guide, such as bus and tram routes, and is essential for visiting the outlying suburbs. The best maps and atlases are published by the Prague firm Kartografie. Old city maps should be used with caution, as many street names honouring famous Communists were abandoned after 1989 in favour of original pre-war names or, in some cases, wholly new ones.

Public transport

Walking is the best way to see the centre of the city. Not only is it faster than public transport, but it allows you to see the large squares, winding alleys and hidden arcades that you might otherwise miss. Some of the outlying sites described in this Guide, however, are best reached using the cheap and efficient public-transport system, which runs 24 hours. The daytime service runs from 05.00 to 24.00 and the night service from 00.00 to 05.00.

Information on the system is obtainable at the information offices of the **Prague Public Transport Company** (Dopravní podnik hl. m. Prahy)—look for the yellow DP sticker. There are offices at the Muzeum (open daily 07.00–21.00) and Můstek (open Mon–Fri 07.00–18.00) metro stations. The staff here will help you find your way around. They speak some English and German and sell travel passes, maps, tram and bus schedules.

Tickets Travel tickets can be used on any form of public transport—bus, tram and metro. A 15-minute ride above ground (no transfers) or one ride on the metro (no more than four stops) costs 8Kč. Unlimited travel on all forms of transport, with transfers, for 60 minutes at peak times and 90 minutes off-peak, costs 12Kč. Children under 6 go free, children under 15 are half-price.

Tickets can be bought at PIS offices (see p 43), newsagents, tobacconists, and anywhere displaying the yellow DP sticker in the window. Once on board a bus or tram, or before entering the 'paid area' of the metro, you must stamp your ticket in a validating machine. Plainclothes inspectors will make fare dodgers pay an on-the-spot fine and will call the police if they cannot pay.

Tickets can also be bought from the vending machines in metro stations, but these are notoriously complicated to use. Generally, a far better option is to buy a **travel pass** (*časová jízdenka*) from one of the DP offices. These cover all forms of public transport and are available for the following periods: one-day, 70Kč; three days, 200Kč; seven-days, 250Kč; 15-days, 280Kč; monthly, 420Kč; quarterly, 1150Kč; annual, 3800Kč. Photos are required only for monthly (or longer) passes. A travel pass is valid from the moment you stamp it in a validating machine—you only need to do this once.

Metro The metro is extremely efficient and runs from 05.00 to 24.00. Trains are clean and frequent. There are three lines: green line A (Skalka–Dejvická), yellow line B (Černý most–Zličín) and red line C (Ládví–Háje). Further extensions are being planned. There are only three transfer (*přestup*) stations: Muzeum (where A and C connect), Florenc (where B and C connect) and Můstek (where A and B connect).

Trams There are 23 tram lines running during the day, and eight at night. Trams run every 7 minutes at peak times, every 15 minutes off peak, and every 40 minutes at night. Remarkably, they respect almost to the second the timetables posted at each tram stop. A good way to see the city is to ride on tram 22, or on 91—the historical tram. This runs from April to October and takes 40 minutes for the journey from the Prague Exhibition Ground (Výstaviště; see p 209) through Mala Straná and Wenceslas Square to náměstí Republiky.

Buses Buses run every 10 minutes at peak times, every 20 minutes off-peak, and every hour at night. There are 196 daytime bus lines and ten night bus lines. You will only need to use buses if you are travelling to the suburbs or out of Prague.

Cycling

Cycling in Prague is not easy. There are no bike lanes, drivers take no notice of you and even pedestrians are hostile if you go anywhere near the pavement. The cobbled streets and tramlines don't help either.

Driving

Driving in Prague is an even worse idea. The narrow streets are difficult to nego-tiate, and you have to deal with trams and the possibility of theft. To drive your own car in Prague, you need a British or EU driving licence as well as Green Card insurance. You must carry your vehicle's registration documents with you. The wearing of seatbelts is compulsory and you are not allowed to have any alcohol in your blood. The car should carry a red warning triangle, replacement bulbs and a first-aid kit. Children under 12 must always sit in the back.

The **speed limit** is 80mph/130kph on motorways, 55mph/90kph on main roads, and 30mph/50kph in towns and villages. Drive on the right-hand side of the road. A yellow diamond sign means you have right of way, a black line through it means you do not have right of way. Give way to pedestrians at lights if turning left or right. Do not drive on tramlines; trams always have right of way.

You must have an authorisation sticker (*dálniční známka*) to drive on any **motor-way** in the Czech Republic. This costs 100Kč (€3) and is valid for ten days. It is available from petrol stations, post offices and border crossings. Failure to display the sticker results in heavy fines. The **emergency road service** number is 154.

Parking in Prague can be very difficult. There is lots of residents-only parking (blue zones), and your car will be clamped or towed away if you ignore regula-tions (the recovery number is 158). Car theft is not that common, but neither is it advisable to leave your car unattended overnight. Use your hotel's own park-ing facilities or any car park with 24-hour security, such as the underground 'Centrum' by the riverside opposite the Rudolfinum (see p 115).

Fuel There are three types of **petrol**: 96 octane (*super*), 90 octane (*special*), and unleaded (*natural*); diesel oil is called *nafta*. Many petrol stations close after 18.00, and most do not accept credit cards.

Car hire

To **rent a car**, you must be over 21 and have a clean driving licence. Insurance is arranged by the rental agency. If you hire from abroad, a small car for a week will cost around €280. The well-known car-hire companies charge much more than local Czech ones.

Avis (www.avis.cz) Klimentská 46, Prague 1, ☎ 221 851 225/6.
Budget (www.budget.cz), Prague airport (Ruzyně), ☎ 220 113 253; náměstí Curieových 5 (Hotel Intercontinental), Prague 1, ☎ 224 889 995.
Czechocar (www.czechocar.cz), Kongresové centrum, 5 května 65, Prague 4, ☎ 261 222 079.
Hertz (www.hertz.cz), Prague airport (Ruzyně), ☎ 233 326 714; Karlovo náměstí 28, Prague 2, ☎ 222 231 010.

Ren Auto, Na příkopě 12 (inside the shopping precinct), Prague 1, ☎ 221 014 630.

Taxis

Prague has plenty of taxis, but these can be very expensive. Prague's taxi drivers are notoriously dishonest and, in spite of recent regulations, you are almost bound to be overcharged. Avoid taking taxis near tourist locations. Agree your fare before you get in, or make sure that the meter is on. When you get in the taxi, the initial fare should read 30Kč at most. The meter rate should be set at 1—that is, no more than 22Kč per kilometre. Ask for a receipt (*paragon*) at the end of your trip. It should have all the details of your journey, including the name of the taxi company and the driver. Only ever use an authorised taxi. The best of way making sure you are not ripped off is to order a taxi by phone. Reputable companies include: **City Taxi**, ☎ 233 103 310, **ProfiTaxi**, ☎ 261 314 151, and **Airport Cars**, ☎ 220 113 892; their operators have a basic understanding of English.

Eating and drinking

'Morning and evening, I endured the atrocious, nauseating cumin-flavoured food. I consequently walked around all day with a constant desire to vomit,' recalled Albert Camus of his rather unsatisfactory visit to Prague in 1935 (see p 80). Nearly one and a half centuries earlier Dr Johnson's friend Hester Lynch Piozzi found instead that the 'eating here is incomparable ... I never saw such poultry even in London or Bath, and there is plenty of game that amazes one; no inn so wretched but you have a pheasant for your supper, and often partridge soup.' Although in the international Prague of today there is food to satisfy all palates, typical Czech cuisine is likely to inspire a response somewhere between Camus' and Piozzi's. It is filling and slightly monotonous food, best appreciated on a cold winter's evening, and washed down with copious quantities of the outstanding local beer.

Dumplings

Bacon and above all caraway seed (rather than cumin, as Camus thought) are the ubiquitous flavourings of Czech food and, as in Polish and Hungarian cooking, soured cream is an accompaniment to numerous dishes. The first thought which comes to mind at the very mention of Czech food, however, is of dumplings (*knedlíky*), which have the same role in Bohemia and Moravia as chips (*hranolky*) do in other countries. There are several types of dumpling, including potato dumplings (*bramborové knedlíky*), plum dumplings (*švestkové knedlíky*) and, most common of all, a type of dumpling known as *houskové knedlíky*, which is made in the shape of a Swiss roll from a mixture of flour, eggs and cubes of white bread, and is served in slices; some of the better restaurants will even provide you with a separate tray piled high with a selection of all of these. A ubiquitous dish is *svíčková*, which consists of bread dumplings served with beef in a delicious creamy sauce.

Starters

Shortly after you sit down in some of the fancier Czech restaurants you are likely to be offered aperitifs from a trolley followed by a tray of unappealing canapés, for which you will be charged individually; the canapés, of glazed, artificial appearance, invariably feature cream or cream cheese, one of the more popular ones being a ham roll (*šunková rolka*) filled with cream cheese and topped with horseradish; others are coated with hard lumps of jelly, and should be avoided at all costs. A normal Czech meal, however, begins with a soup; two common varieties are potato soup (*bramborová polévka*) and a thick white soup known as *kmínová polévka*, both of which are heavily flavoured with caraway seed; a popular clear soup is *polévka s játrovými knedlíčky*, which is beef broth with little dumplings made from liver, garlic, lemon rind, eggs and breadcrumbs.

Main courses

Main courses on restaurant menus are usually divided between *minutky* and *hotová jídla*, the former being dishes that are cooked to order, the latter being ready-cooked ones in heavy sauces. The most typical main dish is pork Frankfurter-style sausage (*klobás*) accompanied by dumplings and sauerkraut. Meat (*maso*) is consumed in vast quantities all over the Czech Republic, and tends to be tough and overcooked. Pork (*vepřové*) is often served with eggs and ham on top and, like veal (*telecí*), is frequently dipped in a mixture of flour, breadcrumbs and eggs to form an escalope or *řízek*; a tastier dish is *vepřová pečeně*, or pork roasted with caraway seeds. Thick fillets of beef (*hovězí*) piled high with cream and cranberries can be found in the more pretentious establishments, but beef is more commonly served as braised slices in a brown onion sauce (*dušená roštěnka*) or else as boiled slices in a delicious dill-flavoured white sauce known as *koprová omáčka*. There are far fewer poultry than meat dishes in the Czech Republic: the most usual one is roast chicken (*pečené kuře*); goose (*husa*) is becoming less common but is traditionally served roast with sauerkraut (*pečená husa se zelím*).

Fish (*ryby*) dishes are few. Carp is by far the most popular fish in the Czech Republic, but even so tends to be eaten mainly as a traditional Christmas Eve dish, when it is served with a near-indigestible black sauce made from fish stock, raspberry juice, beer, lemon rind, sugar, raisins and almonds (*kapr na černo*).

The great joy of Czech cuisine, if such an extreme term can be used, is its game (*zvěřina*), which is sometimes roasted over a wood fire and flavoured with juniper berries. One of the best places to eat it in Prague is the **Myslivna** restaurant in the Vinohrady district (see p 31).

Fresh fruit (*ovoce*) and vegetables (*zelenina*) are now far more widely available than during the Communist era, but for some reason are still only rarely found in restaurants, where tinned fruit (often served as a mixed compote known as a *míchaný ovocný kompot*), sauerkraut (*kyselé zelí*) and pickled vegetable salads such as cucumber salad (*okurkový salát*) dominate. Two cheese specialities sometimes found on menus are *pivný sýr*, a pungent, soft cheese marinated in beer, and *nakládaný hermelín*, a pickled brie stuffed with onion, garlic and chillies, and dowsed in oil. Prague does not cater well to vegetarians, but times are changing and a few dedicated eateries have sprung up in recent years, notably **Country Life** (see p 28) and **Radost FX** (see p 30).

Desserts

Puddings are of the hearty kind, such as plum-jam cake (*povidlový koláč*) or, more commonly, *palačinky*, pancakes that are usually heaped with mountains of cream and chocolate sauce, and occasionally flambéed. The legacy of Austria is fortunately still apparent in the delectable range of cakes and pastries to be found in cafés and bakeries.

Spirits, wine and beer

Spirits and **liqueurs** tend to be drunk neat as an aperitif or as a beer chaser. Two of the most famous are *fernet*, a bitter drink similar to Hungarian *Unicum*, and the greenish, herb-flavoured *becherovka*, a speciality of the Bohemian spa town of Karlovy Vary (Carlsbad) and reputedly far more beneficial to the health than the town's waters. Most spirits, however, come from Moravia and Slovakia and include plum brandy (*slivovice*, one of the more renowned brands being *Jelínec*), and a juniper-flavoured brandy known as *borovička*, a particular speciality of the Slovak town of Trenčín: according to popular tradition a glass of *borovička* drunk half an hour before eating is a considerable aid to the digestion, though its potential beneficial effects are sometimes lost as a result of the hors d'oeuvres that often come with it. At a frightening 170°, *absinthe* is the strongest spirit on the market and one that even many hardened Czechs will keep away from. Prague is the only place in Europe apart from Barcelona where this generally outlawed and potentially lethal drink can openly be found.

The finest Czech **wines** (*vína*) are from Southern Moravia, with excellent Ruländer, Sauvignon, Traminer and Spätburgunder being made in places such as Velké Pavlovice, Mikulov, Musov and Znojmo; Bohemia's small number of wines are grown mainly around Mělník, an area planted with Burgundy grapes during the reign of Charles IV. Wine is less commonly drunk in the Czech Republic than beer, which is by far the most popular local drink, and the usual accompaniment to meals.

When it comes to discussing Czech **beer** (*pivo*), superlatives can at last be used with complete honesty, for it is generally agreed to be the best in the world, and has a reputation going back to the Middle Ages. Beer is made throughout the country, and dark (*černé*) as well as light (*světlé*) beer can be found here, as can a number of small breweries, some of which are attached to their own pubs. However, the general consensus is that the finest beers are the light and creamy ones from the Bohemian towns of České Budějovice (the original Budweiser or Budvar) and, above all, Plzeň, where the bottom-fermented Urquell or Prazdroj brew served as the prototype for Pils-style beers throughout the world. Prague's own beers (slightly more bitter than the ones above) include Staropramen, Braník and Měšťan. The most widely available dark beer is Purkmistr, while slightly treacly home brews are served at two of Prague's most tourist-loved beerhalls—*U Fleků* (see p 36) and *U Zlatého Tygra* (see p 35). Gambrinus, Radegast and, to a lesser extent, Velkopopovický kozel are other popular beers found in pubs around the city. With all this quality on offer, combined with the ridiculously low prices, it is hardly surprising that Czechs are heavy beer drinkers—the average annual per capita consumption is 161 litres, the highest in the world. That said, Czechs handle their drink in an exemplary fashion, and alcohol-related violence is rare. Beer is a very important part of Czech life, and there was even a parliamentary Beer Party in the 1990s, since downgraded to a civic association along the lines of the UK's Campaign for Real Ale. In pubs you will often be given a choice of 10° (*desítka*) or 12° (*dvanáctka*) beers, the latter being darker in colour and slightly more alcoholic (up to 5% by volume).

Restaurants

Since 1989, the standards and choice of restaurant food have dramatically improved, and eating out is no longer the exasperating experience it was during Communist times. The most noticeable change has been the arrival of foreign cuisine, particularly French, Italian, American, Mexican, even Icelandic, providing an alternative to traditional Czech fare. Western fast-food chains and pizzerias are also common. Significantly, the majority of the best-regarded Prague restaurants of today (no fewer than 15 of *Gurmán's* top-20 'winners in meals') are those serving international food.

As a general rule, restaurants specialising in Czech cuisine differ comparatively little in terms of the actual quality of the food, and should be chosen principally for their atmosphere and architectural setting. Modest restaurants, pubs and cellar bars are invariably the liveliest and friendliest of all the eating and drinking establishments in Prague, and their smoke-filled atmosphere, dirty walls and floors, and portly waiters or waitresses—who will slam a large glass of beer on your table often without you even asking for it—are an intrinsic part of their charm; food is served at most of the pubs and cellar bars and is usually no worse, and certainly far cheaper, than in the more pretentious establishments. In such places you will sometimes find yourself sharing a table with others; though your privacy will be respected, it is customary to wish each other *dobrou chuť* (*bon appétit*) when the food arrives. Pubs and cellar bars are often busiest at lunchtimes, when Czechs eat their main meal of the day, while restaurants tend to liven up in the evenings.

The most exclusive Prague restaurants prefer their clients to be formally dressed; booking is now essential in such establishments throughout the year. Occasionally you will come across *vinárna*, or wine-bars, which are smart establishments generally situated in historic cellars; they always provide food, but will rarely serve you with beer. Cellar-style restaurants are common in Prague and have a special ambience, but ventilation can be a problem, particularly for non-smokers.

Listed below are a number of the city's more long-standing establishments, together with several of the more-fashionable places of the moment, some of which—in the rapidly changing Prague of today—might well have closed down or been radically altered by the time you visit them. The best way of obtaining up-to-date recommendations is to buy a copy either of the weekly *Prague Post* or the annually up-dated *Gurmán Choice of Prague Restaurants* (printed locally), which gives points for food, service and atmosphere.

Although many of the restaurants mentioned below are expensive by Czech standards, Western visitors will generally find them significantly cheaper than their equivalents at home. Three price categories are used in this Guide: in 'expensive restaurants', you should expect to pay upwards of €30 for a three-course meal, not including alcohol; in 'medium-price' restaurants, anything from €10-20 is standard; in bottom-end establishments or 'cheap eateries', you can get a three-course meal for under €10.

Tipping Round your bill up to the nearest 10Kč (VAT at 22% is included in the price of your food): this may have been done for you already, so check. Don't leave the tip on the table, but pay it with the bill.

Staré Město and Josefov
Expensive restaurants

Flambée, Husova 5. Top-of-the-range establishment serving game and seafood dishes in a vaulted medieval cellar. Ridiculously expensive, but—with Tom Cruise and Michael Jackson among its former guests—hardly surprising.

Pravda, Pařížská 17 (corner of Červená). Newly revamped and touristy establishment located at the heart of the Jewish Quarter. Cosmopolitan food served by attentive staff.

Rybí Trh, Týn 5. Situated in the busy courtyard (Ungelt) between Malá Štupartská and Týnská. Sea- and freshwater fish specialities prepared to order. Good, but nothing to rival the Kampa Park (see below).

U Červeného Kola, Anežská 2. Charming restaurant with a summer garden in a peaceful part of town. Czech cuisine.

Medium-price restaurants

Kogo, Havelská 27. A good place to stop for pizza before visiting the open-air market on Havelská. There is another branch of Kogo in the courtyard of the Slovanský dům (see p 168).

Le Saint-Jacques, Jakubská 4. Excellent little French restaurant with a candlelit interior and live piano music on most nights.

Red Hot & Blues, Jakubská 12. Ex-pat bar with Czech and American flags above the entrance and a small patio within. Tex-Mex and Cajun food of dubious quality, but the raucous blues nights sort of compensate.

Reykjavík, Karlova 20. Centrally located on the 'Royal Route', the Reykjavík specialises in seafood flown in fresh from Iceland. It's basically glorified fish and chips, but of exceptionally good quality and made the traditional Icelandic way.

Stoleti, Karoliny Světlé 21. Situated in the southern part of the Old Town well away from the crowds, this unpretentious establishment serves decent Czech fare and good salads at very reasonable prices.

Cheap eateries

Chez Marcel, Haštalská 12. French bistro offering inexpensive lunches and a selection of wines in a pleasant Old Town setting.

Country Life, Melantrichova 15. Without doubt the best place for vegetarian snacks in the vicinity of the Old Town Square. Self-service hot and cold dishes, tasty organic soups and salads, freshly squeezed fruit juices and, best of all, smoke-free rooms and a filtered-water dispenser.

Klub Architektů, Betlémské náměstí 5A. In the courtyard opposite the entrance to the Bethlehem Chapel (see p 107). Expect no more than a basic stomach filler.

Pizzeria Roma Due, Liliová 18. Convenient 24-hour snack bar serving pizzas, calzone, and Gambrinus on tap.

Malá Strana
Expensive restaurants

Circle Line, Malostranské náměstí 12. An alternative to the Kampa Park, and usually less crowded, the Circle Line does excellent fish and seafood as well as salads and a good selection of vegetarian dishes. Service can be slightly fussy.

Kampa Park, Na Kampě 8B. Prague's best seafood restaurant with fantastic views of the Charles Bridge from its riverside terrace. Despite being frequented by visiting film stars, the Kampa is not as expensive as it could be, and prices are more than justified by the delicious, beautifully presented fish specialities and intimate candlelit atmosphere. Booking essential (☎ 257 532 685).

U Malířů, Maltézské náměstí 11. The culinary traditions of the 'Painter's House' go back centuries, and today it accommodates Prague's most exclusive French restaurant, with fresh produce flown in daily from France and an entirely French wine list. The food, at prices that few Czechs could afford, is served in beautiful vaulted cellars adorned with 17C frescoes. The exquisite Châteaubriand will set you back around €50.

U Maltézských Rytířů, Prokopská 10. One of the most renowned of the ubiquitous romantically lit 'cellar-style' restaurants. The cuisine is predominantly Czech, comprising game, fish and poultry dishes, finished off with a selection of excellent home-made desserts. Booking advisable (☎ 257 533 666).

Medium-price restaurants

Gitanes, Tržiště 7. Run by a Serbian woman, the Gitanes offers home-made soups and tasty Balkan specialities. Best of all, though, is the extraordinary décor, resembling the interior of a Balkan cottage.

Nebozízek, Petřínské sady 411. Good-to-variable Czech food combined with breathtaking views of Prague. Get off at the half-way stop on the funicular line (see p 136).

Pálffy Palác, Valdštejnská 14. In terms of sheer atmosphere, few Prague restaurants can compete with the Pálffy Palác, an entirely candle-lit Baroque hall with creaking parquet floors and odd snatches of violin music coming from the adjoining conservatoire. Equally romantic is the tiny outdoor terrace, with views over rooftops and gardens. Given the setting, prices could be a lot higher—the €8 and €15 set menus are an absolute bargain. International cuisine.

U Bílé Kuželky, Míšeňská 12. A good-value, no-frills Czech restaurant occupying a historic building (see p 129) close to the Charles Bridge.

U Mecenáše, Malostránské náměstí 10. One of several long-established places for eating and drinking on the Little Quarter Square, U Mecenáše serves steaks, Moravian ragout and other hearty Czech fare in somewhat gloomy and cramped surroundings.

U Tří Zlatých Hvězd, Malostránské náměstí 8. A cheaper alternative to U Mecenáše and certainly better in terms of service. Succulent green-pepper steak and other Czech specialities on offer.

Cheap eateries

Bar Bar, Všehrdova 17. Cosy basement bar that doubles as a crêperie. Ideal for quick snacks, but a bit off the beaten track.

Petřínské Terasy, Seminářská zahrada 13. Like the Nebozízek (see above), situated half way up Petřín Hill, and with equally stunning views. Not worth the trek for the food alone.

Hradčany

Expensive restaurants

U Zlaté Hrušky, Nový svět 3. An intimate 'cellar-style' restaurant located in a small house on one of Prague's most picturesque streets. Czech cuisine, with a heavy emphasis on duck.

Medium-price restaurants

U Ševce Matouše, Loretánské náměstí. A former shoemaker's under the arcades on Loreto Square. Convenient if you've been visiting the Loreto shrine (see p 157) or if U Černého vola (see p 35) is full. Czech cuisine.

Nové Město
Expensive restaurants

Francouzská Restaurace, Obecní dům (see p 88), náměstí Republiky 5. French cuisine served in a splendid Art Nouveau interior replete with gilded chandeliers, wainscotting and allegorical wall-paintings. Guests can chose from the à la carte, gourmet or 'surprise' menus, the latter consisting of seven courses selected by the chef. Booking advisable (☎ 222 002 770/780).

La Perle de Prague, Rašínovo nábřeží 80. Located on the 7th floor of the extraordinary 'Fred and Ginger' building (see p 177), this restaurant offers good-to-excellent French food complemented by breathtaking views from its roof terrace. Unfortunately, the service can be rather frosty if you're not prepared to splash out. Booking advisable (☎ 221 984 160).

Ostroff, Střelecký ostrov 336. Refined Italian cuisine is cooked by Tuscan chef Davide Cannela at this popular establishment superbly situated on Shooter's Island. Prefix your meal with a visit to the sophisticated cocktail bar (see p 36).

Medium-price restaurants

Miyabi, Navrátilova 10. A restaurant and tea-room situated in a quiet backstreet near to the birthplace of Jaroslav Hašek (see p 184). The Miyabi, run by a Czech woman who lived for many years in Japan, offers a curious and delicious mixture of Czech and Japanese cuisine.

Plzeňská Restaurace, Obecní dům, náměstí Republiky 5. Czech cuisine served in the basement of the Municipal House (see p 88). The interior is done in the style of a beer hall, enlivened with ceramic decoration and stained glass.

Radost FX Café, Bělehradská 120. A short walk from the National Museum, the Radost is known primarily as a fashionable dance club. However, the ground-floor café is a haven for vegetarians exasperated with the bland stodgy food served in Czech restaurants. The menu offers a wide selection of vegetarian cuisine arranged by country—from Italian and Greek to French, American and Moroccan. Lunchtimes are particularly busy, and clubbers can refuel on the pasta dishes that are served through the night. Not to be missed is the funky lounge at the back, where hardened ex-pats will regale you with stories from the bad old days.

Zahrada v Opeře (Opera Garden), Legerova 75. Situated behind the State Opera building (Státní opera). Attractive minimalist décor and an international menu that also caters to vegetarians.

Cheap eateries

Kmotra, V Jirchářích 12. Another excellent choice for cheap, well-made pizzas and pasta dishes.

Pizza Coloseum, Vodičkova 32. Avoid the KFC at street level and head straight down to the cellars for a first-rate pizza experience.

Smíchov
Medium-price restaurants

Pravěk, Na bělidle 40. A chain restaurant notable for its weird prehistoric theme: stone rooms filled with stalactites and mammoth tusks, where you can enjoy set lunches for a mere €3.

The Sushi Bar, Zborovská 49 (corner of Vítězná). A very compact and rather pricey establishment. Ideal for a quick snack if you're exploring Petřín Hill or Smíchov, but otherwise not worth the journey.

Vinohrady
Medium-price restaurants
Myslivna, Jagellonská 21. One of very few Czech restaurants worth visiting for the food alone, the Myslivna has for years been virtually unrivalled for its game dishes. The rather tatty interior sports a mass of antlers and animal hides on the walls, but this will hardly deter dedicated carnivores.
Cheap eateries
Pizzeria Grosseto, Francouzká 2. A good and popular pizzeria overlooking Vinohrady's main square—náměstí Míru. Packed at lunchtimes, but worth the wait.

Letná
Expensive restaurants
Belcredi, Letenské sady 341. An upmarket French restaurant located on the upper floor of the Letenský zámeček (see below).
Hanavský Pavilon, Letenské sady 173. Good-to-variable Czech cuisine combined with excellent views of the city. Most impressive is the pavilion itself (see p 201), built for Prague's Jubilee Industrial Exhibition of 1891.
Medium-price restaurants
Brasserie Ullman, Letenské sady 341. Occupying the ground floor of a manor house (Letenský zámeček) in the Letna Park, the Ullman serves an imaginative combination of Czech and French cuisine at reasonable prices. The popular beer-garden in front of the house has wonderful river views.

Holešovice
Cheap eateries
La Crêperie, Janovského 4. An enticing French crêperie just around the corner from the National Gallery (see p 204).

Cafés and tea-houses
As in other Central European cities, café culture was an integral part of social life in Prague from the late 19C onwards. A few of the establishments listed below have a long history behind them as meeting places for artists, writers, intellectuals etc, and still preserve an atmosphere evoking the past. This is especially true of the *Kavárna Obecní Dům* inside the Municipal House and *Café Louvre* on Národní, both of which have impressive turn-of-the-last-century décor. In a bid to win new customers, many cafés have changed their profile in recent years; most now serve alcohol and food, and many stay open late into the evening. Cafés are perhaps best appreciated in summer, when they spill out into the streets, courtyards and secluded gardens.

Traditional cafés are often the best place to eat cakes (*dort*), ice-cream (*zmrzlina*) and dessert (*moučník*). For coffee (*káva*), always insist on espresso (*presso*), as the alternative—'Turkish' (*turecká*)—is simply ground coffee added to boiling water. Black tea (*čaj*) is taken plain or with lemon (*citron*), but never with milk (*mléko*). Specialist tea-houses offer a good range of fruit and green teas.

Staré Město and Josefov
Kavárna Obecní Dům, náměstí Republiky 5. A showpiece café with a grand Art Nouveau interior, located inside the Municipal House (see p 88). An ideal place to begin a tour of the Old Town (walk 1). Lunches served.
Týnská Literární kavárna, Týnská 6. Situated in a pleasant courtyard with

wicker chairs. Frequented by Charles University students and visitors to the art gallery inside the House of the Golden Ring (see p 92).

Dahab, Dlouhá 33. A uniquely decorated tea-room with a Middle Eastern theme, at night inhabited by escapees from the Roxy club next door. There's a vast array of teas to choose from, but the main selling points are the serene ambience and comfortable seating.

Café Montmartre, Řetězová 7. One of Prague's raunchiest meeting-places of the early 20C (see p 100), but its erstwhile Bohemian spirit is now firmly dead and buried. Worth a look if you happen to be passing.

U Prstenu, Jilská 14. Pleasant café with an appealing pre-war feel, situated in a tiny courtyard off the street.

Franz Kafka Café, Široká 12. Pulls in the tourists on account of its Kafka theme and memorabilia, but the lunches are a bit disappointing. It's useful, though, when visiting the Jewish Quarter.

Blatouch, Vězeňská 4. A serious, bookcase-lined student café, with secluded seating in the mezzanine and a delightful small patio at the back.

Le Patio, Haštalská 18 (corner of Rybná). A very chic café, with prices to match, and an adjoining, tastefully appointed shop.

Café Milena, Staroměstské náměstí 22. A passable pastiche of the sort of café Kafka might have frequented, and named after his great love and translator, the journalist Milena Jesenská (see p 190).

Malá Strana

Bohemia Bagel, Újezd 16. Despite its location on a busy street, this is a good place to refuel before ascending Petřín Hill. There are tables and public telephones outside, Internet terminals and a bulletin board within, and, of course, a wide selection of filled bagels served by friendly English-speaking staff.

Malostranská kavárna, Malostranské náměstí (Grömling Palace). A smartly refurbished café with a long tradition behind it (see p 124), situated in the middle of the busy Little Quarter Square. Food served all day, and an extensive wine list, but the traffic may be too off-putting to dine here.

Chiméra, Lázeňská 6. Ground-floor café and modest art gallery in the southern half of Malá Strana.

Cukrkávalimonáda, Lázeňská 7. A little smoke-free gem opposite the Church of Our Lady under the Chain (see p 129). Sandwiches, crêpes and lunchtime specials on offer, as well as good coffee and English-language newspapers.

U Zeleného Čaje, Nerudova 17. An ideal stop-off on your way up to the castle. Few places to sit, but a wide range of herbal, fruit and black teas.

Nové Město

Café Imperial, Na poříčí 15. Situated on a busy thoroughfare, the Imperial boasts an impressive, if now slightly worn, Art Nouveau interior with wood panelling and ornate ceramic decoration. Best avoided on hot days, though, as there's no air-conditioning to speak of, nor any seating outside; there is, however, an on-site play area for kids.

Café Arco, Dlážděná 6 (corner of Hybernská). Experienced its heyday in the early 20C when Brod, Werfel and Kafka were among its regulars (see p 169). Now a downmarket café and busy lunchtime eatery. Convenient if you're travelling to or from Masarykovo station.

Globe Bookstore and Coffeehouse, Pštrossova 6. A legendary ex-pat institution founded at a time when Americans saw Prague as the height of cool and flocked here in their multitudes. The Globe's new premises are more sterile and somewhat less welcoming than the old, but this is still a good place to rub shoulders with the luminaries of Prague's (foreign) literary scene. The bulletin board and high-tech Internet terminals are particularly handy, and you can also peruse books, eat lunch, or stare at photos of Saul Bellow and Susan Sontag.

Café Slavia, Národní 1. A famous riverside café, which has featured in literary works since the early 20C (see p 174), being a meeting-place for writers, artists, and, during the Communist period, political dissidents. Nowadays, the old stalwarts have been replaced by tourists and theatre-goers, but the Slavia still exudes a distinctly unreconstructed feel, with the décor, and particularly the service, failing to move with the times. Don't bother eating here, just be sure to get a table on the embankment side for a picture-postcard view of the castle.

Café Louvre, Národní 20. Traditionalists will enjoy this imposing turn-of-the-last-century café located in the same building as the famous Reduta jazz club (see p 174). There's a pool hall at the back and windows at the front overlooking one of Prague's main shopping streets.

Velryba, Opatovická 24. Large basement café with a very young clientele who come for the dirt-cheap lunches and sociable atmosphere.

Smíchov

Café Savoy, Vítězná 1 (corner of Zborovská). A newly revamped 19C café which also does expensive seafood lunches.

Café Apostrof, Matoušova 9. An elegant café set inside the Portheimka (see p 189), a summer pavilion built by K.I. Dientzenhofer, which overlooks a church garden.

Vinohrady

Dobra Trafiká, Korunní 42. A wonderfully relaxed and friendly café entered through a tobacconist's shop. Tourists hardly ever make it here, and the clientele comprises mainly bookish young Czechs with a few neighbourhood ex-pats thrown in. There is another branch of Trafiká across town at Újezd 37, but the Vinohrady one enjoys the advantage of having a small summer garden. At both places the rule is to pay at the cash desk in the shop.

Medúza, Belgická 17. Another fine café in Vinohrady, this one doubling as a late-night bar. Only bottled beer is served, but this gives you an excuse to try the extensive range of wines and liqueurs. The classical music and 1930s'-style décor make for a pleasant ambience; the rooms are a little dusty, though, so beware if you have allergies.

Late-night bars and clubs

The neighbourhood beer-hall (*pivnica*) is where most Czechs go to drink, and there is still no better place to sample Prague's traditional drinking culture or, for that matter, the famously good local beer. Nowadays, though, there is a much wider choice of drinking establishments—everything from swish cocktail bars populated by young high-achievers to restful café-bars where the clientele seems more absorbed in books than boozing. Whatever the profile, though, Western visitors will find the prices ridiculously cheap and the licensing laws refreshingly sane—03.00 closing is not uncommon. You won't have to walk far to get a drink in Prague: the Old Town, in particular, is teeming with bars, while working-class

Žižkov boasts more pubs per capita than any other place on earth. Most of the bars listed below are well-established, but in these post-Communist times bankruptcies are frequent. Some places close and then reopen under a new name and management; others become intensely fashionable for a few months and then sink without a trace. Consequently, any list of recommended establishments becomes out-of-date almost as soon as it's written. The best policy is simply to ask local cognoscenti for suggestions. If a bar is not to your liking, move on: there's bound to be a good one just round the corner.

Staré Město and Josefov

Barock, Pařížská 24. A restaurant/bar/café decorated with Baroque kitsch where a self-consciously beautiful crowd likes to gather.

Bugsy's, Pařížská 10 (entrance on Kostečna). Lively upmarket cellar bar with a book-length list of cocktails to choose from.

Chateau, Jakubská 2. A big, noisy and hugely popular bar crammed with drunk students looking for love.

Duende, Karoliny Světlé 30. Unobtrusive bar near the riverside populated by an urbane arty crowd. Great place for a quiet one-to-one.

James Joyce, Liliová 10. A raucous Irish pub that pulls in the tourists with its all-day breakfasts and decent, if overpriced, Guinness. For a more sedate experience, try *U Krále Jiřího* next door.

Konvikt, Bartolomějská 11. A small, traditional beer-hall, usually crowded with students. Pilsner, Gambrinus and Kozel on tap, accompanied by a range of snacks—regulars swear by the *nakládaný hermelín* (camembert stuffed with onion, garlic and chillies).

Kozička, Kozí 1. A rowdy cellar bar where locals like to gorge on steak and play drinking games into the small hours.

La Casa Blů, Kozí 15 (corner of Blíkova). A bar-cum-restaurant perched on a raised terrace in a quiet part of town. The Mexican food is nothing to write home about, but the ambience is friendly and the tequila genuine.

Legends, Týn 1. A cavernous 'music bar' in the Ungelt lined with TV screens for homesick ex-pats who can't live without their Premiership football.

M1, Masná 1. Only slightly more restrained than the Chateau (see above), but just as loud and airless. The sign on the door says: 'No stag parties'. You get the picture.

Marquis de Sade, Templová 8. Enormous ground-floor room with a charmingly unkempt Central European feel. Friendly service, cheap drinks, and a twentysomething crowd.

Molly Malone's, U Obecního dvora 4. Definitely the best and friendliest of the Irish pubs, set in a charming backstreet location and with endearingly rambling interior.

Radegast, Templová 2. Long low-ceilinged beer-hall with good pub food at unbeatable prices.

Roxy, Dlouhá 33. A dilapidated former cinema that hosts occasional live gigs but most of the time serves as a very cool and popular dance club spread over several floors.

Tretter's, V kolkovně 3. American-style cocktail bar inhabited by a mix of ex-pats and well-to-do Czechs. Considered pricey by Prague standards, but then even a top-of-the-range, temple-thumping Mojito will set you back only €5. Lively weekend atmosphere enhanced by sharp service and infectious 70s soul of the *Boogie Nights/Car Wash* variety. The same management runs next door's

Ocean Drive, the place to be if you're a lean Czech model looking for a rich husband.

U Medvídků Na Perštýně 7. An unpretentious, authentic Czech beer-hall of medieval provenance. Tasty snacks and excellent Budvar on tap. Turn right as you enter the building.

U Vejvodů, Jilská 4. A huge, centrally located pub/restaurant serving hearty Czech food and a range of local beers, including the somewhat rare Tmavý ležák.

U Zlatého Tygra, Husova 17. The 'Golden Tiger' was once a favourite haunt of the writer Bohumil Hrabal (see p 100), and is now an obligatory stop on every tourist itinerary, much to the annoyance of the regulars. Come early if you want a seat.

Malá Strana

Jo's Bar, Malostranské náměstí 7. A travellers' hang-out serving cheap snacks and bottled beer, and with a noisy dance club in the basement.

Na Kampě 15, Na Kampě 15. Situated on the ground floor of a large, recently restored building, which also houses the U Karlova Mostu hotel (see p 18). This lively pub serves decent Czech food and has a beer-garden at the back, but unfortunately the river views are obscured by a wall. It is, nonetheless, one of the best watering holes in Malá Strana.

Tato, U sovových mlýnů. A newly opened and (for now) trendy student café/bar with adjoining art gallery, scenically located above an old mill in the southern part of Kampa Island.

U Kocoura, Nerudova 2. A celebrated pub that had its heyday in the Communist period when frequented by Havel and his friends. Now oriented towards the tourist market, but still worth visiting on account of its excellent Purkmistr beer.

U Schnellů, Tomášská 2. One of Prague's oldest and most famous beer haunts, today something of a tourist trap.

U sv. Tomáše, Letenská 8. Another decidedly tourist-friendly ale house and restaurant located in the cellars of a former Augustinian friary (see p 128).

Hradčany

U Černého vola, Loretánské náměstí 1. Unlike most Prague pubs, this one closes at 22.00 due to noise regulations in the castle district—a shame, because it is possibly the best pub in the city, and one of the few places in Hradčany where local residents can actually afford to drink. Tourists are not unwelcome, but finding a free table is difficult at the best of times. Wait if necessary, because the *Velkopopovický kozel* they serve here is unrivalled.

Nové Město

Jagr Sports Bar, Václavské náměstí 56. If you're attracted by the idea of eating hamburgers and fries while encircled by chrome fittings and TV screens showing American ice hockey, then this is the place for you.

Jazz Café č. 14, Opatovická 14 (next to the Koruna hotel). Not a live venue and not really a café; rather, a pleasant bar with eclectic furnishings where you can while away the night hours to some cool jazz sounds.

Novoměstský Pivovar, Vodičkova 20. Reached from an alleyway off the main street, the 'New Town Brewery' does its own Novoměstký Kvasnicový Ležák, a fine beer available in light and dark versions and, if you're up for it, 1-litre mugs and barrel-sized take-outs. The food menu is very meat-based, comprising platters, steaks, and tasty beef soup with bacon dumplings.

Ostroff, Střelecký ostrov 336. For an ultra-sophisticated experience look no further than this popular bar on Shooter's Island, where you can sit on stainless-steel chairs sipping exotic cocktails and enjoying superlative views of the floodlit National Theatre.

Pivovarský Dům, Lipová 15 (corner of Ječná). Another New Town micro-brewery, this one making a range of award-winning beers, which are kept on-site in huge copper vats. The food, advertised outside as 'Czech classics', is nothing more than ordinary pub grub, but the flagship brews certainly justify the journey.

Solidni nejistota, Pštrossova 21. An unrepentant pick-up joint, complete with cheesy music, expensive drinks, and a mass of lithe gyrating bodies.

U Fleků, Křemencova 11. The city's most famous beer-hall (see p 177), which exhibits in microcosm the very worst that has happened to Prague since 1989. 'Flek', the excellent house brew, has fortunately not changed with the times, and you can see how it's made at the on-site Brewery Museum.

U Kalicha, Na Bojišti 12. 'The Chalice' gets considerable mileage out of being mentioned in Jaroslav Hašek's famous book, *The Good Soldier Švejk* (see p 183). Were it not for this fortuitous literary connection, the management could surely not justify the inflated prices and bland food. However, after a quart (the standard house measure) of Radegast, you might find this temple of Švejkdom somewhat less galling.

Smíchov

U Buldoka, Preslova 1. A better-than-average pub with a big football screen and hip dance floor downstairs. Perhaps too laddish for some, but at least refreshingly Czech, and this despite a huge flag of St George stuck on the wall. Uncertain whether 'The Bulldog' refers to the British variety or to the head barman, a squat man with bulging biceps and prominent '...she broke my heart' tattoos. Good lunch menu, so long as you avoid the '*Salat à la Buldok*', an appalling concoction of yoghurt and nuts.

Vinohrady

Hapu, Orlická 8. A locals' favourite that looks like a charmingly dilapidated living room. Once installed, you hardly need move, as the friendly Czech couple who run the place will bring cocktails over to your comfy sofa.

Shakespeare and Sons, Krymská 12. An excellent neighbourhood bar/café with a relaxed ambience and backroom bookshop. Pleasantly free of tourists, no doubt because it's so off the beaten track. Even at night, the noise never seems to rise above a murmur.

Žlutá Pumpa, Belgická 11. A boozy, smoky haven for late-night desperadoes.

Žižkov

Akropolis, Kubelíkova 27. The lazy service and depressingly bad décor of the ground-floor restaurant are partially offset by the appetising Devil's pancakes stuffed with meat and veg (*d'ábelský bramborák*). Definitely the place to bring your dog, as there's a separate menu for pets (sadly, no 'Czech specialities' on this one). The human clientele is a mix of foreigners and locals, most of whom head straight for the smoky downstairs club, a converted cinema that has regular live bands and DJs as well as a popular bar and chill-out room.

U Houdků, Bořivojova 110. A traditional workers' pub with a beer-garden and fine selection of brews.

U Vystřelenýho Oka, U božich bojovníků 3. Situated on a grotty terrace at the foot of Žižkov Hill, the wonderfully named 'Shot-out Eye' (a reference to the Hussite general, Jan Žižka; see p 195) is a no-nonsense beer-drinker's paradise, with several smoke-filled rooms and invariably loud music. There is an escape route, though, in the form of a mellow upstairs tea-room known as *Čajírna nad okem* ('Above the Eye').

Holešovice

Bar Práce, Kamenická 9. A tongue-in-cheek shrine to Communism, complete with Socialist Realist portraits of party leaders and assorted memorabilia. Convenient for a well-earned beer after visiting the nearby National Gallery (see p 204).

Cultural events and festivals

The best place to find out about cultural events in Prague is the **PIS** (see p 43), whose offices are dotted around the city. A useful source of listings information is the *Prague Post* (www.praguepost.cz), published weekly, which has news and reviews of films, plays, exhibitions and concerts. The monthly *Prague In Your Pocket* (www.inyourpoc ket.com), available from selected newsstands, is another good source of up-to-date information.

Concerts of classical music, particularly Mozart (see p 70) and the major Czech composers, are very frequent, but you should look out for performances given by the Prague Symphony Orchestra, the Czech Philharmonic or the Prague Chamber Philharmonic. These usually take place at such wonderful venues as the Municipal House (see p 88) and Rudolfinum (see p 115), both of which feature during the unmissable **Prague Spring** festival, the biggest event in the annual music calendar. The best venues for opera are the Estates Theatre (see p 109), with regular performances of *Don Giovanni*, and the National Theatre, which concentrates on Czech opera, especially Smetana and Dvořák.

Czech jazz has been held in high esteem ever since Jaroslav Ježek's big band of the 1930s, producing names such as George Mraz and Jan Hammer. One of the best venues is *AghaRTA* (www.agharta.cz) at Krakovská 5, which organises the city's annual jazz festival and manages to pull in a number of top international acts. It is closely rivalled by *U Staré paní* (www.ustarepani.cz) at Michalská 9, which focuses on contemporary jazz played by first-rate local artists. The *Reduta* (see p 174), at Národní 20, is the most famous of the three, but also the most tourist-oriented, while *U Maélho Glena* (see p 133), at Karmelitská 23, attracts a younger crowd and has regular jazz and blues nights in its tiny basement.

Tickets for cultural events are best bought through one of the city's ticket agencies, such as **Ticket Pro** (www.ticketpro.cz), which has offices on Wenceslas Square, No. 38 (open Mon–Fri 9.30–18:00, ☎ 224 228 454) and at the Old Town Hall (open daily 09.00–18.00, ☎ 224 223 613), or **Bohemia Ticket International** (www.ticketsbti.cz), which has offices at Na příkopě 16 (open Mon–Fri 10.00–19.00, Sat 10.00–17.00, Sun 10.00–15.00, ☎ 224 215 031) and Malé náměstí 13 (open Mon–Fri 09.00–17.00, Sat 09.00–13.00, ☎ 224 227 832). Alternatively, you can buy tickets direct from the venue's box office.

Events calendar

March: Days of European Film (www.eurofilmfest.cz).

March/April: Prague Writer's Festival (www.pwf.pragonet.cz), ☎ 224 931 053.

March–October: Prague Jazz Festival (www.agharta.cz).

May/June: Prague Spring Festival (www.festival.cz), ☎ 257 312 547. Classical music.

June: Prague Fringe Festival (www.praguefringe.com).

May–July: Respect (www.respectmusic.cz). World music.

June: Tanec Praha (www.tanecpha.cz). Modern dance.

Sept/October: Prague Autumn (www.pragueautumn.cz), ☎ 222 540 484. Classical music.

October: Four Days in Motion (www.ctyridny.cz), ☎ 224 809 116. Theatre and dance.

October: Konfrontace (www.divadlo.cz/konfrontace), ☎ 224 809 112. Modern dance.

Museums and galleries

As a rule, museums are open six days a week and are **closed on Mondays**. They open at around 09.00 and close at around 17.00. Times may vary with the season—museums usually operate shorter hours in winter (Oct–March). Tickets are cheap by Western standards, with concessions available for students (proof of identity is required). Exhibits are usually labelled in English or German, but if not, booklets about the displays are usually available from ticket offices. At major sites you can hire an English-speaking guide. All the museums and galleries listed below are described in the main text.

Art Galleries

Kampa Museum, U sovových mlýnů 2, open Tues–Sun 10.00–17.00 (see p 131).

House of the Golden Ring, Týnská 6, open Tues–Sun, 10.00–18.00 (see p 92).

Prague Castle Gallery, Hradčany (second courtyard), open April–Oct daily 09.00–17.00, Nov–March 09.00–16.00 (see p 143).

Strahov Art Gallery, Strahovský klášter, open Tues–Sun 09.00–17.00 (see p 160).

Troja Château, U Trojského zámku 1, open Tues–Sun 09.00–18.00 April–Oct, Sat, Sun 10.00–17.00 Nov–March (see p 210).

Decorative Arts

Mucha Museum, Panská 7, open daily 10.00–18.00 (see p 167).

Museum of Decorative Arts, 17. listopadu, open Tues–Sun 10.00–18.00 (see p 115).

History

Army Museum, U památníku 2, open April–Oct Tues–Sun 09.30–18.00, Nov–March Tues–Sat 09.30–17.00 (see p 195).

City Transport Museum, Patočkova 4, open April–Oct Sat, Sun 09.00–17.00 (see p 197).

Historical Museum, Jiřská 3 (Lobkowicz Palace), open Tues–Sun 09.00–17.00 (see p 150).

Museum of the City of Prague, Na poříčí 52, open Tues–Sun 10.00–18.00 (see p 170).
Museum of Communism, Na příkopě 10, open 09.00–21.00 (see p 166).

Interiors

House of the Lords of Kunštát and Poděbrady, Řetězová 3, open summer only 10.00–18.00 (see p 106).
Maison Müller, Nad hradním vodojemem 14, open Tues, Thur, Sat, Sun 10.00, 12.00, 14.00, 16.00, prior booking only (see p 198).
Municipal House, náměstí Republiky, open Mon–Sat 10.00–18.00 (see p 88).
Old Royal Palace, Hradčany (third courtyard), open April–Sept daily 09.00–17.00, Oct–March daily 09.00–16.00 (see p 151).
Old Town Hall, Staroměstské náměstí, open Mon 11.00–17.00, Tues–Sun 09.00–17.00 (see p 98).

Jewish Prague

Jewish Museum, Josefov (various venues), open April–Oct Sun–Fri 09.30–18.00, Nov–March Sun–Fri 09.30–17.00 (see p 111).
Jubilee Synagogue, Jeruzalémská 5, open Sun-Thur 09.30–18.00, Fri 09.30–17.00 (see p 171).
Old-New Synagogue, Červená, open Sun-Thur 09.30–18.00, Fri 09.30–17.00 (see p 111).

Literature

Kafka Museum, náměstí Franze Kafky, open Tues–Fri 10.00–18.00, Sat 10.00–17.00 (see p 97).
Museum of Czech Literature, Strahovský klášter, open 10.00–17.00 (see p 159).
Museum of Czech Literature, letohrádek Hvězda, Břevnov, open Tues–Sat 09.00–16.00, Sun 10.00–17.00 (see p 200).

Miscellaneous

Lapidarium of the National Museum, Výstaviště Praha, open Tues–Fri 12.00–18.00, Sat, Sun 10.00–12.30 and 13.00–18.00 (see p 210).
Museum of Miniatures, Strahovský klášter, open 09.00–17.00 (see p 160).
National Technical Museum, Kostelní 42, open Tues–Sun 09.00–17.00 (see p 202).
Police Museum, Ke Karlovu 1, open Tues–Sun 10.00–17.00 (see p 182).
Puppet Museum, Karlova 12 open Tues–Sun 10.00–20.00 (see p 104).
Toy Museum, Jiřská 4, Hradčany, open Tues–Sun 09.30–17.30 (see p 150).

Music

Dvořák Museum, Ke Karlovu 20, open Tues–Sun 10.00–17.00 (see p 183).
Mozart Museum, Mozartova 169 (Bertramka), open Tues–Sun 09.30–18.00 (see p 189).
Smetana Museum, Novotného Lávka, open Wed–Mon 10.00–17.00 (see p 105).

National Gallery's collections

Convent of St Agnes, U milosrdných 17, open Tues–Sun 10.00–18.00 (see p 117).
Convent of St George, náměstí U sv. Jiří 33, Hradčany, open Tues–Sun 10.00–18.00 (see p 148).
House of the Black Madonna, Celetná 34, open Tues–Sun 10.00–18.00 (see p 91).
Šternberg Palace, Hradčanské náměstí 15, Hradčany, open Tues–Sun 10.00–18.00 (see p 154)

Trade Fair Palace, Dukelských hrdinů 45, open Tues–Sun 10.00–18.00 (see p 203).
Zbraslav Château, Bartoňova 2, Zbraslav, open Tues–Sun 10.00–18.00 (see p 190).

Natural History and Anthropology
Náprstek Museum of Asian, African and American Cultures, Betlémské náměstí 1, open Tues–Sun 09.00–17.30 (see p 107).
National Museum, Václavské náměstí 68, open May–Sept 10.00–18.00, Oct–April 09.00–17.00 (see p 163).

Churches
Famous Prague churches are often open all day, but sometimes charge an entry fee. Less important churches may be accessible only during mass or at the visiting times indicated outside. It is not considered polite to wander about a church during mass and those who do may get some stern looks or be asked to leave.

 # Additional information

Crime and personal safety
Street crime has risen dramatically in recent years, but Prague is still a lot safer than many Western cities. Petty crime such as pickpocketing is more likely to affect you than anything more serious. Places to be especially vigilant include the Charles Bridge, Old Town Square, and crowded trams and buses. Be sensible: make photocopies of your passport and note down the numbers of your travellers' cheques and credit cards. Carry your valuables in a money belt or leave them in the hotel safe. Report anything stolen to the municipal police, as you will need documentation for your insurance company. If your passport is stolen, you should also contact your embassy (see p 11) to get a temporary one issued.

The main police station is at Bartolomějská 6 and is open 24 hours. *Byl jsem okraden* means 'I've been robbed'. The police are often castigated for taking far too long to arrive at crime scenes and doing little to help the victims; the language barrier may also be a problem. You are technically required to carry identification with you at all times, but the police rarely carry out spot checks. If they do, a photocopy of your passport should suffice.

Accident, *Nehoda*   Doctor, *Lékář*
Passport, *Pas*   Police, *Policie*

Emergency telephone numbers
Police, ☎ 158
Ambulance, ☎ 155
Fire, ☎ 150

Electricity
The Czech Republic uses standard Continental two-pin 220V plugs and sockets. If you are bringing electrical equipment from the UK, you will need to use a three-to-two-pin adapter (available from electrical shops and airports). American appliances will also require a transformer.

English-language bookshops

Most bookshops in Central Prague have a section devoted to books in English, including the excellent translations from Czech produced by the locally based Twisted Spoon Press. However, the main specialist English-language bookshop in the city is the *Big Ben Bookshop* at Malá Štupartská 5 (open Mon–Fri 09.00–18.30, Sat, Sun 10.00–17.00), which also sells English-language newspapers and magazines. An alternative is *The Globe Bookstore and Coffeehouse* (see p 32) at Pštrossova 6, which has slightly shop-soiled products and is based on San Francisco's celebrated *City Lights* shops. It also puts on literary events, with occasional readings by famous authors.

Newspapers

International editions of the *Financial Times* and *Guardian* (printed in Frankfurt) arrive at selected newsstands around noon (try those on Wenceslas Square). The normal editions of the British broadsheets tend to be a day old. The *Wall Street Journal*, *International Herald Tribune* and *USA Today* are also available.

The *Prague Post*, an English-language weekly, appears on Wednesdays and has good entertainment and business sections. You can also check the paper's website (www.praguepost.cz) for useful listings.

Opening hours

The word for open in Czech is *otevřeno*; closed is *zavřeno*.
Banks are open Mon–Fri 08.00–17.00 with a break at lunch.
Government offices are open Mon–Fri 08.30–17.00.
Post offices are open Mon–Fri 08.00–17.00 and Sat 08.00–12.00.
Restaurants generally open for lunch around 11.00 and stay open until 22.00 or 23.00; they are usually open on Sundays.
Shops open Mon–Fri 08.00 or 09.00 to 17.00 or 18.00. Many shops are open until 12.00 Sat. Some close for lunch and many close in August. Late-night shops are called *večerka*; there are also 24-hour shops called, appropriately, 'non-stop'. For museum opening times, see **Museums and galleries**.

Public holidays

1 January (New Year's Day)	6 July (Jan Hus Day)
Easter Monday	28 September (St Wenceslas Day)
1 May (Labour Day)	28 October (Independence Day)
8 May (VE Day)	17 November (Velvet Revolution)
5 July (Cyril and Methodius Day)	24–26 December (Christmas)

Telephone and postal services

Post offices can be confusing because each window has a different service, and you may find yourself queuing unnecessarily. The main post office (*pošta*) is at Jindřišská 14, Prague 1 (open 07.00–20.00), where you can buy stamps (*známky*), send faxes and change money. You can also receive letters (at position 28) if they are addressed Poste Restante, Jindřišská 14, 110 00 Praha 1. Stamps for postcards to the UK cost 6Kč, to the US 8Kč. Sending letters to the UK costs 9Kč and to the US 14Kč. Stamps can also be bought at newsstands and tobacconists. Mail boxes are orange. Post takes up to five working days to reach the UK, and between seven and ten days to the US.

Most **public telephones** now run on cards (*telefonní karty*), which can be bought from post offices, train stations, metro stations, kiosks, large department stores, hotels and anywhere displaying a blue-and-yellow Telecom sticker. They come in 50 units, 100 units and 150 units. In telephones that still take coins, local calls cost a minimum of 3Kč, international calls 5Kč (not recommended).

It can sometimes be a challenge calling AT&T, Sprint and other card companies. Persevere, because some hotel operators may refuse to make the connection and, when they do, will charge you a premium rate. If you have problems, call the international operator, ☎ 133004; to make a reverse-charge call, say '*na účet volaného* London/New York/etc', though most operators understand English.

Dialling codes. All Prague telephone numbers have nine digits and begin with a 2 (the code for Prague, which must always be dialled, even from within the city). The code for the Czech Republic is 420

Calling Prague from the UK: 00 420 + nine-digit number
Calling Prague from the US and Canada: 011 420 + nine-digit number
Calling Prague from Australia and New Zealand: 0011 420 + nine-digit number
Calling Prague from elsewhere in the Czech Republic: 0 + nine-digit number

When calling abroad from Prague, drop the first zero of the local area code, e.g. to call London, dial 00 44 20 followed by the eight-digit number.
Calling the UK from Prague: 00 44
Calling the US and Canada from Prague: 00 1
Calling Ireland from Prague: 00 353
Calling Australia from Prague: 00 61
Calling New Zealand from Prague: 00 64

Internet
To log on to a PPP server from your laptop, phone 971 103 333 (username: quick, password: quick). You will be charged for a local call. Many upmarket hotels now provide Internet access. Failing this, you can always check your e-mail at one of the many Internet cafés around the city, such as the Globe Bookstore and Coffeehouse (see p 32).

Time zone
The Czech Republic lies within the Central European time zone (CET). Prague is one hour ahead of the UK and six hours ahead of US Eastern time. The clocks go forward one hour in the summer (usually April/May) and back one hour in the winter (usually September).

Toilets
Public conveniences (*záchody* or WC) are few and far between. Those that do exist are usually clean and have attendants. A charge of 5Kč is standard. 'Ladies' is *Dámy* or *Ženy*, 'Gents' is *Páni* or *Muži*. If desperate you can always use the toilets in a restaurant or hotel.

Tourist information and tour operators
The quality of tourist offices (*informační centrum*) varies, but most will at least sell information brochures, guide books, catalogues, maps and plans. In the better offices, you can get information about local places of interest, travel, accommo-

dation, sports-equipment rental, and entertainment. Nowadays, the staff will often speak English and/or other foreign languages. One of the best tourist offices is the **Prague Information Service** (*Pražká informační služba*), or PIS, listed below. Hotel receptions are sometimes a good source of information, as is www.expats.cz, a bulletin board useful for finding jobs and flats in Prague. Many offices sell the **Prague Card**, which costs around €25 and gives you free entry into over 40 sites around the city, as well as free travel on all public transport, for a period of three days.

E-Travel (www.travel.cz), Ostrovní 7, Prague 1, ☎ 224 990 990-9, open daily 08.00–22.00. Formerly known as Tom's Travel, this extremely helpful organisation will arrange every aspect of your visit to Prague. The company also has a London office, ☎ (020) 7681 2362.

Čedok (www.cedok.cz/incoming), Na příkopě 18, Prague 1, ☎ 224 197 242, open Mon–Fri 09.00–19.00, Sat, Sun 09.30–14.30. The former state travel agency is a good place to buy bus, train and air tickets.

Martin Tour (www.martintour.cz), Štěpánská 61 (Lucerna Palace), Prague 1, ☎ 224 212 473, 224 239 752, open Mon–Fri 09.00–16.30. Guided tours for groups and individuals.

Prague Information Service (www.prague-info.cz), **Na příkopě 20**, Prague 1, open April–Oct Mon–Fri 09.00–19.00, Sat, Sun 09.00–17.00, Nov–March, Mon–Fri 09.00–18.00, Sat 09.00–15.00; **Old Town Hall** (Staroměstská radnice), Prague 1, open April–Oct Mon–Fri 09.00–19.00, Sat, Sun 09.00–18.00, Nov–March Mon–Fri 09.00–18.00, Sat, Sun 09.00–17.00; **Central Railway Station** (Hlavní nádraží), open April–Oct Mon–Fri 09.00–19.00, Sat, Sun 09.00–16.00, Nov–March Mon–Fri 09.00–18.00, Sat 09.00–15.00.

Czech words and phrases

The basics

Do you speak English? *Mluvíte anglicky?* [mloo-vee-te ang-glits-ki]

I don't understand Czech. *Nerozumím česky.* [ne-ro-zoo-meem che-ski]

Do you understand? *Rozumíte?* [ro-zoo-mee-te]

I am English. *Jsem Angličan(ka)*. [Y-sem An-gli-chan(ka)] (the 'ka' ending is used if the speaker is a woman)

Yes, *Ano* [a-no]

No *Ne*, [ne]

Please, *Prosím* [pro-seem]

Thank you (very much), *Děkuji (mockrát)* [dye-koo-yi mots-kraht]

Thanks, *Díky* [dyee-kil]

How do you do, *Dobrý den* [do-bree den] (lit. 'good day', general-purpose greeting)

Goodbye, *Na shledanou* [na-skhle-da-noh]

Goodnight, *Dobrou noc* [dob-roh nots]

When? At what time?, *Kdy? v kolik hodin?* [gdi] [fko-lik ho-dyin]

How long? (i.e. time), *Jak dlouho?* [yak dloh-ho]

Where? *Kde?* [gde]

Where can I buy...? *Kde mohu koupit...?* [gde mo-hu koh-pit]

What? *Co?* [tso]

How? *Jak?* [yak]

How do I get to...? *Jak se dostanu k...?* [yak se do-sta-nu k]

May I...? *Smím...?* [smeem]

Have you got...? *Máte...?* [mah-te]

I would like... *Chtěl bych (chtěla bych)...* [khytyel bikh/khtye-la bikh] (the 'a' on the end is used if the speaker is a woman)

How much (does it cost)? *Kolik (stojí...)?* [ko-lik sto-yee]

Please write. *Prosím napište...* [pro-seem na-pish-te] (this may be helpful if you are getting an answer in Czech that is an address, a number, a date or time of day)

Excuse me. *Promiňte* [pro-min-te] (as in English, this can be used either when accosting or interrupting someone, or as a mild apology)

I'm (very) sorry *Je mi (velice) líto* [ye mi ve-li-tse lee-to]

Not at all. *Není zač* [ne-nyee zatch] (lit. 'there is nothing for which', a polite response to thanks or apologies)

Have you got a menu in English? *Máte lístek v angličtině?* [mah-te lees-tek van glitch-ti-nye]

The bill please *Prosím, platit* [pro-seem pla-tyit] (lit. 'please, to pay')

Mr, Mrs, Miss *Pane, Paní, Slečno* [pa-ne, pa-nyee, sletch-no] (like 'Monsieur' or 'Madame' in French, they can be used with or without a proper name following. They are given here in the vocative case, which is used when you are talking to someone rather than about them)

Numbers

Intermediate numbers work like English, or, more precisely, like American English: 127 is said as 'one hundred twenty-seven', *sto dvacet sedm* (there is no 'and'). Czechs may, however, reverse the order of tens and units when saying or writing the words, e.g. 'seven-and-twenty', *sedmadvacet* (the same words in reverse order, with an 'a' in the middle) as this avoids some grammatical complications. You may therefore hear 'sto sedmadvacet' for 127. If in doubt, ask for the number to be written down.

0 *nula* [nu-la]

1 *jeden* [ye-den]
2 *dva* [dva]
3 *tři* [trzhi]
4 *čtyři* [chti-rzhi]
5 *pět* [pyet]
6 *šest* [shest]
7 *sedm* [se-dum]
8 *osm* [o-sum]
9 *devět* [de-vyet]
10 *deset* [de-set]
11 *jedenáct* [ye-de-nahtst]
12 *dvanáct* [dva-nahtst]
13 *třináct* [trzhi-nahtst]
14 *čtrnáct* [chtr-nahtst]
15 *patnáct* [pat-nahtst]
16 *šestnáct* [shest-nahtst]
17 *sedmnáct* [se-dum-nahtst]

18 *osmnáct* [o-sum-nahtst]
19 *devatenáct* [de-va-te-nahtst]
20 *dvacet* [dva-tset]
30 *třicet* [trzhi-tset]
40 *čtyřicet* [chti-rzhi-tset]
50 *padesát* [pa-de-saht]
60 *šedesát* [she-de-saht]
70 *sedmdesát* [se-dum-de-saht]
80 *osmdesát* [o-sum-de-saht]
90 *devadesát* [de-va-de-saht]
100 *sto* [sto]
1000 *tisíc* [tyi-seets]

Days and months

Sunday, *neděle* [ne-dye-le]
Monday, *pondělí* [pon-dye-lee]
Tuesday, *úterý* [oo-te-ree]

Wednesday, *středa* [strzhe-da]
Thursday, *čtvrtek* [chtvr-tek]
Friday, *pátek* [pah-tek]
Saturday, *sobota* [so-bo-ta]
January, *leden* [le-den]
February, *únor* [oo-nor]
March, *březen* [brzhe-zen]
April, *duben* [du-ben]
May, *květen* [kvye-ten]
June, *červen* [cher-ven]
July, *červenec* [cher-ve-nets]
August, *srpen* [sr-pen]
September, *září* [zah-rzhee]
October, *říjen* [rzhee-yen]
November, *listopad* [lis-to-pad]
December, *prosinec* [pro-si-nets]
Note that days and months do not have
capital letters in Czech.

Tourist glossary

Cesta, Path
Chrám/katedrála, Cathedral
Divadlo, Theatre
Galerie, Gallery
Hrad, Castle
Hřbitov, Cemetery
Kaple, Chapel
Kašna, Fountain
Kavárna, Café
Klášter, Monastery
Knihovna, Library
Kopec, Hill
Kostel, Church
Most, Bridge
Muzeum, Museum
Náměstí, Square
Národní, National
Ostrov, Island
Palác, Palace
Památky, Monuments, historic buildings
Pošta, Post office
Průvodce, Guide (either a person or a
guidebook)
Restaurace, Restaurant
Sad, Garden

Silnice, Road
Socha, Statue
Staré město, Old town
Svatý, Saint
Trh, Market
Třída, Avenue
Tržište, Market-place
Ulice, Street
Ulička, Alley
Věž, Tower
Vrch, Hill
Výstava, Exhibition
Zámek, Château
Zahrada, Garden

Signs and notices

Dámy, Ladies
Informace, Information
Kouření zakázáno, No smoking
Letiště, Airport
Muži, Men
Nádraží, Railway station
Nástupiště, Platform
Obsazeno, Reserved (table), full up (bus),
taken (seat)
Odjezd, Departure
Otevřeno, Open
Páni, Gentlemen
Pitná voda, Drinking water
Platte u pokladny, Pay at the desk
Pozor, Attention, warning, mind out for...
Příjezd, Arrival
Samoobsluha, Self-service
Šatna, Cloakroom
Vstup zakázán, No admittance
Vchod, Entrance
Vlevo, Left, to the left
Volný, Free (i.e. vacant, not taken)
Vpravo, Right, to the right
Východ, Exit
Zavřeno, Closed
Záchod, WC
Zakázán, Forbidden
Ženy, Women

BACKGROUND INFORMATION

The history of Prague

Appropriately for a city of such fairy-tale appearance, there is a legend connected with the founding of Prague. In around AD 800, **Princess Libuše**, a woman with great powers of divination, sent her henchmen into the forest with instructions to found a town at the spot where they saw a ploughman (*přemysl*) constructing the threshold (*práh*) of a house. She married the ploughman (thus establishing the Přemyslid dynasty) and from her palace at Vyšehrad, situated on a rocky outcrop above the right bank of the Vltava, predicted that the new town, later to be called Praha or Prague, would have a future so glorious that its fame would reach the stars.

The Přemyslids

The real origins of Prague are rather more prosaic and are connected with Slavic settlers occupying the left bank of the Vltava (to the north of Vyšehrad) about the beginning of the 6C AD. The citadel established here at the end of the 9C by the first documented member of the Přemyslid family, Prince Bořivoj, became the first seat of the dynasty, and not Vyšehrad, as legend would have us believe. Bořivoj and his wife Ludmila were baptised by the missionaries **Cyril and Methodius**, who had arrived from Byzantium to spread **Christianity** among the Slavs; Prague was made a bishopric in 973, during the reign of Boleslav the Pious. In the course of the same century, numerous Jewish, German, Italian and French merchants settled on the right bank of the Vltava, at the meeting-place of several trade routes and directly opposite the Slavic settlement on the left bank; the two areas were connected by a wooden bridge at the end of the century. The first known traveller's description of Prague dates from c 965, when the town was visited by Ibrahim ibn Ya'qub, an erudite Spanish Jew who had been sent by the Cordoban caliph al-Hakam II as a member of a diplomatic mission to Emperor Otto I in Merseburg. He described in detail the lively international mercantile life of Prague, a town that belied its relative smallness by seeming to him to have been made 'richer by commerce' than all the other places he visited in Central Europe.

Prince Vratislav II (from 1085 King Vratislav I) transferred his residence to **Vyšehrad**, which was to remain the seat of the Czech rulers until 1140, when the seat was moved back to its original location. The importance of Vyšehrad Castle greatly declined thereafter, but the area of the right bank to the north of it, where the merchants had settled, became an increasingly bustling commercial centre, particularly from the 1170s onwards, when the wooden bridge across the Vltava was replaced by a stone one—the so-called Judith Bridge—and special privileges were granted by Prince Soběslav to encourage more Germans to stay here. This commercial settlement, featuring a walled merchants' court known as the Týn, formed a separate township that was granted a municipal charter c 1230 and is called today the Staré Město or **Old Town**; the extensive

Jewish community was contained from the early 13C within its own walled ghetto attached to the northern side of this settlement. Meanwhile, on the left bank of the Vltava, in the sparsely populated outer bailey of the castle, King Přemysl Otakar II founded in 1257 the township later to be called the Malá Strana or **Little Quarter**, the population of which was originally made up largely of German colonists summoned by the king. In the early 13C the district of **Hradčany** was founded just to the west of the castle, and Prague emerged as one of the most important and densely populated cities in Europe.

The 'Golden Age'

The highpoint of Prague's medieval development was to be reached during the reign of **Charles IV** (1344–78), who was to turn the city in 1355 into the capital of the Holy Roman Empire. Under Charles IV Prague became the 'Rome of the North', attracting scholars and artists from all over Europe, including the Italian poet Petrarch. Elevated to archbishopric in 1344, Prague became in 1348 the seat of the first university in Central Europe, an institution that bears to this day the name of **Charles University**. In that same year Charles greatly increased the size of Prague by founding yet another township, the Nové Město or **New Town**, which incorporated the former horse and cattle markets (respectively today Wenceslas and Charles Squares) and came eventually to extend from Vyšehrad all the way to the northeastern corner of the Old Town. Numerous churches and other monuments were founded by Charles, most notably the Gothic **St Vitus's Cathedral**, on which there worked one of the outstanding architects of medieval Europe, **Petr Parléř**, who was summoned to Prague by Charles in 1353. In 1357, to replace the Judith Bridge, another of Prague's great landmarks was created—the Charles Bridge.

With the succession of Wenceslas IV to the throne in 1348, social and religious tensions led to a period of cultural and economic decline. Urged by the religious reformer **Jan Hus**, Wenceslas curtailed the rights of the Germans at the Charles University, thus leading to the exodus of 2000 students and many professors. The peculiarly Czech tradition of throwing people to their deaths from high places—initiated by Wenceslas with the ejection of the prelate John of Nepomuk (Jan Nepomucký) from the Charles Bridge in 1379—continued in 1419 with the shoving of two Catholic councillors out of the window of the New Town Hall, an event that sparked off the Hussite Wars and was later dignified with the absurd and pompous name of the **First Defenestration**. Renewed stability and building activity set in with the reign of George of Poděbrady (1458–71), but Prague's importance as a trading centre continued to decline. George's successor, the Polish king Vladislav II (1471–1516), brought the Renaissance to Prague by inviting here the outstandingly original architect **Benedikt Ried**, whose idiosyncratic Vladislav Hall in Prague Castle is the earliest example in Bohemia of the influence of contemporary Italian architecture. Vladislav also consolidated the political decline of Prague, however, by transferring his court in 1490 to the Hungarian capital of Buda.

The Habsburgs and decline

Through most of the period of Habsburg rule, which began in 1526, Prague continued to play a secondary role in European politics, the city being now subservient to Vienna. It experienced a brief political and cultural revival during the rule of **Emperor Rudolph II** (1576–1612), who established his court at Prague, and indulged here his passions for collecting, lavish festivities, astronomy and the occult. He attracted to Prague artists associated with the so-called Mannerist style (most notably Bartolomaeus Spranger, Adriaen de Vries and Giuseppe Arcimboldo), as well as such leading and controversial European scientists as the astronomers Tycho Brahe and Johannes Kepler, the alchemists Edward Kelley and John Dee, the surgeon Jan Jessenius (who conducted the first public dissection in Prague) and the mathematician Jost Bürgi, the inventor of logarithms. In 1612 he was forced to abdicate in favour of his brother Matthias, who brought the court back to Vienna in 1617. On 23 May 1618, over 100 members of the Bohemian nobility rose up in revolt against the Habsburgs and made their way to Prague Castle, where they perpetrated the **Second Defenestration**, an incident giving rise to the **Thirty Years War**. After the defeat of the Protestants at the Battle of the White Mountain in 1620—which took place on the western outskirts of Prague, near the star-shaped hunting lodge of Hvězda—27 of the Protestant leaders were executed on the Old Town Square. Occupied by Saxons in 1631–32, Prague was later besieged by the Swedes, who managed to take possession of the Little Quarter just before peace was declared in 1648.

As with the rest of Bohemia, Prague was left in a state of devastation at the end of the Thirty Years War. Yet the process of rebuilding the city (beginning with the reconstruction from 1630 onwards of the Little Quarter), together with the spectacular reassertion of the Catholic Church following years of religious strife, led to the transformation of Prague into one of the great Baroque centres of Europe. The highpoint of the city's Baroque development was reached during the early 18C, during the period of architectural supremacy of the prolific **Kilian Ignaz Dientzenhofer**, who was responsible for the vast Clementinum and countless palaces and churches, most notably that of St Nicholas in the Little Quarter, which is comparable to Longhena's Church of the Salute in Venice in dominating the skyline of the city. This same century saw the burgeoning of palace gardens in the Little Quarter, the creation of the wooded parks of Letná, Troja and Petřín, and the extension, between 1753 and 1775, of Prague Castle into the complex of buildings and courtyards that is to be seen today. In place of the medieval fortifications around the Old Town there was laid out between 1760 and 1781 Prague's first boulevard, comprising Na příkopě and its continuation, Národní. Prague's development into a bustling modern city was consolidated in 1784 with the bringing together into a single administrative unit of the four hitherto separate townships of the Old Town, New Town, Little Quarter and Hradčany.

The 19th century, Czech nationalism and the arts

The rapid industrialisation of Prague in the 19C, and the increase in the city's population from 80,000 to well over 200,000, went hand-in-hand with a mood of growing **Czech nationalism**, and ever greater tensions between the Czechs and Germans in the city. In 1848 a Czech national uprising centred on Prague was crushed, but in that same year there also took place here the first Pan Slavic Congress. Germans lost their majority in the Prague Municipal Parliament for the first time in 1861, and in 1882 the Charles University was divided up according to nationality. In the latter years of the century the city's skyline was enriched by two massive neo-Renaissance buildings that expressed the aspirations of the Czech people: one was the **National Theatre** at the western end of Národní avenue, the other was the National Museum, situated above what was now emerging as the new focal point of Prague life—**Wenceslas Square**. Other major urban changes occurring in Prague at this time included the demolition of the city's remaining ramparts in 1874–76, and the destruction of the **Jewish Quarter** through the creation in the 1890s of a long street named after the city of Paris and lined, as its name would suggest, with grand apartment blocks and fashionable shops. An important industrial exhibition held in Prague in 1891 confirmed the city's position as one of the main industrial and commercial centres of the Habsburg Empire.

By the early years of the 20C, Prague was already becoming a leading European centre of the avant-garde, and the visionary achievements of a writer such as **Kafka** were matched by the construction of exceptionally original 'Cubist' buildings by the likes of Gočár and Chochol. However, it was the establishment of the **Czechoslovak Republic** in 1918 that led to one of the richest and liveliest periods in the cultural history of Prague. Pioneering poets, painters, designers, photographers and architects were all brought together by the Prague-based group Devětsil, which was closely associated with the city's developing reputation as the European centre of Constructivism and Functionalism. Uncompromising structures in concrete and glass grew up in the very centre of the city, while suburbs such as Podbaba and Barrandov became showpieces of Modernist architecture.

Communism and democratic future

The German occupation of 1939–45, followed by the repressive years of Communism, drove the city's cultural life underground but by no means extinguished it, as became evident in the great burst of literary, cinematic and theatrical talent in the 1960s, culminating in the '**Prague Spring**' of 1968. World attention was drawn once again to Prague, but admiration turned to horror in August of that year, when television cameras showed Soviet tanks entering Prague's Old Town Square. On 16 January 1969, at a spot near Wenceslas Square, the student **Jan Palach** set fire to himself in protest against the Soviet invasion. The subsequent years, up to the signing in 1977 of **Charter 77**, were among the greyest in the city's history, though they were also ones of rapid urban growth: in 1974 the underground railway system was opened, and the city boundaries were greatly increased by the incorporation within them of 74 outlying communities, bringing the total population of Prague up to 1,200,000 inhabitants. The new architecture was generally drab and mediocre, reducing the exciting Functionalism of the 1920s to unimaginative uniformity; a lively literary culture, however, continued to exist in the city, thanks principally to *samizdat* publishing—typewritten articles and books that circulated from hand to hand within a wide illicit network. Leading dissident meeting-places included jazz clubs, the Café Slavia, and the back-rooms of the Magic Lantern theatre, the latter coming to play a vital role in the '**Velvet Revolution**' of November 1989, a revolution that had begun on 17 November with a large student demonstration making its way from the Vltava down Národní avenue and eventually settling in Wenceslas Square. Among the first acts of the Civic Forum Government led by the playwright president **Václav Havel** was, in January 1990, to rename Red

Army Square after Jan Palach. The renaming of numerous other squares and streets in Prague gathered momentum in the course of 1990, and in November of that year the remains of Jan Palach were brought back to the Olšany Cemetery in the Prague district of Vinohrady.

The problems of popularity

With the return of democracy, Prague has had to face the inevitable physical consequences of the sudden onslaught of capitalism and **mass tourism**. Václav Havel, though coming himself from a family of architects and developers, frequently expressed his concern that the foreign investors swarming into Prague would overcrowd the city with crass office-blocks, hotels, conference centres and shopping malls: in 1995 he praised as 'the first victory for common sense' the City Council's decision to call off an architectural competition for the design of a 180-room hotel to be built near the Charles Bridge. But a problem even more worrying than new development is the way in which so much of old Prague is being turned through insensitive and haphazard renovation into a Disneyland designed to please tourists. **Façades** that had been left to crumble during the Communist period are now being covered in garish colours that are often not only historically inaccurate but also potentially destructive when the wrong types of paint are used. In 1997 the director of the city's Centre for the Preservation of Architecture successfully petitioned the New York-based **World Monument Fund** to include the city's historic centre on its list of the 100 most endangered sites in the world. Without financial assistance, he claimed, few of Prague's original façades and roofs would soon be left, and the whole city would be turned into a characterless reconstruction like Nuremberg.

Perhaps an even greater threat to Prague's physical appearance was presented by the massive **floods** of August 2002, which made headline news around the world. When the Vltava burst its banks, large tracts of the Little Quarter and Old Town became submerged in several feet of muddy water, causing untold damage to museums, galleries and historic buildings, not to mention homes and businesses; initial estimates put the bill for the clean-up operation at more than 2 billion US dollars. Among the places to be worst hit was Kampa Island, where the infrastructure had to be rebuilt practically from scratch and where, in one particularly dramatic incident, a giant sculpture that stood in front of the Kampa museum was washed more than 45km downriver. The cellars and beautiful gardens of the Troja château also fell victim to the flood waters, and in 2003 ....res rescued from the château were put on display in the House at the ....Prague's Old Town Square. By some cruel irony the City of Prague had in spring 2002 put on an exhibition entitled 'Floods of Prague', ...ting, in an historical context, the floods that have affected the city since the Middle Ages. But for many who witnessed the catastrophic events later that August, the most heartbreaking moment was the death of Nadir, a 35-year-old Indian elephant at Prague Zoo. A photograph taken by René Jakl (which won Czech Press Photo of the year) shows the animal hoisting its trunk above the floodwaters in a desperate last attempt to breathe.

A chronology of Czech rulers

Czech State

The Přemyslids (870–1306)
Princes

Bořivoj I	? –c 890
Spytihněv I	? –915
Vratislav I	915–21
Wenceslas (Václav) I	921–935 (St Wenceslas)
Boleslav the Cruel (I)	935–972
Boleslav the Pious (II)	972–999
Boleslav the Red (III)	999–1002 and 1003
Vladivoj	1002–03
Jaromír	1003, 1004–12 and 1033–34
Boleslav the Brave (IV)	1003–04
Oldřich (Ulrich)	1012–34
Břetislav I	1035–55
Spytihněv II	1055–61
Vratislav II	1061–92
Konrad I	1092
Břetislav II	1092–1100
Bořivoj II	1101–07 and 1117–20
Svatopluk	1107–09
Vladislav I	1109–17 and 1120–25
Soběslav I	1125–40
Vladislav II	1140–72
Bedřich I	1172–73 and 1178–89
Soběslav II	1173–78
Konrad II	1189–91
Wenceslas (Václav) II	1191–92
Přemysl Otakar I	1192–93 and 1197–1230
Jindřich (Henry) Bretislav	1193–97
Vladislav Jindřich (Henry)	1197

Kings

Wenceslas (Václav) I	1230–53
Přemysl Otakar II	1253–78
Wenceslas (Václav) II	1278–1305
Wenceslas (Václav) III	1305–06

Miscellaneous Houses (1306–1310)

Rudolph (Rudolf) I	1306–07
Jindřich Korutanský (Henry of Carinthia)	1307–10

The Luxemburgs (1310–1437)

John (Jan) of Luxemburg	1310–46
Charles (Karel) I	1346–78 (H.R. Emp. as Charles IV)
Wenceslas (Václav) IV	1378–1419
Sigismund (Zikmund)	1419–20 and 1436–37

The Habsburgs (1437–1457)

Albert (Albrecht) of Habsburg	1437–39
Ladislav the Posthumous (Pohrobek)	1453–57

The Hussites (1458–1471)

George (Jiří) of Poděbrady	1458–71

The Jagiellons (1471–1526)

Vladislav II	1471–1516
Louis (Ludvik) I	1516–26

The Habsburgs (1526–1918)

Ferdinand I of Austria	1526–64
Maxmilian I	1564–1576
Rudolph (Rudolf) II of Austria	1576–1611
Matthias (Matyáš) I	1611–19
Frederick of the Palatinate (Bedřich Falcký)	1619–1620 ('the Winter King')
Ferdinand II of Austria	1620–37
Ferdinand III	1637–46 and 1654–57
Ferdinand IV	1646–1654
Leopold I of Austria	1657–1705
Joseph (Josef) I	1705–11
Charles (Karel) II of Austria	1711–40 (H.R. Emp. as Charles VI)
Maria Theresa (Marie Terezie), Queen	1740–80
Joseph (Josef) II	1780–90
Leopold II of Austria	1790–92
Francis (František) I of Austria	1792–1835
Ferdinand V	1835–48
Francis Joseph (František Josef) I	1848–1916
Charles (Karel) III	1916–18 (Charles I of Austria)

Czechoslovak Republic
Presidents

T.G. Masaryk	1918–35
E. Beneš	1935–38 and 1945–48
E. Hácha	1938–45
K. Gottwald	1948–53
A. Zápotocký	1953–57
A. Novotný	1957–68
L. Svoboda	1968–75
G. Husák	1975–89
V. Havel	1989–92

Czech Republic
Presidents

V. Havel	1993–2003
V. Klaus	2003–

Art and architecture

Few Westerners coming to Prague for the first time are likely to be familiar with the names of most of the great artists and architects whose works make this one of the European cities with the richest concentration of monuments. Understandably for a city at the confluence of so many cultures, Prague is a place of exceptional stylistic diversity where you need only walk the shortest of distances to be confronted in turn by Gothic arches, Renaissance gables, Baroque statuary, Art Nouveau canopies, Cubist columns, and pioneering sheets of plate glass. But it is also a place where influences from France, Italy, Austria and Germany have often been distorted to strange and fantastical effect, as in the richly decorated gables crowning the toy-like houses, the exhilaratingly inventive vaulting of Petr Parléř and Benedikt Ried, the swollen-formed Cubist buildings of Gočár and Chochol, and the near uncategorisable anti-Modernist structures of Jože Plečnik. Prague, in short, is a city that will constantly excite the curious, open-minded visitor in search of novel cultural experiences.

From Romanesque to Gothic

Among the earliest and most distinctive survivals of Czech architecture are a number of **rotundas** ranging in date from c 900 to c 1225, the oldest being probably that of Levý Hradec near Prague, which appears to have been founded by Prince Bořivoj, the first of the Přemyslid princes to be converted to Christianity. Of slightly later date is St Vitus's Rotunda in Prague, the foundations of which were discovered between 1911 and 1925 in the course of excavations below the Wenceslas Chapel in St Vitus's Cathedral: built by St Wenceslas (who was buried in its southern apse) this 13m-wide structure soon came to attract so many pilgrims on St Wenceslas's Day that in the mid-11C Prince Spytihněv I was forced to build a large new basilica to contain them all. There are three other, heavily restored, Romanesque rotundas in Prague, the earliest of these being St Martin's at Vyšehrad, which is the only intact survival of the palace founded there in the late 11C by Prince Vratislav II, the future first king of Bohemia; the second of the rotundas is that of the Holy Cross (in the middle of the Old Town, at the intersection of Karoliny Světlé and Konviktská), while the third is the late-11C St Longinus Rotunda on Na Rybníčku in the New Town. But the most interesting and extensive Romanesque survival in Prague is the early 12C **Basilica of St George**, which is the second-largest church within Prague Castle: containing rare remains of Czech Romanesque painting, this building is in the shape of a Roman basilica but with heavy walls and small openings that suggest the influence of Ottonian Germany.

A **French style** of art and architecture was introduced into Bohemia and Moravia with the arrival in the early 13C of the Cistercians, whose influence first became apparent in the Convent of St Agnes, the oldest early-Gothic complex in Prague. A comparable Cistercian-Burgundian style can also be found in the magnificent **Old-New Synagogue**, which—given the law forbidding Jews from becoming architects—was probably built by the same Franciscans who had worked at St Agnes. In the meantime important advances were being made in Bohemian **town planning**, with Prague acquiring the first of its pre-planned quarters—the Havelské Město, and the areas around Ovocný trh, Uhelný trh, and Rytířská street. As with Bohemia's many towns of 13C foundation that were laid out on a regular ground-plan, Prague came to acquire as its central feature a large market-place (today's Old Town Square) lined with arcaded houses.

But it was during the reign of **Charles IV** that Prague was to experience the first great flowering of its art and architecture. Charles had been brought up in France, and it was thus not surprising that for the first major commission of his rule—the rebuilding of St Vitus's Cathedral in Prague—he should have called in a French architect, Matthew of Arras (?–1352). Matthew, who had previously worked at Avignon under Charles's friend Clement VI, produced a plan with radiating chapels in the ambulatory that was closely based on the French cathedral at Narbonne. However, Matthew died only eight years after work had begun on the building, and in 1352 Charles summoned to Prague an architect of a very different background, **Petr Parléř** (1330–1405/6).

Parléř, one of the outstanding builders of the Middle Ages, had been born to a family of architects in Cologne in 1330, and had probably received most of his training in the Rhineland. Within the limits imposed by Matthew of Arras's plan, Parléř introduced into St Vitus's Cathedral elements that look ahead to the German *Sondergotik* or Late Gothic. Among his achievements here was the creation of a bold, openwork staircase that was to be copied in the cathedrals at Ulm and Strasbourg; but his principal contribution was his exceptionally inventive vaulting, which included a dazzling star-shaped formation and a system of freestanding ribs spread out like a fan.

The age of Charles IV saw the development of an important local school of painting, to which much impetus was given by Charles's large collection of French and Italian illuminated manuscripts, and by the numerous foreign artists who were attracted to his court, such as the Italian painter Tommaso di Modena. Italian and in particular Sienese influence can be felt in the work of many of the early Bohemian artists, for instance, the Master of Vyšší Brod and the anonymous painter of the votive panel of **Jan Očko of Vlašim**, a work that shows the Virgin and Child flanked by the donor and Charles IV in a way that recalls an Italian *sacra conversazione*. The leading and most idiosyncratic painter in Charles's circle was **Master Theodoric**, who is best known for a series of 129 panels painted between 1357 and 1365 for the Holy Cross Chapel at Karlštejn Castle: his solid but softly modelled figures are set here against a background studded with semi-precious stones, an unusual feature—also to be found in the Wenceslas Chapel in St Vitus's Cathedral—which reflects Charles's passionate love of jewellery. At the end of the century, during the reign of Charles's successor Wenceslas IV, the dominant Bohemian painter came to be the **Master of the Třeboň Altarpiece**, whose art, with its strong sense of colour and feeling for linear rhythm, turned not to the south but to the west, and had strong affinities with contemporary Burgundian artists such as Melchior Broederlam.

The period of intense building and cultural activity that Charles IV had initiated was cut short in 1420 with the outbreak of the Hussite Wars, and was not to be renewed until the end of the century, when the kingdoms of Bohemia, Hungary and Poland were united under the rule of Vladislav the Jagiellon. Vladislav's rule saw some of the more spectacular achievements of the late-Gothic style, as well as a budding influence from Renaissance Italy. Exuberant late-Gothic ornamentation can be seen in the fantastical **Royal Oratory** in St Vitus's Cathedral and in the structures associated with Matěj Rejsek (c

1450–1506), for instance, the public fountain at Kutná Hora and the Powder Gate in Prague.

The Renaissance period

Later in his life Vladislav was to move his court to Buda and surround himself with Italian artists and architects, but before doing so c 1480 he invited to Prague a German architect of extraordinary originality, **Benedikt Ried** (c 1454–1534). Ried, who came probably from South Germany and would soon supersede all other architects in Bohemia, was given the monumental task of extending the fortifications of Prague Castle and rebuilding the Royal Palace there. For the latter he constructed in 1493 the vast **Vladislav Hall** in which Renaissance features (in the doors and windows) are to be found in Bohemia for the first time but combined eccentrically with late-Gothic vaulting of a fantasy and complexity virtually unparalleled in the rest of Europe. Similarly elaborate vaulting was created by him in **St Barbara's Cathedral** at Kutná Hora, which he took over in 1515 from Matěj Rejsek, whose own vaulting here, though complex, lacks the flowing energy of Ried's.

The main painter at Vladislav's court in Prague was the **Master of the Litoměřice Altarpiece**, who is sometimes identified with the German artist Hans Elfelder; he was at any rate someone who had been brought up in South Germany and might also have had first-hand knowledge of North Italian art. The altarpiece from which he derives his name was painted c 1500 for the chapel adjoining the Vladislav Hall (currently in the North Bohemian Gallery at Litoměřice), and is characterised by its lively and detailed realism. Artists from his workshop are often said to have been responsible for the frescoes of c 1509 on the upper walls of the **Wenceslas Chapel**, which reveal an Italianate sense of composition and perspective, as do the slightly earlier frescoes in the Smíšek chapel at Kutná Hora.

After the Habsburgs came to power in 1526, the art and architecture of Bohemia and Moravia came to be dominated by Italians, most of whom were from the Como region. From the time of Benedikt Ried, Classical detailing had sometimes been applied to Gothic structures, but it was not until the 1530s that work was begun in Prague on a truly Italianate building. This, the so-called **Belvedere** in the Hradčany, was commissioned by Ferdinand I from Paolo della Stella, and is surrounded by a most elegant arcaded loggia decorated with exquisitely carved mythological and Classical scenes. The only feature that singles the building out as a work executed outside Italy is its bizarre copper roof in the form of the upturned hull of a ship, an addition of the mid-16C by the Bohemian court architect **Bonifác Wohlmut** (?–1579). Wohlmut's architecture represents a curious synthesis of Italian and Czech elements, and indeed he created for the same belvedere an upper floor inspired by Bramante's Tempietto in Rome; another work of his is the organ loft in **St Vitus's Cathedral**, which seems at first wholly in the spirit of the High Renaissance and yet conceals Gothic vaulting behind its Classical arches. Such a synthesis was to typify the spirit of the Czech Renaissance, and even the many Italian architects and craftsmen who were to come to Bohemia in the wake of Paolo della Stella were to adapt to local building traditions.

Dormer windows, as well as fantastical parapets and stepped gables of every conceivable shape and size, are among the main distinguishing characteristics of the Czech Renaissance, as is the tendency to cover the exteriors of buildings with **sgraffito** decorations. This style of architecture was applied as much to grand palaces, such as the magnificent Šternberg Palace in Prague's Hradčany, as to modest burghers' dwellings, and was to be current in Bohemia right up to the late 17C.

The last great period of court patronage in Bohemia took place under **Rudolph II** at the turn of the 16C. Rudolph's mania for art, and his habit in later life of shutting himself up in his *Schatzkammer* to contemplate obsessively the accumulated treasures therein, gave him much in common with his Spanish cousin Philip II, with whom he also shared a taste for the bizarre and the erotic. However, unlike Philip II, the artists whom Rudolph admired tended to be precious and ultra-refined, the eroticism of Correggio's *Io*, for instance, being apparently preferred to the more full-blooded sensuality characteristic of Titian's mythologies. His favourite sculptor was the Flemish-born Italian Mannerist Giambologna, in whom he showed an interest that was one-sided and hardly subtle: after amassing almost all this artist's statuettes of Venus he wrote to him to ask for 'another naked female figure of the same size'. Rudolph tried unsuccessfully to lure Giambologna to Prague, but succeeded instead in attracting here from Italy the latter's pupil **Adriaen de Vries** (1546–1626), as well as two other Flemish-born artists, the painters **Hans von Aachen** (1552–1615) and **Bartolomaeus Spranger** (1546–1611), both of whom could combine precious eroticism with the sort of allegorical subject-matter that appealed to Rudolph's love of the esoteric.

As for Rudolph's taste for the bizarre, this was amply satisfied by the Milanese artist, **Giuseppe Arcimboldo** (1527–93), who had been first summoned to Prague in 1566 by Ferdinand I, and who was so admired by Rudolph that in 1592 he was given the title of Count Palatine. Arcimboldo, who worked at Prague not only as a painter but also as an organiser of lavish festivities, developed a speciality in 'visual punning'. This was dismissed after his death as a mere curiosity but was to be greatly appreciated in the 20C by the Surrealists: he portrayed members of the court with appropriate still-life objects, thus turning the royal gardener into a composite of flowers, or the court historiographer Wolfgang Lazius into an accumulation of books.

In comparison to Rudolph's patronage of the visual arts, relatively little has been written about the architectural commissions associated with him, though these were in fact considerable. Mention, above all, should be made of the **Italian Chapel** in Prague's Clementinum, which was designed in 1590 by Ottaviano Mascharino and was the first church in Bohemia with an oval ground-plan, a form that was to be much used by Bohemian architects of the Baroque period.

Bohemian Baroque

It is ironic that a country with such strong Hussite and Protestant traditions as Bohemia should have ended up as one of the great Baroque centres of Europe. The devastation caused by the Thirty Years War led to a rebuilding campaign on a vast scale, and today most of Bohemia's old towns, in particular Prague, have a predominantly 17C and 18C look. A vital role in the artistic and architectural renewal of the country was played by the **Jesuits**, who were determined to create resplendent buildings and works of art that would embody the spirit of the triumphant Catholic Church. In many ways their propaganda was quite subtle, for in their attempts to give a fresh image to the country, they turned to Bohemia's past and formed out of this a new national mythology that they hoped would counteract the Protestant one. A particular stroke of genius was to have discovered an obscure prelate called **John of Nepomuk** who had fallen foul of Wenceslas IV in 1393 and been thrown into the river Vltava. In the course of the 17C legends began circulating about him—that he had refused to betray the queen's secrets in the confessional, that a constellation of stars had hovered above his floating body—and eventually in 1693 he was canonised, thus inspiring the consecration of many new churches and providing the subject of much of the religious statuary to be seen around the Czech Republic.

A truly Baroque style of architecture was slow to develop in Bohemia, and was not in fact to emerge until the arrival of the Dientzenhofers towards the end of the 17C. Most 17C architects continued to be from the Como region, and they were for the most part deeply conservative. Shortly after the Catholic victory at the Battle of the White Mountain, a former Lutheran church in Prague's Little Quarter was transformed into Our Lady of Victory, which was little more than a gloomy, impoverished version of the Mannerist Jesuit Church in Rome. During the same decade the Duke of Wallenstein commissioned for himself a building misleadingly referred to as Prague's 'first Baroque palace', though it is actually a structure wholly in the spirit of the Florentine High Renaissance.

The two leading Como architects of the middle and late years of the century were **Carlo Lurago** (1615–84) and **Francesco Caratti** (?–1677/9), both of whom achieved their effects of splendour largely through the unsubtle means of repeating the same elements over enormously long façades, the masterpiece in this style being Caratti's façade of the **Černín Palace** in Prague. The main architect to break the Comasque hegemony at this time was **Jean-Baptiste Mathey** (c 1630–c 1695), a Burgundian by birth who had trained in Rome not as an architect but as a painter. The elegance and low relief of much of the detailing of his work are very French, and at the **Troja Château** on the outskirts of Prague he broke away from the block-like or quadrangular Italian villa through the introduction of a French pavilion system and projecting wings. An admirer of Mathey was the outstanding Viennese architect **Johann Bernard Fischer von Erlach**, whose own work was none the less essentially Italian in inspiration. Though active mainly in Austria, he executed one of Prague's most magnificent palaces, the **Clam-Gallas Palace** (1713), which reveals the influence of Palladio while at the same time accommodating statuary by the most dynamic of Bohemia's Baroque sculptors, Matthias Braun.

The major architects of the Bohemian Baroque were virtually all of foreign origin, and it seems possible that nationalist tensions within Bohemia led to difficulties being put in the way of indigenous Czech architects, whether Czech- or German-speaking. Significantly, the greatest of these indigenous architects, Balthasar Neumann (who was born in 1687 in the Bohemian town of Cheb) worked entirely in Germany, while the foremost German architects active in Bohemia, **Christoph** and **Kilian Ignaz Dientzenhofer**, originated from Bavaria. Remarkably little is known about Christoph Dientzenhofer (1655–1722), other than that he settled in Prague at some time in the late 1670s, married there in 1685 and died there at the age of 67; there is also a document of 1689 which refers to him as someone who 'understood his art very well ... despite an inability either to read or write'. It is not always easy to distinguish his works from those of his extraordinarily prolific son, Kilian Ignaz (1689–1751), but it is generally agreed that he was the more brilliant and innovative of the two. The two architects can at any rate claim together to have popularised in Bohemia a dynamic architectural style indebted to the work of both Francesco Borromini and, above all, Guarino Guarini, who had himself produced a design in 1692 for Prague's Theatine **Church of Our Lady of Unceasing Succour**. The hallmarks of the Dientzenhofer style include undulating façades and interiors, plans based on intersecting ovals, a rich play of convex and concave surfaces, piers that project diagonally into the nave, and Gothic-inspired cross-vaulting such as Guarini had advocated. The supreme expression of this style is the **Church of St Nicholas** in Prague's Little Quarter (1703–55), the most dominant landmark in this city after the castle, and as such a particularly eloquent assertion of resurgent Catholicism.

Though Guarini and in turn the Dientzenhofers had revived the use of a Gothic system of vaulting, it was left to Bohemia's most original Baroque architect, **Jan Balzej Santini-Aichel** (1677–1723), to devise a new style of church architecture, later christened 'Baroque Gothic'. Born in Prague, Santini was the crippled grandson of an immigrant mason from Como, whose family later added the name Aichel. As with Mathey, under whom his father had worked, Santini's training was as a painter, and he seems to have had no building to his credit when in 1702 he was chosen to replace the architect Pavel Bayer in the rebuilding of the Cistercian abbey church at Sedlec (now a suburb of Kutná Hora). Santini's adoption of a Gothic style for this and the later Bohemian monasteries that he was to rebuild can be linked to the same motives that had led the Jesuits to create the cult of St John of Nepomuk. Sedlec had been burnt down by the Hussites, and by reconstructing it in a medieval manner Santini was looking back to a past as yet uncontaminated by Utraquism and later heresies. The brilliance of Santini's work at Sedlec lies above all in the vaulting, which was certainly inspired by that of Benedikt Ried at Kutná Hora and combines the latter's elegance and complexity with Baroque dynamism. To appreciate the full originality of Santini's later architecture one has to travel beyond Central Bohemia, notably to the Benedictine abbey of Kladruby in Western Bohemia (where, in the words of the abbot, he evolved 'a hitherto unseen Gothic style') and to the town of Žďár in Eastern Bohemia, where a bizarre climax to his art was reached in a symbolically formed pilgrimage chapel commemorating the rediscovery of the undecayed tongue of St John of Nepomuk. Santini, a prolific architect, displayed a more conventional if none the less lively Baroque manner in his various works in Prague, for instance the neighbouring Thun-Hohenstein and Morzin Palaces (which are particularly striking for their sculptural decorations by Braun and Brokoff respectively) and the recently restored **gardens of the Ledebour Palace**—one of a number of Baroque terraced gardens that give the Little Quarter so much of its charm.

The great surge of building activity in Bohemia from the late 17C onwards was accompanied by a renaissance in local schools of painting and sculpture. Few artists of interest were active in the first half of the century, with the exception of **Karel Škréta** (1610–74) who, though not the genius that is often claimed by Czech art historians, was a painter of great energy and versatility, who led an intriguing early life. Born to a Protestant family in Záborice in 1610, he and his mother fled to Freiburg in Saxony in 1628. From there he went to Italy, and spent time in Venice and Bologna before completing an artistic training in Rome, where he met and made a portrait of the French painter Nicolas Poussin in 1634. Whether out of genuine conviction or a longing to return to his native Bohemia, he converted to Catholicism shortly after leaving Italy, and eventually settled in Prague, becoming there a prolific painter of altarpieces. As a painter he owes nothing to Poussin but embraces a whole spectrum of Italian Baroque artists from Caravaggio to Guercino and Annibale Carracci. His dark and dramatic canvases sometimes display an impressive realism, which is particularly evident in his portraits, of which the most famous is a lively and informal group portrait of the gem-carver Dionisio Miseroni and his family (now in the Convent of St George at Prague Castle). Two painters of a slightly later generation are **Michael Willmann** (1630–1706) and the latter's stepson and pupil Jan Liška (c 1650–1712), the former working in a strongly Rubens-inspired manner, the latter evolving a loosely handled and vividly coloured style, which is sometimes described as proto-Rococo.

The leading painter active in Bohemia at the beginning of the 18C was **Petr Brandl** (1668–1735), who, like the sculptor Matthias Braun, enjoyed the patronage of the eccentric and visionary Count Špork. Brandl was an artist as varied in his style and subject-matter as Škréta, painting portraits in an heroic French manner one moment and the next dark, religious canvases in which the paint is handled with an agitation reminiscent of the sculptural effects of Braun. A contemporary of Brandl was the portraitist **Jan Kupecký** (1667–1740), in many ways the greatest of all Bohemian painters, but who neither studied nor worked in his native Bohemia. An active member of the Moravian Brethren, he was born in Prague but was forced to emigrate with his Protestant parents to Pezinok, in western Slovakia. When he was 15 he ran away from home to avoid being apprenticed to a weaver, and entered a painter's workshop in Vienna before going on to Italy. After suffering years of hardship he was finally able to establish a workshop in Rome and stayed there until 1729, when he accepted an invitation from Prince Adam von Liechtenstein to settle in Vienna. His friend, the portraitist Johann Caspar Füssli (the father of the Swiss-born English painter Henry Fuseli), described Kupecký's portraits as combining 'the power of Rubens, the delicacy and spirituality of Van Dyck, the sombreness and magic of Rembrandt'. Another contemporary, Anton Graff, gave a better idea of Kupecký's pictures when he wrote that you found in them 'true nature, life itself'. The realism of his portraits is certainly remarkable and gave much inspiration to the Bohemian artists at the end of the century who were trying to get away from the pleasing but shallow Rococo manner of painters such as Norbert Grund (1717–60).

The great specialists in large-scale **decorative painting** in Europe were the Italians, but relatively few of these worked in Bohemia. At the end of the 17C two obscure Italians, Francesco and Giovanni Marchetti, were invited to decorate the **Troja Château** near Prague but suffered the humiliation of being replaced there by the Dutch artist **Abraham Godyn**, who covered its main hall with one of the most spectacular examples of Italian-inspired illusionistic painting to be seen in this country. One of the main Italian exponents of this heavily architectural style of decorative painting was Padre Pozzo, who moved in later life to Vienna, where he influenced a number of Bohemia's artists, among them Johann Hiebel (1681–?) and the prolific Václav Reiner (1689–1743). A more painterly and colourful style of ceiling painting was practised by the great Austrian decorators, all of whom were active at some stage in Bohemia and Moravia, including Johann Michal Rottmayr, Paul Troger and, above all, **Franz Anton Maulbertsch**, whose ceiling in the **Philosophical Hall** at Prague's Strahov Monastery (1796) is one of the culminating works of the Bohemian Baroque. Among the indigenous decorators to be influenced by the Austrians were Franz Palko (1727–67) and **Johann Lucas Kracker** (1717–79), the latter being responsible for the masterly ceiling paintings in the **Church of St Nicholas** in Prague's Little Quarter.

Few countries in Europe have such a wealth of **public statuary** as Bohemia, and much of this was the creation of the Baroque period, when palace façades were embellished with struggling giants and atlantes, bridges such as Prague's remarkable **Charles Bridge** lined with gesticulating saints, and almost every town square in the country adorned with tapering piles of statuary that offered thanksgiving to the Virgin for protection during times of plague. The earliest of the great Baroque sculptors working in Bohemia was **Johann Georg Bendl** (c 1620–80), who is sometimes thought of as the sculptural equivalent of Škréta, combining as he does Baroque drama with powerful realism; though intimate with the sculpture of the Roman Baroque, he seems to have been trained in his native South Germany, which perhaps explains his particular genius for limewood carving. All the other main sculptors of the Bohemian Baroque took part in the decoration of the Charles Bridge, including Jan Brokoff (1652–1718) and Matěj Jäckel (1655–1738), both of whom were influenced by Bernini. Brokoff's son, **Ferdinand Maxmilián Brokoff** (1688–1731), began his career collaborating with his father on the Charles Bridge, but soon surpassed him both in technique and imagination, evolving a heavy monumental style enlivened with vivid touches of realism.

Brokoff would have been without equal in Bohemia if his career had not coincided with that of **Matthias Bernard Braun** (1684–1738), one of the most brilliant sculptors of the European Baroque. Born in the Oetz Valley in North Tirol and trained probably in Italy, Braun came to Prague in about 1710. *The Vision of St Luitgard*, which he executed that year for the Charles Bridge, is a dynamic sculptural group of astonishing technical virtuosity, and so painterly in its approach to stone that you can well believe the tradition that ascribes its design to the painter Petr Brandl. In later years the agitated, almost hysterical energy of his art was to make the work of Bernini seem quite restrained in comparison.

Braun had a large workshop, but his influence on the Bohemian sculptors of the late 18C was slight. The leading sculptor of this later generation was **Ignác František Platzer** (1717–87), whose art owes less to Braun than to the more Classical style of Austria's foremost 18C sculptor, Georg Raphael Donner.

The late 18C brought with it major changes in the structure of **patronage** in Bohemia. The expulsion by Maria Theresa of the Jesuits in 1775 and Joseph II's dissolution of most of the country's monasteries in the course of the 1780s greatly diminished the political and economic power of the Church. The country's artists and architects could thus no longer depend on what had once been their most stable source of income, and were forced to rely more on the nobility, who came to be based for much of the year in Vienna and would come to Bohemia principally for summer stays on their country estates.

From neo-Classicism to Art Nouveau

An elegant neo-Classicism of French derivation became the dominant architectural style in Bohemia from the 1770s onwards, to be followed after about 1800 by an '**Empire style**' inspired not so much by France as its name would suggest but by Viennese architects such as **Georg Fischer**, who was himself responsible for the design of Prague's most striking Empire building, the austerely impressive customs house known as **U Hybernů** (Hibernians' House; 1808–11).

Later in the 19C, when an at times fantastically over-blown eclecticism came to characterise the architecture of Central Europe, nationalist sentiments found a partial expression in the **neo-Gothic**, of which one of the principal Czech exponents was **Josef Mocker** (1835–99), Bohemia's answer to Viollet-le-Duc, and a man known for his drastic restoration and rebuilding of many of this country's medieval monuments, including **Karlštejn Castle** and Prague's Powder Gate. The major buildings of this period associated with the nationalist revival were in a **neo-Renaissance** style, which was initiated in Bohemia by **Josef Zítek** (1832–1909). Zítek was trained in Vienna under the architects of the Vienna Opera House, E. van der Nüll and A. von Sicardsburg, and devoted much of his life to the building of Prague's **National Theatre** (1867–81); his style was perpetuated by his one-time collaborator **Josef Schulz** (1840–1917), who was the author of this city's equally grandiose, if rather less eloquent, **National Museum** (1881–83). A variant of the style was the **Czech neo-Renaissance**, which, at the turn of the century, brought back a fashion for stepped gables and sgraffito decorations.

Though Bohemia cannot boast Art Nouveau architects of the same calibre as Hungary's Ödön Lechner or Austria's Otto Wagner, there are numerous fanciful buildings in this style to be seen here, most notably Prague's newly (and disastrously) restored **Municipal House**, which was built between 1903 and 1911 by Antonín Balšánek, Osvald Polívka and Josef Chochol. The later development of **Art Nouveau**, when decorative exuberance gave way to more rationalist tendencies, is represented in Bohemia principally by Jan Kotěra (1871–1923), a pupil of Otto Wagner and the Viennese Secessionists, whose works helped to pave the way for the remarkable generation of pioneering architects active in Bohemia in the early 20C.

Nationalism and 19th-century Czech art

The **nationalist revival** of the 19C provided a great rallying point for painters and sculptors, and gave them necessary encouragement at a time when the conditions for producing art here were generally unfavourable. The situation for Bohemia's artists at the end of the 18C could in fact hardly have been worse, thanks to a combination of the Church's diminished role as a patron and Prague's decline into a provincial backwater. Concern with the provincial nature of Prague's cultural life led finally in 1796 to a group of Bohemian nobles and rich Prague citizens founding The Society of Patriotic Friends in Art. To help compensate for the loss to Vienna of Prague's imperial collections, this society began amassing a collection of paintings and sculptures that would later form the basis of the **Czech National Gallery**. Of more immediate consequence to the city's art life was the foundation by the society in 1796 of the **Prague Academy of Fine Arts**, an institution at which most of Bohemia's leading artists of the 19C were to receive their basic training.

The majority of Bohemia's painters in the early years of the 19C were highly conventional, including the academy's first director, Josef Bergler (1753–1829)—who painted stiff mythologies and Baroque-style portraits—and its first professor of landscape painting, Karel Postl (1769–1818), an artist in the Claude tradition. The portraitist Antonín Machek (1775–1844) delicately portrayed the leading figures associated with the nationalist revival, while the landscapist Antonín Mánes (1784–1843)—the father of a great dynasty of painters—is notable principally for his romantic landscapes of sites associated with Bohemia's past. A more remarkable painter than either of these was **Josef Navrátil** (1798–1865), who painted still-lifes of extraordinary freshness and realism that only came to light long after his death. But by far the most important painter of the first half of the century was Mánes's son, **Josef Mánes** (1820–71), an artist of great versatility, equally adept at portraiture, landscape painting, nudes, Romantic historical works, and Classical allegories. His central position in Czech art is also due to his fascination with Slavic country-folk and close involvement with the nationalist revival. A tour around Silesia in 1846 first aroused his interest in traditional rural life, and this interest was further stimulated in the course of numerous stays after 1849 with the Silva Tarouca family at their estate in the Haná region, a part of Moravia known for its strong folk culture; in 1854 he undertook a long journey through Moravia, Slovakia and Silesia with the specific aim of recording folk costumes and traditions. He designed banners for patriotic organisations and, in the last years of his life, ensured his lasting popularity in Bohemia through his delightful scenes of the Czech and Slovak countryside for the **astronomical clock** on Prague's Old Town Hall.

Vienna and Munich were the principal art centres to which Bohemian artists were attracted in the first half of the 19C. By the middle of the century, however, Paris had superseded these places in popularity, and a number of the leading artists of this generation spent a long period of their lives there, including the Courbet-inspired portraitist and still-life painter Karel Purkyně (1834–68), the landscapist and genre painter Soběslav Pinkas (1827–1901) and Viktor Barvitius (1834–1902), who abandoned an early career as a history painter to devote himself to the portrayal of urban life. The only painter of this period to gain an international reputation was **Jaroslav Čermák** (1830–78), who painted scenes from Czech history in a style indebted to French artists such as Delacroix and Fromentin; as well as spending many years in France, he travelled extensively around Dalmatia, and produced a large body of work documenting the struggle of the Montenegrin people against Turkish domination.

From the 1870s onwards, the situation for artists wishing to work in Bohemia itself was greatly improved and, following a pattern widespread throughout Europe, many of the artists who had lived for a long time in France began returning to their home country. The ambitious buildings erected in Prague in the last years of the century, such as the National Theatre, involved the collaboration of virtually all the country's important artists, and indeed this whole generation is referred to today as the **National Theatre Generation**. Two of these painters, František Ženíšek (1849–1916) and Vojtěch Hynais (1854–1925) produced spirited interpretations of often ridiculous Classical subject-matter, involving numerous female nudes; another, Václav Brožík (1851–1901), after specialising in quiet landscape studies in France, made a name for himself in Bohemia with two large canvases representing *Master Jan Hus before the Council of Constance* and *The Election of George of Poděbrady as King of Bohemia* (1898). The major landscapists to have worked in the National Theatre were Julius Mařák (1832–1899), famous for his romantic woodland scenes, and Antonín Chitussi (1847–91), who spent much of his early life working in and around the Fontainebleau forest near Paris, and later applied a Barbizon School manner to the depiction of his native Czech-Moravian Highlands. The central figure of this generation was **Mikoláš Aleš** (1852–1913), whose works can be paralleled with the historical novels of his contemporary, Alois Jirásek. He endlessly depicted scenes from Bohemian history and folk-tales, and at the National Theatre collaborated with Ženíšek on a great patriotic cycle entitled *My Country* (now in the castle of Moravský Krumlov). Lively and very decorative, his style was ideally suited to book illustration and after 1882 he virtually abandoned oil painting to devote himself to graphic work, a move which may also have been connected with his constant financial difficulties.

Aleš today is little known outside the Czech Republic, in contrast to his contemporary **Alfons Mucha** (1860–1939), most of whose life was spent in Paris, where he gained enormous fame for his luxuriously flowing Art Nouveau posters, in particular a series of the 1890s featuring the actress Sarah Bernhardt. Though an essentially decorative artist, he worked in fact in many different fields, and was sponsored by a Chicago industrialist and Slavophile, Charles Richard Crane, to paint a series of 20 enormous canvases called the *Slav Epic* (also now in Moravský Krumlov). An immensely wealthy and celebrated artist, he settled permanently in Czechoslovakia in 1922, taking up residence in a Renaissance palace in Prague's Little Quarter and continuing his varied career through such activities as designing stamps and banknotes. Mucha's fame in his home country has been further perpetuated by the museum to him right in the heart of Prague's New Town.

To the end Mucha's art remained deeply rooted in the world of the *fin-de-siècle*, as did that of the later artist **Max Švabinský** (1873–1962), another highly successful figure working in many fields, from oil painting to the design of stained-glass windows and mosaics. The strong Symbolist elements in Švabinský's paintings are also evident in those of Jan Preisler (1872–1918), who executed decorative works reminiscent of those of Pierre Puvis de Chavannes and designed mosaics for a number of Art Nouveau buildings in Prague. The principal exponent in Bohemia of an Impressionist style of landscape painting was Antonín Slavícek (1870–1910), while Post-Impressionist tendencies can be seen in the work of **Jakub Schikaneder** (1855–1924), whose highly subtle paintings mark the transition between Czech art of the 19C and the experimental generation of the early 20C. Schikaneder began his career painting peasant genre scenes in the tradition of the French painter Jules Bastien-Lepage, but ended it with haunting and almost abstract evocations of dusk scenes in Prague.

Bohemian sculpture, after a period of decline in the late 18C, was to enjoy during the following century a gradual renewal in vitality that led eventually to one of the livelier periods in its history. The Prague Academy of Fine Arts was not to have its own sculpture school until 1896, but a number of aspiring sculptors went there to study drawing from the Antique, including Václav Prachner (1784–1832), who evolved a robust Classicism. Romantic historical subjects were the speciality of the brothers Josef Max (1803–54) and Emmanuel Max

(1810–1901), artists of German origin who, while often portraying scenes from Czech history, did so in a stiff and linear manner that owes more to German than to Czech sculptural traditions. Very sensual modelling, which was to be one of the main characteristics of later Czech sculpture, was shown instead in the early works of Václav Levý, whose bronze of the legendary Czech bard Lumír (1848) is sometimes regarded as one of the first eloquent manifestations in sculpture of Czech national consciousness. However, Levý was unable to compete success-fully with the Max brothers in Prague and in 1854 settled in Rome, where he fell under the cold and sterile influence of the religious art of the Nazarenes.

The second half of the century was dominated by **Josef Václav Myslbek** (1848–1922), a sculptor whose richly worked bronzes were to be admired by Auguste Rodin. In Myslbek's work a romantic Slavonic fervour vied with a strong neo-Renaissance element, and in the course of the slow evolution of his **St Wenceslas Monument** in Prague a wild and romantic portrayal of the saint gave way to a statelier and more sober one. One of the greatest of Myslbek's pupils was **Stanislav Sucharda** (1866–1916), who displayed particular bril-liance as a sculptor of Symbolist metal reliefs, and was also responsible for one of the most exciting of Prague's monuments, the **Palacký Monument** (1898–1912), a work with a pictorial verve worthy of Matthias Braun. The other outstanding monument from turn-of-the-20th-century Prague was the **Monument to Jan Hus** (1900–15) by **Ladislav Jan Šaloun** (1880–1946), one of the few sculptors of this period to have developed independent of Myslbek. This much-neglected and misunderstood work revealed a painterly approach to bronze that was anathema to Myslbek, who had instilled in his pupils a rigorous tectonic approach to sculpture and had encouraged them to avoid the more extreme forms of Art Nouveau. A comparably isolated artist who had rejected both Myslbek's training and principles was František Bílek (1872–1941), the author of elongated Art Nouveau works of great expressive power. The more mainstream Czech sculptors at the turn of the century were heavily influenced by Rodin, including two of Myslbek's more important later pupils, Josef Mařatka (1874–1937) and **Bohumil Kafka** (1878–1942). The former organised a major exhibition of Rodin's work in Prague in 1902, while the latter entered Rodin's studio in Paris in 1904; in later years Kafka was to devote himself to Romantic historical works, culminating in his **Jan Žižka Monument** on Prague's Žižkov Hill, which is claimed to be the largest statue in the world. Another of Myslbek's pupils was Jan Štursa (1880–1925), who achieved partic-ular notoriety for his exceptionally sensual female nudes, executed in a great range of styles, from the Classical to the highly realistic.

The 20th century

The vital role that Czech and Slovak artists played in the art and architecture of the 20C has come to be recognised only recently, and is likely to become ever more widely appreciated thanks to Prague's magnificent Gallery of Modern Art housed in the former Trade Fair Palace. The towering genius of the early years of the century was **František Kupka** (1871–1957), one of the pioneers of abstract painting in Europe, but someone whose work was greatly neglected in Czechoslovakia after the Second World War. After studying at the Prague Academy of Fine Arts, and later in Vienna, Kupka settled in Paris in 1895 and was thereafter to live mainly in France. In his early years he painted a number of vividly coloured Symbolist canvases, but worked principally as a satirical artist and book illustrator. From the start he had been fascinated by spiritualism and the occult, and from this had grown an interest in the spiritual symbolism of colour. Soon he began experimenting with linear rhythms and colour schemes that attempted to approximate to the effects of music, and even started to call himself a 'colour symphonist'. Inspired by high-speed photography after 1909, he went on to portray effects of movement, and this was to lead in 1912 to the pure abstraction of *Fugue in Two Colours* (now in the Gallery of Modern Art), which created a sensation at the Salon d'Automne of that year. The lyrical abstraction of these years, which can closely be related to the work of Robert Delaunay and the Orphists, gave way in the 1920s to a more geometric abstract style. In 1923 he published in Prague an influential theoretical work entitled *Creation in Plastic Art* (*Tvoření v Umění výtvarném*), and in 1931 was one of the founder members of the French-based Abstraction-Création Group.

In the years immediately before the First World War, when Kupka had been engaged in his experiments in Paris, Prague had emerged as one of the main centres of the European avant-garde. The more modern tendencies in Czech art had been represented for many years by the **Mánes Association of Artists**, which had been founded in 1887 in opposition to the Prague Academy of Fine Arts, and had organised several highly influential exhibitions in the early years of the century. One of these was an exhibition in 1905 of the Norwegian artist Edvard Munch, which had been derided by both the public and critics alike and yet had been a decisive influence on the formation in 1907 of Bohemia's first avant-garde group of artists—**Osma** ('The Eight'). Four years later, members of the short-lived group were to found the **Association of Plastic Arts**, the membership of which included all the painters, sculptors and architects who were to be associated with **Czech Cubism**. A knowledge of French Cubism among Czech artists was at first derived largely from visits to Paris, but an important part in its dissemination here was also played by the art historian and future director of the National Gallery, **Vincenc Kramář**, an avid collector of the works of Picasso and Braque. The main Cubist painters in Czechoslovakia were Vincenc Beneš (1893–1979), Josef Čapek (1887–1945), Emil Filla (1882–1963), Antonín Procházka (1882–1945), Václav Špála (1885–1946) and the aptly named Bohumil Kubišta (1884–1918); most of these artists were to remain faithful to the principles of Cubism for the rest of their lives. Filla, the principal spokesman of this group, made two attempts at Cubist sculpture, but the leading artist in this style was **Otto Gutfreund** (1889–1927), perhaps the most outstanding Czech sculptor of the century. After evolving an idiosyncratic 'Analytical Cubist' manner by 1911, later in the decade Gutfreund moved closer to 'Synthetic Cubism' before abandoning Cubism altogether after 1920 and producing works in a style that came to be known as 'Objective Realism'. In these last years Gutfreund devoted himself to the realistic but dignified portrayal of the everyday world, which he represented with simple, stately forms, often making use of colour and terracotta; these works were to have an enormous influence on Czech sculptors of the 1920s, including Karel Dvořák (1893–1950), Jan Lauda (1898–1959), Karel Pokorný (1891–1962) and Bedřich Stefan (1892–1982).

A phenomenon unique to Bohemia and Moravia was the impact of Cubism on architecture. Believing that the ever more severe brick and concrete structures of the Secessionist architect Jan Kotěra had become far too rationalist, a group of architect members of the Association of Plastic Arts attempted to create a more self-consciously artistic architecture, using a simplified ornamental vocabulary comparable to the forms employed by Cubist painters such as Braque and Picasso. Pavel Janák (1882–1956) was the leader of this group, but some of the finest buildings in the style were those created between 1911and 1914 by **Josef Chochol** (1880–1956) at the foot of Prague's Vyšehrad: the façades of these structures were covered in faceted diamond-shaped forms that owed a debt not only to Cubism but also to the diamond or 'cellular' vaulting of the Bohemian architects of the late-Gothic period. Another of the Cubist architects was **Josef Gočár** (1880–1945), who was inspired instead by the ordering of Bohemian façades of the Empire period, and came to evolve in the 1920s an academic Cubist style made up of cylindrical forms, most notably in the former Legio Bank in Prague.

The optimism and excitement that followed the creation of the Republic of Czechoslovakia in 1918 led to a period of quite exceptional cultural vitality and experimentation. Thanks to its location at the heart of Europe, Czechoslovakia became a melting pot for all the conflicting cultural fashions of the time, and appropriated and transformed such influences as Constructivism and Productivism from Russia, Dadaism from Zürich and Berlin, Futurism from Italy, the Bauhaus from Weimar and Dessau, and Purism and Surrealism from Paris.

The great focal point of the Czech avant-garde of this period was a left-wing group formed in Prague's Union Café in 1920, and given the mysterious name of **Devětsil**, which is both the name of an obscure flower and a composite of two words meaning 'nine' and 'forces', the forces in question being probably the nine Muses of Parnassus. It was a group that experimented with most of the 'isms' of the 1920s, and included progressive figures active in all cultural fields, from architecture and the fine arts to design, poetry, music, drama, and film; honorary memberships were even given to Charlie Chaplin and Douglas Fairbanks, though it is unlikely that these two actors were aware of the honour. Its leader was the witty and charismatic **Karel Teige**, an experimental poet and collage artist who believed in the integration of all the arts, and whose theoretical writings included an article on the work of art in the age of mechanical reproduction, which anticipated by some ten years Walter Benjamin's famous essay on this subject. Teige's aesthetic was based essentially on the reconciliation of the opposing extremes of utilitarianism and lyrical subjectivity, a dichotomy which he described in terms of '**Constructivism and Poetism**': 'Constructivism', he wrote, 'is a method with rigorous rules, it is the art of usefulness. Poetism, its living accessory, is the atmosphere of life ... the art of pleasure.' The Marxist utopianism of Devětsil was not to survive the growing totalitarianism of the 1930s, but when the group finally folded, in 1931, it had managed to maintain its delicate unity longer than all the other European avant-gardes of the 1920s.

One of the principal ideals behind Czech **avant-garde architecture** of the inter-war years was a belief in the beauty of the industrial age, and it is significant that several of the Devětsil architects, such as Jaromír Krejcar (1895–1949), were inspired by transatlantic steamers and other modern forms of transport, incorporating into their buildings such elements as portholes, the rounded windows of express trains, and terraces balustraded with railings as on a ship's deck: such conceits were typical of Devětsil, the geometry of the architecture being invested with a strong element of poetry, in this case derived from the glamorous associations of long-distance travel. However, with the rapid growth of Devětsil's architectural membership, the poetry of the buildings was made increasingly subservient to their utilitarian and purely abstract elements, Constructivism becoming replaced by an international **Functionalism** of a type promoted by Le Corbusier, Gropius and Mies van der Rohe. An intermediary building was the wonderful structure now housing Prague's Gallery of Modern Art —the **Trade Fair Palace**: built between 1924 and 1928 by Josef Fuchs and Oldřich Tyl (1884–1939), this incorporates a strong element of poetry (evident above all in the atrium) into a monument that Le Corbusier claimed to have shown him how Functionalism could be applied on a pioneeringly large scale. A more brutally Functionalist structure of similarly vast proportions was Prague's Pensions Institute building of 1929–34, a gaunt concrete structure by Josef Havlíček (1899–1961) and Karel Honzík (1900–60).

An architect of these years whose work ran contrary to all the prevailing Modernist trends was **Jože Plečnik** (1872–1957), a Slovenian who had been invited to Prague by Jan Kotěra in 1911 to teach at the School of Decorative Arts. Later Plečnik formed a close friendship with President, Tomáš Masaryk, who commissioned from him in the 1920s the restoration of Prague Castle. His interest in the architecture of the past, as well as in traditional craftsmanship and materials, has led him to be hailed in recent years as a precursor of Postmodernism, though in reality his work was so idiosyncratic as to defy rigid categorisation. His Prague **Church of the Sacred Heart** (1929–33) is certainly one of the more bizarre masterpieces of Czech architecture between the wars, taking elements from such diverse sources as an Early-Christian basilica and an Egyptian temple, and treating them with a boldness that is thoroughly modern.

The artists of **Devětsil**, in common with the Dadaists, rejected the notion of high art, though in their case they at first expressed this disdain through taking an interest in popular culture, devoting themselves at the beginning of the 1920s to what they termed '**Poetic Naivism**'. Inspired by ex-votos and anonymous shop signs, but also by Henri Rousseau, the Czech Cubists, and the child-like figures in the paintings of the Czech artist Jan Zrzavý (1890–1977), several of the Devětsil members, such as the painter and art historian Adolf Hoffmeister (1902–73), created self-consciously naive works. Soviet-style Constructivism had little impact on the painters of this generation, though it did influence one of the most original of the Devětsil sculptors, **Zdeněk Pešánek** (1896–1965), who experimented with kinetic art and also made a number of works involving electric light. Constructivism was also an important force behind the works of the pioneering **photographers** Jaroslav Rössler (1902–90) and Jaromír Funke (1896–1945), both of whom were technically adventurous and flirted with pure abstraction. Two other outstanding photographers of these years were František Drtikol (1883–1961) and the one-armed **Josef Sudek** (1896–1976), the former specialising in female nudes in disturbing, geometrical settings, the latter concentrating on the abstract qualities of everyday scenes and objects, and also creating some of the most evocative images ever produced of Prague. The Devětsil leader **Karel Teige** employed photographs in his spirited and mysterious collages, which he described as 'Pictorial Poems'.

The free rein given to the poetic impulse and to the subconscious in the work of Teige and other Devětsil members created effects of pure Surrealism, which was perhaps the lasting legacy of the Devětsil artists. Not surprisingly, when Devětsil eventually closed, many of its members went on to found the **Czech Group of Surrealists**. The French Surrealist, André Breton, described Prague as 'the magic metropolis of old Europe', and it was only fitting that this city should have become between the wars one of the main European centres of Surrealism. The Czech Surrealists included the sculptor **Ladislav Zívr** (1909–80), who devised a number of strange assemblages, and **Zdeněk Rykr** (1900–40), an artist remarkable above all for his delicate collages made out of thread, tissues and other ephemeral materials. Among the other Surrealists were the versatile Jindřich Štyrský (1899–1942) and the morphological painters Josef Šíma (1881–1971) and Toyen (1902–80). Another of the painters was Kamil Lhoták (1912–), who was to be one of the most interesting Czech artists active in the 1940s and 1950s, executing strange and sinister landscapes that beautifully evoked the uncertainty of the war years and their aftermath.

As a whole the art and architecture of **Communist Czechoslovakia** was unmemorable, and certainly cannot be compared in quality to the literature, theatre and cinema of those years. The revolutionary Functionalism of the 1920s and 1930s led under Socialism to the drabbest of housing schemes and civic buildings, while the visual arts of this period suffered from a lack both of imaginative patronage and a true spirit of communal endeavour. Inevitably, the most interesting artists were the dissident figures who used a subversive and characteristically Czech sense of humour to mock at officialdom: one such person was **Jiří Kolář**, who began as a banned poet in the 1950s before going on in the early '60s to produce witty Teige-inspired collages involving words, images and political comment. With the thaw leading up to the 'Prague Spring' of 1968 the Czech avant-garde was able once more to assert itself, with artists such as Milan Knižak introducing Prague to the 'happening' by slaughtering chickens to the sounds of loud rock music.

In today's post-Communist world many of the dissidents of old have become part of the new establishment, with even a figure such as Knižak being appointed to the directorship of the National Gallery in Prague. Fortunately, even in this new era of near-unrestricted freedom there still remains a place for wittily subversive figures such as the 'Situationist artist **David Černý**, who achieved considerable notoriety in 1991 by painting the Soviet memorial tank in the Prague district of Smíchov a bright pink (which was, as he explained to journalists, the colour of an infant babe in arms, a symbol of innocence). Another of Černý's efforts was to place a giant red metronome on top of the granite plinth in Prague that once supported a massive statue of Stalin. The novelist Bohumil Hrabal only regretted that the statue itself had not been around for Černý to have applied his pink paint to that as well: 'Can you imagine', he wrote, 'what a wondrous sight that would've been ...? In one fell swoop this would have made Prague the world centre for pop art; a happening like this here in Prague would have set the crown on that American school initiated all those years ago by Allan Kaprow, Claes Oldenburg and the rest ...'

Music

'The music claimed me there a long time', wrote the American traveller Bayard Taylor on a visit in 1846 to the exuberant Baroque church of St Nicholas in the Little Quarter of Prague. Most visitors to Prague today are likely to have a similar experience, and to find themselves transfixed by the sounds of classical music that seem to emanate from so many of this city's churches and palaces. For this is a part of Europe that has not only given birth to an exceptional number of composers, but that has also enjoyed a reputation for its vibrant musical life since at least the late 18C, when the English musical historian Dr Burney came here and opined that 'Bohemia is the conservatory of Europe.'

Early Czech music and the Church

The early history of Czech music is centred around St Vitus's Cathedral in Prague, which is documented as acquiring a new organ as early as 1245, and as already extending its choral resources by 1250. With the flowering of the arts initiated by Charles IV in the following century, the cathedral choir came to possess up to 100 singers, and a richly varied tradition of **liturgical music** began gradually to develop. The course of Czech music would soon, however, be altered radically by the rise of the Hussite movement.

With their opposition to anything in religion that might detract from the primitive simplicity of early Christianity, the Hussites disapproved both of the 'decadent' art of polyphony and of the use in churches of organs and other instruments; they encouraged instead **congregational music** and the abandonment of Latin songs in favour of ones in Czech, a language previously forbidden in church music. In 1561, when the fashion for choral music was at its height, as many as 750 new Czech hymns were brought together in the *Šamotulský kancionál* by the future bishop of the Hussite Church, Jan Blahoslav (d. 1571). Three years earlier he had published the pioneering *Musica*, which was not only the first musical textbook in Czech, but also the first theoretical treatise of any description in this language. The powerful and often folk-influenced melodies of these songs—later a rich source of material for the 19C national school—would be perpetuated over the centuries by Bohemia's numerous **singing societies**, of which over 100 were still in existence near the end of the 18C, despite the ban after 1620 on all but Catholic ones. In few other countries were social singing societies to proliferate so early or to exist so long.

But the Hussite abolition of the Latin liturgy, and the partial and temporary ban on instrumental church music, had the additional effect in the early 16C of cutting off Bohemia from the innovatory developments of the Flemish school, whose impact was so enormous on the music of the European Renaissance. Bohemia had little contact with these developments until the reign of Rudolph II, who turned his court into a truly cosmopolitan centre by inviting to Prague such musical celebrities as the German Hans Leo Hassler (1564–1612), the Italian Filippo di Monte (1521–1603) and the Slovenian-born Jacob Handl (1550–91), who, despite his place of birth, is sometimes regarded as Bohemia's first polyphonic composer of European standing. Though Rudolph's court orchestra (which numbered about 60 musicians) had little direct influence on Czech music generally, it seems to have served as a prototype for the many **domestic bands** that were established in the 17C and 18C in the châteaux and town-houses of the Czech nobility.

Czech music in the 18th century

The musicians employed by these aristocrats were usually liveried servants whose duties extended beyond music to humdrum domestic activities, as was the case with František Václav Míča (1694–1744), who, while employed by Count Johann Adam Questenberg as valet at Jaroměřice, organised the other servants into an orchestra and composed in 1730 the first Czech opera—*The Origin of Jaroměřice*. The most famous employee of this kind was the Bohemian-born violinist and composer **Heinrich Biber** (1644–1704), who, as a teenager, worked in the orchestras founded by Prince-Bishop Karl von Liechtenstein-Castelcorno at Kroměříž and Olomouc. Biber was an extraordinarily original composer who retuned stringed instruments to produce unusual notes (an effect known as *scordatura*), and used these to great naturalistic effect in the evocation of battle scenes, or even—on one occasion—a gall-bladder operation.

In 1670 Biber left Olomouc on a mission to collect violins from the Austrian town of Absam, and never returned to Bohemia. Most other, but by no means all, Czech composers of the 17C and 18C followed Biber's example and spent the greater part of their careers working in German lands. Of those who stayed behind several made fascinating use of local folk motifs, notably the Czech composer **Jan Jakub Ryba** (1765–1815), whose delightful and unconventional *Christmas Mass* of 1796 is still regularly performed every Christmas Eve in the Prague **Church of St James**. This work, with its rich folk influences, is sometimes said to have paved the way for 19C nationalist composers such as Smetana.

In the meantime, Czech composers were making a considerable name for themselves throughout Europe. **Jan Dismas Zelenka** (1679–1745)—one of several distinguished composers to have studied at Prague's Clementinum (another was Christoph Willibald Gluck)—was employed for the last 35 years of his life as a musician at the Court of Dresden: the author of stunningly inventive works that made considerable demands on instrumentalists (especially the windplayers), he acquired such a reputation at Dresden that he was invited in 1723 to compose music for the coronation in Prague of the Habsburg emperor Charles VI.

Two of the best-known operatic composers largely active abroad were **Jiří Benda** (1722–95) and **Josef Mysliveček** (1737–81): the former—one of a large family of Bohemian musicians—worked in Berlin for 28 years as a *Kappellmeister* to the Duke of Gotha, pioneering during this period the dramatic use of the spoken word against a musical background (that is, 'melodrama' in the original meaning of this term); Mysliveček, meanwhile, settled in Italy aged 26 and wrote operas there that earned him the title of *Il divino Boemo*, or 'The divine Bohemian'.

Mozart in Prague

A large number of Czech composers were inevitably drawn to Vienna, including the prolific Jan Křtitel Vaňhal (1739–1813)—the author of more than 100 symphonies and 90 masses—and Leopold Koželuh (1747–1818), who succeeded Mozart as chamber composer to the Viennese court. Mozart himself was particularly influenced by the family of Mannheim-based Bohemian musicians led by **Johann Stamitz** (1717–57), who was born Jan Václav Stamic in the

Czech town of Hávlíčkuv Brod. The symphonic compositions of Stamic and the 'Mannheim School', with their change in emphasis away from strictly observed counterpoint towards harmonic contrasting of attractive melodies, were fundamental to Mozart's musical development.

Mozart's debt to Bohemian music would be amply repaid, for it was perhaps thanks above all to the great composer that the Czechs today are so famed internationally as a music-loving nation. Though Mozart went as a child to Bratislava, Olomouc and Brno, he did not have any real contact with Bohemia until as late as January 1787, when he came to Prague with his wife Costanza to attend the production of his *Marriage of Figaro*, a work that had been improperly understood in Vienna. His English biographer Edward Holmes, writing in 1845, said of this production that 'the success of Le Nozze di Figaro, so unsatisfactory at Vienna, was unexampled at Prague, where it amounted to absolute intoxication and frenzy.' All this proved understandably exhilarating to Mozart, whose rapturous response to the city and its people was evident in a letter he wrote describing to his Viennese friend Baron Gottfried von Jacquis his attendance at a ball where 'the cream of the beauties of Prague is wont to gather':

> You ought to have been there my friend! I fancy I see you running, or rather, limping, after all those pretty girls and women! I neither danced nor flirted with any of them, the former because I'm too tired, and the latter arising from my natural bashfulness. I looked on, however, with the greatest pleasure while all these people flew about in sheer delight to the music of my Figaro arranged for contredanses and German dances. For here they talk nothing but Figaro. Nothing is played, sung or whistled but Figaro. No opera is drawing like Figaro. Nothing, nothing but Figaro. Certainly a great honour for me!

Shortly afterwards he composed, while still in the city, his *Prague Symphony*; and he returned here with Costanza later in the year to perform and to compose his opera *Don Giovanni*, which he dedicated to the 'good people of Prague', who, it would seem, were equally taken by him ('The people of Prague', wrote his contemporary biographer Niemetschek, 'were charmed by his affability of manner and unassuming behaviour'). On this second visit, in the autumn, he stayed at first at an inn called *The Three Lions* before moving on to the house of the Czech composer František Xaver Dušek and his wife Josefa, an accomplished singer. This house on the outskirts of Prague (it survives today as the Mozart Museum) proved almost an over-congenial setting for the composer, who found himself constantly distracted from his work by all the laughter, conversation and playing of bowls that took place in this most unusually warm autumn. Finally, in the course of an animated party given here at the end of October, one of the guests is said to have reminded Mozart that the première of *Don Giovanni* was scheduled for the following night, and that the overture for this had still not been written. The story then goes that Mozart duly retired to his room at about midnight, ordered some punch and asked Costanza to try to keep him awake by talking. Though the overture was ready by the time the copyists came to collect it at seven in the morning, the copyists were not as quick as the composer had been, and the audience had to wait 45 minutes for the performance to start, at 7.45 that evening. Whether this story is true or not, *Don Giovanni* was certainly composed at remarkable speed, and its overture must have been performed sight unseen.

'My opera Don Giovanni', recorded Mozart, 'was received with the greatest applause.' Some time later, Josef Haydn, replying to a letter sent to him by the director of the opera house, wrote that 'Prague ought to retain him, and reward him well too; else the history of great genius is melancholy, and offers posterity but slight encouragement to exertion ... I feel indignant that this unique Mozart is not yet engaged at some royal or imperial court.'

Mozart came back to Prague in August 1791, alone and in such poor health that he was observed continually taking medicine. Commissioned to compose an opera to accompany the coronation of the Emperor Leopold, he began this work—*La Clemenza di Tito*—in the carriage in which he had travelled, and completed it in Prague 18 days later. He stayed again with the Dušeks, where he was side-tracked this time not so much by any activity organised by his hosts but by the billiards in a neighbouring coffee-house. Yet even when playing billiards, Mozart's creative mind was busily at work, and he kept on interrupting the game to take out a pocket book and scribble down notes while humming away: he later astonished everyone at the Dušek household by performing here soon afterwards the quintet from the first act of what would be his last work, *The Magic Flute*.

The Prague public, worn out by all the revelry that the emperor's coronation had entailed, did not respond to *La Clemenza di Tito* with the enthusiasm that had been hoped for by the composer, who died in Vienna later in the year. An enormous affection for Mozart has none the less been maintained in Prague over the centuries, and he has now come to be treated here not only as an honorary Czech, but also as a person integral to the stereotypical image of the city—a status enormously enhanced by the filming here in 1984 of Miloš Forman's film, *Amadeus*.

Mozart's visits to Bohemia have been given so much emphasis that it is easy to forget the important stays here made by other leading European composers from the late 18C onwards. The spa towns of Teplice, Mariánské Lázně and Karlovy Vary were especially lively musical centres, and attracted such figures as Beethoven, Chopin, Brahms and Wagner (who began conceiving *Tannhäuser* while staying at Teplice in 1843). Prague too had a great appeal to composers of the Romantic generation, beginning with Beethoven, who paid at least four visits to the city between 1796 and 1812. From 1813 to 1816 the German composer Carl Maria von Weber was musical director of the German Opera House that was founded here in 1807; and from 1840 onwards Franz Liszt became a regular visitor to the city, meeting up here with, among others, Hector Berlioz, Robert Schumann and a Czech composer who drew heavily on Liszt's work and that of Wagner to formulate a truly national Czech style—Bedřich Smetana (1824–84).

Smetana and Czech nationalism

The eldest son of a successful brewer from Litomyšl, Smetana grew up a German-speaker, and was never fully to master the Czech language despite a life-long dedication to the Czech nationalist cause. Whereas Liszt and Chopin were only able to flourish in Western Europe, Smetana found in his homeland a perfect environment for the nurturing of his talents: here he could follow closely the great revival of interest in Czech culture and history while being exposed to the latest developments in European music. After attending schools in Jindřichův Hradec, Jihlava, Prague and Plzeň, he settled in Prague, where he immediately revealed his political sympathies by composing in 1848 a work entitled *The*

March of the Prague Students' Legion. In that same year he composed his piano work *Six Characteristic Pieces*, which he dedicated to Liszt, who became a friend and mentor, and indeed advised him in 1856 to move to Sweden, where many other Czechs had taken refuge in the wake of 1848.

It was after his return to a more liberal Bohemia in 1861 that Smetana composed the works that would soon turn him into a national figurehead. The country's new mood of optimism was epitomised by the inauguration in 1862 of a provisional Czech National Theatre for the performance of opera, ballet and plays. Encouraged by this, and swearing allegiance to the school of Wagner, Smetana set himself the task of creating a repertory of **Czech operas**, starting off with *The Brandenburgers in Bohemia*, which, though composed in 1863, was not performed until 1866, when he was appointed director of the National Theatre. Later in that same eventful year he produced here the even more successful *The Bartered Bride*, which remains to this day the most popular Czech opera.

Smetana's national consciousness was expressed not only in his subject-matter but also in his lofty and monumental compositions, which attempted to merge the achievements of European pioneers such as Wagner, Liszt and Schumann with a highly personal language derived from Czech folk music: in contrast to other 19C Romantics, he never quoted or imitated folk-melodies but tried to capture instead their essential spirit. A stirringly patriotic climax to his work was reached with his cycle of six 'symphonic poems' collectively known as *My Country* (*Má Vlast*, 1874–79). *Vltava* and *Z českých luhů a hájů* celebrated the beauties of the Bohemian landscape, while *Tábor* and *Blaník* evoked two of the greatest periods in Bohemian history. The two remaining works of the cycle, *Vyšehrad* and *Šárka*, turned to the same legendary past that inspired his opera *Libuše*, the première of which in 1883 was chosen to open the magnificent neo-Renaissance structure constituting the new National Theatre. Remarkably, this last decade of critical triumph for Smetana was marked by rapid physical and mental deterioration: made suddenly deaf as early as 1874, he died insane ten years later.

Antonín Dvořák

After Smetana's death, the role of inspirational figure to the new generation of Czech musicians was inherited by a composer 17 years his junior, and with a notably different background and character—Antonín Dvořák (1841–1904). Born in the village of Nelahozeves, just to the north of Prague, he was the son of the village butcher and publican, and began his career as a butcher boy. Lacking the education and resources of the young Smetana, he gained his interest in music entirely through his zither-playing father, who conducted the village band. After becoming a violin-player in this band from the age of nine, Dvořák went to Prague when he was 16, and became a pupil of the organ school attached to the Bohemian Church Music Society. So poor that he had to keep himself by playing the viola in cafés and the organ in a mental home, he was even unable to afford to go to concerts ('As for Mozart and Beethoven', he later reminisced, 'I only just knew that they existed.'). In 1862, at the age of 21, he was accepted as viola player in the provisional National Theatre orchestra conducted by Smetana, and in 1875 he was awarded a grant for impecunious musicians by an Austrian government committee that included Brahms, who became thereafter a keen promoter of his music.

Dvořák's roots in Czech peasant culture, and his lack of early exposure to classical music, gave him far greater credentials than Smetana as a musician closely wedded to the Czech soil. And yet, ironically, his aims as a composer were more overtly international than those of Smetana, and the folkloric elements of his music more integrated still into compositions betraying strong influences from Beethoven, Schumann, Brahms and, above all, Wagner. International success came with the publication in 1878 of his *Moravian Duets* and *Slavonic Dances*, the latter drawing on folk-dances from all the Slav countries but without ever borrowing existing tunes. Invited thereafter to England and the United States (where he held the post of artistic director of the New York Conservatory between 1892 and 1895) he became known especially for his symphonic works. Though he even referred to his famous symphony in E minor, subtitled *From the New World*, as 'genuine Bohemian music', his symphonies at their best transcend personal and national sentiments to achieve a truly universal significance.

Working under the shadow of both Smetana and Dvořák, but likewise considered as one of the founders of Czech national music, was **Zdeněk Fibich** (1850–1900), who wrote Wagner-inspired operas and concert melodramas. Unlike his more famous Czech contemporaries, he took almost no interest in folk music, and has since become virtually unknown outside the Czech Republic, where his works are still regularly performed.

Janáček's new musical language

Though barely four years younger than Fibich, the composer Leoš Janáček (1854–1928) was a late developer whose music belongs essentially to the 20C. Born in the North Moravian town of Hukvaldy, he became at the age of ten a choir-boy at the Augustinian Monastery at Brno, where he was greatly influenced by the monk Pavel Křížkovský (1820–85), a Moravian composer of strongly nationalistic tendencies who was an ardent transcriber of folk-songs. Janáček went on to pursue his studies in Prague and Leipzig, but remained so attached to his native Moravia that he returned afterwards to Brno, where he stayed for the rest of his life.

Isolating himself in this way from Prague led to his being treated at first as a composer of essentially provincial importance; but it was also the avant-garde nature of his work that hindered its early appreciation. In addition to collecting and notating the folk-songs of Bohemia, Slovakia and Moravia, he embarked in the early 1890s on the far more unusual task of recording on paper the melodic and rhythmic characteristics not only of the spoken word but also the sounds made by animals and inanimate objects. Calling these musical descriptions of real sounds '**Speech Melodies**' or 'Melodic Curves', he later boldly announced that 'no-one can become an opera composer who has not studied living speech'. 'Speech Melodies' encouraged him to abandon verse for prose in his own operas, the most famous of which was written in 1903, just after the death of his daughter Olga, whose dying rattle he had naturally recorded. Known originally as 'Her Stepdaughter' (*Její pastorkyňa*), this was first performed in 1904 in Brno, where it was a complete failure. Not until 1916, when it was premièred in Prague under the catchier title of *Jenůfa*, was its greatness finally recognised and Janáček acknowledged as an avant-garde composer of the stature and originality of Claude Debussy, whose new musical language had much in common with his own independently created one.

Stimulated by this late success, the elderly Janáček went on to produce the other works for which he is best remembered today, including the ope Makropulos Affair (1926), The Cunning Little Vixen (1923), and The Excur Mr Brouček, a proto-Surrealistic piece based on the tales of the 19C author Svatopluk Čech. Just one year before he died he wrote his most important choral work, the Glagolitic Mass, an exultant work of almost barbarous joy in which 'Melodic Curves' are combined with the old Slavonic rite.

Whereas Janáček managed eventually to achieve a reputation as both an avant-garde and a popular composer, the same was not true of the far more pro- lific **Bohuslav Martinů** (1890–1959), who, despite being the only other 20C Czech composer of major international status, was greatly neglected during the Communist era, and is only now beginning to feature more regularly in the Czech classical repertory. The son of a Moravian bell-ringer, and indeed brought up in the village bell-tower of Polička, he was a largely self-taught composer much drawn in his mature music to the works of Debussy, Igor Stravinsky and Albert Roussel. Moving to France in 1923, where he came to be regarded as a leading light of the Paris School, he was to spend almost all his remaining life away from Czechoslovakia while continuing to write music that expressed both his yearnings for his homeland (most poignantly in his Fifth Symphony of 1946) and his deep attachment to its musical traditions.

The persistent influence of folk music on Czech classical composers in the 20C is also illustrated in the work of Martinů's contemporary **Alois Hába** (1893–1973), who was a professor of composition at the Prague Conservatory from 1923 to 1953 and, like almost all the important Czechoslovakia-based musicians of the inter-war years, a member of the Přítomnost Society for Contemporary Music. Haba's main contribution was as one of the 20C's most convinced exponents of composing in semi-tones, quarter tones and sixth tones (**microtone music**). Interestingly, he was originally prompted to embark on his life-long study of 'micro-intervals' largely as a result of his encounter with the modified scales used by Czech and Slovak folk-singers.

Jazz and dissent

A major new influence on Czech music from the 1920s onwards was jazz, which soon developed into a national mania. One of the classical composers affected was **Ervín Schulhoff** (1894–1942), who, in addition to the challenge of com- posing an oratorio on the subject of The Communist Manifesto (1932), wrote a Jazz Oratorio and other jazz-related works. He was also a member of the Jazz Orchestra founded in 1936 at the celebrated avant-garde venue known as The Liberated Theatre (Osvobozené Divadlo), which was associated with the Devětsil actor-playwrights Jiří Voskovec and Jan Werich. The orchestra director was Jaroslav Ježek (1906–42), who wrote jazz music to accompany Voskovec's and Werich's absurdly satirical pieces, and to whom there is a small museum in Prague at Kaprova 10.

The jazz-obsessed novelist Josef Škvorecký, in his books The Bass Saxophone (1980), Talking Moscow Blues (1989) and Heading for the Blues (1998), has beau- tifully recorded how jazz in Czechoslovakia was transformed from the Second World War onwards from a music of pure entertainment into a **music of protest**—'a sharp thorn in the sides of the power-hungry men, from Hitler to Brezhnev'. The Nazis, for reasons largely of misleading propaganda, allowed former Jewish members of the Jazz-Quintet Weiss to regroup at the Terezín ghetto as 'The Ghetto-Swingers'. However, they generally considered jazz, with its African rhythms, as decadent music, as did their Communist successors, under whom musical life in Czechoslovakia reached its lowest point.

During the Stalinist era Czech composers were not allowed to stray far from an officially sanctioned Romantic style often incorporating folk music: the orthodox *Wallachian Symphony* (1952) by the previously experimental Hába is a typical example of this. A more liberal attitude to musical expression set in during the early 1960s, and a number of interesting classical composers emerged during the last three decades of Communist power, including the electronic specialist Miloslav Kabeláč (1908–79), and the jazz-inspired Alexej Fried (b. 1922).

But the role of music as a symbol of personal freedom was assumed principally by **popular music**, which acquired in the 1960s and '80s some of the same emotive, epoch-making qualities that had characterised the works of Smetana and other nationalist composers of the 19C. The spirit of the 'Prague Spring' of 1968 was epitomised in the mini-skirted figure of the singer Marta Kubišova, whose impromptu planting of a kiss on Dubček's lips was one of the key images of her generation. And it was, strangely enough, the censoring of a punk group unpromisingly named 'The Plastic People of the Universe' that led to the creation of Charter 77, the most sustained charter of human liberties in the history of Communist Europe.

Visions of Prague

The city through the eyes of travellers and writers

Prague, a city so frequently described as 'the golden' or 'the beautiful' or even 'the most beautiful city in the world', is a place that inevitably raises enormous expectations in the first-time visitor. But despite the glowing appraisals found in most travel literature, native writers have generally agreed that this is a city where beauty, melancholy and anguish have tended to exist in almost equal measures. 'There are evenings', wrote Miloš Jiránek in 1908, 'when Prague, our filthy, gloomy, tragic Prague, is transformed by the golden light of sunset into a blonde fairy-like beauty, a miracle of light and brilliance.' André Gide referred to Prague as 'a glorious, suffering and tragic city', while the level-headed historian Peter Demetz prefaced his recent book on the city with the words 'I love and hate my hometown.'

In attempting to define the 'spirit of Prague', one of its leading novelists of today, Ivan Klíma, concluded that this is a 'city of paradoxes'. Indeed, one need only reflect on the extent to which the rapturous epithet of 'city of the hundred spires' is due to the four centuries of building work undertaken by the country's Catholic oppressors. But one should also consider the contrast between the city famously characterised by the French Surrealist André Breton as the 'magic capital of old Europe', and the pragmatic, down-to-earth, beer-drinking city that Kafka and other intellectuals found irritatingly small and cramped.

Perhaps no city but Prague could have nurtured such opposing literary contemporaries as the ascetic, teetotal vegetarian Franz Kafka (the ultimate representative of the city's German-Jewish intellectual community) and the fat, inebriated philistine Jaroslav Hašek (the creator of the quintessentially Czech anti-hero, Švejk). Revealingly, even two of the greatest books ever written about Prague are works that take a diametrically opposed approach to the city. One is Angelo Maria Ripellino's *Magic Prague* (1973), a brilliant, difficult and densely argued book that takes off occasionally into flights of fictional fantasy; the other is Peter Demetz's *Prague in Black and Gold* (1997), a solid work of revisionist history that avoids imaginative simplifications and gives greater emphasis to Rabbi Löw's pedagogical reforms than to his golem, to the sober philosophy of Tomáš Masaryk than to the *fin-de-siècle* fantasists and mystics beloved by Ripellino.

'I catch myself wondering whether Prague really exists or whether she is not an imaginary land like the Poland of King Ubu', confesses Ripellino, who is severely criticised by Demetz for having promoted the fanciful, distorted vision of Prague that had been created by foreigners, developed by turn-of-the-20th-century Czech and German Decadents, and then taken up again in the 1960s by the dissident left in reaction to the drab uniformity of Socialist Realism. But, as the Canadian translator Paul Wilson pointed out in his excellent *Prague: A Traveller's Literary Companion* (1995), 'Prague is far more than the sum of its physical parts or its history. It is a city of the mind and the imagination, a city that exists as vividly in poetry and painting and music and legend as it does in brick and stone.'

In the eyes of foreigners this rich imaginary city does not begin properly to take shape until well into the 19C. Until then foreign conceptions of Prague had to rely largely on sober descriptions that did not bear out any exotic notions that might have been formed on the basis of the city's remoteness and important history. **Hester Lynch Piozzi**, an adventurous member of Dr Johnson's circle, recalled how her mentor had lost his temper once at a man 'for not being better company' despite his having 'travelled into Bohemia and seen Prague': '"Surely", added Dr Johnson, "the man who has seen Prague might tell us something strange, and not sit silent for want of matter to put his lips in motion."' But when Piozzi herself finally visited Prague in the 1780s, she had to confess to 'have brought away nothing very interesting I fear; unless that the floor of the opera-stage there is inlaid.' Among her only other observations was that the food here was 'incomparable' (see p 24) and that 'here everything seems at least five centuries behind-hand.'

During the Romantic era, too, with its taste for the medieval and the bizarre, foreign accounts of Prague remained at first remarkably low-key, even when written by the future gushing author of *Tales of the Alhambra*, **Washington Irving**. Irving came here in November 1822, at a time when many of the palaces of the Little Quarter had fallen into ruins after their owners had departed for Vienna. In his diary notes he commented on the 'curious' architecture of many of the houses, and on how he found the people 'better looking than any we had seen yet in Moravia'; and he revealed a typically Romantic fascination with decayed splendour in his evocation of the collapsing, geese-ridden Černín Palace. But otherwise all he could say about Prague was that it had 'a fine, old continental look'.

Much more eloquent and forthcoming was Irving's contemporary and fellow Hispanophile, the **Vicomte de François-René Chateaubriand**, who arrived on a May evening in 1833 and embarked on a walk up to the Hradčany: 'I climbed up silent, gloomy streets, without street-lamps, to the foot of the tall hill which is crowned by the immense castle of the Kings of Bohemia. The building outlined its black mass against the sky; no light issued from its windows: there was there something akin to the solitude, the site and the grandeur of the Vatican, or of the Temple of Jerusalem, seen from the Valley of Johoshaphant ... As I climbed I discovered the town below me. The links of history, the fate of men, the destruction of empires, the designs of Providence presented themselves to my recollection, identified themselves with the memory of my own destiny ...'.

By the following decade, when the city was visited by **J. Bayard Taylor**, the author of *Views A-Foot. Or Europe Seen with Knapsack and Staff* (1846), Prague had already come to be perceived in a largely fantastical light. Under the blue haze that was present when Bayard Taylor made his own ascent up to the Hradčany, Prague looked 'like a city seen in a dream'. After eccentrically describing Prague as a 'half-barbaric, half-Asiatic city', he went on to write that the 'fantastic Byzantine architecture of many of the churches and towers gives the city a peculiar oriental appearance; it seems to have been transported from the hills of Syria. Its streets are full of palaces, fallen and dwelt in now by the poorer classes. In a word, it is, like Venice, a fallen city.' Like so many later 19C travellers, he acquired a certain morbid fascination with the then horribly decrepit Jewish Quarter, which he stumbled on by chance, and left hurriedly, pursued by beggars and other more sinister types.

The nightmarish quality of Prague hinted at by Bayard Taylor was exploited by **George Eliot**, whose visit to the city in 1858 led the following year to the writing of her short novel about the supernatural, *The Lifted Veil*, a novel so strange that no-one would publish it until nearly 20 years later. This work begins with the narrator relating a disturbing vision he has had of Prague's Charles Bridge under harsh sunlight: 'The city looked so thirsty that the broad river seemed to me a sheet of metal; and the blackened statues, as I passed under their blank gaze, along the unending bridge, with their ancient garments and their saintly crowns, seemed to me the real inhabitants and owners of this place ...'. What is particularly unsettling is that he had yet to go to Prague, and—presumably like most Victorians—had only the haziest idea of what it must be like: 'I had seen no picture of Prague: it hung in my mind as a mere name, with vaguely remembered historical associations—ill-defined memories of imperial grandeur and religious wars.' Eventually, when he finally comes to the city and escapes from his party to rush off and see for himself the Charles Bridge, he finds his vision to be borne out entirely by the reality. It is indicative perhaps of the tourist priorities of the time that the people he is with should want to start their tour of the city not with its famous bridge, nor even with the Hradčany, but with the Jewish Quarter—a part of the city that now comes to be central to the nascent image of Prague as a centre of magic, mystery and evil.

The ever more feverish interest taken by foreigners in Prague from the mid-19C (culminating in Marion Crawford's best-selling novel of 1882, *The Witch of Prague*) coincided with the emergence of a native literary tradition inspired by this city. The Prague-born **Jan Neruda**, in his *Tales from the Little Quarter* (1878), celebrated with ironic concision and humour the often eccentric everyday lives of those living in his own picturesque home district below the castle; the satirist Svatopluk Čech, meanwhile, used the setting of a well-known beer cellar in the castle precinct as the drunken starting-point for the fantastical exploits of one Mr Brouček, who even travelled to the moon and back to the 15C.

The lightheartedness and gentle wit of Czech authors such as these stood in contrast to many of the writings of Prague's Germans and Jews, who captured in their works the dark, sinister and claustrophobic city that the Prague-born poet Rainer Maria Rilke found unbearable in its 'heaviness' and in its 'incomprehensible and confusing' presence. Egon Erwin Kisch dedicated himself to the city's under-world, night life and labyrinth of covered passages, while Gustav Meyrink, in his enormously successful novel *The Golem* (1915), took over from Marion Crawford in popularising the city's many alchemists and practitioners of the occult.

But the writer whose works did most to establish the image of a nightmarish Prague was of course **Franz Kafka**, who, as an agnostic in a German-speaking Jewish community that faced prejudices from both Czechs and Germans alike, was ideally placed to explore alienation and paranoia. The centre of his world was the Old Town Square and its surroundings, where he spent most of his child-hood and youth, witnessing during these years the destruction of the decayed ramshackle Jewish Quarter where he was born. 'The unhealthy old Jewish town within us', he once commented, 'is far more real than the hygienic town around us.' This phrase is indicative not only of his morbid obsessiveness but also of his trans-formation of the city's topography into a geography of the heart and the mind.

Kafka's only fictional work specifically to mention places in Prague was his novella *Description of a Struggle* (1904–05), which deals with two strangers leav-ing a party and walking by moonlight across the Charles Bridge and up on to the Petřín Hill: more concerned with mood than with plot, this is an hallucinatory account of a journey through a deserted nocturnal Prague that has rarely been so brilliantly evoked as a city of the dead. In all his other works, notably the posthumously published novels *The Trial* (1925) and *The Castle* (1926), the set-ting, though unspecified, can easily be imagined as Prague, with the cathedral referred to in the first of these novels being taken as St Vitus's Cathedral and the eponymous castle as the Hradčany—an association that would acquire an added resonance during the Communist era, when the place was the focal point of cor-rupt power and monstrous bureaucracy.

Whereas the humdrum reality of modern Prague was glossed over in Kafka's expressionistic vision, it frequently impinged on the fantasies of the growing number of foreign travellers now coming to the city. One of the more critical of these was the poet and essayist **Arthur Symons**, who, while finding little to admire in the city's 'over-emphatic, unaesthetic ... bastard kind of architecture' ('Renaissance crossed with Slavonic'), was able to let his imagination loose in the Jewish Quarter, especially in the cemetery, where 'it seemed to me as if one were seeing all the graves of all the people who had ever died.' For him the Jewish Quarter was the one corner of Prague that had 'kept more than any other its medieval aspect'; however, by the time his essay on the city eventually appeared (in 1903), this district had already been pulled down, making more noticeable still the modern Prague which had been 'growing up in the image of Vienna, with tall characterless buildings, and modish shops'.

The clash between the real and the imagined Prague, the old and the new city, was highlighted by the popular novelist **Vernon Lee**, who confessed in her book

The Sentimental Traveller (1921) that ever since childhood the 'mere name of Prague had awakened emotions of mystery and wonder'. Inevitably she had to pay for such 'imaginary raptures' in the course of 'three dreary, chilly autumn days in the Prague which exists outside the fancy ...'. However, there were moments of escape from this Prague of 'electric trams' and 'intolerably gloomy' weather: walking at dusk into the 'silent emptiness' of the Hradčany, she was able to relive her childhood imaginings through an encounter there with a strange and fascinating woman whom she romantically perceived as a princess.

Extremes of elation and depression were reached in the respective responses towards Prague of the writers **Patrick Leigh Fermor** and **Albert Camus**, both of whom were here in the mid-1930s. Leigh Fermor, looking back on his visit over 40 years later, remembered how the city had seemed to him 'not only one of the most beautiful places in the world, but one of the strangest'. Camus instead perceived a Prague of unrelieved grimness: lonely, frightened and constantly sickened by the 'cumin-flavoured food' (see p 24), he would later retain of the city little more than the 'smell of cucumbers soaked in vinegar, which were sold at every street corner to eat between your fingers, and whose bitter piquant flavour would awaken and feed my anguish as soon as I had crossed the threshold of my hotel.'

The one foreign writer of the early years of the 20C who managed successfully to bring together the conflicting moods of Prague was the French poet **Guillaume Apollinaire**, who, though paying only a brief visit to the city in 1902, profoundly influenced the Prague avant-garde of the 1920s and '30s; he is commemorated today by a street named after him. Apollinaire's experiences in Prague—the subject of his prose story *Prague Flâneur*—were distilled to their essence in the poem *Zone*, which appeared in 1918 in a Czech translation by Karel Čapek, with illustrations by the latter's brother Josef. The short section of this long and innovative poem that deals with Prague opens with the poet sitting happily in a suburban garden, where he is distracted from his writing of *Prague Flâneur* by the sight of a beetle asleep inside a rose. The next lines recall a panic attack the poet had while visiting the Wenceslas Chapel in St Vitus's Cathedral: looking here for the precious stone that is said to bear the features of Napoleon, Apollinaire discovered instead his own sad face. The image of the famous backward-moving clock in the Jewish Town Hall then sets him on a journey into his own past, which continues as he climbs up to the Hradčany and listens in the evening to 'Czech songs being sung in the taverns'.

Apollinaire's technique of compiling apparently disconnected images was emulated by the writers associated with Poetism, a major Czech movement of the inter-war years that—under the influence of French Surrealism—advocated free association and the impulse of the subconscious. The leading writer associated with the movement was **Vitězslav Nezval** (1900–58), who, after beginning his career as a 'proletarian' poet, reacted against doctrinaire rhetoric in favour of a style that was better able to express what was contradictory and paradoxical in experience. Prague, the ultimate symbol of this contradictoriness, provided him with one of his major themes, and inspired perhaps his finest collection, *Prague with Fingers of Rain* (1936). His love for Prague was by no means immediate though, as indicated in his poem *Walker in Prague*, which evokes the Camus-like state of solitude and depression in which his days were spent here after first arriving in April 1920.

Another poet whose early development was comparable to that of Nezval was **Jaroslav Seifert**, who also moved from Proletarianism to Poetism, and was similarly influenced by Apollinaire, to the extent even of fantasising about sitting next to the French poet in Prague's *Café Slavia* (see p 174). He too was an obsessive lover of Prague, which, at dusk, seemed to him 'more beautiful than Rome'. In later years, when he went on to confirm his unofficial status as Czech national poet after becoming the first Czech recipient of the Nobel Prize for Literature, he came to perceive Prague through an increasingly romantic haze, as is illustrated in his poem *View from the Charles Bridge*.

The complex spirit of Prague is one that in recent times has been evoked more vividly in fiction than in poetry, including works by such disparate foreign authors as Philip Roth and Bruce Chatwin. The former's *The Prague Orgy* (1985) is an absurdly funny yet deeply serious portrayal of the city's dissident scene in the 1970s, while the latter's *Utz* (1989) is a sparsely told tale set near the Jewish Cemetery and commenting obliquely on the golem story. Prague has also been a powerful presence in the works of the many Czech authors who, since the 1960s, have made their nation's literature one of the most translated into English. Though the city has been evoked only partially by both Milan Kundera (who is far more concerned with ideas than with specific places) and Josef Škvorecký (whose novels are set mainly in rural eastern Bohemia, with the major exception of his marvellous *Miss Silver's Past*, 1969), the place is of paramount importance to those other two leading Czech writers of modern times, **Ivan Klíma** and **Bohumil Hrabal**.

In his stimulating essay *The Spirit of Prague* (1994), Klíma gave particular emphasis to this city's intensely human aspects—the absence in its centre of any tall building or triumphal arch, the local dislike of ostentatiousness, the paucity of public monuments and memorials. This is exactly the modest Prague that serves as the background to his largely autobiographical works, such as *My Golden Trades* (1992), which describes with quiet humour and delicious irony the ridiculous variety of jobs he was forced to undertake during the Communist period. Communism, as Klíma himself has acknowledged, at least enabled Czech writers to have a far greater insight than they might otherwise have had into the everyday lives of the city's inhabitants. This was certainly true of Hrabal, whose work experiences compacting wastepaper and books were put to brilliant allegorical and humorous use in his short work, *Too Loud a Solitude* (1976). Indeed, Hrabal regarded himself less as a writer than as a teller of stories related to him either at work, or, more usually, in the numerous Prague bars that he used to frequent. Yet, in contrast to Klíma's delicate and understated approach to the city, Hrabal's vision of Prague was one in which a Hašek-like earthiness merged at times into the zany and the fantastical, as in his profoundly entertaining *I Served the King of England* (1989), which is an account of Bohemia's 20C history as seen from the grotesquely distorted viewpoint of a diminutive waiter with a preternatural gift for survival and the giving of sexual pleasure.

Younger Czech writers, whose works are only now beginning to be known outside the Czech Republic, have continued to perpetuate a vision of Prague based on such polarities as the magical and the coarse, the disturbing and the ludicrous, the intimate and the broadly expressionist. One of the more imaginative of these new talents is **Michal Ajvaz**, whose Kafkaesque novel *The Other City* (1993) includes a particularly powerful nocturnal scene set high up in the tower of the Little Quarter Church of St Nicholas. Here, as he observes the deserted moonlit cityscape around him, the narrator meets a mysterious beautiful young woman, on kissing whom he is suddenly attacked by a shark: 'I remained alone with the shark on the gallery of the tower above the sleeping city.'

In the post-Communist Prague of today, in a city that is daily becoming more crowded, more garish, more Americanised, and more like any other European capital, one might have expected writers to have observed the place in a more normal light. And yet the very speed with which all these changes have come about has appeared to many to contain its own element of magic and the unreal, so much so that Daniela Hodrová, in her essay *I See a Great City* ..., asked herself whether 'this had all been just a dream—the kind in which the prisoner dreams that he has become king?' The bizarreness and surreal absurdities of the city's sudden recent transformation have been sharply chronicled by **Jáchym Topol**, a former singer and songwriter and co-founder of the *samizdat* publication, *Revolver Review*.

'The city was changing', runs the refrain of Topol's short story *A Trip to the Train Station* (1993). 'Iron grills and shutters pulled down for years and gone to rust were given fresh coats of paint and often a sign with somebody's name on it. Dusty cellars and dirty beer joints in what used to be the Jewish Quarter were cleverly converted into luxury stores. You could find steamer trunks from the last century, a book dictated by Madonna herself with a piece of her chain included, pineapples and fine tobacco, diaries of dead actresses and trendy wheels from farmers' wagons, whips and dolls and travel flasks with adventurers' blood in them, coins and likenesses of Kafka, shooting galleries with all the proletarian presidents as targets, rags and bones and skins, anything you could think of.'

Appropriately, the narrator observes this changing Prague in the state that epitomises the city's maelstrom of conflicting emotions in which painful reality comes fast on the heels of hearty indulgence, good humour and magical intoxication—a violent hangover.

Further reading

General, travel literature, fiction and poetry

Few European cities have been the recent subject of so many **general books** as Prague. The two that stand out head and shoulders above the rest are Angelo Maria Ripellino's *Magic Prague* (first English paperback edition 1995) and Peter Demetz's *Prague in Black and Gold* (1997). The former, though a difficult read and almost oppressively erudite, is filled with exciting, fanciful ideas and wonderful esoteric information; the latter, in contrast, is a clear, sturdy and eminently readable work of scholarship that does its best to deprive the city of its 'magical' reputation. Those in search of a lightweight, romantic and old-fashioned account might be better off with Count Francis Lützow's *The Story of Prague* (London, 1902). The most famous photographic introduction to the city is Josef Sudek's stunning *Praha* (Prague, 1948).

Among **early travellers**' impressions of the city are those contained in Hester Lynch Piozzi's *Observations and Reflections Made in the Course of a Journey through France, Italy and Germany* (1789; edited by Herbert Barrows, Ann Arbor, Michigan, 1967); Volume 5 of the *Memoirs of Chateaubriand* (1833; translated by Alexander Feixara de Mattos, 6 volumes, London, 1902); *The Journals of Washington Irving* (1822; edited by William P. Trent and George S. Hellman, Boston, 1919); and J. Bayard Taylor's *Views A-Foot. Or Europe Seen with Knapsack and Staff* (1846). Mozart's stay in the city is documented in *The Letters of Mozart and his Family* (edited and translated by Emily Anderson, Basingstoke, 1985), as well as in such early accounts as Edward Holmes' *The Life of Mozart* (1845; reprinted with introduction and additional notes by Christopher Hogwood, London, 1991) and Edward Moricke's *Mozart's Journey to Prague* (1850–51; translated by Leopold von Loewenstein-Wertheim, London, 1957).

Of the travellers' accounts that proliferated from the late 19C onwards, one of the most interesting if also misguided ('the Bohemians have produced nothing beautiful in any of the plastic arts' runs a typical sentence) is Arthur W. Symons's eloquent essay on Prague in his book *Cities* (London, 1903); a wholly uncritical approach towards the city is taken instead in B. Granville Baker's *From a Terrace in Prague* (London, 1923), which is almost contemporary with Vernon Lee's similarly romantic *The Sentimental Traveller. Notes on Places* (Leipzig, 1921). Albert Camus' bitter tale of his experiences in the city, included in his *Selected Essays and Notebooks* (Harmondsworth, 1984), is a good antidote to the ecstatic reminiscences featured in Patrick Leigh Fermor's *A Time of Gifts* (London, 1979), which is written in the author's characteristically indigestible flowery style. Accounts of a more recent Prague include those that appear in V.S. Pritchett's *Foreign Faces* (London, 1964), Stephen Brook's *The Double Eagle: Vienna, Budapest and Prague* (London, 1988), Rory Maclean's semi-fictional *Stalin's Nose: Across the Face of Europe* (London, 1992) and Geoffrey Hodgson's readable if pedestrian *A New Grand Tour. How Europe's Great Cities Made our World* (London, 1995).

Undoubtedly the most enjoyable preparation you can make before visiting Prague is to immerse yourself in the wealth of **novels** and **poems** written about the city. F. Marion Crawford's occult classic *The Witch of Prague* (London, 1976), Philip Roth's amusing *The Prague Orgy* (Harmondsworth, 1985) and Bruce Chatwin's beautifully enigmatic *Utz* (London, 1989) are perhaps the three best-known foreign works of fiction set in Prague; also worth reading is Martha Gellhorn's autobiographical novel *A Stricken Field* (London, 1986), which deals with the experiences of an American journalist working in Prague after the Munich pact of 1938. Apollinaire's influential poem *Zone*, with its famous section on Prague, is featured in Oliver Bernard's *Apollinaire: Selected Poems* in the Penguin Modern European Poets series (Harmondsworth, 1965).

For English translations of **Czech poetry** inspired by Prague see *Three Czech Poets: Vitězslav Nezval, Antonín Bartušek, Josef Hanzlík* (translated by Ewald Osers and George Theiner, Penguin Modern Poets, Harmondsworth, 1971) and *The Selected Poetry of Jaroslav Seifert* (translated by Ewald Osers, London, 1986).

Two classics of **Czech fiction** are Jan Neruda's *Prague Tales* (1878; translated by Michael Henry Heim, with an introduction by Ivan Klíma, London, 1993) and Alois Jirásek's *Old Czech Legends* (1890s; translated by Marie K. Holeček, London, 1992). The best-known works of historical fiction by Prague-born authors are Gustav Meyrink's *The Golem* (1913–14; translated by M. Pemberton, London,

1985) and Leo Perutz's *By Night Under the Stone Bridge* (1953; translated by Eric Mosbacher, London, 1991), both of which are set in Rudolphine Prague. Franz Kafka's *The Complete Novels* (London, 1992) and *The Complete Short Stories* (London, 1994) are available as Minerva paperbacks.

One of the most outstanding Czech writers active at the beginning of the Communist period was Jiří Weil, whose *Life with a Star* (1947; first published in English in 1988) and *Mendelssohn is on the Roof* (posthumously published in 1960, and translated into English by Marie Winn in 1988) are unforgettable evocations of Jewish experience in Prague during the Second World War: moving and bleak at times, they are also savagely ironic and blackly humorous.

Among the more recent Czech novels, short stories and essays that have particular relevance to Prague, some of the most entertaining are Bohumil Hrabal's *The Death of Mr Baltisberger* (1990), *I Served the King of England* (London, 1989) and *Total Fears* (Prague, 1998); Ivan Klíma's *My Merry Mornings: Stories from Prague* (London, 1993), *My Golden Trades* (London, 1992) and *The Spirit of Prague* (London, 1994); and Ludvík Vaculík's *A Cup of Coffee with my Interrogator: the Prague Chronicles of Ludvík Vaculík* (London, 1987). Elena Lappin's excellent anthology *Daylight in Nightclub Inferno: Czech Fiction from the Post-Kundera Generation* (North Haven, Connecticut, 1997) includes extracts from Jáchym Topol's *City Sister Silver* (1994) and from *The Other City* (1993), a haunting novel by Michal Ajvaz, who is also featured in Paul Wilson's admirable *Prague: A Traveller's Literary Companion* (San Francisco, 1995), a collection of Czech writings about the city.

Details of other literary works describing Prague are given in James Naughton's useful *Traveller's Literary Companion to Eastern and Central Europe* (Brighton, 1995), as well as in Susie Lunt's *Prague* (World Bibliographical Series, Volume 195, Oxford, 1997), which is the most important bibliography of the city as yet available in English.

History

One of the best general introductions to Czech history remains Robert Seton-Watson's *A History of Czechs and Slovaks* (second edition, Hamden, Connecticut, 1965). Bede Jarrett's *The Emperor Charles IV* (London, 1935) serves as a readable introduction to the greatest of Prague's medieval rulers, while Howard Kaminsky clarifies many of the complexities of the Hussite period in *A History of the Hussite Revolution* (Berkeley and Los Angeles, 1967). **Rudolphine Prague** is especially well chronicled in English, notably by R.J.W. Evans in his celebrated *Rudolf II and his World: A Study in Intellectual History, 1572–1612* (Oxford, 1984), and by the many authors of the massive exhibition catalogue *Rudolph II and Prague* (edited by Eliška Fučíkova, London, 1997). Other studies relating to this latter period include Frederick Thieberger's *The Great Rabbi Loew of Prague* (London, 1955); *The Prague Ghetto in the Renaissance Period* (edited by Otto Muneles, Prague, 1965); Max Caspar's *Kepler* (London, 1959); and John Alleyn Gade's *The Life and Times of Tycho Brahe* (Princeton, 1947).

Useful background material for the **later history of Hapsburg rule** in Prague is provided by C. Veronica Wedgwood's fascinating and scholarly *The Thirty Years War* (London, 1992), Michal Šroněk and Jaroslava Hausenblasova's *Gloria & Miseria 1614–1648: Prague During the Thirty Years War* (Prague, 1998), Lawrence D. Orton's *The Prague Slav Congress of 1848* (Boulder, Colorado, 1978),

G.B. Cohen's *The Politics of Ethnic Survival: Germans in Prague 1861–1914* (Princeton, 1981), and Zdeněk Zeman's *The Break-up of the Habsburg Empire* (Oxford, 1963). Zeman was also the author of *The Masaryks: The Making of Czechoslovakia* (London, 1976), which, together with Karel Čapek's *Masaryk Tells his Story* (London, 1951) and Paul Selver's *Masaryk: A Biography* (London, 1949), helps chart some of the most exhilarating years in Prague's 20C history. Further details of the historical and cultural background are given in such splen-did literary biographies as Ernst Pawel's *Franz Kafka: The Nightmare of Reason* (London, 1984), Lionel B. Steinman's *Franz Werfel: The Faith of an Exile* (Waterloo, Ontario, 1985) and Sir Cecil Parrot's *The Bad Bohemian: The Extraordinary Life of Jaroslav Hašek* (London, 1978), which is almost as entertaining as anything that Hašek himself wrote. A useful survey of Prague cultural life from the 1880s right up to the 1960s is Peter Hrubý's *Daydreams and Nightmares* (New York, 1990).

Among the numerous works in English documenting aspects of Prague's history from the **Second World War** right up to the **Soviet invasion** of 1968 are two very readable books by Callum McDonald, *The Killing of SS-Obergruppenführer Reinhard Heydrich* (London, 1989) and *Prague in the Shadow of the Swastika: A History of the German Occupation, 1939–1945* (London, 1995), Meir Cotic's *The Prague Trial. The First Anti-Zionist Show Trial in the Communist Bloc* (London, 1987), *Stalinism in Prague: The Loebl Story* (New York, 1969) and Harry Schwartz's *Prague's 200 Days: the Struggle for Democracy in Czechoslovakia* (London, 1969). These works can be supplemented by a wide range of personal memoirs, above all Heda Margolius Kovaly's *Prague Farewell* (London, 1988), Rosemary Kavan's *Love and Freedom: My Unexpected Life in Prague* (London and New York, 1988), Elizabeth Wiskemann's classic *Czechs and Germans* (London 1938), written during the build-up to the Munich crisis, Sir Cecil Parrot's *The Serpent and the Nightingale* (London, 1977), Edwin Muir's *An Autobiography* (London, 1980), Alexander Dubček's *Hope Dies Last: The Autobiography of Alexander Dubček* (London, 1993) and Alan Levy's engrossing accounts of his harrowing involvement in 1968 and its aftermath, *Good Men Still Live (I Am the Other Karel Čapek)* (Chicago, 1974) and *So Many Heroes* (Sagaponach, New York, 1980).

Václav Havel's *Living in Truth* (London 1990), a collection of essays including the seminal *Anatomy of a Reticence* and *The Power of the Powerless*, is a tour de force of political writing, which brilliantly dissects the inertia, dilemmas and anxieties of life in 1970s Czechoslovakia; equally engaging are his *Letters to Olga* (London 1989), written from his prison cell in the 1980s, and the autobiographical *Disturbing the Peace* (London 1991). For an excellent analysis and eyewitness description of the '**Velvet Revolution**' of 1989, see Timothy Garton Ash's *We the People: The Revolution of 89 Witnessed in Warsaw, Budapest, Berlin and Prague* ... (Cambridge, 1990) and *The Uses of Adversity. Essays on the Fate of Central Europe* (Cambridge, 1989).

Art and architecture

Remarkably, there is still no good general history of Czech art and architecture written in English. However, those interested specifically in architecture can turn to Brian Knox's *The Architecture of Prague and Bohemia* (London, 1962), which remains an invaluable introduction to the subject. There are also a number of detailed **architectural guides** to Prague, notably the densely and tediously written *Prague: Eleven Centuries of Architecture* (various authors, Prague, 1992), which nevertheless provides most of the necessary facts, as well as a wealth of useful plans, elevations and line drawings. A more accessible architectural work is Léon and Xavier de Koster's *14 Promenades dans Prague*, which is useful even to those who do not understand French, thanks to the exceptional clarity of its layout and admirably concise information.

The **medieval period** is covered by a number of poorly translated and barely readable books such as V. Denkstein and A. Matouš's *Gothic Art of South Bohemia* (Prague, 1955), Eric Bachmann's *Gothic Art in Bohemia: Architecture, Sculpture and Painting* (Oxford, 1977) and Václav Mencl's *Czech Architecture of the Luxemburg Period* (Prague, 1955). Far better, but in French, is Karel Stejskal's *L'Empéreur Charles IV: L'Art en Europe au XIVe siècle* (Paris, 1980). But the definitive work for some time to come on 14C Czech art is likely to be the enormous exhibition catalogue *Magister Theodorious, Court Painter of Emperor Charles V* (ed. Jiří Fajt, Prague 1998).

Thomas da Costa Kauffmann has written a difficult but stimulating account of the Czech **Renaissance and Baroque periods** in *Court, Cloister and City: The Art and Culture of Central Europe 1450–1800* (London, 1995); he is also the author of *The School of Prague: Painting at the Court of Rudolph II* (Chicago, 1988). Jiřina Hořejší's *Renaissance Art in Bohemia* (London, 1979) and Oldřich Blažícek's *Baroque Art in Bohemia* (London, 1968) are to be enjoyed largely for their illustrations, as is also the case with Milan Pavlík and Vladimír Uher's superlatively produced *Prague Baroque Architecture* (Amsterdam, 1998).

The city's **Art Nouveau** monuments are beautifully photographed in Petr Wittlich's *Prague—Fin de Siècle* (London, 1992), while the exhibition catalogue *Czech Modernism, 1900–1945* (Phoenix, Arizona, 1989) provides the best overview of early-20C Czech art and architecture. The most detailed architectural survey of Prague during this period is Rostislav Šacha's *The Architecture of New Prague, 1895–1945* (Boston, 1997), which, though difficult to read as a continuous text, serves as an especially useful guide to the city's modern buildings. A portable alternative to this massive tome is Ivan Margolius's literally pocket-sized *Prague: A Guide to Twentieth-Century Architecture* (London, second edition 1996). More specialist works for the enthusiast of the modern city are Karel Teige's *Modern Czechoslovak Architecture* (London, 1947), the exhibition catalogue *Czech Cubism: Architecture, Furniture and Decorative Arts, 1910–1925* (edited by Alexander von Vegesack, Montreal, 1992), the guidebook *Cubist Prague 1905–25* (various authors, Prague, 1995), and Damjan Prevlovšek's *Jože Plečnik, 1872–1957—Architectura perennis* (Yale University Press, 1998).

1 The Old Town (Staré Město) and the Jewish Quarter (Josefov)

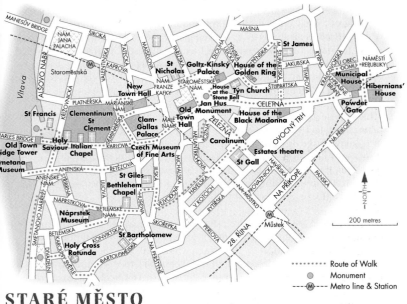

STARÉ MĚSTO

Along the Royal Route

The **Staré Město**, or Old Town, is bordered to the north and west by the River Vltava, and to the south and east by a long thoroughfare (comprising Národní, Na příkopě and Revoluční) marking the line of the medieval fortifications.

The Powder Gate

The *Powder Gate (Prašná brána) stands on the **náměstí Republiky**, which divides the pedestrian Na příkopě from its northern continuation, Revoluční. Open daily 10.00–18.00.

> Originally known as the New Tower, the dark and sinister Powder Gate, 65m tall, was commissioned in 1475 by Vladislav the Jagiellon on the site of one of the 13 gates forming part of the Old Town's defensive system, a system that had been made redundant following the founding of the New Town in 1348. The Gate, adjoining at one time the building that served from 1383 to 1484 as the seat of the Royal Court of Bohemia, was intended purely as a monumental entrance to the Old Town, and marked the beginning of the Royal Route used by the Czech kings on their way to be crowned in St Vitus's Cathedral. When in 1484 Vladislav the Jagiellon moved the Royal Court back

to Prague Castle, work on the gate was abandoned, and the incomplete structure was given a temporary roof and put to use—until the end of the 17C—
as a storehouse for gunpowder. Heavily damaged during the Prussian siege of
Prague in 1737, it was left in a ruined state until the late 19C. Its present
appearance is due largely to reconstruction work carried out between 1875
and 1886 by Josef Mocker, who provided the structure with its turreted upper
gallery, steeply pitched roof and flamboyant Gothic decoration. The writer
Max Brod recalled how every afternoon at 2 o'clock he would wait at the foot
of the newly restored tower for his friend Franz Kafka, who invariably would
arrive late: 'My anger', wrote Brod, 'at his lateness would rapidly dissolve as
soon as the tall, thin figure appeared, who, more often than not, would be
wearing an embarrassed smile.'

The profuse neo-Gothic ornament that covers the Powder Gate contains,
alongside late-19C statues of Czech kings and other pseudo-medieval figures,
fragments of the original sculptural decoration carried out by Matěj Rejsek of
Prostějov after 1478. Ascend the steep winding stairs to the cash desk on the
first floor, where you can buy tickets to the tower's upper gallery, the best point
from which to study the layout of Prague's Old Town (open summer only
10.00–18.00).

Before entering the Old Town, you should take a look at two of the other monuments on náměstí Republiky. Facing the gate, at the eastern end of the square, is
the **Hibernians' House** (U Hybernů), which occupies the site of a former
church and monastery belonging to the Hibernian Order (Franciscans of Irish
origin). The monastery building (No. 3), erected in 1637–52, is a simple structure now used for offices; far more impressive is the adjoining former church (No.
4), which was transformed by Georg Fischer in 1810 into a grandiose Customs
House, inspired in its design by the former Mint in Berlin, and constituting one of
the finest examples in Prague of the Empire style. The building, until recently
used for ambitious art exhibitions, now awaits renovation and is currently closed
to visitors.

Municipal House

Meanwhile, flanking the northern side of the Powder Gate, and indeed dominating the whole square, is the ****Municipal House** (Obecní dům), still the most
remarkable Art Nouveau building in the Czech Republic despite recent restoration that has made its beauty seem somewhat tawdry. Open Mon–Sat
10.00–18.00.

The Municipal House stands on the site originally occupied by the Royal
Court of Bohemia, a building dating back to the late 14C and later converted
first into a seminary, then into a barracks, and finally into a cadets' school,
which was pulled down in 1902–03. The idea of erecting the Municipal
House was that of the Czech Patriotic Society, which envisaged a building
that would serve as a social and cultural centre for the Czech community in
Prague, complete with café, restaurant, concert hall, and rooms for civic
functions and assemblies. The architects chosen for the task, after a public
competition that closed in 1905, were Antonín Balšánek and Osvald Polívka.

Work on the building was undertaken between 1906 and 1912, and involved the collaboration of many of the leading Czech painters and sculptors of the turn of the century, including Ladislav Šaloun (the sculptor of the Hus Monument in the Old Town Square; see below), Max Švabinský (who created the stained-glass windows in St Vitus's Cathedral) and Alfons Mucha, who had accepted the commission in the mistaken belief that he had been asked to carry out all the decoration (a protracted and heated correspondence in the press concluded that it would not be fitting for a single artist to assume responsibility for the whole work). The most important meetings to have taken place in the building were held at the end of the First World War, concluding with the proclamation here, on 28 October 1918, of the independence of Czechoslovakia and the issuing of the new republic's Constitution. As for the concert hall, this continues to be one of Prague's most important cultural venues, hosting each year the inaugural concert of the Prague Spring Festival (see p 37); among the famous musicians to have performed in the hall are Sviatoslav Richter, David Oistrakh, Yehudi Menuhin, Mstislav Rostropovitch and Pablo Casals.

This large irregularly shaped building, once so wonderfully evocative of the city's turn-of-the-20th-century splendour, now has the garish, artificial look of some modern pastiche. The restoration that took place between 1989 and 1997 has been rightly described by Daniel Špička, director of the Prague Centre for the Preservation of Architecture, as a textbook case of how not to renovate the city's buildings. This is especially unfortunate given that the building was deliberately left to rot for several decades, first by the Nazis and then by the Communists, on account of its associations with Czech nationalism and independence. Fortunately, however, no amount of crude restoration can entirely disguise the genuine decorative brilliance of the structure, the exterior of which is impressive above all for its central **ironwork canopy**, which is coloured with stained glass and topped by bronze figures of lamp-bearers. Above the canopy is a large lunette decorated by Karel Špillar with a mosaic, *Homage to Prague*; crowning this is a cupola, while on either side are sculptural groups by Ladislav Šaloun representing respectively the *Humiliation and Rebirth of the Czech Nation*. Numerous other sculptures adorn the exterior, including a statue by Čeněk Vosmík of the main architect of the adjoining Powder Gate, Matěj Rejsek, and, below the statue, a relief by Šaloun commemorating the first assembly in 1918 of the National Committee of the Czechoslovak Republic.

Inside the building you find yourself in a vestibule adorned with bronze reliefs of *Flora* and *Fauna* by Bohumil Kafka. To the right a door leads into a French restaurant (*Francouzská restaurace*; see p 30), whose

The ironwork canopy of the Municipal House

impressive interior includes gilded chandeliers, wainscoting and allegorical wall-paintings, most notably Josef Wenig's *Prague Welcoming its Visitors* on the side wall; to the left of the vestibule is a similarly elegant café (*Kavárna Obecní dům*; see p 31), featuring at one end a niche containing a statue of a nymph made of white Carrara marble; the Art Nouveau lights, however, are replicas. A further restaurant (*Plzeňská restaurace*; see p 30), serving Czech cuisine, is situated in the basement and is notable for its vivid mosaic by Jakub Obrovský entitled *Harvest Time*. Next door to it is the small and rather characterless *American Bar*, with coloured drawings by Mikoláš Aleš on the walls.

The Concert Hall and Civic Rooms are on the first floor, and can be visited during the day by guided tour. Temporary exhibitions are also held in some of the newly renovated rooms. Tickets for the English-language tour, which begins at 10.00, 12.00, 14.00 and 16.00 (times subject to change), can be bought from the Cultural and Information Centre, just off the vestibule, where there is also a souvenir shop and café (open 10.00–18.00).

The large, ochre-coloured **Concert Hall**, named after the composer Smetana, has a central section domed in stained glass, and two wide balconies flanked by large murals by Karel Špillar representing Music and Dance (right) and Poetry and Drama (left). Between the stage and two prominent boxes at the front of the hall are two dynamic sculptural groups by Ladislav Šaloun portraying scenes from Dvořák's *Slavonic Dances* (left) and Smetana's opera *Vyšehrad* (right). Among the other first-floor rooms are the small and exquisitely tasteful neo-Classical pastiche called the **Sweetshop**, the rather brasher **Oriental Room**, and the **Němcová Salon**, decorated all over with stuccowork inspired by folkloric themes. Other rooms on this floor have ambitious large-scale paintings: for instance, the **Rieger Hall** has two long painted panels by Max Švabinský (*Czech Spring*) containing portraits of leading Czech writers, artists and musicians such as Jan Neruda, Božena Němcová, Josef Myslbek, Josef Mánes, Mikoláš Aleš, Bedřich Smetana and Antonín Dvořák.

Pride of place among the Civic Rooms must go to the **Hall of the Lord Mayor**, the windows of which occupy the central position on the building's façade. All the furniture and furnishings, and every detail of the decoration of this circular room are by Alfons Mucha, including allegorical murals on the walls and shallow ceiling, the pale-blue stained-glass windows, the Lord Mayor's chair, and the elaborately embroidered curtains.

After leaving the Municipal House, turn left and then left again into the narrow side-street, U Obecního domu, which flanks the northern side of the building. On its right-hand side is another fine edifice from the turn of the last century, the brashly revamped **Hotel Paříž** (see p 16), regarded in its time as a model example of the Art Nouveau style. There are colourful figurative decorations on the corner façade of its gabled, Gothic-inspired exterior, while inside you will find the attractively panelled *Café de Paris* and the mirrored *Sara Bernhardt Restaurant* with blue mosaics. A fantastical description of this hotel appears in Bohumil Hrabal's novel, *I Served the King of England*: 'The Hotel Paříž was so beautiful it almost knocked me over. So many mirrors and brass balustrades and brass door handles and brass candelabras, all polished till the place shone like a palace of gold.' It is here that the picaresque narrator of the novel meets the head waiter who 'served the King of England', and where he himself makes his reputation by serving Haile

Selassie at a Gargantuan banquet centred around a stuffed and roasted camel.

At the end of U Obecního domu turn left into the short U Prašné brány, where you will pass at No. 1 an Art Nouveau apartment block (now offices) built by Bedřich Bendelmayer in 1903–04, and featuring inside an elegant semi-circular staircase. The street brings you back to the Powder Gate and to the eastern end of Celetná.

The pedestrianised ***Celetná**, at the start of the Royal Route (*Královská Cesta*), is one of the Old Town's showpiece streets, lined principally with recently restored houses of medieval origin that were given pastel-coloured façades during the Baroque period.

House of the Black Madonna

At No. 34 is one of the more interesting modern buildings in the Old Town—the **House of the Black Madonna** (Dům U černé Matky Boží). Built as a department store in 1911–12 by Josef Gočár, this corner house is one of the master-pieces of Czech Cubism, and has two prominent cornices as well as heavy prism-shaped forms painted a dark maroon; its name is derived from a curious survival of the Baroque building it replaced—a 17C statue of the Virgin that in 1921 inspired Jaroslav Seifert's poem 'Prayer on the Pavement' ('I raised my eyes towards the Black Virgin / Standing there / and keeping her protecting hand over my head / and I prayed ...'). Major restoration carried out in 1993–94 attempted to bring back as much as possible the look of the original interior: partition walls and ceilings were demolished, revealing rein-forced-concrete beams reminiscent of Gothic vaulting.

Between 1994 and 2001 the building housed an exhibition of Czech Cubism administered by the Czech Museum of Fine Arts (České muzeum výtvarných umění), but these collections have been temporarily moved to the National Gallery pending the completion of further renovation work, which is set to finish in 2004. The project will include the reopening of the original Cubist café in the basement of the building. For now, you can visit the 'Kubista' museum shop on the ground floor, which sells expensive reproductions of Cubist applied art, and the adjoining bookshop, with a good selection of albums, art books and guides.

Continuing down Celetná, you will reach at No. 22 (left) a pale-green, late-18C building with a German inscription dating back to the days when the royal jeweller Gindle had his shop here; the ground floor houses the popular *U Supa* beer-cellar and restaurant. Directly facing you, on the opposite side of the street, is a covered passageway leading through to Malá Štupartská, on which stands the former **Monastery Church of St James** (sv. Jakuba). Founded by Minorites in 1232, the church was completely remodelled by Jan Šimon Pánek between 1689 and 1702. Its tall west façade has rich stuccowork executed in 1695 and featuring representations of Sts James, Francis and Anthony of Padua.

The enormously long and imposing interior, which has retained the medieval three-aisled plan and tall, Gothic proportions, is profusely whitewashed and gilded, and contains ceiling frescoes of the *Life of the Virgin* (1736) as well as 22 altars. The main altarpiece, supported by an exuberant gilded framework of angels high above the chancel, is a painting by Václav Reiner of the *Martyrdom of St James*. Three of the altars on the right-hand side of the nave are by Petr Brandl, and were executed c 1710; another work by Brandl (the St Joseph Altar of 1708) is on the left-hand side of the nave, where an altar by Jan Liška representing *St Valburg* can also be found. This side of the nave also boasts one of Prague's grandest funerary monuments, the *Monument to Jan Vratislav of Mitrovice*, designed by Johann Bernard Fischer von Erlach in 1721 and containing sculpted figures by Ferdinand Brokoff.

The building's most gruesome feature is a 400-year-old decomposed human forearm that hangs high up on the west wall. It was put there both as a warning and as a record of a miracle involving the Virgin's tight-fisted response to a man who had attempted to steal her jewels from the high altar: the thief's arm, unable to free itself from the Virgin's grip, had eventually to be cut off by a local butcher.

Unfortunately, at most times the interior of St James's is policed by some exceptionally rude and suspicious security staff, who will spy on your every move and ask you to make a 'voluntary' contribution to the collection box if you stay too long. A better bet, therefore, might be to attend the sung High Mass on Sunday, which is followed by a free organ recital, allowing you to marvel at the church's famous acoustics. Likewise, the Christmas Day service featuring the *Christmas Mass* by the Czech composer Jan Jakub Ryba is well worth attending.

Across the street from St James's, at No. 5 is the *Big Ben Bookshop*, with a good selection of English-language newspapers, magazines, paperbacks and guides. Heading north along Malá Štupartská and taking the first turning to the left, Týnská, you will reach (at No. 6) the medieval **House of the Golden Ring** (dům U zlatého prstenu), which has now been taken over by the collection of 20C Czech art belonging to the **Prague City Gallery**. The long and rambling building, with its whitewashed vaulted rooms and views of the Týn Church, provides the setting for a comparatively small permanent exhibition of 20C Czech art, arranged over three floors, with temporary exhibitions being held in the basement. The works include Max Švabinský's powerful *Destitute Land* (1900), sculptures and paintings by František Bílek, boldly handled landscapes by Antonín Slavíček (among which is an unfinished view of St Vitus's Cathedral of 1909), Indian-inspired paintings by Otakar Nejedlý (who spent several years in Southern India and Ceylon at the beginning of the 20C), delicate fantasies by Josef Šíma and Toyen, including *Woman with a Mandolin* (1932), Cubist and other works by Emil Filla, and Surrealistic photomontages by Jiří Kolář. The labelling and information panels are in Czech and English, and the works themselves are divided thematically into three sections: 1) Dream, Myth, Ideal; 2) In the Mirror, Behind the Mirror; 3) Utopia, Vision, Order, then further subdivided under such enigmatic and unhelpful headings as 'Rigid Unrest'. Open Tues–Sun 10.00–18.00.

After finishing your tour you could stop for refreshments at the convenient *Týnská Literární kavárna* (see p 31) in the courtyard at the back.

Instead of visiting just now the Týn Church (the apse of which directly faces the gallery's entrance), turn left down Štupartská to return to the covered passage leading to Celetná. Continuing west along Celetná, you will come, at No. 12 (left), to the elegant **Hrzán Palace** (Hrzánský palác), a building of Romanesque origin remodelled by Giovanni Alliprandi in 1702, with sculptural decorations on the façade by pupils of Ferdinand Brokoff; Franz Kafka's father, Hermann, had a haberdashery shop on the premises after 1882. Further down the street, at No. 2, is the house, now boarded up, where the Kafka family lived in 1888–89, and where Albert Einstein is said to have first explained his Theory of Relativity. Between 1896 and 1901 the Kafka family lived on the opposite side of the street, at No. 3, where the writer's street-facing bedroom inspired one of his earliest stories, *The Window onto the Street*.

Old Town Square

Celetná comes to an end at the spacious ****Old Town Square** (Staroměstské náměstí), one of Europe's most beautiful squares.

Situated at what was formerly the junction of several trade routes, the Old Town Square served as a market place in the 11C and 12C. An important point on the traditional processional route of the Bohemian kings, and overlooked by the former Hussite Church of Our Lady before Týn, the square was later to witness some of the most significant—and tragic—events in the history of Prague, and came almost to symbolise the struggles and aspirations of the Czech people. Jan Želivský—the Hussite leader whose storming of the New Town Hall in 1419 had sparked off the Hussite Wars—was executed here in 1422; 56 other Hussites, including the officer Jan Roháč of Dubé, were executed on the square 15 years later. At the Old Town Hall, George of Poděbrady was elected King of Bohemia in 1458 (see p 98), and in 1621, 27 of the Protestant leaders who had taken part in the Battle of the White Mountain were beheaded outside the building. One of these was the pioneering surgeon Jan Jessenius, an ancestor of Kafka's great love, Milena Jesenská. Before his tongue had been taken out prior to the execution he had said, 'You are treating us shamefully, but I want you to know that others will come who will bury with honour our heads, which you have desecrated and put on show.' In 1945 large crowds welcomed the arrival of Soviet troops, and three years later Klement Gottwald proclaimed from the balcony of the Goltz-Kinský Palace (see p 96) the accession of the Communists to power. A rather different response to the Red Army was shown in 1968, when, at the end of the 'Prague Spring', Soviet tanks advanced on the square, their arrival being greeted not by applause but by Molotov cocktails.

The square is surrounded by a picturesque jumble of historic buildings, to which recent restoration has given a toy-like cleanliness and cheerful range of light and vivid colours. Though most of the square is now traffic-free, it is the tourist heart of Prague, and you would be best advised to come here early in the day to appreciate the place before it fills up with a vast and noisy crowd in which buskers, street-vendors and money-changers now jostle with the visitors. The western side of the square, with its array of stalls selling tacky souvenirs and crafts, rather disrupts the harmony of what is still a beautiful urban space, and indeed testifies to the changing appearance of the Old Town since the onslaught of

Monument to Jan Hus

commercialisation in the 1990s.

Rising on steps near the centre of the square and dominating the whole space is the extraordinary bronze **★Monument to Jan Hus**, a disgracefully undervalued work of the early 20th century. Considered by some to be completely out of place in the square, it is nonetheless one of the most powerful public monuments in any European city, and one which brilliantly complements its surroundings.

The Monument to Jan Hus was the masterpiece of the idiosyncratic sculptor Ladislav Šaloun, who began planning the work as early as 1898, and struggled with it for the next 17 years, making constant changes throughout this period of gestation. The monument was intended to be unveiled in 1915, on the occasion of the 500th anniversary of the burning of Jan Hus for heresy. The unveiling went ahead as planned, but few worse moments could have been chosen for the completion of a highly emotive monument symbolising the Czech national consciousness and the fight for Czech independence. The Austrian authorities did not permit any ceremony to take place, but within a few days the work was completely covered with flowers, and all that showed of it was a solitary finger pointing menacingly to the sky. At this time there still stood next to the monument a Marian column erected in 1650 to commemorate the Peace of Westphalia—the treaty that brought the Thirty Years War (1618–48) to an end. In 1918, only five days after the declaration of independence, this symbol of Catholic and Habsburg dominance, with its sculpted angels trampling over devils, was pulled down, leaving only Jan Hus to preside over the square. The continuing power of the latter monument was attested in the wake of the Soviet invasion of August 1968, when it was shrouded in black drapes.

Šaloun's monument to Hus, which bears at its base the preacher's words, 'The truth will prevail', features the figure of Hus rising above a struggling sea of gesticulating people, in a defiant posture reminiscent of one of Rodin's Burghers of Calais; the power of this detailed yet unified composition lies to a large extent in the way in which—even on the brightest of days—it forms against the light and cheerful background of the square a dark and menacing profile, vividly reminding the spectator of the bleaker moments in Czech history.

Church of Our Lady Before Týn

The eastern end of the square is overshadowed by the most prominent building in the Old Town, and one of those most closely associated with the Hussite cause—the **★★Church of Our Lady Before Týn** (Matky boží ped Týnem). As with most medieval churches in Bohemia, it does not rise directly above the square, but is set back behind a row of arcaded houses, comprising in this case a house of Romanesque origin with a tall late-18C façade (No. 15, at the southeastern end of the square), and the attractive **Týn School** (No. 14), which has a late-14C ground floor and a pair of stepped 16C gables recalling those of the Scuola Grande di San Marco in Venice; the architect Matěj Rejsek of Prostějov was a teacher at the school in the late 15C. Walking through the second of the school's four arches will take you to the west portal of the church. For many years access to the building has been extremely limited and can only be guaranteed at times of services (currently Sat 8.00 and Sun 11.00), and this situation is likely to persist for the foreseeable future.

The origins of the Týn church lie in a Romanesque building first mentioned in 1135 as the property of the foreign merchants' hospice on Celetná. Work on the present structure was begun in 1365, and by the 1380s the north portal, the side aisles, the walls of the nave and much of the east end had been completed. The reformist preachers Konrád Waldhauser and Jan Milíč of Kroměříž were preaching in the building by the end of the 14C, and early in the following century the place had become the main church of the Hussites in Prague; it was to remain associated with the followers of Jan Hus until 1621. The nave was vaulted by 1457, a year before the accession to the throne of the Utraquist monarch George of Poděbrady, who was to be one of the church's greatest benefactors. Under his reign the northern of the west façade's twin towers were erected (the southern one dates from the early 16C), as was this façade's tall gable. The gable was adorned with a statue of George and a gold chalice symbolising the Utraquist cause, but these were removed after the Battle of the White Mountain in 1620, and replaced with an image of the Virgin whose halo was made from the gold of the chalice. A fire in 1679 led to the rebuilding of the nave vault and extensive remodelling of the interior.

The twin-towered exterior of the church is a gloomy pile of exposed masonry, the principal decoration being concentrated on the north portal, where there is a late-14C tympanum of the Crucifixion from the workshop of Petr Parléř (the original is now in the Lapidarium of the National Museum—see p 210). The north portal can be reached along the narrow Týnská, which runs along the northern side of the Týn School, and off which there is a gateway (just to the east of the church) leading into the merchants' courtyard which gave this area its name (*týn* means 'enclosure'); the courtyard, better known by its German name of *Ungelt*, was used from the 11C to the 18C for the stocking and selling of goods, and as a customs house, but today only the ground-plan is medieval (the oldest surviving part is a mid-16C loggia). Cafés, restaurants and bars now fill the pleasant cobbled space.

The interior of the Týn church is a three-aisled hall with unadorned plaster from the Baroque period. At the western end of the north aisle is a fine Gothic baldachin by Matěj Rejsek (1493), but the outstanding work of art in the building is the intricately carved **Baptism of Christ** by the Monogramist I.P.

View of the Týn Church

(c 1526), on the pier immediately to the right of the south portal. Attached to the south-aisle pier directly in front of the main apse is the red marble tombstone of the Danish astronomer Tycho Brahe, who died in 1601 as a result of trying to hold back his urine while in the presence of Emperor Rudolph II ('I don't want to die like Tycho Brahe' is the Czech expression for 'I'm desperate for a pee'). The high altar of the *Ascension* (1649) is by Karel Škréta.

Returning to the Old Town Square and continuing to walk north along its eastern side, you will come next to the **House at the Stone Bell** (Dům U kamenného zvonu) at No. 13, a narrow-fronted structure, the Baroque cladding of which was recently removed to reveal its original late-14C stonework. The interior, which features a small chapel with fragments of 14C murals, is used by the **Prague City Gallery** as an exhibition space and is the venue of the *Zvon* biennial of young Central European artists. Open Tues–Sun 10.00–18.00.

Adjoining the house, at No. 12, is one of the most elegant of the city's 18C palaces, the richly stuccoed **Goltz-Kinský Palace** (1755–65), which was built by Anselmo Lurago to a design supplied by K.I. Dientzenhofer. The twin pediments of the façade are a clever solution to the building's position at the corner of the square, and show how the architects were anxious not to destroy the unity of the multi-gabled square by providing a single enormous pediment.

Goltz-Kinský Palace

One of the many distinguished visitors to have stayed in the palace was the Swedish dynamite magnate Alfred Nobel, who fell in love here with the future Bertha von Suttner (née Kinský), whose early years were spent in the building: Bertha, who became famous as a pacifist and as the author of *Down with the Weapons*, was said to have been very influential in determining Nobel's decision in later life to found the Nobel Peace Prize, of which she herself was one of the first recipients. In the late 19C part of the palace was turned into a state-run German-language secondary school, one of whose pupils was Franz Kafka, who came here in September 1891 and—despite irrational fears of failing his final exams—graduated from the institution ten years later; between 1912 and 1918 a ground-floor room on the southern side of the palace served as the new premises of his father's ever-more-successful haberdashery business. But the palace's eminence in modern Czech history was not finally sealed until 21 February 1948, when, from one of its main balconies, Klement Gottwald proclaimed to an assembled crowd of thousands the coming to power of the Communist regime. At his side was a man called Clementis who was executed four years later for high treason, and later airbrushed from all the many photographs of the scene; this incident is recalled in the opening passages of Milan Kundera's novel *The Book of Laughter and Forgetting* (first published in English in 1980).

The Kafka family's former premises have been converted into an excellent bookshop (*Knihkupectví Franze Kafky*), and there are plans to open above this a museum and library devoted to the writer. For the time being the **National Gallery** continues to hold temporary exhibitions on the upper floors of the palace. These are often well worth the admission fee, and have in recent years included a retrospective of the Mánes family, as well as displays of graphic art and drawings from the Gallery's extensive collections. Open Tues–Sun 10.00–18.00.

The northern side of the square was radically altered at the end of the 19C, at around the same time that the pompous Pařížská Avenue was built. Standing in its northeastern corner, adjacent to the Goltz-Kinský Palace, is the late-17C former Pauline Monastery (Klášter paulánů), but the space between here and Pařížská is now taken up by an enormous neo-Baroque building housing the Ministry for Regional Development. The *Church of St Nicholas (sv. Mikuláš) was once tucked away at the very corner of the square, at the junction of Pařížská and Mikulášská, but, since the destruction in the Second World War of the northern wing of the Town Hall, has now a prominent, exposed position, and indeed is one of the square's great glories. Open Tues–Fri 10.00–12.00, Wed 14.00–16.00.

The original Church of St Nicholas was founded by merchants in the late 13C, and served until the building of the Týn church as the parish church of the Old Town. The reformist preacher Jan Milíč of Kroměříž gave sermons here in the 1360s, and in the following century the building was taken over by the Utraquists, who were to keep it for over two centuries. In 1635 the church was presented to the Benedictines, who had it rebuilt between 1650 and 1660. During the rule of Abbot Anselmo Vlach it was demolished and replaced by the present structure, which was erected in 1732–35 by K.I. Dientzenhofer (who also designed its sister church in Malá Strana—see p 124). The monastery was abolished in 1787, and for a while the building was used as a concert hall before being handed over to the Russian Orthodox Church in 1871. Since 1920 it has been the property of the Czechoslovak (now Czech) Hussite Church, which was founded in that same year. A thorough restoration of the building was completed in 1990.

The church is a centrally planned structure with an unusual design that was determined to a large extent by the once-cramped nature of the site. Dientzenhofer, wishing to create a structure that would powerfully reaffirm the Catholic faith in the wake of the building's Utraquist past, was forced by the restricted site to put the emphasis on verticality. The twin-towered façade, adorned with sculptures from the school of Matthias Braun, has an arrangement recalling that of Borromini's Sant' Agnese in Rome, but the architectural elements have been elongated in the creation of soaring proportions.

The impressive, albeit spartan interior is dominated by the tall central dome, from which a chandelier in the shape of a Czar's crown is suspended; made in the Harrachov glassworks in 1860, the chandelier was given to the Orthodox church to be hung here by Czar Nicholas II. The ceiling has fine frescoes depicting scenes from the Old Testament and the lives of Sts Nicholas and Benedict but—unusually for Dientzenhofer—the painted decorations are subservient to the exceptionally rich stucco framework by Bernard Spinetti. Classical concerts are held inside the church, which indeed seems mostly geared to this purpose, with barriers and 'Do not enter this zone' signs restricting visitors' access.

On the square (náměstí Franze Kafky) adjacent to the west façade of St Nicholas is the site of the house where **Franz Kafka** was born on 3 July 1883; not until 1965, when the Communist regime finally accepted Kafka as a 'revolutionary critic of capitalist alienation', was the present bronze commemorative bust attached to it. The house, known as **At the Tower** (U Věže), originally belonged to the Benedictines, but by Kafka's day had been turned into a warren of small apartments at the southernmost end of the Jewish ghetto; largely destroyed by fire in 1887, but replaced in 1902 with a new structure that retained the original Baroque portal, the building now features a small museum devoted to the writer, with photographs and quotations from his works. Open Tues–Fri 10.00–18.00, Sat 10.00–17.00.

Old Town Hall

The heavily restored *Old Town Hall (Staroměstská radnice), which projects into the southwestern corner of the Old Town Square, is the square's principal tourist attraction. Its history is a complex one, the place being an assemblage of several buildings, the earliest of which dates back to the beginning of the 14C. Open Mon 11.00–17.00, Tues–Sun 09.00–17.00.

To understand the Town Hall's genesis you should walk slowly around the exterior, beginning with the eastern end, which incorporates part of the ground floor of the original building—a private house that the civic authorities purchased from one Wolflin of Kámen in 1338. A tower was added to this in 1364, and a chapel—with an oriel window projecting east—built on its first floor by 1381; on the wall underneath the oriel is a plaque bearing the names of the 27 Protestants executed on the square in 1621, the exact place of the execution being marked by white crosses on the paving stones nearby. The block that was attached to the northern end of Wolflin's house was a late-15C addition, rebuilt in the late 18C, and again in the early 20C; it was burnt down by the Nazis on the penultimate day of the Second World War, and plans to put up a modern extension on its site seem to have been abandoned. Walking the length of the southern side of the Town Hall, from east to west, you will come immediately to the famous *Astronomical Clock, which was added to the south façade of Wolflin's house in 1410.

Installed originally by the master clocksmith Mikoláš of Kadaň in 1410, the clock was rebuilt in 1490 by a teacher at the Charles University, Master Hanuš of Růže. According to legend, Hanuš was blinded to prevent him from creating another such marvel in Prague, but the blind man then climbed up the tower and stopped the clock. The true story is that the clock's mechanism was not to be perfected until Jan Táborský repaired it between 1552 and 1560, after which it required no further alterations. Only its decorations changed, the painted calendar on the lower level being executed by Josef Mánes in 1865 (the original is kept in the Museum of the City of Prague—see p 170). The middle level comprises the clock proper, which tells the time according to three conventions (Central European, Old Bohemian, Babylonian) and gives the position of the sun and moon in relation to the signs of the zodiac, thus telling the date. At the striking of each hour an impressive spectacle which begins with a figure of Death raising an hour glass and pulling a funerary bell. Windows subsequently open on the upper level, and a procession of Apostles files past, bowing to the onlookers. At the corners of the clock are three more allegorical figures perched on pinnacles—Vanity, the Ottoman Turk, and Greed (represented by a Jew gloating over his sack of gold)—reflecting the anxieties of the medieval mind. Below these are a further four figures representing Astronomy, History, Philosophy and Religion.

West of the clock is a fantastically ornate portal of 1470–80, attributed to Matěj Rejsek, and constituting the main entrance to the building. Further west is the former Kříž House, purchased by the civic authorities in 1360 and featuring a fine Renaissance window of 1520 bearing the Latin inscription *Praga caput regni* ('Prague, capital of the kingdom'). In 1458 the Town Hall was extended by the purchase of the house now attached to the west, a property belonging previously to Mikeš the Furrier and which was to be remodelled in a neo-Renaissance style in 1878. The complex was enlarged yet further in 1835 with the purchase of the adjoining **Cockerel House** (Dům U kohouta), an originally Romanesque structure given an Empire façade in 1830. Finally, in 1896, the Town Hall bought the splendid property adjacent to the western end of the Cockerel House—**At the Minute** (Dům U minuty), a house where the Kafka family had lived from 1889 right up to the time of its purchase. The exterior of the house is covered with sgraffito decorations that are among the finest in Prague; these monochrome works, representing Classical and Biblical scenes and allegorical figures of the Virtues, were executed c 1611 and restored in 1919 by Josef Čapek, the brother of the writer Karel (they were restored again after the 1945 fire).

The interior of the Town Hall can only be visited on a guided tour, which takes place at irregular intervals throughout the day, attracting great crowds of tourists. Though it has been much altered over the centuries and was badly gutted in 1945, it retains on the second floor the late-Gothic **Council Chamber** of 1470. The late-19C **Assembly Room** on the same floor was dominated until recently by two large canvases by Václav Brožík, *Master Jan Hus before the Council of Constance* and *The Election of George of Poděbrady as King of Bohemia*. The Gothic vaulting in the vestibule of the building has a mosaic decoration of 1937, executed after designs by Mikoláš Aleš and representing the story of the mythical Princess Libuše, while the recently opened dungeon has evidence of fire damage from the Second World War, when the building was used by the Czechoslovak Resistance. Also worth seeing is the reconstructed Gothic chapel, designed by Petr Parléř, with remnants of medieval frescoes. A visit to the Town Hall is complemented by a climb up its 70m-high **tower** (a separate ticket is required), from where an excellent view can be had. The lift is designed for wheelchair access.

Karlova

The Old Town Square leads at its narrow southwestern corner into the quieter and triangular **Small Square** (Malé náměstí), which is centred around a small **fountain** surrounded by a Renaissance ironwork grille of 1560. One of the oldest spaces in the Old Town, this was inhabited in the 12C by French merchants; fruit markets were held here during the Middle Ages. Though a number of the houses have Romanesque cellars, the present appearance of the square is due mainly to 18C and 19C remodelling. One of the most prominent of the buildings is the one at No. 3, which was rebuilt in a neo-Renaissance style in 1890 for the ironmongery firm of V.J. Rott; the name of Rott appears on the recently repainted façade, which is covered all over with figurative and ornamental motifs based on designs supplied by Mikoláš Aleš, while the ground floor is now a shop selling Bohemian cut glass. An excellently preserved neo-Baroque pharmacy of the last

No. 3 Malé Náměstí, with ornamental designs by Mikoláš Aleš

century is incorporated into the late-18C house at No. 13, adjoining which, at the southwestern corner of the square, is the site of the former American Reception Centre—a landmark in the history of Prague's post-1989 transformation, and a place where you could buy T-shirts inscribed with the words, 'Prague. Czech it out'.

Although this reception centre is long gone, Americanisation of the worst kind has done much to destroy the character of the neighbouring **Karlova*, along which you can continue heading west along the processional route of the Bohemian kings. As much of a showpiece as Celetná, but narrower and more winding, and with houses that are picturesquely askew, this street has sadly lost much of its former fairy-tale charm through its recent encrustation of competing neon signs, souvenir shops and exchange offices. In summer, the street becomes oppressively crowded, and you should beware of the gangs of pickpockets that operate in this area.

At the junction of Karlova and **Husova**, the first street that you cross, three interconnected buildings form another branch of the **Czech Museum of Fine Arts** (České muzeum výtvarných umění), this one devoted entirely to temporary exhibitions, mainly of 20C Czech art. The part of the gallery on Karlova is an elegant 18C structure, but the building where the gallery's main entrance is situated, at No. 21 Husova, is a Renaissance house crowned by an attractive pair of stepped gables; the interior of the gallery, featuring a Romanesque cellar, successfully incorporates the surviving medieval elements into a bright modern setting (open Tues–Sun 10.00–18.00). Just to the south of the entrance, at No. 17 Husova, is the beer-cellar called ***The Golden Tiger*** (U zlatého tygra; see p 35), a popular former haunt of the writer Bohumil Hrabal, and mentioned in several of his writings, for instance in a short piece entitled *The Magic Flute* (1989): 'And I was at The Golden Tiger, deep in thought, saying to myself, as I always do, that if the Gods loved me I would expire in front of a glass of beer ...'. In fact, Hrabal died in 1997 by falling out of a hospital window, though whether this was some wilful act of (self-)defenestration in the time-honoured Czech tradition or merely a tragic accident is still unknown. The bar has certainly lost some of its allure since the great man's death, but his memory lives on in the form of a phantasmagorical oil painting that hangs on one of the walls. There is also a colour photograph of Hrabal having a beer here with President Clinton in 1994.

One of Prague's raunchiest Bohemian meeting-places of the early 20C, the **Cabaret Montmartre**, was situated around the corner from here, at No. 7 Řetězová (the first turning to your right as you continue south down Husova). The ground floor of the building is now the disappointing *Café Montmartre* (see p 32) which, a few old photographs aside, pays scant homage to the colourful traditions of the building. More worthy of a visit is the *Bayer & Bayer* commercial gallery upstairs (open Tues–Sat 12.00–18.00), which shows work by Czech artists in beautiful rooms with painted beamed ceilings.

Cabaret Montmartre

It was founded in 1911 in a seedy beer-cellar forming part of a then-run-down building appropriately known as **The Three Wild Men** on account of a popular local legend claiming that a strange trio of cannibals lived here in the late 17C (hence the mural on the building's exterior of what looks like a group of Hell's Angels). The interior consisted originally of two large rooms with a dance-floor, grotesque Cubist parodies by V.H. Brunner, and—according to one of its *habitués*, Egon Erwin Kisch—'mysterious Cubist and Futurist images' left by some of the clients in lieu of paying their bills; the place was rebuilt after 1918 to Cubist–Futurist designs by Jiří Kroha, who created rooms nicknamed 'Heaven', 'Hell' and 'Purgatory'. The clientele comprised a wide variety of the city's literary and artistic coteries, including the German-Jewish writers in the circle of Kafka and Brod, gypsy painters and actors from the Lucerna Cabaret, and Czech anarchist poets; inevitably, another of the regulars was the ubiquitous Hašek, who generally turned up late and drunk, splattering beer over a wide radius, and often creating such a stir that he had to be thrown out. Soloists from the National Theatre sang here during their off-hours, while Kisch made a name for himself inventing dances such as the 'Ape Man' and the 'Paralytic's Dance' (also known as the 'Holešovice Apache'). Accompanying these on the piano was a local celebrity with the wonderful name of Emča Revoluce (Emma Revolution), who also danced the tango with the famous head-waiter known as Hamlet, an ex-actor with a mass of curly hair. Presiding over all this was the cabaret's owner and founder Josef Waltner, an actor and variety singer who, attired in the long robe of a 'high priest' and flanked by two female 'acolytes', would read from a book that brought together local anecdotes, quips and repartee.

Returning to Karlova along Husova, and deviating this time to the north, you will pass almost immediately the most celebrated of Prague's Baroque palaces, the **Clam-Gallas Palace**. Built between 1713 and 1719 for Count J.W. Gallas, it was the work of the great Viennese architect Johann Bernard Fischer von Erlach, aided by two of the leading artists of his day, the sculptor Matthias Braun and the Italian painter Carlo Carlone. The main façade, hemmed in on the narrow Husova, is in many ways remarkably Classical, with its large central pediment, simple fenestration, and largely undecorated walls. At the same time, however, it is given a dynamic Baroque quality by Braun's sculptural additions—the row of figures (replaced mainly by copies) along the attic and, above all, the powerful, struggling atlantes who support the two portals, which are unusually situated at the sides of the façade. The building is now home to the city archives, but temporary exhibitions (Czech art and design) are also held on the first floor, reached via a grand staircase with murals, stuccowork and views onto the courtyard. Open Tues–Sun 10.00–18.00

The northern side of the palace abuts into Mariánské náměstí, where you will find, immediately on turning right into the square, a **fountain** attached to the palace's garden wall. Within its niche is a copy of a famous sculpture executed in 1812 by the Romantic artist Václav Prachner (the original has now been taken to the National Gallery in Zbraslav, see p 190): entitled **Vltava** but popularly called 'Terezka', it is a vigorous portrayal of a female nude, and tradition has it that an old man living in the neighbourhood fell in love with this image and left all his money to her in his will.

The rest of the square is taken up by the northeastern corner of the vast Clementinum (see below), the grim Municipal Public Library (1934–28) and, on the eastern side of the square, the **New Town Hall**. The latter, built in 1908–11 by Osvald Polívka, is a grey and heavy Art Nouveau structure enlivened by some fine and prominent statuary: the allegorical figures and reliefs around the main portal are by Stanislav Sucharda and Josef Mařatka, while the niche figures at the bottom two corners of the façade are by Ladislav Šaloun, and include a wonderful sandstone representation of the 16C Talmudic scholar Rabbi Löw (1910). Despite its unpromising exterior, the Municipal Public Library has a series of newly renovated rooms where modern art exhibitions are put on by the **Prague City Gallery**. Open Tues–Sun 10.00–18.00.

The short Seminářská, at the southwestern corner of the square, will take you back to Karlova, passing, at the junction of the two streets, the toy-like **House at the Golden Well** (Dům U zlaté studny), a Renaissance structure later adorned with stucco figures of saints by Ulrich Mayer; the latter were added in 1701, shortly after an outbreak of plague, and include two saints normally invoked at times of plague—Sts Anthony and Roch. The building is now a hotel (see p 16) with a restaurant inside a 16C Gothic cellar.

Continue walking west along Karlova and you will find at No. 18 (at the junction with the next street, Liliová), the Renaissance **House at the Golden Serpent** (U zlatého hada), all decked out in striking red, with a 19C plaque of a snake on the outside. In the early 18C the house was occupied by the Armenian coffee-merchant Deodatus Damajan, who sold coffee in the streets of Prague before opening here the first coffee-shop in Prague (later he opened another shop at the Three Ostriches' House across the river, see p 129); the place today is an unappealingly decorated restaurant, which loses out to the far better *Reykjavík* across the street (see p 28). Alternatively, there is a cheap but decent pizzeria further down Liliová, at No. 18 (*Pizzeria Roma Due*, see p 28).

Further west along the southern side of Karlova, at No. 4, a plaque marks the house where the German astronomer Johannes Kepler lived between 1607 and 1612, formulating during this period his first two laws concerning the movement of the Earth around the Sun; he is said to have used the tower within the courtyard of the house as an observatory.

The Clementinum and its churches

The whole northern side of the Karlova, from Seminářská to the end of the street, is lined by the former Jesuit College of the Clementinum (Klementium), the largest complex of buildings in Prague after the Castle, and covering 2 hectares.

House at the Golden Serpent

As part of his campaign to strengthen the Catholic faith in Bohemia, the Habsburg Emperor Ferdinand I summoned the Jesuits in 1556 to Prague where they took over the former Dominican church and monastery of St Clement. At the western end of Karlova, overlooking Knights of the Cross Square, the Jesuits began building in 1593 the Church of the Holy Saviour, the construction of which was later to involve two of the leading architects of the early Baroque in Bohemia, Anselmo Lurago and Francesco Caratti. By the middle of the 17C the teaching establishment that the Jesuits had founded alongside the church had been turned into a university college, endowed with an important library. From 1653 onwards Caratti began work on the university buildings, a task that was to entail the pulling down of much of the Old Town and was not to be completed until 1748, under the direction of František Kaňka. With the expulsion of the Jesuit order in 1773, the Clementinum was given over to the Charles University, which shortly afterwards transferred its library here.

The library of the Charles University has now been amalgamated into the Czech National Library, which takes up most of the complex and boasts such precious works as the Vyšehrad Codex of 1085, and the world's largest collection of works by the English religious reformer John Wycliffe, to whom the Hussites were greatly indebted. Open Mon–Fri 08.00–22.00, Sat 08.00–19.00.

Walking down Karlova from Semínářská you skirt the southern side of the former Dominican **Church of St Clement** (sv. Kliment), which is incorporated into the southern walls of the Clementinum. The church was rebuilt in 1711–15 by František Kaňka, and is now used by the Greek Catholic Church (open only for Sunday services at 08.00 and 10.00). The recently restored interior is covered with ceiling paintings depicting the life of St Clement by Johann Hiebel, who was also responsible for the illusionistic framework in the chancel, a work clearly inspired by the Italian *quadratura* specialist Padre Pozzo. More remarkable are the outstanding and emotionally charged series of statues of the *Evangelists and Fathers of the Church* by Matthias Braun and his workshop, decorating the niches of the piers.

Adjacent to the western end of St Clement, and attached to the apse of the Holy Saviour church, is the **Italian Chapel** (Vlašská kaple), the rounded exterior of which affects the course of Karlova, and gives drama to the street; built by Ottaviano Mascharino in 1590 (but with an interior redecorated in the 18C), it is the earliest example in Central Europe of an elliptically planned structure.

The grandest of the churches associated with the Clementinum is the **Church of the Holy Saviour** (sv. Salvátor), which was begun in 1593 and not completed until 1714. The Italianate west façade, facing Knights of the Cross Square, is inspired by that of the Jesuit's mother church in Rome, but has a three-arched portico added by Francesco Caratti in 1653–59; the sculptures on the portico's balustrade, as well as those on the pediment above, were executed by Johann Georg Bendl in 1659. The interior, with alterations by both Carlo Lurago and František Kaňka, has rich stucco decorations by Bendl and a ceiling painting of the *Four Continents* (1748); among the furnishings is a confessional (1675), which Bendl decorated with sculptures of the Apostles (the church is open only for Sunday mass at 08.00). Running north of the church of the Holy Saviour along Křižovnická is the earliest and most grandiose of the Clementinum's façades, begun by Caratti in 1653 and featuring stucco medallions of Roman emperors.

You can enter the **Clementinum complex** from Karlova, though there are also entrances on Mariánské náměstí and next to the Church of the Holy Saviour (see above). Inside, you will find four large courtyards, one of which (currently closed to the public) has a statue by Emmanuel Max of a *Prague Student* (1847), a work commemorating the role played by students in defending the Charles Bridge during the siege of Prague by the Swedes in 1648.

The only way of seeing the interiors of the Clementinum is to take the 30-minute guided tour (head for the visitors' entrance in the second courtyard), which starts on the hour between 10.00 and 19.00 Sat, Sun, and between 12.00 and 17.00 Mon–Fri. The tour encompasses the two chief attractions of the complex: the **Baroque library hall** (Barokní sál) and 18C **observatory tower** (Astronomická věž). The first of these is a sumptuous gilded space of 1727, designed by František Kaňka, with a ceiling painting of *The Temple of Wisdom*, and walls enlivened by salomonic columns. The 52m-high observatory tower, reopened in 2000, has a rather pedestrian display of astronomical equipment, but the magnificent view of Prague to be had from the top is well worth the climb. Nearby, though not included on the tour, is the **Chapel of Mirrors** (Zrcadlová kaple), built in 1725 and presently used for chamber concerts on account of its fine acoustics (closed at other times).

Returning to Karlova, you could pay a brief visit to the **Puppet Museum** (Muzeum loukářských kultur) at No. 12. Set in Gothic cellars, the museum traces the history of Czech puppetry from the 17C to the 19C, with many fine examples on show. Open Tues–Sun 10.00–20.00.

Karlova ends at Křižovnická, an extremely busy thoroughfare, which separates it from the small **Knights of the Cross Square** (Křižovnické náměstí). The latter derives its name from the hospice brotherhood to which the protection of the Judith Bridge, the predecessor of the Charles Bridge, was entrusted in the 13C. The former **monastery and church of St Francis**, which once belonged to this order, stand adjacent to the church of the Holy Saviour, and were rebuilt in the late 17C. Designed by Jean-Baptiste Mathey, and carried out by Carlo Lurago, the centrally planned church has a dome based closely on that of St Peter's in Rome. The interior is ringed with dark Slivenec marble altars, and adorned with a ceiling painting of the *Last Judgement* (1722–23) by Václav Reiner; in the crypt are the foundations of the original three-aisled structure of the 13C. Just outside the church stands a cast-iron **Memorial to Charles IV**, erected in 1848 to commemorate the fifth centenary of the foundation of the Charles University.

The western end of the square is marked by the **Tower of the Old Town Bridge**, a late-14C structure that served as a model for the Powder Gate and has rich sculptural decorations from the workshop of Petr Parléř, including, above the gate, representations of St Vitus (the bridge's patron saint) flanked by St Wenceslas and Charles IV; the structure was heavily restored and considerably embellished by Josef Mocker in the 1870s. The view from the top is in many ways the finest in all Prague, embracing the Old Town, the Little Quarter and a grand sweep of the Vltava. Open daily June–Sept 10.00–18.00; Oct–May 10.00–17.00.

The southern Old Town

The arch of the Tower of the Old Town Bridge leads on to the Charles Bridge, along which the coronation processions would pass on their way to St Vitus's Cathedral. Leave the Royal Route and head south from Knights of the Cross Square along the **Smetana Embankment** (Smetanovo nábřeží) to visit the southern half of the Old Town. The first turning to the right is the short Novotného Lávka, which takes you on to a tiny spit of land jutting out into the Vltava and dominated by the former **municipal water tower** (a structure of 1489 reconstructed at the end of the 19C). The furthermost building, originally a part of the municipal waterworks, was built in 1885 in a Czech Renaissance style, and is covered with sgraffito decorations representing the *Siege of the Old Town by the Swedes*, and executed after designs by, among others, Mikoláš Aleš and František Ženíšek. On its first floor (open daily except Tues 10.00–17.00) is a drably modern display of exhibits relating to the life and work of the composer **Bedřich Smetana** (Muzeum Bedřicha Smetany), who is also

Tower of the Old Town Bridge

commemorated outside by a statue that bizarrely shows him with his back turned to one of his principle sources of inspiration, the Vltava. The weirside terrace on which the museum stands becomes a hive of activity at night, chiefly on account of its two dance clubs—*Klub Lávka*, a glorified student disco, and the huge and slightly trendier *Karlovy Lázně*, which is set in a former bathhouse. Between these two establishments are restaurants and bars that put out tables on the terrace in summer, though you may find your dining experience ruined by a plague of mosquitos.

Across the Smetana Embankment from Novotného lávka is Anenská, which leads after a few metres into the intimate Anenské náměstí. Immediately to your right on entering the square, at No. 4, is a Rococo palace built c 1765 for Count Hubert Karel Pachta of Rájov. The Pachtas were great patrons of music, and Mozart, his wife Costanza, and Beethoven were among those who have stayed here. Attached to this palace, at No. 5, is an early-19C building that was transformed in the late 1950s into one of Prague's most influential small theatres, the **Theatre on the Balustrade** (Divadlo na zábradlí).

The Theatre on the Balustrade rose to prominence in the early 1960s under the directorship of the visionary, dictatorial and totally impractical director Ivan Vyskočil, whom Václav Havel recalls in his book *Disturbing the Peace* (1990): 'Sometimes his behaviour was outrageous: for example, he'd say, "Tomorrow we're going to try out whatever comes into our minds", but then he wouldn't come to the rehearsal, although he was the only person in the troupe capable of that kind of creativity.' Jan Grossman took over the directorship of the theatre shortly afterwards (1962–68), and it was under him that it experienced its greatest years, putting on acclaimed productions of Jarry's *Ubu Roi*, Beckett's *Waiting for Godot*, and a dramatisation of Kafka's

The Trial. The theatre is perhaps best remembered today for its associations with Václav Havel, who worked here between 1960 and 1968, establishing himself as a playwright through such works as *The Garden Party*, *The Memorandum* and *The Increased Difficulty of Concentration*. After the events of November 1989, Havel's plays and those of his banned contemporaries returned to the repertory here, with Grossman doing another four-year stint as director (1989–93). The new programme alternated for a while with the mime productions of Ladislav Fialka and his troupe. Fialka's internationally renowned Pantomime, which acquired in later years the status of a tourist attraction, was housed in this theatre from the time the place was founded up to Fialka's death in the spring of 1991.

On the opposite side of the square to the theatre is the former **Convent of St Anne** (Klášter sv. Anny), which was founded by Dominican nuns in 1313 inside a monastery that had belonged up to then to the Order of the Knights Templar. After 1330 the nuns built a Gothic church on the site of the Templars' Romanesque rotunda, the foundations of which were excavated in 1954–57; the convent itself was rebuilt in the late 17C, and has an imposing main façade of 1676. The church—where Christoph Willibald Gluck used to play the organ in the early 18C—survives to this day, though it has been put to other uses since the abolition of the convent in 1782; the whole complex, for many years the centre of the printing works of Schönfeld, is used today partly as lithographic studios and partly as rehearsal rooms for the National Theatre.

The former convent extends east of the square all the way to the continuation of Anenská, Řetězová, on which stands, at No. 3, the **House of the Lords of Kunštát and Poděbrady** (Dům pánů z Kunštátu a Poděbrad), one of the more remarkable survivals in Prague of Romanesque domestic architecture. From the courtyard, you enter what was originally the first floor of the 12C house, later rebuilt in the Gothic period. The display here consists of Latin documents relating to the former owner, the 15C Hussite king George of Poděbrady, though unfortunately only translated into Czech. Downstairs in the completely bare and dimly lit cellars you can visit the original ground floor of the building, which has remained little changed since c 1200. Open summer only 10.00–18.00.

Returning along Anenská to the Smetana Embankment, and walking south by the side of the Vltava, you will shortly come to a small garden containing Prague's answer to London's Albert Memorial—a neo-Gothic **Monument to the Emperor Franz I**, who died in 1846. Erected in 1844–46 by Josef Kranner, it features at its base a series of allegorical figures by Josef Max, executed in a style that owes nothing to Czech art but much to German sculpture and engravings of the late 15C and early 16C; the equestrian statue of Franz I that once crowned the monument was taken down in 1918 and now languishes in the Lapidarium of the National Museum (see p 210).

Due east of the garden, along Konviktská, is the tiny **Holy Cross Rotunda** (Rotunda sv. Kříže), one of Prague's oldest buildings. Dating back to the early 12C, it was well restored by Vojtěch Ullmann in 1862–65, and ringed by an attractive ironwork grille designed by Josef Mánes; the interior, restored again in the late 1970s, contains fragments of 14C wall-paintings, including a scene of the *Coronation of the Virgin*. Open only for services, Sun 17.00, Tues 18.00.

Head south from the Rotunda down Karolíny Světlé and turn left into

Bartolomějská, an eerily quiet street that still strikes fear into the hearts of many Czechs, as it was the headquarters of the Communist Security Police (StB). The cell block where detainees were held was located inside the former convent building at No. 9, which was restored to the Sisters of Mercy after 1989. The enterprising nuns now lease out their property to the *Penzion Unitas* (see p 16), which offers accommodation in whitewashed cells with iron doors, including the famous Room P6 where Václav Havel was incarcerated. Next to the convent stands the former Jesuit church of **St Bartholomew** (sv. Bartoloměje), which was built by Kilian Ignaz Dientzenhofer in 1726–31, and has ceiling paintings by Václav Reiner (open only for mass, 11.30 daily).

Continuing up Bartolomějská, you should turn left into the easily missed alleyway (Průchodní) that leads into Betlémské náměstí (Bethlehem square). On the western side of the square is the **Hálanek House** (U Halánků), which was formed of three 15C houses that were remodelled at the end of the 16C.

In the middle of the 19C the Hálanek House came into the hands of Vojta Náprstek (1826–94), a manufacturer and academic who was responsible, among other things, for introducing to Prague such modern appliances as the refrigerator, the washing machine and the sewing machine. An enthusiast of anthropology, he arranged lectures on the subject in his house, and opened here first a library and then a museum of anthropology. Thanks to numerous bequests from Czech travellers, Náprstek was soon able to build at the back of his house a large modern extension to this museum, designed in 1886 by, among others, Bedřich Münzberger.

Náprstek's institution, subsequently administered by the National Museum, is known today as the **Náprstek Museum of Asian, African and American Cultures** (Nápstrkovo muzeum asijských, afrických a amerických kultur), and is housed in its entirety in the extension of 1886; this grand yellow block forms a complete contrast to the intimate arcaded courtyard that precedes it. The collections are clearly displayed and, in the case of those on the top floor dedicated to Australasia, with considerable imagination. Open Tues–Sun 09.00–17.30.

Bethlehem Chapel

The north side of the Betlémské náměstí is dominated by the austere twin-gabled ***Bethlehem Chapel** (Betlémská kaple), which gives the square its name. Open April–Oct Tues–Sun 10.00–18.00; Nov–March 10.00–17.00.

In 1391 followers of the reformist preacher Jan Milíč of Kroměříž decided to build a church where the Mass would be said in Czech. The Catholic authorities agreed only to the construction of a chapel, but when it was completed in 1394 the building turned out to be large enough to contain a congregation of 3000. The fame of the place was secured in the following decade when it became associated with the extraordinary rise of Jan Hus, leader of the Hussite movement.

The Bethlehem Chapel was to remain the spiritual centre of Hus's followers long after their master's death. His friend, Master Jakoubek of Stříbro, succeeded him as preacher here from 1414 to 1429, and in 1521 the German peasant leader Thomas Münzer proclaimed from the chapel's pulpit his

Utopian social views; from 1609 up to the Battle of the White Mountain in 1620, the chapel belonged to the Union of Czech Brethren, one of whose preachers was the future father-in-law of the educational reformer Comenius. Taken over subsequently by the Jesuits, the building was destroyed three years after the expulsion of the Jesuit Order in 1773, and a private dwelling put up in its place. In 1919 part of the chapel was unearthed under the house, and further archaeological excavations in 1949 revealed that all except the southern wall of the chapel had been used in the construction of the later building. The decision was then taken to reconstruct the Bethlehem Chapel in its original state, the idea being to create a memorial to the Hussites who, according to remarks made at this time by Klement Gottwald, were already 'fighting for Communism' 500 years ago. A rather cynical view of the place during the Communist period was expressed by one of the characters in Josef Škvorecký's novel *The Miracle Game*: 'Petrofim couldn't even work up any plausible enthusiasm for the Bethlehem Chapel, reconstructed—mainly to attract tourists—on a spot where it was thought the great Jan Hus might once have preached.'

You enter the chapel from the courtyard by the side of the building, opposite the **Klub Architektu** restaurant (see p 28). The impressive box-like interior, reconstructed in 1950–52 by Jaroslav Fragner, has pseudo-medieval wall-paintings mixed up with restored 14C fragments of Biblical scenes, and is focussed on the pulpit rather than the altar; the wooden furnishings and the southern wall are modern. As in many other Prague churches, rows of chairs are laid out for the concerts that take place here, but daytime visitors are forbidden to sit on them. From the foyer you can go up to the first floor, where there is display relating to the history of the chapel and the Hussite movement in general.

Jan Hus

Born in 1373 of peasant parents in the south Bohemian village of Husinec, Hus studied at Prague University before entering the Church, where he soon made such a name for himself that he became confessor to King Wenceslas IV's wife, Queen Sophia. He was at first unwavering in his devotion to the Church of Rome, but the papacy's corruption at the time of the Schism—as exemplified in its selling of indulgences in the streets of Prague—was to turn Hus into one of its most violent opponents. In 1402 he began denouncing the morals of the clergy from Prague's Bethlehem Chapel, finding international support for his views two years later following the arrival in Prague from England of two disciples of the English reformer John Wycliffe, James and Conrad of Canterbury. Hus would continue preaching from the chapel up to 1413.

The preachings of Hus won him an enormous following among the Czech people and, at Prague University, led to the development of a great rift between the Czechs and the Germans, the latter all taking the side of the Church of Rome. In 1409 Hus scored a major victory when he managed to persuade Wenceslas IV to impose the Decree of Kutná Hora, whereby the voting system in the university was changed greatly in favour of the Czechs, a decision that led to an exodus from Prague of 2000 German students and many professors, who went on to found the University of Leipzig in Saxony.

The success of the Czech reform movement incited the new pope at Rome, Alexander V, to authorise the archbishop of Prague to destroy all the writings of Wycliffe and to punish those who read and preached his doctrines. When Hus persisted in his preachings, he was excommunicated, and all those who supported him were threatened with the same fate, even if they only offered him food and drink; it was further stipulated that all religious services were to be suspended in every town he entered. Wenceslas IV persuaded Hus to leave Prague for a while, in the hope that his absence from the city would help to calm the situation. In his 20 months of voluntary exile Hus produced most of his finest writings, but also continued to preach, finding his congregations in the villages and farms around his native Husinec. In the meantime, Wenceslas's brother Sigismund induced the church authorities to call a Council at Constance to settle the dispute between the rival pontiffs. Sigismund also suggested that Hus should attend this council to refute the charges of heresy, promising him a safe-conduct and a free return to Bohemia whatever the outcome. Hus was burnt at the stake at Constance on 6 July 1415.

After leaving the building turn left and then left again into Husova, on which stands—a short way to the north on the right-hand side—the **Church of St Giles** (sv. Jiljí). Founded in the 13C and rebuilt between 1310 and 1371, this church has a sturdy, twin-towered west façade that has been little altered since the 14C, when the building was the principal base of the reformist preacher Jan Milíč of Kroměříž; the tall interior, however, was remodelled after 1733 and has been cloaked with massive gilded capitals, stucco decoration by Bernard Spinetti and ceiling frescoes by Václav Reiner comprising a central panel of the *Celebration of the Dominican Order*, and two flanking ones representing the *Legends of St Giles and St Thomas Aquinas*.

The area to the east of the church is a veritable maze of streets filled with bars and shops. Proceed along the tiny Zlatá, turning right into Jilská, and then immediately left into Vejvodova; this will take you into Michalská, where you should turn right again, and then first left into **Havelská**. This street, enlivened today by one of Prague's best open-air markets, widens at its northeastern end into a narrow square, dominated by the **Church of St Gall** (sv. Havla). The latter, a 13C foundation, was remodelled c 1722 by Pavel Bayer and Jan Santini-Aichel, who gave the church its powerful, undulating façade. After visiting the church, you could stop for a bite to eat at the conveniently located *Kogo* pizzeria (see p 28), which has another branch in the Slovanský dům (see p 168).

On the former Fruit Market (Ovocný trh) northeast of the church stands the ***Estates Theatre** (Stavovské divadlo), an elegant neo-Classical building designed by Antonín Haffenecker in 1781.

The oldest theatre in Prague, the Nostitz Theatre opened in 1783 with a performance of Lessing's play *Emilia Galotti*. Four years later the first-ever performance of Mozart's opera *Don Giovanni* took place here, and early in the following century the place acquired further musical renown when the German composer Karl Weber was director of its operatic ensemble. The property after 1799 of the Czech Estates, the theatre was known up to 1945 as the Estates Theatre, after which it was renamed in honour of the Czech dramatist Josef

Kajetán Tyl (1808–56), whose comedy *Fidlovačka*—from which the song and future Czech national anthem, 'Where is my Home', is taken—had been premièred here in 1834. Today, the building is a popular venue for ballet and modern-dance productions put on by the National Theatre, as well as opera, including, inevitably, frequent performances of *Don Giovanni*. Despite major refurbishments, the basic structure of the building has changed little over the past two centuries, and the concert scenes for Miloš Forman's *Amadeus* were filmed here. The name reverted to the Estates Theatre in 1990.

Adjoining the theatre, at No. 9 Železná, is the **Carolinum**, the original building of the oldest university in Central Europe. Founded by Charles IV in 1348, the university building is also claimed to be the oldest still in use in Europe, though in fact very little of the medieval structure remains, the principal survival being the charming oriel window on the southern side, facing Ovocný trh. The structure was extensively rebuilt by František Kaňka after 1718, at the time when the university was in the hands of the Jesuits; further major reconstruction took place after the Second World War. Today, the building houses the Charles University's administrative offices.

Continue north up Železná, and turn left into the narrow Kožná, where, at No. 1, is a house with a beautiful Renaissance portal featuring two bears. A plaque indicates that the house was the birthplace of the journalist Egon Erwin Kisch (1885–1948), who devoted much of his writing to accounts of his native Prague, including *Prague Adventures* and *Tales from Prague's Streets and Nights*. Another of his works was dedicated to the city's covered passages, and until recently you could walk through such passages from No. 10 Kožná all the way back to Jilská. Kisch's birthplace stands at the corner of Melantrichova, where you turn right to rejoin the southern side of the Old Town Square.

The Jewish Quarter (Josefov)

A good starting-point for a tour of the northern half of the Old Town, encompassing the former Jewish ghetto of Josefov, is **Pařížská**, which runs off the Old Town Square towards the river. This long tree-lined avenue, built at the end of the 19C, is lined with large, oppressively ornamented blocks, featuring fantastical corners composed of irregularly shaped balconies and openings piled up one on top of the other. Its creation constituted one of the few major acts of urban renewal within the Old Town of Prague, cutting as it did a great swathe through a slum area crammed with picturesque but decayed old houses inhabited largely by the city's Jewish population. Today, Pařížská is lined with stylish boutiques and several overpriced bars and restaurants catering to the vast numbers of tourists that visit the area.

The Monuments of Jewish Prague

Immediately beyond the junction with Červená there is a sudden interruption in the line of Pařížská's turn-of-the-20C-century blocks to reveal incongruously, just below the pavement level on the left-hand side, three of the main survivals of Jewish Prague—the Jewish Town Hall, High Synagogue, and Old-New Synagogue. The first two buildings, returned to the Jewish community in 1994, are used for religious services and are closed to the public. Tickets to the Old-New

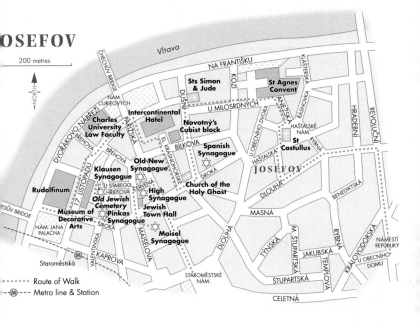

Synagogue can be bought from the ticket office/gift shop on Červená; the ticket also covers entry to the Jubilee Synagogue (see p 171), situated outside the area of the former ghetto.

The **Jewish Museum** is a wholly separate institution that encompasses several historic buildings and monuments, including the Maisel Synagogue, Klausen Synagogue, Ceremonial Hall, Pinkas Synagogue, Old Jewish Cemetery and Spanish Synagogue, which are described in this chapter. An entrance ticket covering all the various parts of the museum can be purchased from any of the quarter's ticket offices (male visitors are provided with skullcaps). The Jewish Museum is today one of the city's obligatory tourist sights, and the throngs of visitors who descend upon this restricted area lead to unpleasant congestion and long queues to enter some of the monuments. To add to the confusion, because of recent flood damage, the entry points have in some cases been relocated (e.g. for the Old Jewish Cemetery), and some monuments, such as the Pinkas Synagogue, are closed altogether for renovation.

- **Admission** The sites in the Jewish Museum are open (with some variations) April–Oct Sun–Fri 09.30–18.00; Nov–March Sun–Fri 09.30–17.00.

Architecturally and historically the most important site of the former ghetto is the ****Old-New Synagogue** (Staronová synagoga), which is also Prague's most outstanding early-medieval building. Unfortunately, parts of it were damaged during the floods of 2002, and a painstaking renovation programme is currently underway. It is the oldest functioning synagogue in Europe, dating back to the middle of the 13C, and owes its unusual name to the fact that it was originally called the 'New Synagogue' until another 'new' one was built in the vicinity. You enter through a narrow barrel-vaulted vestibule that was originally the main hall of the synagogue until the present one was added after c 1270 (it later became the women's gallery); in the 17C metal boxes were placed in this vestibule for the collection of Jewish taxes.

The actual main hall, one of the finest examples in Central Europe of the Cistercian Gothic style, is reached through a 13C portal with an exquisitely carved vine tree bearing 12 bunches of grapes that refer to the 12 tribes of Israel. There are numerous further references to the figure 12 both in the decoration and in the plan of the vaulted double-naved hall itself. Leaf ornament of the 13C decorates the tympanum of the shrine on the east wall containing the Torah (a parchment scroll of the five Books of Moses, or Pentateuch). In the middle of the hall stands a pulpit or *bema*, surrounded by a beautiful Gothic grille; it was from here that the Jewish community's most famous son, Rabbi Löw, would read from the scrolls of the Torah (see below). Above the *bema* hangs a flag donated to Prague's Jews in 1648 by the Emperor Ferdinand, who wanted to thank them for helping him fight off the Protestant Swedes. The benches lining the walls are early 19C, while on the walls themselves are traces of medieval frescoes and inscriptions of 1618 recording certain sections of the Psalms. Open Sun–Thur 09.30–18.00, Fri 09.30–17.00.

Directly facing the south portal of the building is the entrance to the **High Synagogue** (Vysoká synagoga), which was built in 1568, extended at the end of the 17C, and remodelled and given its present façade in the 19C. It is now a functioning synagogue and is closed to the public, though the gift shop in the foyer is a good place to pick up books and postcards connected with Jewish Prague.

Adjoining the synagogue, and until the 19C connected to it by a door, is the picturesque **Jewish Town Hall** (Židovská radnice), founded by Maisel in the late 16C, but completely rebuilt in 1763 when it was given its wooden turret, complete with an Hebraic clock (on the north gable) that tells the time backwards ('The hand of the clock in the Jewish quarter is turning backwards /And you are passing slowly backward through the history of your life', wrote Apollinaire in his visionary poem 'Zone'). The building is closed to the public.

Walking south from here along Maiselova you will soon come to the **Maisel Synagogue** (Maiselova synagoga), which was commissioned and paid for by Mordechaj Maisel in 1590, later rebuilt in a Baroque style, and then given a wholly neo-Gothic appearance between 1893 and 1905; the building contains a well-labelled but uninspiring display relating to the history of the Jews in Bohemia and Moravia from the 10C up to the period of their emancipation in the 18C.

Heading instead due west of the Old-New Synagogue along U Starego Hřbitova, a street lined with souvenir stalls, you will shortly reach the **Klausen Synagogue** (Klausová synagoga), which dates back to 1694 and has a stuccoed, barrel-vaulted interior containing today a large collection of Hebraic manuscripts and prints, as well as silverware and religious objects. It is flanked on its western side by the former **Ceremonial Hall** (Obřadní síň), built in 1906 for the Jewish Burial Society: taking the form of a tiny neo-Romanesque castle, it features a dull display of items connected with burial ceremonies in the Jewish tradition.

The entrance to the Old Jewish Cemetery is usually next to the Ceremonial Hall, but since the floods of 2002 it has been moved to Široká, with the old entrance now becoming the exit. This situation is set to remain until renovation work on the Pinkas Synagogue is complete.

The Ghetto, the Golem and the Nazi Occupation

Jews began settling in Prague from at least the 10C onwards, though it was not apparently until the mid-13C that they began forming a ghetto in the district around the Old-New Synagogue; in accordance with the Third Lateran Council of 1179 this ghetto was separated from its Christian surroundings by a wall. Despite fires, pogroms and even a law of 1541 banishing Jews from the whole of Bohemia, the ghetto flourished, and by the 17C an estimated 7000 people were crowded into the area. Two of its most influential figures were active during the reign of Rudolph II, one being the emperor's finance minister, Mordechaj Markus Maisel, who was responsible for the paving of the ghetto and the building of the Maisel Synagogue and the Jewish Town Hall. The other great Jewish figure of this period was the Rabbi Löw, a man much respected by Rudolph II and the leading aristocratic families of the time, and under whose influence the Jewish community in Prague enjoyed the most privileged period in their history. A prominent theologian, Löw was the author of many writings that became an inherent part of Hasidic teaching, such as his homily *On the Hardening of Pharaoh's Heart*. But Löw was to be remembered above all for his reputed supernatural powers, a reputation doubtless enhanced by his being a passionate devotee of the Cabala, whereby he believed that the whole of human history, past, present and future, could be read in the Torah. Numerous fanciful tales are told of Löw, but none more famous than that of his creation—from the mud of the Vltava—of Yossel the Golem. Though sometimes portrayed as a guardian of the ghetto and even as a figure of fun, Yossel has usually been imagined as a figure like Frankenstein's monster, who ends up running amok (as in Gustav Meyrink's sinister novel *The Golem* of 1915 and in the German Expressionist film of the same name by Paul Wegener).

The law requiring the Prague Jews to be contained in the ghetto was abolished in 1781 by Emperor Joseph II, whose ultimate intentions were to assimilate Jews fully into the rest of the population, destroying their language and culture by forbidding Hebrew and Yiddish for business transactions, and forcing the Jews to Germanise their names (it was not until 1867 that Jews were assured all civil rights equal to those guaranteed to Czechs and Germans). In 1850, when the ghetto had been almost entirely infiltrated by outsiders and only 10 per cent of the former Jewish population was left, this area of Prague was turned into a municipal district known as Josefov in honour of Joseph II. The emperor would not, perhaps, have entirely appreciated the honour, for this district was by now a festering slum, more over-populated than any other area in the city, without water-supply or drainage, and with a notorious reputation for low life: decrepit smoke-filled bars and brothels, marked by poles hung with red lanterns, stood provocatively alongside the houses of the remaining Orthodox Jews, whose Sabbath chants would sometimes be interrupted by the shouts and songs of drunken revellers and prostitutes.

Despite the protests of poets, students, architects and others, this whole area was largely razed in 1895, leaving only the buildings of historical interest still standing (the 21,700 wagonloads of rubble were used as landfill to protect a district that was still constantly under the threat of floods). Later, the Nazis, far from wishing to destroy these surviving monuments, planned to turn them into a 'Museum of Jewry', so as to record for posterity the culture of what they believed would soon be an extinct race. A museum of Jewish art had existed since the beginning of the century but, as a result of the Nazis' confiscation of Jewish property, its holdings were swelled to become the largest collection of synagogical art in the world. The museum's growth coincided with the dwindling of the Jewish population of Bohemia and Moravia to a tenth of its former size: a memorial in Prague's Pinkas Synagogue records the names of 77,297 Jews killed during the Nazi occupation of the country. Today, only a small community of Orthodox Jews remains in the traditional Jewish Quarter of Prague.

The former Jewish ghetto has always held a strong fascination for visitors to Prague, and a number of foreign writers have evoked the place in their works, for instance the popular 19C American novelist, Marion Crawford. In her novel, *The Witch of Prague* (1882), Crawford evokes the ghetto with an unsavoury mixture of romantic fascination and deep repellence: 'Throngs of gowned men, crooked, bearded, filthy, vulture-eyed, crowded upon each other in the narrow, public place ... a writhing mass of humanity, intoxicated by the smell of gold, mad for its possession, half hysteric with the fear of losing it, timid, yet dangerous, poisoned to the core by the sweet sting of money, terrible in intelligence, vile in heart, contemptible in body, irresistible in the unity of their greed—the Jews of Prague two hundred years ago.' More recently the former ghetto provided the main setting for the English novelist Bruce Chatwin's compelling novella, *Utz* (1988), which deals with a collector of Meissen porcelain figurines living in the same district where the Rabbi Löw had fashioned his golem.

Within the ****Old Jewish Cemetery** (Starý židovský hřbitov)—the Jewish Museum's most popular attraction—are 20,000 tombstones jumbled together among trees. Though established in the late 15C, it contains tombs transferred from an earlier cemetery, the oldest being that of the Rabbi Abigdor Kar (d. 1389); the last person to be buried here was Moses Beck in 1787. The tall, cracked and often perilously leaning stones are engraved with symbolic reliefs referring either to the occupation or the name of the deceased, for instance, a stag in the case of someone named Hirsch, or a pair of scissors in the case of a tailor. One of the most richly decorated stones is that of Heudele Bassevi (d. 1628), who was the wife of the first Prague Jew to be raised to the nobility; among the graves of other distinguished Jews are those of Mordechaj Maisel (d. 1601), the astronomer David Gaus (d. 1613), the scientist Josef Delmedigo (d. 1655) and the bibliophile David Oppenheimer (d. 1736). Pebbles and scraps of paper with messages are often left on the graves as a gesture of respect towards the dead. The grave with the greatest accumulation of these is that of the most famous person to be buried here, the Rabbi Löw (d. 1609), a renowned Talmudic scholar whose devotion to the scriptures enabled him to evade Death on several occasions; he finally succumbed when Death hid in a rose given to him unwittingly by his granddaughter. A beautiful description of the cemetery appears in Bruce Chatwin's novella, *Utz*: 'It was now early evening and we were sitting on a slatted seat in the Old Jewish Cemetery.... The sunbeams, falling through sycamores, lit up spirals of midges and landed on the mossy tombstones, which, heaped one upon the other, resembled sea-weed-covered rocks at low tide.' Sadly, the cemetery is today no longer the oasis of calm and contemplation so evocatively described by Chatwin, and in high season fills up with noisy tour groups marching in single file along the designated trail.

Attached to the cemetery's southern wall is the **Pinkas Synagogue** (Pinkasova synagoga), founded in 1479. It was rebuilt in 1535, and enlarged and remodelled by Juda Goldsmid de Herz in 1625. The hall, turned after the Second World War into a holocaust memorial, was closed after the Arab-Israeli war of 1967, apparently for restoration, though this was interminably and suspiciously protracted by the Communists. Reopened in the 1990s, it closed again following the floods of 2002, which destroyed the wall inscriptions list-ing the names, personal data, and home

Ceremonial Hall by the Old Jewish Cemetery

towns and villages of the 77,297 Jews killed by the Nazis in Bohemia and Moravia (of this number, 36,000 were from Prague). The inscriptions are cur-rently undergoing restoration. When the synagogue reopens, the exhibition will also include children's drawings depicting conditions at the Terezín ghetto near Prague, where many perished.

Heading west along Široká you will come, at the end of the cemetery wall, to the large riverside square—formerly Red Army Square— which since 1989 has been named after Jan Palach (see p 49), to whom there is a small memorial containing a bust made from a death mask (by the corner of the Philosophy Faculty build-ing on the east side of the square). The four-span Mánesuv bridge that leads from here to Malá Strana dates back to 1911–14 and includes reliefs by such leading sculptors of the time as František Bílek and Jan Štursa. On the northern side of the square stands the imposing late-19C **Rudolfinum**, which, despite its con-ventional neo-Renaissance detailing, was greatly admired for the boldness of its layout by the Cubist architect Pavel Janák, who featured it in his book *Art Treasures of Bohemia* (1913). Built between 1875 and 1884 by Josef Zítek and Josef Schulz, it functioned originally as an art gallery and concert hall before serving from 1918 to 1939 as the seat of the Czechoslovak parliament. After the war it was used again for cultural purposes and is now one of the main venues of the annual music festival known as the Prague Spring (see p 37). From the river-side entrance you can walk upstairs to visit the café set in a superb columned hall, where art exhibitions are also held.

Turning right as soon as you enter the square from Široká, and walking north from it along 17. listopadu, the next building you come to is the recently revamped ***Museum of Decorative Arts** (Umělecko průmyslové muzeum), a French-style neo-Renaissance structure rising above the western side of the Old Jewish Cemetery. Open Tues–Sun 10.00–18.00.

Founded in 1885 with a largely didactic purpose, the museum was at first housed in the Rudolfinum while awaiting its eventual transfer to the present building, which was completed by Josef Schulz in 1900; the façade is covered with reliefs by Bohuslav Schnirch and Antonín Popp representing the different branches of the decorative arts in Bohemia, and the coats of arms of the Bohemian towns most renowned for these arts.

The museum itself, frequently empty, is one of the great little-known attractions of Prague. The ground floor is taken up by a café and rooms devoted to excellent temporary exhibitions, with the main permanent display—somewhat uninvitingly called 'Stories of Materials'—being contained on the first floor. The exhibits have English labelling, and audio-guides are also available.

Despite the great size of the building, only a small proportion of its objects is on display, with others having been moved to the Trade Fair Palace (see p 203). The collections, ranging from the Middle Ages up to the present day and with the main emphasis on Bohemia and Moravia, include glass, ceramics, porcelain, woodwork, furniture, metalwork, clocks, textiles, costumes, prints, posters and photographs. The rooms have ceilings attractively decorated with turn-of-the-20C-century grotesque work, and the layout is endearingly old-fashioned and crowded, the overall effect—enhanced by the occasional dramatic lighting—being that of great wealth and variety, as in a Netherlandish still-life painting. Among the finest of the objects permanently on show are the numerous pieces of Bohemian Baroque glass, and the superlative collection of Meissen porcelain figurines. There is also a selection from the museum's unrivalled holdings of Czech Cubist art.

Continuing north along 17. listopadu will take you to náměstí Curieových, a riverside square standing at the northern end of Pařížská, and bordered to the south by the fussy modern block of the luxurious Hotel Intercontinental (1968–74), and to the west by the Law Faculty of Charles University, an Art Deco structure designed by Jan Kotěra in 1919. To the north, the Čechův Bridge leads across the river to the Letná Park, which is described in the next chapter. For now,

head south of the square along Pařížská and turn left beyond the Hotel Intercontinental to reach, on the eastern side of a small garden, Elišky Krásnohorské; here, at Nos 10–14, overlooking the square, is a remarkable 'Cubist' block built by Otakar Novotný in 1919–21 as the Prague Teachers' Co-operative.

Continuing south along this street, you will shortly rejoin Široká, passing on your left the **Church of the Holy Ghost** (open only for Sunday mass at 08.00 and 09.30), a single-aisled structure of 1346 remodelled after a fire in 1689; in front of the building stands a statue of St John of Nepomuk (1727) by Ferdinand Brokoff.

Turn left along Široká, then left again into

'Cubist' building in Elišky Krásnohorské by Otakar Novotný, 1919–21

Dušní, where, directly facing the eastern end of the Church of the Holy Ghost, is the **★Spanish Synagogue** (Španělská synagoga), a neo-

Moorish structure built in 1882 for the city's Sephardic Jews. The beautiful interior, replete with vividly coloured floral patterns and stained glass, has elaborate stucco decorations inspired by those of the Alhambra in Granada. Contained on the ground floor and in the women's gallery is an interesting permanent exhibition documenting the history of Prague Jews from the mid-19C up to 1945.

Walking north along Dušní in the direction of the river you reach the Baroque **Church of Sts Simon and Jude**, famous for its organ on which both Mozart and Haydn played.

Convent of St Agnes

U milosrdných, which runs east of the church, will take you to the present entrance of the former ***Convent of St Agnes** (Klášter sv. Anežský české), a large and important medieval complex situated at the corner of Anežská. The convent, which is sometimes known by the ridiculous name of the 'Bohemian Assisi', was founded for the Poor Clares by Wenceslas I in 1233, probably on the request of his sister, Agnes of Bohemia, who would become the first abbess, as well as the patron saint of Bohemia. Open Tues–Sun 10.00–18.00.

The museum installed in the convent is centred around a large cloister, which has largely retained its mid-13C appearance, apart from the upper level of the eastern side, which features a Renaissance arcade built by the Dominicans. At the cloister's southeast corner is a door leading into the convent's two adjoining churches (at the time of writing both were closed due to flood damage): the earlier of the two was dedicated to St Francis and completed by the mid-13C; however, only its presbytery has survived, and this is known today as the **Mánes Hall** and is used for concerts. Projecting east of this structure is the spacious and elegant **Sanctuary of St Saviour**, which dates from the 1280s, and is a fine example of French Gothic influence; it is also the resting place of St Agnes.

Until recently, the convent contained the 19C Czech paintings belonging to the National Gallery, but these have now moved to the Trade Fair Palace in Holešovice (see p 203), and in their place the convent has received the collections of **medieval Bohemian art** from the Convent of St George (see p 148) at Prague Castle. This seems to have been a wise move by the National Gallery as the collections, comprising Gothic altarpieces, painting and sculpture, seem very much at home in their new setting. The arrangement is chronological, beginning in the mid-14C and ending approximately in the mid-16C.

The first major Bohemian painter represented in the museum is the anonymous **Master of the Vyšší Brod Altarpiece**. This altarpiece of c 1350, originating from the former Cistercian monastery at Vyšší Brod in Southern Bohemia, was probably commissioned by Petr I of Rožmberk; it comprises nine panels of scenes from the life of Christ and the Virgin: Annunciation, Nativity, Adoration of the Magi, Christ on the Mount of Olives, Crucifixion, Lamentation, Resurrection, Ascension of Christ and Pentecost. A more distinctive personality of slightly later date, and one of the earliest Bohemian artists known by name, was **Master Theodoric**, who is best known for his panels and murals painted in the Holy Cross Chapel at Karlštejn Castle in 1357–65; he is represented here by six large and luminously modelled heads of saints and Church fathers: St Luke, Charlemagne, Catherine, Matthew the Evangelist, Ambrose and Gregory the Great. A work of great historical interest is the votive panel of Jan Očko of Vlasim, which portrays the enthroned Madonna flanked by what are sometimes considered to be the earliest examples of Bohemian portraiture—remarkably realistic representations of Charles IV, Wenceslas IV and the panel's donor, Jan Očko, Archbishop of Prague, himself.

The last years of the 14C are dominated by the **Master of the Třeboň Altarpiece**, whose principal work, from which he derives his name, is to be found here. Only three panels of this work—which was painted c 1380 for the former Augustinian church of St Giles in the southern Bohemian town of Třeboň—have survived: these panels, painted on both sides with the most vivid colours and charming naturalistic detail, represent (1) Christ on the Mount of Olives, (2) Sts Catherine, Mary Magdalene and Margaret, (3) The Entombment, (4) Sts Augustine, Giles and Jerome, (5) the Resurrection, and (6) Sts James, Bartholomew and Philip.

Saint Agnes

Born in 1211 as the third and youngest of King Přemysl Otakar II's daughters from his second marriage, Agnes spent most of her childhood being used as a pawn to try to secure useful political alliances. After being promised at the age of three to a Silesian prince who subsequently died, she was offered to the ten-year-old son of Emperor Frederick II, who was then taken away from her by the daughter of Duke Leopold VI of Vienna; marital negotiations were later entered into with Henry III of England, but after being protracted for several years, these were finally dropped, mostly on account of the dowry. When, finally, Frederick II himself tried on two occasions to marry her, she decided she had had enough of worldly suitors and made the sensible decision to betrothe herself instead to Christ. She was 23 at the time.

She entered the Prague convent of the Poor Clares in 1234, one year after its foundation, after her hair had been shorn off and all her riches given away; she remained here until her death in 1292, by which time the present large complex was almost complete. Throughout her many years at the convent she remained fanatically devoted to her order's ideals of poverty, while accepting the concessions necessitated by their transference from Italy to the cold climate of Prague: papal permission was eventually given for fasting hours to be shortened and wool stockings and double or fur-lined tunics to be worn. The story of her legendary life, written 50 years after her death, praised the simplicity of her lifestyle, her humble devotion to her fellow nuns (whose clothes she washed and mended) and her frugal diet of raw onions and fruit.

Agnes's arguments against a Church too deeply involved in worldly power and magnificence did not prevent her convent from being taken over by the Hussites in 1420 for use as an arsenal. Occupied again after 1555 by the Dominicans, and then partially rebuilt in the wake of the Old Town fire of 1689, the convent was dissolved for good by Joseph II in 1782, after which the whole complex fell into decay and its buildings were usurped as craft workshops. Extensive restoration work was begun in the 20C, and in the course of this the foundations of a neighbouring Franciscan monastery of the early 13C were discovered. Agnes herself, beatified in 1874, was finally canonised on 12 November 1989, four days before the 'Velvet Revolution'. Restoration of her convent is at last nearing completion.

The last of the outstanding Bohemian painters represented here is the anonymous **Master of the Litoměřice Altarpiece**. The altarpiece itself is in the North Bohemian Gallery at Litoměřice (though it seems originally to have come from St Vitus's Cathedral in Prague), but the National Gallery has a number of other impressive works associated with him, most notably a series of panels from the Týn church (c 1510) showing Sts Barbara and Catherine, and a triptych of *The Holy Trinity* of 1515–20. Of the later sculptures, special mention should be made of the expressive relief of the *Lamentation of Žebrák* (early 16C) by the artist known as the Monogramist I.P., who seems to have come from the Passau or Salzburg region. This artist was also responsible for the Votive Altarpiece from Zlíchov—a series of eight intricately carved reliefs, including a superb central one of *Christ the Saviour*.

After leaving the Convent of St Agnes head south down the short Anežská, at the end of which you will come to the **Church of St Castullus** (sv. Haštal), which dates back to the early 14C. Though the main nave and chancel were remodelled following the fire of 1689, the south aisle has been preserved in its medieval state, as has the remarkable twin-aisled extension that was added to the north side of the church in 1375; the extension features a fine net vault with bosses decorated with masks and leaves. The walls of the sacristy are covered with medieval murals, comprising a series of Apostles' heads of c 1400 and scenes of the *Crucifixion* and the *Last Supper* of c 1500.

The quiet and picturesque streets to the south and west of the church boast several good places to eat and drink where the atmosphere is more relaxed and slightly less tourist-oriented than in the vicinity of the Old Town Square. Places you might try include: *Chez Marcel*, Haštalská 12, *Le Patio*, corner of Haštalská and Rybná, *La Casa Blů*, Kozi 15, *Blatouch*, Vězeňská 4, and *Molly Malone's*, U Obecního dvora 4.

Heading south of the church you will reach **Dlouhá**, a street that follows the early-medieval route connecting the Old Town Square with the colony of German merchants at Poříčí (see p 170). Going left, at No. 33 is the *Roxy*, a former cinema that is now generally regarded as Prague's best dance club, and next door to it is *Dahab*, an excellent Turkish-style tea-room with sofas to recline on. The historic building at No. 37 is known as the **House at the Golden Tree** (Dům U zlatého stromu), with a fine late-16C courtyard dating from the time when the house belonged to the mayor of the Old Town, Václav Kročín.

At the eastern end of Dlouhá you will come to Revoluční, where you turn right, shortly afterwards re-entering náměstí Republiky.

2 The Little Quarter (Malá Strana)

Across the Vltava

The Little Quarter or Malá Strana, founded in 1257 by King Přemysl Otakar II in the outer bailey of Prague Castle, was known up to the early 14C as The New Town below Prague Castle. Later in the century Charles IV considerably extended this town with the creation of new fortifications incorporating the Petřín Hill to the south. Today this hill forms part of a large wooded park, the northern sides of which are fringed by lush gardens attached to Baroque palaces. Gardens and palaces, many of which now serve as embassies, are the dominant feature of the Little Quarter, the most genuinely picturesque area of a city steeped in the picturesque, and the one that can most truly be compared to a stage set. Although overprettified in parts in recent years, and today largely lacking the romantically decayed corners of old, it has so far escaped the worst of the commercialisation now affecting the Staré Město. Furthermore, in comparison to the flat Staré Město, this steeply pitched district offers an enticingly variegated profile when viewed from a distance. Despite the now almost oppressive congestion of pedestrians that can mark the Royal Route as it crosses the Charles Bridge, it is difficult not to feel an acute sense of drama and expectation while being drawn by the bridge's gesticulating statuary towards the Little Quarter's turreted entrance gate, behind which rises the massive dome of St Nicholas and, higher still, the dramatic silhouette of Prague Castle.

Charles Bridge

The **Charles Bridge** (Karlův most), one of Europe's most beautiful bridges, is not simply the visual centrepiece of Prague, but has also played a central role in the life and history of the city.

The first bridge to span the Vltava at this point was a wooden construction, first mentioned in 1118 and destroyed by flood in 1157. At the instigation of Queen Judith, the wife of Vladislav I, a 21-arch stone bridge was built in its place between 1158 and 1160 but, in 1342, this too collapsed after a flood. In 1357 Charles IV entrusted the architect Petr Parléř with the construction of a new bridge, which was to be known as the Stone or Prague Bridge up to 1870, and only thereafter as the Charles Bridge. Built of sandstone blocks, this 16-arch structure runs a slightly irregular course due to the fact that, while the bridgeheads of the Judith Bridge were retained, new piers were constructed in the middle of the river, just to the south of the old ones. The new structure, which was completed in the early 15C, has been damaged a number of times by floods, and two of its arches had to be rebuilt in 1890, but it has never collapsed.

As well as serving as part of the processional route of the Bohemian kings, the Charles Bridge was a place where commerce took place, tournaments were held, customs duties collected, law suits settled, criminals executed, and delinquents punished by being dipped in the Vltava in wicker baskets. The most famous incident in its history occurred on 20 March 1393 when the future St John of Nepomuk (see p 57) was bound hand and foot and thrown

MALÁ STRANA AND THE CASTLE DISTRICT (HRADČANY)

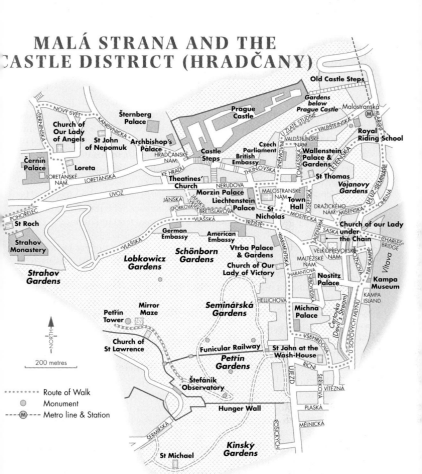

Old Castle Steps

Gardens below Prague Castle

Malostranská

Prague Castle

Sternberg Palace

Church of Our Lady of Angels

St John of Nepomuk

Archbishop's Palace

HRADČANSKÉ NÁM.

Castle Steps

Czech Parliament

British Embassy

Royal Riding School

Wallenstein Palace & Gardens

Černín Palace

Loreta

LORETÁNSKÉ NÁM.

LORETÁNSKÁ

KE HRADU

Theatines' Church

THUNOVSKÁ

St Thomas

Vojanovy Gardens

ÚVOZ

NERUDOVA

Morzin Palace

Liechtenstein Palace

MALOSTRANSKÉ NÁM.

Town Hall

DRAŽICKÉHO NÁM.

St Roch

POHOŘELEC

JÁNSKÁ

ŠPORKOVÁ

BŘETISLAVOVA

VLAŠSKÁ

St Nicholas

MOSTECKÁ

Church of our Lady under the Chain

CHARLES BRIDGE

Strahov Monastery

German Embassy

American Embassy

TRŽIŠTĚ

SASKÁ

Strahov Gardens

VLAŠSKÁ

Schönborn Gardens

Vtrba Palace & Gardens

Church of Our Lady of Victory

HARANTOVA

VELKOPŘEVORSKÉ NÁM.

MALTÉZSKÉ NÁM.

Nostitz Palace

Vltava

Kampa Museum

Lobkowicz Gardens

HELLICHOVA

Seminářská Gardens

Michna Palace

KAMPA ISLAND

Petřín Tower

Mirror Maze

Čertovka (Devil's Stream)

ÚSOVYCH MLÝNŮ

Church of St Lawrence

VŠEHRDOVA

Funicular Railway

St John at the Wash-House

Petřín Gardens

ÚJEZD

ŘÍČNÍ

SERKOVA

Štefánik Observatory

VÍTĚZNÁ

Hunger Wall

PLASKÁ

MĚLNICKÁ

ŠERMÍŘSKÁ

Kinský Gardens

St Michael

ROSICKÝCH

NORTH

200 metres

· · · · · · · · Route of Walk

○ Monument

-- Ⓜ -- Metro line & Station

from its parapet into the river where, according to legend, his body floated for an unnaturally long time, a group of five stars hovering above it. In 1683, at a time when the Jesuits were beginning to promote the Nepomuk cult, a statue to him by Jan Brokoff was placed on the bridge, near the supposed point from where he was flung. This led to several religious orders commissioning other statues for the bridge, from, among others, Jan and Ferdinand Maxmilián Brokoff, Matěj Jäckel and Matthias Braun. The Baroque statues, which were all in place by 1714, were joined in the mid-19C by works by Emmanuel Max; between 1908 and 1937 a number of other statues were added, and some of the more worn ones removed to the Lapidarium of the National Museum (see p 210), being replaced by copies. On 9 February 1911 the bridge witnessed one of the many extravagant incidents in the life of the great hoaxer and comic writer Jaroslav Hašek. A newspaper of the time reported that 'in the small hours of this morning Jaroslav Hašek wanted to throw himself from the parapet of the Charles Bridge into the Vltava ... The theatre dresser, Mr Edward Bräuer, pulled him back. The police doctor diagnosed a pronounced neurosis, and he was taken to a mental home.'

The bridge, which is closed to traffic, is overwhelmed during the day by hordes of tourists and all manner of street artists; it is also a haven for pickpockets. The views on all sides are uninterruptedly beautiful, and the place becomes especially evocative on a winter's night when, in the dim light of lanterns, a freezing mist rises from the river, and isolated groups of pedestrians glide past and disappear into the gloom.

Another of the bridge's attractions are of course its **statues**, which turn the whole structure into a museum of Bohemian sculpture. On the first pier to the right immediately beyond the Tower of the Old Town Bridge (see p 104) stands the *Madonna and St Bernard* (1709) by **Matěj Jäckel**, a sculptor who introduced to Bohemia the dynamic high-flown style of the Italian artist Bernini. This style was used to far more expressive effect in the work of **Matthias Braun**, an Austrian-born sculptor who first came to Bohemia in 1710, invited by the Cistercians of Plasy to execute statues for the Charles Bridge; a copy of the second statue that he did here, representing *St Ivo* (1711), the patron saint of lawyers, can be seen on the left-hand side of the bridge, directly facing Jäckel's *Madonna*. The other outstanding Bohemian sculptor of this period was **Ferdinand Brokoff**, an artist noted for his realism and who carried out several works for the bridge, including the sculptural group of *Sts Barbara, Margaret and Elizabeth* that adorns the second pier on the left-hand side.

The first monument to be placed on the bridge was a gilded bronze crucifix, which was set up on the third pier to the right in 1657; the two stone figures were executed by Emmanuel Max in 1861, while the Hebrew inscription on the cross ('Holy Holy Holy is Our Lord'), dating from 1696, is said to have been paid for by a Jew as a fine for mocking this Christian symbol.

Between the sixth and seventh piers on the right you will pass a small cross marking the supposed spot where St John of Nepomuk was thrown into the Vltava in 1393; the bronze statue of the saint, with a gold-leaf halo, stands on the eighth pier to the right, and was executed by **Jan Brokoff** in the 1680s; the relief at the base of the statue depicts a now-weathered scene of St John's martyrdom; it is believed that touching it will bring good luck.

Towards its western end the bridge crosses the picturesque Kampa Island (see p 131), which is separated from the left bank by a narrow canal, and is sometimes referred to as the 'Venice of Prague'. Above the steps leading down to it, on the twelfth pier to the left, is a sculpture of *The Vision of St Luitgard* (1710), the first work that **Matthias Braun** made in Prague, and in many ways the most powerful and emotionally compelling on the bridge; tradition has it that the work was based on a design by Petr Brandl, and there is certainly something very painterly in its wildly agitated drapery. Two piers further along to the left is another sculptural masterpiece, a group by **Ferdinand Brokoff** featuring *Sts John of Matha, Felix de Valois, and Ivo*, with a Turk guarding a group of captured Christians (1714), the whole carved with Brokoff's characteristic realism (note, in particular, the face of the Turk); the work was commissioned as a gesture of thanks to the Trinitarian Order for having redeemed Christians from Turkish captivity. Directly opposite this group is Brokoff's *St Vitus* (1714), the only marble work on the bridge, the other stone sculptures all being sandstone.

The bridge ends picturesquely at a gate of 1410 flanked by two **towers**, the taller of which was built in 1466 at the behest of George of Poděbrady, and is closely similar to the tower of the Powder Gate (see p 87); the shorter tower, a survival of the Judith Bridge fortifications, dates back to 1166 but was remodelled in 1591. Once through the Little Quarter gate the royal processional route headed west along **Mostecká**, today a busy shopping street featuring a number of fine Renaissance and Baroque palaces, most notably, at No. 15, the **Kaunic Palace** (Kauniců palác), which was built in 1773–75 and has a façade richly decorated with stuccoes by Ignác František Platzer; it is now home to the Yugoslav Embassy.

Little Quarter Square

Mostecká leads into the sloping **Little Quarter Square** (Malostranské náměstí), which is divided in two by the massive Church of St Nicholas and adjoining buildings.

The square, surrounded today by buildings of largely 17C and 18C appearance, formed originally the nucleus of Prague Castle's outer bailey, and in the middle there once stood the Romanesque Rotunda of St Wenceslas. The site of a market and town hall for many centuries after the foundation of the Little Quarter in 1257, the square remains to this day the lively heart of this area, with an important tram junction at its lower, eastern end.

The eastern half of the square, known as the Lower Square, features on its eastern side (at No. 21) the former **Town Hall**, which was founded in the late 15C. Here, in March 1575, a group of Habsburg opponents comprising neo-Utraquists, Lutherans and members of the Union of Czech Brethren formulated the so-called Czech Confession, a plea for legal recognition of

Smiřický-Montág Palace, Malostranské náměstí

Evangelical trends. This meeting is recalled in a plaque on the building's façade, the present appearance of which is due to reconstruction work carried out in 1617–22. The elegant façade, divided by cornices into three main floors, is articulated by pilasters flanking paired windows crowned by broken pediments; the interior is now used for lectures, concerts and theatrical performances.

Dominating the northern side of the Lower Square is the imposing **Smiřický-Montág Palace** (No. 18), which dates back to 1606 but was rebuilt in late-Baroque style c 1763; the building is famous as the place where, on 22 May 1618, Albrecht Smiřický and an invited group of leaders of the anti-Habsburg opposition hatched the plot that was to lead on the following day to the 'Second Defenestration', the incident that sparked off the Thirty Years War. Adjacent to this, on the western side of the Lower Square, is the enormous and rather severe bulk of a former Jesuit college, which is attached to the northern side of the Church of St Nicholas, and was built between 1674 and 1691 on a site previously occupied by a group of 20 burghers' houses. In front of the east end of the church, and projecting out into the Lower Square, is the 18C **Grömling Palace**. In 1874 there was installed here one of Prague's larger and more popular cafés, the *Radetzky*, which was later supplanted by the equally successful *Malostranská*; this celebrated institution has recently reopened (see p 32), and is a convenient if rather noisy place to stop for refreshments.

Dům U zlatého lva: The Golden Lion House

Walking up from the southeastern corner of the Little Quarter Square to the square's upper, western half, you will skirt to your right the southern side of the Church of St Nicholas and to your left a group of tall, narrow-fronted houses of Renaissance and medieval origin, where you will find several long-established places for eating and drinking. No. 10, **The Golden Lion House** (Dům U zlatého lva), is the only building in the whole square to have completely retained its Renaissance appearance, and houses one of Prague's better-known restaurants, *U mecenáše* (see p 29), located on the site of a tavern dating back to the reign of the Emperor Rudolph II. A few doors down is the newly-opened *U tří zlatých hvězd* (see p 29), which serves good, moderately priced food in pleasant surroundings; further down still is the backpacker's favourite—*Jo's Bar* (No. 7), with loud music and a friendly atmosphere.

The upper and quieter half of the Little Quarter Square is known as the Upper or Italian Square, and has in its centre a **plague column** put up by Giovanni Alliprandi in 1715 in place of a fountain. Its western side is taken up entirely by the neo-Classical façade of the **Liechtenstein Palace** (1791), today used by the Charles University's Faculty of Music and as a venue for concerts and art exhibitions. Facing this is the west façade of the ****Church of St Nicholas** (sv. Mikuláš), one of the outstanding Baroque buildings of Central Europe, and rivalled only by Prague Castle as the dominant element in the city's skyline.

The present church occupies the site of a 13C three-aisled structure that was handed over to the Jesuits shortly after the Battle of the White Mountain in 1620. Later in the 17C the Jesuits built a college alongside it, and in 1673 laid the foundations of a new church, the construction of which was not begun until 1703, under the direction of Christoph Dientzenhofer. The church was roofed by 1705, but work was subsequently interrupted through lack of funds, and was only continued between 1709 and 1711, when the west façade was completed and the nave vaulted. Further financial difficulties led to the east end being closed by a provisional, illusionistically painted wooden screen until 1737, when work was resumed under the direction of Dientzenhofer's son, Kilian Ignaz, who built the chancel and domed crossing; the tower alongside the dome was added by Anselmo Lurago in 1755. The finished church, the largest Jesuit church in Bohemia if not in the whole of Central Europe, was to inspire some effusive prose by the French Catholic dramatist Paul Claudel in the early 20C. In the introduction to his religious drama, *The Satin Slippers* (1929), Claudel referred to the building as a 'sanctuary where everything is suffused by inner life and eloquence, where the whole structure is an act of grace which immediately draws us in, where everything is peace, joy, and not simply a smile, but an outburst of laughter ...'

Despite the protracted history of its construction, the church of St Nicholas has an impressive unity, and its undulating west façade, with its remarkably rich play of concave and convex surfaces, is a powerful preparation for the dynamic interior. The latter can be viewed in its entirety, and is open daily, with last visits beginning at 16.45. You will be charged a small admission fee unless you intend to pray (though how you prove this is unclear).

The interior of this single-aisled building is a truly astonishing array of pinks and pastel greens. The nave walls, with their undulating balconies and giant, obliquely set pilasters, exude an extraordinary sense of movement, and create a flowing line that culminates in the enormous oval of the crossing. The originality of the nave vaulting, with its intersecting ribs as in a Gothic building, is obscured by the vast ceiling painting by Johann Lukas Kracker representing *The Apotheosis of St Nicholas* (1760–61); the dome meanwhile is covered by *The Celebration of the Holy Trinity* (1752–53) by Franz Palko, who also did many of the wall-paintings in the chancel. The magnificent statuary was largely the work of Ignác Platzer the Elder, who was responsible for the statue of St Nicholas at the High Altar, the agitated saints along the nave, and the four overblown figures of the Church Fathers in the corners of the crossing. The remarkable pulpit (1765), a gilded Rococo confection in pink marble, is by Richard and Petr Prachner. Of the paintings, special mention should be made of the Chapel of St Barbara (first left), where there is an altarpiece of the Holy Rood (right) by Karel Škréta, and an altarpiece of St Barbara by Ludvík Kohl; a painting of St Michael by the Neapolitan painter Francesco Solimena is found in the Chapel of St Aloise (second left), while the Chapel of St Francis Xavier (third right) contains *The Death of St Francis* by Palko. In the summer months you can also climb the belfry (open 10.00–18.00), which affords fine views over Prague.

After leaving the church, head to the northern end of the Upper Square, turn right, and, just before entering the Lower Square once again, turn left into the narrow **Sněmovní**. Among the old palaces and houses on this street, which lies almost in the shadow of Prague Castle, is a large neo-Classical building at No. 4, whose political traditions reach back to the 19C when it served as a provincial Diet; since 1993, it has been used as the lower house of the **Czech parliament**. Equally impressive is the gabled and well-preserved Renaissance structure at No. 6 called **The Golden Swan House** (Dům U zlaté labutě), built by Ulrico Avostalis in 1589, which overlooks a treed square. At its upper end the street is continued in the once picturesquely shabby cul-de-sac with the exotic name of '**U zlaté studně**' (At the Golden Well); the recently restored house at No. 3 belonged to the turn-of-the-last-century artist Karel Klusáček, who painted on its façade a decoration featuring St Methodius. Adjoining the house, at No. 4, is one of Prague's most romantically situated hotels—*U zlaté studně* (see p 17)—with views from its terrace café onto fountains, flowerbeds and gardens rising up the hill to the Castle.

Albrecht of Wallenstein

One of the most colourful figures in Czech history, Albrecht of Wallenstein (known to the Germans as Albrecht von Waldstein, and to the Czechs as Albrecht z Valdštejna) was born in Prague on the afternoon of 14 September 1583, and was thus—according to the imperial astrologer Johannes Kepler—destined by his birth chart to be deceitful, avaricious, unloved and unloving. An opportunist of whom even Macchiavelli might have been ashamed, Wallenstein embarked on his life of dubious reputation after being expelled from his Lutheran school for the killing of a servant. Taking refuge in Italy, he married a wealthy widow and converted to Catholicism; the widow died soon afterwards, leaving him a considerable fortune, and his new-found Catholicism stood him in good stead while cultivating his friendship with the future Habsburg emperor Ferdinand II.

As a general in the imperial army, Wallenstein was able to prosper sensationally at a time when his home country was going through one of the darkest moments in its history: by appropriating the properties of the Protestant aristocrats defeated at the Battle of the White Mountain of 1620, he succeeded in amassing within five years over 50 Bohemian castles and villages. With his continuing military successes and entrepreneurial dealings, his titles and privileges multiplied, and by 1630 he had even earned the right to keep on his hat in the presence of the emperor. His increasing demands, combined with the growing resentment towards him on the part of the emperor's supporters, led him briefly to be deprived of his position as general; however, the occupation of Prague by the Saxons in 1631 forced Ferdinand to call once again on his services.

Then in 1634, amid rumours that he had ambitions to crown himself King of Bohemia, Wallenstein openly rebelled against Ferdinand—a gesture almost certainly undertaken for purely personal gain, but which nonetheless assured his future reputation as a great Czech hero. He, and several of his loyal officers, were murdered soon afterwards at the West Bohemian town of Cheb. His megalomaniac life and inevitably tragic end have been of understandable fascination to numerous writers, most notably Schiller, whose *Wallenstein* is one of the outstanding works of German Romantic drama.

The gardens of Malá Strana

Backtracking along the cobbled street, take the first turning to the left, which leads you into Wallenstein Square (Valdštejnské náměstí). This narrow square is named after the **Wallenstein Palace** on its eastern side, which was built in 1623–30 for the great Albrecht of Wallenstein, whose family seat it was to remain until 1945.

Wallenstein's suitably imposing palace in Prague—built by Giovanni Pieroni to designs supplied first by Andrea Spezza and then by Niccolo Sebregondi—was the earliest of the many grand palaces erected in this city in the 17C and 18C. Its interior, now home to the upper house of the **Czech parliament**, can be visited by guided tour (Sat, Sun 10.00–17.00) and features a splendid main hall with a stuccoed ceiling incorporating a fresco by Baccio del Bianco representing Wallenstein himself dressed as Mars and riding in a chariot; the work was executed in 1630, only four years before Wallenstein's ignominious murder. Architecturally the finest feature of the building is the *sala terrena* overlooking the palace's wonderful gardens, which can be reached either from the palace's main entrance or through the archway on Letenská (see below). A brief visit could be paid to the **Museum of Education** (Pedagogické muzeum) situated off the palace courtyard, which has a didactic display devoted to the life and work of the Protestant educational reformer, John Comenius (1592–1673). Open Tues–Sun 10.00–12.00, 13.00–16.30.

The *Wallenstein Palace Gardens** (Valdštejnská zahrada), laid out in the early 17C, have at their centre an avenue of bronze statues copied after works by Adriaen de Vries that were stolen from here by the Swedes in 1648 and have been standing since then outside the Swedish Royal Palace at Drottningholm. The most impressive structure, however, is the tall and magnificent loggia, or *sala terrena*, built by Giovanni Pieroni in 1623–27, and decorated inside with painted scenes by Baccio del Bianco of the Trojan Wars (1629–30), set in a stucco framework. Elsewhere in the gardens are fountains, an aviary, a weird 'stalactite wall', and a large well-stocked fishpond; the bronze of Hercules standing in the middle of the pond is an original by de Vries.

On summer weekends the gardens are used by artists for the display of their works, while the former **Royal Riding-School** (Valdštejnská jízdárna) overlooking the pond houses temporary exhibitions organised by the National Gallery (open Tues–Sun 10.00–17.00). The entrance is actually on the other side of the building, by the Malostranská metro station (see below).

Several other important palaces and gardens are found to the north of the Wallenstein Palace, beginning with the **Ledebour Palace** (Ledeburský palác), in the northwestern corner of Wallenstein Square. This late-Baroque palace, designed by Ignác Jan Palliardi in 1787, is remarkable above all for its wonderful gardens, which were laid out by Santini-Aichel in 1716 and rise steeply in terraces from a *sala terrena* up to a belvedere, the whole enlivened by fountains and a statue of Hercules. The gardens, restored thanks to help from the Prague Heritage Fund, today form part of a public park known as the *Gardens Below Prague Castle** (Zahrady pod Pražským Hradem) that also comprises the terraced gardens of two adjoining palaces to the north, on Valdštejnská. The first of these, at No. 14, is the early-18C **Pálffy Palace** (Pálffy palác), now a music academy that also houses one of the best and most atmospheric restaurants in Prague (see p 29), an absolute must-see, where you can enjoy your meal while admiring the views from the beautiful terrace. The Pálffy gardens themselves feature three terraces linked by a covered staircase and a loggia; on the middle one is a sundial bearing a Latin inscription and the date 1751. Next along is the **Kolowrat Palace** (palác Kolowrat), situated at No. 10. This was designed in 1784 by Palliardi, who was also responsible for laying out its gardens, which are perhaps the finest of them all, comprising a luxuriant Rococo complex of staircases, terraces, fountains, loggias, balustrades and pools. The last of the great palaces along Valdštejnská is the **Fürstenberg Palace** at No. 8, built in 1743–47 by an unknown architect clearly influenced by K.I. Dientzenhofer; it is now the Polish Embassy, and its attractive 18C gardens are closed to the public.

Return to Wallenstein Square and continue south along **Tomášská**, where, just before rejoining Malostranské náměstí (Little Quarter Square), you will pass on the left-hand side one of Prague's best-known beer-cellars, *U Schnellů* (see p 35); this long-established and recently revamped tourist bar and restaurant has décor dating back to 1787.

Turn left at the end of the street into **Letenská**, where you will find to your left the dazzlingly restored **Church of St Thomas** (sv. Tomáše), which was founded in 1285 for the Order of Augustinian Hermits. The medieval church, partially rebuilt in the 16C and 17C, was remodelled by K.I. Dientzenhofer in 1722–31. Its main façade, featuring a portal of 1617 and a sandstone statue of St Thomas by Hieronymus Kohl (1684), was given a dramatic Borromini-inspired appearance through the addition of massive, projecting forms intended both to strengthen the structure and to make the most of the restricted site.

To get inside the church, walk to the end of the short side street (Josefská) and enter through the Augustianian friary, which has a beautiful inner courtyard with trees and shrubs. The chancel of St Thomas's retains some of the medieval masonry and has ceiling paintings by Václav Reiner representing scenes from the lives of Sts Augustine and Thomas, and (on the dome) *The Four Continents*. In the first chapel on the right is a painting of *St Thomas* (1671) by Karel Škréta, by whom there are two further paintings in the chancel (an *Assumption* and a *Holy Trinity*, both of 1644). Paintings by Rubens of *St Augustine* and the *Martyrdom of St Thomas* were recently transferred from here to the Šternberg Palace and replaced by copies (see p 154).

The Augustinian hermits produced fine dark beer in the cellars of their friary from the mid-14C onwards, and their former brewery (entered at No. 8 Letenská) continues to function as an ale-house known as *U sv. Tomáše* (see p 35). This establishment is today a popular tourist attraction with prices to match; earlier this century, however, it was the place to which the rowdy literary club known as Syrinx transferred its allegiance after tiring of the now equally spoilt *U Fleků* in the New Town (see p 36).

Continuing to walk north along Letenská, you will skirt to your left the walls of the Wallenstein Palace Gardens (see above), before reaching the broad and busy Klárov, which marks the northeastern edge of the Little Quarter. Turning left here will bring you immediately to the Malostranská station, the most elegant in Prague; erected in 1978, it has a small forecourt with a café, fountains and statuary copied from 18C models, and a vestibule containing a copy of Matthias Braun's statue of *Hope* from the Baroque complex at Kuks in Eastern Bohemia.

Turning right at the end of Letenská will bring you into U lužického semináře, which was named after a seminary (at No. 13) built in 1726–28 for Lusatian students. To your right you will skirt the high whitewashed walls of the **Vojanovy Gardens** (Vojanovy sady), founded in the 17C, which today are much closer in appearance to a public park than the carefully manicured palace gardens in the district. At the next junction you could make a brief detour left to the parallel Cihelná, where at No. 2b, by the riverside, is the recently opened Prague Jewellery Collection (Pražský cabinet šperku) with a display of jewellery and luxury decorative items dating from the 17C onwards (open 10.00–18.00). Turning instead right into Míšeňská, you will find at Nos 1 and 12 two appealing corner houses designed respectively by K.I. Dientzenhofer and his brother Christoph. The latter house is occupied by the *U bílé kuželky* restaurant (see p 29), an unpretentious ground-floor establishment offering decent Czech cuisine.

Míšeňská opens out onto Dražického náměstí, a mere stone's throw from the Charles Bridge. The chief building of interest here is the **Three Ostriches' House** (U tří pštrosů), whose exterior has fragments of mural decorations of ostrich feathers, as well as a house-sign with ostriches, all dating back to 1606.

The building owes both its name and decoration to a merchant called Jan Fux, who rebuilt the house after 1597, and made a living partially by selling ostrich feathers, then a fashion novelty. The building was already functioning as a tavern in Fux's time, and was acquired early the following century by the Armenian coffee-salesman Deodatus Damajan (see p 102), who in 1714 opened here the first coffee-shop in the Little Quarter. Between 1972 and 1976, the place was restored and transformed into a luxury restaurant and tiny, exclusive hotel; returned recently to its pre-war owner, the place is now known principally as a hotel—*U tří pštrosů* (see p 17), with beamed ceilings, 17C paintings and other antique furnishings in the bedrooms.

The southern Little Quarter

After returning to Mostecká you should turn left immediately into **Lázeňská** to begin a tour of the southern half of the Little Quarter. On this short street were once situated the workshops of **Adriaen de Vries** and other foreign sculptors who came to Prague during the reign of Rudolph II. Later in the 17C the street came to have a hotel, known as **The House at the Baths** (dům U lázních; No. 6), which was to host until the early 19C some of the most distinguished visitors to Prague, including Peter the Great of Russia in 1698, the pioneering balloonist Jean-Pierre Blanchard in 1790–91 and, in 1833, the French writer Chateaubriand. The ground floor is now an arty café—the *Chimera*—but a better place to stop for coffee is *Cukrkávalimonáda* (literally: 'sugarcoffeelemonade'; see p 32) across the street at No. 7, an airy ground-floor room where you can peruse the foreign newspapers put out for guests or look out onto the beautifully serene Maltézské náměstí.

At the southern end of the street begins a small area originating in plots of land that in 1169 were given over by Vladislav II to the Order of the Maltese Knights (the Johannites). The church that formerly belonged to this order, **Our Lady under the Chain** (Panny Marie pod řetězem), dominates the area, standing at the junction of Lázeňská and the narrow, connected **Maltese Square** (Maltézské náměstí) and **Grand Priory Square** (Velkopřevorské náměstí). Its unusual name derives from the fact that the Knight's were responsible for guarding the nearby Judith (later Charles) Bridge. The original three-aisled Romanesque structure of the 12C, the oldest church in the Little Quarter, was pulled down in the middle of the 14C, and work was begun on a new building. The latter was abandoned by the end of the century, the only parts to be completed being the western vestibule and its two austere and fortress-like towers, which form such an incongruous presence in the middle of this intimate part of town. The former nave of the Romanesque church serves now as a forecourt to a Baroque church built largely by Carlo Lurago in 1640–60; within the latter is a high altar of the 1660s by Karel Škréta, representing the Virgin Mary and St John the Baptist coming to the assistance of the Knights of Malta during the Battle of Lepanto of 1571.

Facing the church, at the northeastern end of Maltézské náměstí, is a building dating back to 1531, and known as **The Painter's House** (Dům U malířů) after the painter Jiří Šic, who lived here in the late 16C, and whose name, when pronounced in English ('Shits'), was an unfortunate one in view of the place's later function: the building, remodelled c 1690 and restored in the 1930s, now houses Prague's most exclusive French restaurant—*U malířů* (see p 29), with fresh produce flown in daily from France, and an entirely French wine list.

A number of fine 17C and 18C palaces line the rest of the square, at the centre of which is a sculptural group by Ferdinand Brokoff featuring St John the Baptist, erected as a plague memorial in 1715. On the western side of the square, at No. 6, is the **Turba Palace** of 1767–68, a beautiful Rococo structure articulated with giant pilasters and serving today as the Japanese Embassy. Giant pilasters feature also on the façade of the large and freshly renovated **Nostitz Palace** (Nostický palác) at No. 1 (south side), today the Czech Ministry of Culture. It was built in 1660–70 by Francesco Caratti, who was later to perfect such an ordering of a façade in the Černín Palace on Loreto Square (see p 157).

Make your way back to Our Lady under the Chain, and turn right into Velkopřevorské náměstí, a quiet cobbled square shaded by trees. Immediately to your left is the main façade of the **Grand Prior's Palace**, which was rebuilt to a design by Giuseppe Bartolomeo Scotti in 1726–28, and has a fine portal with vase decorations from the workshop of Matthias Braun. The building formerly housed the Museum of Czech Musical Instruments, which was closed for good in 1990 following the theft of its priceless Stradivarius violins. The Maltese Knights reclaimed their building shortly thereafter, and are currently restoring it. So far they have reluctantly allowed the survival of the so-called **John Lennon Wall**, an improvised multi-coloured homage to the Beatle that was first daubed on the building's garden wall following his death in 1980, and that has now been redone by a new generation of Beatles' fans. Lennon has enjoyed a saint-like status among the predominantly atheist Czechs, who regarded him in the Communist era as the ultimate anti-authoritarian figure and constantly resisted police attempts to remove the graffiti. Later, when the disapproving Maltese Knights took over the building, the wall was saved yet again following the intervention of the French ambassador, a Beatles fanatic, who resides in the **Buquoy Palace** (Buquoyský palác; No. 2) across the square. Today, on the anniversary of Lennon's death (14 December), crowds of long-haired guitar players gather here and on the neighbouring Kampa Island to celebrate his life.

At the eastern end of the square, on the left-hand side, is the gabled **Grand Prior's Mill** (Velkopřevorský mlýn), a Renaissance structure complete with medieval waterwheels (closed in 1936), which is one of several mills built on the narrow branch of the Vltava called the Čertovka, or Devil's Stream. This stream, separating the Little Quarter from Kampa Island, was first referred to simply as 'The Ditch', and only acquired its present, more romantic name towards the end of the 19C, when the Straka Palace on the nearby Maltese Square (No. 14) came to be known as 'The Devil's House' after an eccentric woman owner.

Kampa Island

The bridge beside the Grand Prior's Mill leads over the Čertovka stream to the beautiful *Kampa Island, an area once taken up entirely by vineyards, gardens and fields, and that only acquired buildings from the late 16C onwards. Successive floods have changed the shape of the island over the centuries, and the narrator of Jiří Weil's novel *Life with a Star* (1964) even recalls frequent arguments with his mistress when she 'claimed that Kampa was a peninsula and I said it was an island'. Most of the houses on this so-called Venice of Prague are concentrated in the northern half of the island, on either side of the quiet and tree-lined Na Kampě, where, at No. 11, there is a bronze plaque and bust marking the house where the composer Bohuslav Martinů lived. At its northern end the street broadens out into a picturesque square from which steps lead up to the Charles Bridge; a pottery market was regularly held here up to 1936.

Kampa Island is host to several good places to eat and drink, including the superb *Kampa Park* (see p 28), Prague's best seafood restaurant with fantastic views of the Charles Bridge, and *Na kampě 15* (see p 35), a large and lively riverside pub, ideal for lunchtime snacks.

Walk south down Na Kampě, and its continuation—U sovových mlýnů—which cuts through a pleasant park. Just before it, on the left-hand side, is the excellent *Kampa Museum, set inside a converted 14C mill. The collections here were amassed over several decades by the Washington-based couple, Jan and Meda Mládek, and include a permanent display of works by František Kupka (whom Meda Mládek knew from her student days in Paris), Otto Gutfreund, Jiří Kolář, and others. At the time of writing the museum was unfortunately closed due to flood damage, but is set to reopen in 2004; in a particularly dramatic incident during the floods of 2002, a giant sculpture that stood in front of the museum was washed almost 45km downriver!

Continuing south through the park you will pass, on the right-hand side, the **Works Mill** (mlýn Huť), another of the old mills on the Čertovka. Inside it is the recently-opened *Tato café* (see p 35), a slightly tatty lounge inhabited by art students, where you can sip beer while watching the mill-wheel turn.

Leaving the island at its southernmost point, and turning right into Říční, you will soon pass on your right the **Church of St John at the Wash-House** (sv. Jana Na prádle), named in reference to the washerwomen who would rinse their linen on the banks of the Vltava. The church, which dates back to the 13C, is a structure of rustic simplicity, and contains inside fragments of late-14C wall-paintings. On the opposite side of the street, at No. 11, a plaque marks the turn-of-the-century building to which the brothers Josef and Karel Čapek moved after settling in Prague in 1907.

The Čapek brothers

The brothers Čapek were to stay in their Říční house until 1925, living, according to their friend Václav Štech, 'a simple life in an old-fashioned household, probably quite wealthy, but still very money-conscious.' An inseparable pair who kept their distance from the city's artistic community, they were described by another friend, František Langer, as 'invariably entering rooms together, sitting next to one another, and ordering a cup of coffee and a roll each'.

It was while living in this house that Karel wrote, in the early 1920s, the plays that were to establish his reputation as a dramatist, most notably his science-fiction work *RUR* (Rossum's Universal Robots) (1921) and his morality play *From the Life of the Insects* (1922), which he wrote in collaboration with his painter brother Josef. The Scottish poet and translator Edwin Muir befriended Karel at this time, and published a short memoir of him in his autobiography, *The Story and the Fable* (1940).

From the Church of St John at the Wash-House, head northwest along Všehrdova, which eventually joins the long and busy **Újezd**, where you will find, immediately to the right at No. 40, the **Michna Palace** (Michnův palác), a large complex dating back to the late 16C, and with a Baroque wing built by Francesco Caratti between 1640 and 1650. This wing, which overlooks Újezd, is covered both on its rear façade and inside with Italianate stucco decorations by Domenico Galli. The interior, now occupied by a private health clinic, was until recently the venue for a small but very evocative Sports Museum (Tyršovo muzeum tělesné výchovy). At the time of writing the museum had moved to the Lobkowicz Palace at Prague Castle (see p 150), but only temporarily, as the administrators are still tying to find a permanent home for the collection.

Walk north along Újezd into its northern continuation, **Karmelitská**, on which stands, on the left-hand side, the **Carmelite Church of Our Lady of Victory** (Panny Marie Vítězné). Built originally for the German Lutherans between 1611 and 1613, it came into the possession of the Carmelites in 1624, who subsequently had it rebuilt as a thanksgiving for the Habsburg victory at the Battle of the White Mountain. Though generally referred to as the first Baroque church in Prague, it would be better described as one of the many dreary European imitations of the Gesù in Rome, and has little of architectural interest. Its rather plain interior, however, is much visited on account of a tiny votive image of the Infant Christ displayed in a chapel on the right of the nave.

The Carmelite nuns have taken pains to exploit the full commercial potential of the image, setting up a religious souvenir shop behind the chancel, and regularly changing the outfits of this ecclesiastical Barbie doll for the benefit of tourists; you can see some of these outfits in the small upstairs museum (open 09.30–17.30), where there is also video show of the famed *Bambino*. Of greater artistic interest than the image itself is the gilded wooden altar on which it has been placed, a Rococo structure carved by Petr Prachner in 1776; elsewhere in the church are a number of dramatic canvases of saints by Petr Brandl.

The Bambino di Praga

The celebrated wax image of the Infant Christ lifting his arm in blessing is a Spanish work of the 16C, which for some reason—perhaps confusion between the Spanish and Italian languages—is popularly known by the Italian name *Bambino di Praga* ('Pražské Jezulátko'; 'Child of Prague'). Brought over from Spain in the mid-16C by María Manríquez de Lara, the Spanish wife of Vratislav of Pernštejn, it was later presented to her daughter Polyxena on the occasion of the latter's marriage to the High Chancellor Zdeněk Popel of Lobkowitz. The widowed Polyxena gave the work to the Carmelites in 1628, since when the statue, with its numerous changes of clothing, has acquired a growing mythical status, and inspired countless reproductions in dubious taste. The absurd and kitsch qualities of the *Bambino di Praga* have been wittily exploited by the writer Bohumil Hrabal, whose novel *I Served the King of England* (1989) includes a fantastical tale of a successful Bolivian plot to replace the work surreptitiously with a copy and take the original back to South America, where it was supposed to be so popular 'that millions of South American Indians wore replicas of it on chains around their necks and had a legend that Prague was the most beautiful city in the world and that the infant Jesus had gone to school there.'

Continuing north up Karmelitská, you will pass on your left, at No. 25, the **Vrtba Palace** (Vrtbovský palác), which František Kaňka remodelled c 1720 and endowed with some of the most beautiful if also most hidden gardens in Prague. The ***Vrtba Gardens** (Vrtbovská zahrada), reached by way of a passage running through the palace, today form a small and quiet park at the edge of a great sweep of verdant parkland covering Petřín Hill. After passing through a court-yard adorned with statues by Matthias Braun of Atlas and two female allegorical figures, you will come to a *sala terrena* decorated with painted mythological scenes by Václav Reiner. Ascend the balustraded double staircase, where mytho-logical figures alternate with Greek vases; from the highest of the gardens' ter-races there are wonderful views of Prague Castle and the Church of St Nicholas.

Further up Karmelitská, at No. 23, is a good little bar/café called *U Malého Glena*, named after its founder Glen Spicker, which serves cheap American-style food and has regular jazz and blues nights in the basement.

The approach to Prague Castle

Karmelitská will bring you back at its northern end to the Little Quarter Square (Malostranské náměstí), from where you begin the steep walk up to Prague Castle, passing through what is in many ways the most attractive part of the Little Quarter (see map, p 121). There are three main ways of climbing up to the castle from the square.

The Castle Steps

The shortest and steepest route, and the one offering the finest roof-top views, is the ascent up the Castle Steps (Zámecké schody). From the northwestern corner of the Lower Square turn right into Sněmovní, and then immediately left into Thunovská, off which stands at No. 14 the large **Thun Palace** (Thunovský palác), a building of 17C origin with a façade of 1716–27 by Antonio Giovanni Lurago; at this palace, now the seat of the British Embassy, Mozart and his wife Costanza stayed during their first visit to Prague in 1787.

Further west up Thunovská, on the right-hand side of the street, the Castle Steps begin. They pass to the left, at No. 25 Thunovská, the greyish-white **Palace of the Lords of Hradec**, which dates back to the late 16C and is crowned by a group of small Renaissance gables; this building, now connected to the Italian Embassy on Nerudova (see below), was from 1911 to 1928 the house of the artist Alfons Mucha, who is commemorated here by a plaque. The Castle Steps, which lead directly up to Hradčany Square, were built originally in the 15C on the site of a path of 13C origin. A number of small buildings grew up alongside them, and in the 16C and 17C artists and craftsmen used to sell their wares here (the wide stone ledges of some of the windows were once used for display).

The Royal Route

The tourist shops today are not to be found on the Castle Steps but are concentrated instead along *****Nerudova**, which is the main and most traditional approach to the castle, and the one that was favoured by the royal coronation processions. Nerudova begins at the upper western end of the Little Quarter Square, and is lined along its whole length with 16C–18C buildings, many of which have shop fronts displaying crafts products and souvenirs. The first building on the right (at No. 2) houses the once lively *U kocoura* (see p 35), a famous haunt of the city's pre-1989 underground musicians, writers and hangers-on; it is still a good place to drink Pilsner and Purkmistr beer. Further up the street, on the left-hand side at No. 5, is the **Morzin Palace** (Morzinský palác; now the Romanian Embassy), which was built by Santini-Aichel in 1713–14, and has magnificent sculptural decoration by Ferdinand Brokoff on its façade: its two portals are surmounted by statues of Day and Night, while in between these is a balcony supported by figures of Moors (a pun on the family's name), executed with Brokoff's customary realism.

The Italian Embassy, slightly higher up Nerudova on the opposite side of the street (at No. 20), occupies another splendid Baroque building by Santini-Aichel, the **Thun-Hohenstein Palace** (Thun-Hohenštejnský palác): raised between 1716 and c 1725, its portal was decorated c 1730 with two deeply and vigorously carved eagles by Brokoff's great rival, Matthias Braun. Santini-Aichel seems also to have been responsible for the portal of the adjoining **Church of Our Lady of Unceasing Succour at the Theatines** (Panny Marie ustavičné pomoci u kajetánů); the rest of the church, built in 1691–1717, has been attributed to Jean-Baptiste Mathey. Across the street is a small and pleasant tea-room—*U zeleného čaje* (see p 32), with views down the sloping Nerudova, and a fine selection of herbal, fruit and black teas.

At the top of the Nerudova, at No. 47 on the left-hand side, is the **House at the Two Suns** (Dům U dvou slunců), a building of Renaissance origin with attractive late 17C gables. Attached to its façade is a large memorial plaque recording that the poet and journalist after whom the street is named, Jan Neruda, lived in this house (between 1845 and 1857); the everyday life and pub culture of this part of Prague—now all but destroyed through tourism—provided Neruda with the subject matter of his delightful short-stories, *Tales from the Little Quarter* (1878). In the 1970s the ground-floor bar was a favourite haunt of the underground rock band Plastic People of the Universe, whose banning by the Communist authorities—an event recalled in Václav Havel's brilliant essay, *The Power of the Powerless*—led to the formation of Charter 77 and the rise of Czech 'dissidence'. To complete the journey up to the castle, you should turn sharp right at the end of Nerudova and walk up the street named Ke Hradu, which means 'Towards the Castle'. Turning instead to the left you enter Úvoz, which climbs up slowly towards the Strahov Monastery (see p 150) and Loreto Square (see p 156); the street is bordered to the right by another fine succession of 16C–18C houses, and to the left by a shaded balustrade commanding excellent views of the Petřín Gardens (see below).

South of Nerudova

Another way of climbing up to the castle from the Little Quarter Square is to follow the streets running parallel to Nerudova to the south, beginning with **Tržiště**, which starts at Karmelitská, by the side of the Vrtba Palace (see above). A short way up it, at No. 7, you could stop for a bite to eat at the *Gitanes* restaurant (see p 29), which offers traditional Balkan cuisine in a romantic, cottage-like setting.

By far the grandest building on this dark and quiet street is the **Schönborn Palace** (Schönbornský palác) at No. 15, which was raised in the mid-17C on a site previously occupied by five houses, and remodelled c 1715, probably by Santini-Aichel. Franz Kafka, while keeping a work-room in Golden Lane (see p 149), rented in this building from March 1917 the apartment of his dreams; unfortunately it was also here, on the night of 12–13 August, that he suffered the haemorrhage that would confirm his long-suspected tuberculosis. The palace is now the American Embassy, and its impressive gardens laid out in the late 17C—'The gardens!', exclaimed Kafka, 'When you enter the gateway of the palace you can hardly believe your eyes'—are not open to the public.

Tržiště veers to the right after the palace, and after tunnelling through a group of houses, joins up with Nerudova at a point directly in front of the Thun-Hohenstein Palace (see above). Alternatively, you could turn left at the Schönborn Palace on to Vlašská, or take the second turning to the left, and walk up the narrow street parallel to Vlašská—Břetislavova. The building at No. 2 **Břetislavova** is an early-18C structure known as **The House of the Baby Jesus** (Dům U Ježíška) and attributed to Santini-Aichel. However, those who visited the street in the past generally did not do so for architectural reasons.

Břetislavova

Until comparatively recently Břetislavova was known popularly as Corpses' Street, for it was along here that funeral processions would pass on their way to the now-demolished cemetery on St John's Hill. This was also one of the main brothel streets of Prague, and the poet Jaroslav Seifert recalled in his charming memoirs how as a schoolboy he timidly paid a visit to the street from his faraway home district of Žižkov, his interest in the place having been excited by the report of one of his friends. The street was deserted, and the disappointed Seifert was on the point of leaving when, outside a house to be identified with that of The Baby Jesus, he heard a soft knock on a window, and was tempted to peer inside. 'The curtains parted, and a girl stood by the window with a dark braid hanging over her shoulder...' Later he was

> to evoke the street in his elegiac poem, 'View from Charles Bridge': 'A few steps from the Royal Road was a dark corner,/where tousle-haired prostitutes appeared/to walkers in the evenings,/luring into their dead wombs/young inexperienced boys,/as I was then./Now all is silent there./And only television aerials haunt/the ridges of the roofs.'

Břetislavova leads into Jánský vršek, where, on turning right, you reach the upper end of Nerudova. Turning instead to the left you will come to Vlašská, at a point just below this street's most important building, the **Lobkowicz Palace** (Lobkovický palác) at No. 19 (now the German Embassy). Begun by Giovanni Alliprandi in 1703 and completed by Ignác Jan Palliardi in 1769, this palace took as its main inspiration Bernini's unrealised plan for the Louvre in Paris, and features an entrance hall leading to a large oval vestibule projecting out on to the palace's gardens. After 1793 these gardens were given an informal English look by Václav Skalník, who is best known for his landscaping of the spa at Mariánské Lázně (Marienbad). The newest addition to the gardens is a sculpture of a Trabant on legs by the controversial 'Situationist artist' David Černý. Entitled *Quo Vadis?*, it pays homage to the scores of East Germans who scaled the walls of the embassy building back in the heady days of 1989 to demand West German citizenship, the first in a series of events that culminated in the fall of the Berlin Wall. Unfortunately, the gardens are now closed to the public.

From the palace you can reach the upper end of Nerudova by walking due north along the narrow Šporkova, which curves around a picturesque group of houses before ending up at Jánský vršek (see above). Continuing instead to walk west along Vlašská, you will pass to your left the northern walls of the Lobkowicz Gardens and, to your right (at No. 34), a hospital and chapel founded in the early 17C by Prague's Italian community, which was centred in this area.

Petřín Hill

At the western end of Vlašská you enter the large area of beautiful parkland covering *Petřín Hill**, and can either turn right in the direction of the Strahov Monastery (see p 158), or else turn left and make your way to the top of the hill, which is crowned by trees. Peering up above the summit is the **Petřín Tower** (Petřínská rozhledna; open 10.00–21.30), a slightly decrepit imitation of Paris's Eiffel Tower, which was erected for the Jubilee Exhibition of 1891. It commands a remarkably extensive panorama of the city, with particularly fine views towards the castle. Immediately to the south of this is another building created for the Jubilee Exhibition, a crenellated neo-Gothic structure containing a hilarious **Mirror Maze** (Zrcadlové bludiště; open 10.00–21.30) as well as a large tableau with waxwork figures representing Czech students defending the Charles Bridge against the Swedes in 1648. The Mirror Maze is recalled in Josef Škvorecký's novel *The Cowards* as the place where the book's hero, Danny Smiřický, asks to be kissed by the girl he loves so that 'it would be like a thousand kisses all at once'.

Just to the south of this, also among trees, is the twin-towered **Church of St Lawrence** (sv. Vavřinec), a Romanesque structure remodelled in the 18C. Further south still is the upper station of a **funicular railway** (lanová dráha;

every 15 mins, daily 09.00–23.30); it descends down to the long Újezd Street at the bottom of the hill, passing through the **Petřín Gardens** (Petřínské sady), where there is a statue to the poet **Jan Neruda** and a restaurant—the *Nebozízek* (see p 29)—with excellent views of the city (get off at the half-way stop on the funicular line).

The Nerudas

This statue of Jan Neruda held a particular significance for the latter's great Latin-American namesake, the Nobel Prize-winning poet Pablo Neruda. The real name of this Chilean poet was Ricardo Eliecer Neftalí Reyes, but he changed his name at the very start of his career, for reasons that have both mystified and irritated Czech writers (including Josef Škvorecký). The Czech satirist Erwin Kisch, whom the Chilean had befriended in Madrid in the 1930s, decided one day to ask him why he had changed his name, but he simply replied: 'My dear Kisch, you who have discovered the mystery about Colonel Redl will never clarify the mystery surrounding my being called Neruda.' The answer was in fact quite simple, as he himself admitted in his autobiography, *I Confess to Have Lived*. His father, a train-driver, was not at all happy with the idea of his son becoming a poet, and so the young man searched for another name under which to publish his first collection of verse. 'I happened upon the name Neruda in a Czech magazine without having the slightest idea that it belonged to a Czech writer, worshipped by all his people, author of the most beautiful ballads and romances, and who was commemorated by a statue in the district of the Little Quarter in Prague. As soon as I arrived in Czechoslovakia, many years later, I placed a flower at the foot of his bearded statue.'

Still at the top of the hill, you could walk south from the funicular station to visit the **Štefánik Observatory** (Štefánikova hvězdárna; open Tues–Fri 14.00–19.00, 21.00–23.00, Sat, Sun 10.00–12.00, 14.00–19.00, 21.00–23.00), situated by a well-tended rose garden. The enthusiastic staff will show you around the modest display of astronomical equipment before allowing you gaze at the sun and planets through two giant telescopes on the uppermost floor.

The green and wooded slopes of the Petřín Hill are interrupted by the so-called **Hunger Wall** (Hladová zed'), which was erected by Charles IV in 1360–62 and marks the southeastern boundary of the Little Quarter; it derives its curious name from the fact that the poor of the city were employed in its construction, and were thus able to secure a livelihood. On the bosky slopes that stretch south of the wall into the district of Smíchov can be seen the charming if rather neglected wooden **Church of St Michael** (sv. Michal), an 18C structure brought here in 1929 from a remote Carpathian village near the Ukrainian town of Mukatchevo.

3 Prague Castle and the Hradčany

The Citadel

'A spell hangs in the air of this citadel', wrote Patrick Leigh Fermor in *A Time of Gifts* (1977), 'and I was under its thrall long before I could pronounce its name.' The enormous Prague Castle (Pražský hrad) rises above the Little Quarter like a town in its own right, its elegant Classical casing holding together a veritable architectural treasury from which project the fantastical Gothic spires of St Vitus's Cathedral. More than any other monument in the Czech Republic, the 'Hrad' has, over the centuries, come to symbolise the changing fortunes of the Czech nation. Its former inhabitants constitute an impressive list, ranging from pious martyrs and mad emperors, through enlightened despots and benign philosophers, to Nazi colonisers and elected dissidents; history literally seems to seep from every nook and cranny of the place. Unsurprisingly, the Castle tops all the tourist itineraries as the quintessential 'must-see'. It is impossible to avoid the crowds completely, but you can limit the damage by arriving early in the day. See as much as you can, or can bear, then head out to the Castle District (Hradčany), which offers respite in the form of lush gardens and quiet lanes, as well as being home to several important sites, all of which are described in this chapter.

- **Admission** You are free to walk through the castle grounds and its three courtyards, but you will need a ticket to enter any of the buildings. These can be purchased at the respective entrances, but a cheaper and more convenient option is to buy one of the special tickets (A, B or C) covering groups of buildings within the castle complex:

  Ticket A St Vitus's Cathedral (chancel, royal crypt, tower; entrance to the nave is free), Powder Tower, Basilica of St George, Old Royal Palace, Golden Lane
  Ticket B St Vitus's Cathedral (chancel, royal crypt, tower; entrance to the nave is free), Old Royal Palace, Golden Lane
  Ticket C Golden Lane

  Special tickets are available from the main information centre in the third courtyard, or from the vestibule of the cathedral. Choosing which ticket to buy depends on how much time you have to spare. To see all the sites on ticket A, for instance, would require at least half a day, while Golden Lane (ticket C) could be visited in less than an hour. The information centre has audio-guides, maps and an ATM; you can also book guided tours here.

  - Grounds open daily April–Oct 05.00–24.00; Nov–March 05.00–23.00
  - Gardens open daily April–Oct 10.00–18.00; Nov–March closed
  - Buildings open daily April–Oct 09.00–17.00; Nov–March 09.00–16.00

  There are also several other important sites within the castle complex that are run by different institutions and therefore not covered by the above tickets. These sites include the Prague Castle Gallery (second courtyard), Convent of St George (náměstí U sv. Jiří), Toy Museum (Jiřská), Historical Museum (Lobkowicz Palace), Sports Museum (Lobkowicz Palace) and Royal Riding School (U Prašného mostu). Tickets for these buildings can be bought at the respective entrances; admission times vary.

Rather confusingly, the 'Ticket Office' in the Chapel of the Holy Rood (second courtyard) is in fact only a box office selling tickets for concerts and other events, but not to any of the buildings within the castle complex.

The complex history of Prague's citadel goes back to around AD 870 when Prince Bořivoj, founder of the Přemyslid dynasty and first prince of Bohemia, erected on top of a hill a modest but strategically situated fortified settlement. This became the seat of the Přemyslid princes, later kings, replacing the previous one at Levý Hradec, further north along the Vltava. In the early 10C the Church of St George and the Rotunda of St Vitus were founded here, and in 973, when the citadel became also the seat of the Prague bishopric, Bohemia's oldest convent was established alongside St George's. A devastating fire in the early 11C led Prince Břetislav I to replace the former earthen ramparts of the citadel with stone ones in 1041, but 26 years later the Bohemian princes were temporarily to abandon the citadel in favour of Vyšehrad, where they were to remain until 1139. In preparation for the return here of the Přemyslids, Soběslav I constructed a new palace and rebuilt the fortifications, the line of which is largely preserved in the citadel of today. The importance of the citadel was to reach its zenith in the 14C, during the reign of Charles IV, when the place was transformed into an imperial residence and work was begun on the great Gothic cathedral of St Vitus. Later in the century, though the citadel was to remain the seat of Bohemia's government, its role as a residence of the country's rulers was to be greatly diminished as a result of Wenceslas IV's decision to move to the Royal Court in the Old Town. King Vladislav the Jagiellon turned the place once more into a royal residence in 1484, and brought Benedikt Ried to Prague to rebuild and extend the castle's palace and fortifications; however, later in his reign, he and his court were to be based mainly in Budapest.

Bohemia's first Habsburg rulers, beginning with Ferdinand I, renewed the building activity in the citadel, and in the course of the 16C, the place was to become an impressive Renaissance complex, with pioneering Italianate structures such as the Summer Palace (Belvedere), and the Ball-Game Court. With Rudolph I, and the international group of scientific and artistic luminaries that he gathered around him, the castle was once again, if only briefly, the seat of one of Europe's most brilliant courts. His successor, Matthias, vaunted the glories of the Habsburgs through the commissioning in 1614 of the imposing triumphal arch known today as the Matthias Gateway. Yet it was only four years later that the Habsburgs were to suffer here a profound humiliation when two of their councillors were ejected from one of the palace windows. Following this incident, which sparked off the Thirty Years War, the rebelling Czech Estates made the castle the seat of their government, though they were only to remain here for two years, their cause being momentously defeated at the Battle of the White Mountain in 1620. Reduced subsequently to the status of secondary residence the castle declined, and little important work was to be carried out here until the reign of Maria Theresa, who initiated a major rebuilding campaign that gave the complex the late-Baroque and neo-Classical framework that it has largely kept to this day.

The last important building campaign in the castle took place after 1918, when Tomáš Masaryk turned the complex into the presidential seat of the newly created Republic of Czechoslovakia. St Vitus's Cathedral was finally brought to completion, and the lively and idiosyncratic architect Jože Plečnik was entrusted with the relaying of gardens and the remodelling of courtyards and interiors. Plečnik's additions are bright and cheerful, but in the 20C the castle has acquired sinister connotations, thanks partially to the popular identification of the place with the novel of this name by Franz Kafka, who indeed worked here after 1916 in a house rented by his sister on Golden Lane. Kafka's vision of faceless tyranny and monstrous bureaucracy seems at any rate to have been prophetic of the years when the castle served as the seat of Czechoslovakia's Communist rulers.

The whole complex was given a more human image during the presidency of Václav Havel, who on occasion could be seen riding around here on his scooter. The once-drab costumes of the castle's guards were replaced by a colourful garb designed by a friend of Havel's whose previous most important job had been as costume designer for Miloš Forman's film *Amadeus*. More importantly, areas of the complex once rigorously closed and guarded by machine-gun-carrying soldiers have now been opened up to the public.

There is so much to see in the castle that the better part of a day is required to begin to do justice to the complex. To conserve their energy, many people prefer to reach the castle by public transport and save the beautiful walks through the Little Quarter for the afternoon descent. The easiest access by public transport is to take the underground to the Malostranská station, and from there catch a No. 22 tram to the junction of Mariánské hradby and U Prašného mostu, where you are left with a five-minute walk, arriving eventually in the citadel's second courtyard. If you decide to walk all the way up the hill to the castle, the quickest ascent is up the **Old Castle Steps** (Staré zámecké schody), which begin the climb at a point just to the north of the Malostranská station, and enter the citadel at its narrow eastern end. Those travelling by taxi should ask to be dropped off on Hradčany Square (Hradčanské náměstí), by the main gates to the castle.

First and Second Courtyards

Whatever route or means you choose to reach the castle, a tour of the place is best begun at its western end, which faces Hradčany Square. Railings and a gate flanked by copies of two overblown sculptural groups of *Battling Giants* by Ignác Platzer (1786) mark the entrance to the **First Courtyard**, which is guarded by soldiers who perform an hourly **Changing of the Guard** ceremony, best seen at midday, when it is enlivened with a fanfare and parade.

On the other side of the courtyard to the gate is the **Matthias Gateway** (Matyášova brána), a large Roman-style triumphal arch inspired, if not actually designed, by the Mannerist architect Vicenzo Scamozzi and executed by Giovanni Maria Philippi in 1614. Originally a freestanding structure rising directly above the ramparts of the citadel, it was later incorporated into the palace's monumental west façade, which was built to designs by the court architect Niccolo Pacassi in 1763–71. Further modifications to the courtyard were made in 1920–22 by Jože Plečnik, who designed the two 25m-high flagpoles (tapering structures made out of pine trees taken, symbolically, from the Czechoslovak frontier), pierced the main block with openings on either side of the Matthias

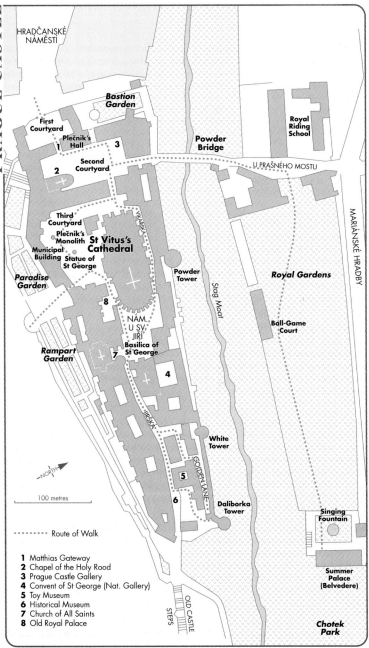

PRAGUE CASTLE

HRADČANSKÉ NÁMĚSTÍ

Bastion Garden

First Courtyard

Plečnik's Hall

Second Courtyard

Powder Bridge

Royal Riding School

U PRAŠNÉHO MOSTU

Third Courtyard

Plečnik's Monolith

St Vitus's Cathedral

Municipal Building

Statue of St George

Paradise Garden

Powder Tower

Stag Moat

Royal Gardens

MARIÁNSKÉ HRADBY

Ball-Game Court

NÁM. U SV. JIŘÍ

Rampart Garden

Basilica of St George

VIKÁŘSKÁ

JIŘSKÁ

White Tower

GOLDEN LANE

Daliborka Tower

NORTH

100 metres

Singing Fountain

Summer Palace (Belvedere)

OLD CASTLE STEPS

Chotek Park

········· Route of Walk

1 Matthias Gateway
2 Chapel of the Holy Rood
3 Prague Castle Gallery
4 Convent of St George (Nat. Gallery)
5 Toy Museum
6 Historical Museum
7 Church of All Saints
8 Old Royal Palace

Gateway, and ingeniously planned to reduce the importance of the latter—a symbol of Habsburg dominance—by laying across the courtyard two paths of darker coloured paving stones that direct the eye to the new side entrances. Inside the gateway, a staircase climbs up to the presidential reception rooms, while to the left is a recently installed glass opening affording a view of Plečnik's greatest work for the castle—an enormous hall built in 1927–31 and featuring a ceiling of copper panels and walls articulated by three superimposed rows of Ionic columns.

To enter the castle's Second Courtyard you can either go through the Matthias Gateway or the arch just to the left of the First Courtyard; adjacent to the latter, at the northern end of the castle's west façade, is a small **Bastion Garden** (Zahrada na Baště) laid out by Plečnik in 1927, and arranged on two levels that are joined by an ingenious circular stairway. The *Café Poet* inside the garden serves breakfasts and lunches, and is a convenient place to stop before proceeding to the castle proper.

The **Second Courtyard**, dating back to the late 16C, and given its present unified appearance in the late 18C, is centred around a Baroque fountain adorned with statues by Hieronymus Kohl (1686). The southern side of the courtyard comprises the western end of a long edifice known as the **Municipal Building**, which extends all the way up to the Old Palace in the Third Courtyard; its monotonous, uniform façade shields a series of rooms dating back to 1534 and currently used as presidential offices. Attached to the southeastern corner of the Second Courtyard is the **Chapel of the Holy Rood** (kaple sv. Kříže), which was built in 1756–63 by Anselmo Lurago after a plan by Pacassi, and remodelled in 1852–56. Now partly transformed into a box office and shop, it previously housed for many years the greater part of the treasury of St Vitus's Cathedral.

The main rooms on the northern side of the Second Courtyard comprise the **Spanish Hall** (Španělský sál) and the **Rudolph Gallery** (Rudolfova galerie), two mirrored and richly stuccoed halls dating back to the late 16C but remodelled in a neo-Baroque style in 1866 for the coronation of Emperor Franz Josef I, who never showed up! Generally closed to the public, except for the occasional concert, the rooms are used today mainly for governmental meetings and receptions. The Rudolph Gallery originally housed the extraordinary art collection belonging to Rudolph II, the sorry remnants of which can once again be seen in the ground-floor rooms below, which were formerly the imperial stables: these rooms, comprising what is now the Prague Castle Gallery, were closed for many years after a couple of visitors brazenly walked off with one of the paintings.

Rudolph II ranked with his cousin Philip II of Spain as one of the greatest of the Habsburg collectors, but many of his pictures were transferred after his death to Vienna, and others were seized by the Swedes in 1648. In the mid-17C Ferdinand III built up a new collection at Prague chiefly made up of works acquired from the collection of the Duke of Buckingham, which was auctioned at Antwerp in 1648–49. The new gallery remained intact until 1721, when Charles IV began removing many of the better works to Vienna; later in the century Maria Theresa sold off many more of the paintings, as did her son Joseph II in 1782. The dispersal of the collection continued throughout the 19C, and by the end of the First World War it was thought that all the paintings had gone from Prague. Investigations carried out in 1962–64 revealed that in fact much had remained in the city, and in 1965 the surviving works were brought together to form the Prague Castle Gallery.

The **Prague Castle Gallery** (Obrazárna Pražského hradu) occupies a series of newly modernised rooms, but the works on show are largely minor ones, doing scant justice to the magnificence of the original collection. Works by artists of Rudolph's time include paintings by Bartolomaeus Spranger, Hans von Aachen and Cornelisz von Harlem. There are works by the Bohemian artists Jan Kupecký and Petr Brandl, the latter's *A Mismatched Couple at the Notary* (1700) showing a young man and an elderly woman about to be married, as well as a painting by Rubens of the *Assembly of the Gods at Olympus*, executed probably in Mantua in 1602; his *Annunciation* (c 1610) is currently on loan. The bulk of the collection is of the Italian 16C and 17C, including a *Flagellation* and an *Adoration of the Shepherds* by Tintoretto, a *Young Woman at her Toilet* by Titian (a version of a painting in the Louvre), *St Catherine of Alexandria and an Angel* and *Christ Washing the Feet of His Disciples* by Veronese, and a peculiarly erotic *St Sebastian* by Saraceni, with a single arrow placed directly in the groin; among the other Italian paintings are works by Bernardo Monsu, Viviano and Niccolò Codazzi, Orazio Gentileschi, and Leandro, Jacopo, Francesco and Gerolamo Bassano. Open daily April–Oct 09.00–17.00; Nov–March 09.00–16.00.

Third Courtyard ~ the Cathedral of St Vitus

Entering the third and principal castle courtyard, you find yourself directly facing the west front of ****St Vitus's Cathedral**, one of the finest and most richly endowed in Central Europe.

The Cathedral has its origins in a rotunda founded by St Wenceslas c 925, and transformed in 973 into the cathedral church of the Prague bishops; in 1060 this was replaced by a three-aisled Romanesque basilica. On the occasion of Prague's elevation from bishopric to archbishopric in 1344, Charles IV ordered the construction of the present Gothic building, for which he summoned from the papal court at Avignon the architect Matthew of Arras. Matthew had laid the foundations of the building and completed its east end up to the triforium level by the time of his death in 1352. In search of an architect to complete Matthew's work, Charles IV turned this time to Germany, and found there **Petr Parléř**, who had been born c 1330 to a family of Cologne builders and whose father had been responsible for the great town church at Schwäbisch-Gmünd. From 1353 up to his own death in 1399 Parléř was to be engaged on the building, completing the east end, doubling the St Wenceslas chapel in the southwestern corner of the ambulatory, constructing the south portal and its adjoining open staircase, and beginning the nave; his work was to be continued by his sons Václav and Jan, who began work on the south tower. When the Hussites occupied the castle in 1421 the cathedral was greatly damaged and many of its furnishings destroyed; building activity was subsequently suspended for many years, the completed east end being closed off by a temporary wall.

Work on the cathedral was only resumed towards the end of the 15C, during the reign of the Polish king Vladislav the Jagiellon: the strange Royal

Oratory was put up on the south side of the ambulatory in the 1480s, the upper walls of the Wenceslas Chapel were painted in 1504, and the foundations of the north tower were laid in 1509–11. At the same time Vladislav the Jagiellon's principal architect, the great **Benedikt Ried**, formulated grandiose plans for the completion of the nave but, sadly, lack of funds led to their having to be abandoned in 1511. The main additions to the cathedral later in the century were the work of **Bonifác Wohlmut**, who was responsible in the 1560s for the Renaissance organ loft in the north transept and for crowning the Gothic south tower with a Renaissance gallery and bulbous domes (the top part of the tower was later destroyed by fire and rebuilt by Niccolo Pacassi after 1770). A new attempt to complete the nave was made by Giovanni Domenico Orsi in 1675, but this too was thwarted, and it was not until after the formation in 1861 of the 'Union for the Completion of the Cathedral' that work was begun in earnest to try to finish the building. This new campaign was begun by Josef Kranner, and taken over by Josef Mocker—Czechoslovakia's answer to Viollet-le-Duc—who was responsible for the 'restoration' and pseudo-Gothic remodelling of many of Prague's other medieval monuments, such as the Powder Gate. The last architect to work on the cathedral was Kamil Hilbert, who finally completed the fabric of the building in 1929.

Exterior The most recent and dullest part of the cathedral is the twin-towered west façade, which features a large rosette window with stained-glass by František Kysela and three portals with tympana containing carved reliefs executed between 1948 and 1952 to designs by, among others, Karel Dvořák. The high point of the exterior is undoubtedly the **south façade**—the work of Petr Parléř, who wanted to give particular emphasis to the side of the building that both housed St Wenceslas's tomb and faced the city. This façade is dominated by its 96m-high **tower**, the tapering Gothic part of which was begun by Parléř's sons in the early 15C and has a main window protected by a wonderfully intricate gilded Renaissance grille; the arcaded gallery above this is a mid-16C addition by Bonifác Wohlmut, while the crowning steeple was designed by Palassi in 1770.

Immediately to the right of the tower are the three arches of Petr Parléř's South Porch or **Golden Portal**, which is decorated on the outside with a much-restored mosaic of the *Last Judgement* executed in the late 14C by Venetian artists; in the spandrels of the central arch are the work's donors, Charles IV and his wife Eliška Pomořanská. One of Petr Parléř's main contributions to the cathedral was his inventive vaulting, as can be seen inside the porch, where a skeletal system of ribs is spread out like a fan. Above the porch, to the right, is a further example of Parléř's structural daring—a complex, openwork staircase that was to be imitated in the cathedrals at Ulm and Strasbourg. Sadly, you can no longer enter the cathedral through the south porch to see how Parléř creates an ingenious progression from three arches to a double doorway, and, finally, to a single portal.

Interior Enter the cathedral through the western vestibule and proceed directly to the south transept, from where one of the best views of the interior can be had. The plan and proportions of the building clearly reflect the work of a French architect, and indeed the arrangement of the chancel, with its radiating chapels, seems to have been inspired by that of Narbonne Cathedral, which was completed early in the 14C by Jean Deschamps. Petr Parléř provided the chancel with

ST VITUS'S CATHEDRAL

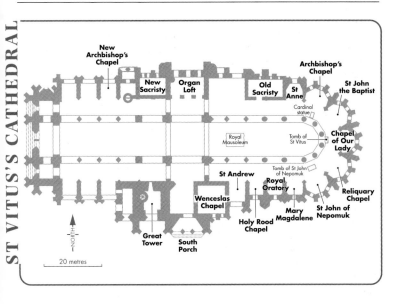

its elegant vaulting system of parallel diagonal ribs, and also began the triforium, which runs round the whole building and has inside it a celebrated series of **portrait heads** representing all those involved in the building of the cathedral, including Parléř himself and members of Charles IV's family. Twenty-one of these busts—which are so high up that they can scarcely be seen—were executed by members of Parléř's workshop, but the rest (mainly in the nave) are modern works portraying recent figures such as the sculptors Bohumil Kafka and Jan Štursa. The whole west end of the nave is a lifeless imitation of the east end, and bears little relation to the ambitious structure that Benedikt Ried would have created.

The finest of the modern contributions to the building are the **stained-glass windows**, executed mainly by František Kysela, Karel Svolinský and Max Švabinský, the latter's largest work here being the *Last Judgement* window in the south transept.

Attached to the north wall of the north transept is Bonifác Wohlmut's **Organ Loft** (1557–61), which curiously combines an harmonious Renaissance front taken from the pages of Serlio with Gothic vaulting inside. The finest of the chapels in the nave is the third on the left-hand side, the **New Archbishop's Chapel**, which has been the burial place of Prague's archbishops since 1909, and also houses the tomb of the art-historian bishop Antonín Podlaha, whose research played an important part in the last phase of the cathedral's construction. The chapel is adorned with a vivid stained-glass window by Alfons Mucha of the *Lives of Sts Cyril and Methodius*. Nearby, in the north aisle, is a wooden altar with a powerful sculpture of the *Crucifixion* (1899) by František Bílek.

Chancel You will need a ticket to enter the east end of the church. Begin your tour of the ambulatory from its northwestern end, by the **Old Sacristy** (closed), the vaulting of which (begun in 1356) shows Petr Parléř at his most daring, featuring a dramatically suspended boss supported by four skeletal ribs. To the north of it is **St Anne's Chapel**, displaying on its altar a silver reliquary of 1266, decorated with enamels and precious stones. In the ambulatory passage in front of this chapel is Myslbek's over-life-size bronze statue of the kneeling Cardinal Bedřich Schwarzenberg (1891–95), the most important of the 19C sculptures in the cathedral.

The five radiating chapels of the apse begin with the **Archbishops' Chapel**, featuring the plain brown marble tomb of Vratislav of Pernštejn, a work of the 16C by Hans Vredeman de Vries. Tombs from the Parléř workshop (1370s) of prominent members of the Přemyslid family are to be found in the next three chapels: the tombs of Princes Břetislav II (d. 1100) and Bořivoj II (d. 1124) are in the **Chapel of St John the Baptist**, where there can also be seen the so-called Jerusalem candelabrum, a fine example of Rhenish craftsmanship of the early 12C; the tombs of Princes Břetislav I (d. 1055) and Spytihněv II (d. 1061) are in the **Chapel of Our Lady** (the chapel where work on the cathedral was probably begun in 1344); and those of Kings Přemysl I (d. 1230) and Přemysl Otakar II (d. 1278) are in the **Reliquary (Saxon) Chapel**. Behind the High Altar, and directly in front of the Chapel of Our Lady, stands the **tomb of St Vitus**, with a statue of the saint by Josef Max of 1840.

Next comes the **Chapel of St John of Nepomuk**, which contains the marble tomb of Jan Očko of Vlašim, a work of 1370 from the Parléř workshop; fragments of late-14C wall-paintings can be seen here, as they can in the following **Chapel of Mary Magdalene**, containing the wall tombs of the cathedral's two main architects, Matthew of Arras and Petr Parléř. The **tomb of St John of Nepomuk** stands in the ambulatory passage opposite the first of these two chapels, and is unquestionably the finest of the Baroque furnishings in the cathedral: an elaborate silver structure under a canopy hung with draperies supported by angels, the tomb was made in Vienna between 1733 and 1736 to the designs of the great Johann Bernard Fischer von Erlach.

One of the more remarkable additions to the ambulatory is the subsequent **Royal Oratory**—a balcony decorated with characteristic late-Gothic fantasy and naturalism, the architectural members imitating the branches of a tree; this highly entertaining work, dating back to the early years of Vladislav the Jagiellon's reign, is sometimes attributed to the Frankfurt sculptor Hans Spiess. Fragments of 14C murals can be seen in the **Chapel of the Holy Rood**, which is followed by the more interesting **Chapel of St Andrew**, containing the tombstone (to the left, under the window) of Jaroslav von Martinic (d. 1649), one of the two Habsburg councillors thrown out of the Old Royal Palace window in 1618 (see below).

The ambulatory comes to an end at the Cathedral's chief attraction: the **Wenceslas Chapel** (Svatováclavská kaple), which Parléř enlarged by pushing out its southern and western walls, the latter at the expense of the transept. Visitors are no longer allowed inside the chapel, and have to content themselves with the views from the railings. The chapel, containing the much-restored 14C tomb of St Wenceslas (d. 929 or 935), has a door of 1370 incorporating a Romanesque lion's-head knocker to which Wenceslas is said to have clung when he was attacked and murdered by his brother Boleslav. The interior, reflecting perhaps Charles IV's love of jewellery, is studded on its lower level with more than a thousand semi-precious stones, one of which was later thought to resemble the head of Napoleon (the French poet Apollinaire, on being shown this particular agate in 1902, was shocked to recognise his own features in the stone, and began fearing for his sanity).

On this same level is a series of paintings of the Passion by an anonymous Czech artist of 1372 (identified variously as Master Theodoric and Master Oswald). The story of St Wenceslas is portrayed above these, in elaborately detailed works of 1504 generally attributed to the Master of the Litoměřice Altarpiece; the room is further enhanced by Parléř's splendid ceiling, comprising parallel diagonal ribs springing from eight corbels to form a star-shaped dome.

The Bohemian Crown Jewels (shown to the public only on special occasions) are kept in a room above the chapel, and constitute the main survival of the extraordinary **treasury** founded by Charles IV. One of the most important cathedral treasuries in Europe, this contained numerous objects that had been brought by Charles to Prague from the court of France, and many others that were given to him as gifts by the leading dignitaries of his time. Others still were commissioned from his own jewellers and goldsmiths, including the dazzling Royal Crown of Bohemia, which was made in 1346 out of pure gold, 91 precious stones and 20 pearls; a copy of this work can be seen today in the Historical Museum installed in the Lobkowicz Palace (see below).

In the middle of the long east end of the cathedral stands the **Royal Mausoleum**, a large memorial in white marble, executed in 1571–89 by the Netherlandish sculptor Alexander Collin, and surrounded by a Renaissance grille by Jörg Schmidthammer: on its upper slab are reliefs of the Emperor Ferdinand I, his consort Anna the Jagiellon, and his son Maximilan II, while on the sides are shown Charles IV and his four consorts, and the kings Wenceslas IV, Ladislav Pohrobek and George of Poděbrady. The actual tombs of these monarchs, as well as those of Rudolph II and members of the Přemyslids, can be seen in the **Royal Crypt**, the entrance to which is in the Chapel of the Holy Rood; within the crypt are also displayed the excavated remains of the cathedral's foundations, including masonry from the 10C and 11C. Behind the mausoleum is the uninspired High Altar, a neo-Gothic work of 1868–73, designed by Josef Kranner and later altered by Josef Mocker. If you're feeling fit, you can make the arduous ascent up the cathedral's Great Tower for a magnificent view over the city and its environs; the entrance to the tower is in the south aisle.

You leave the cathedral through its western door, where you should turn right, touring the rest of the castle complex in a clockwise direction. Skirting the northern side of the cathedral is the narrow Vikářská, where at No. 2 is the former Deanery, remodelled after 1705 by Santini-Aichel. Also on this street was a famous beer-cellar in which the 19C writer Svatopluk Čech set his very popular tale about Mr Brouček—a man who, under the influence of beer, goes on a series of imaginative adventures, including to the moon and back to the 15C.

A nearby alley leads from the street to the castle's northern bastions, which were renewed by Benedikt Ried in 1485 and include the round tower known as the **Powder Tower** (Mihulka). The two floors of this building contain a rather tedious exhibition on Renaissance life at the castle, the highpoint of which is an elaborately detailed bronze bust of Rudolph II by Adriaen de Vries; the exhibits are labelled only in Czech.

Vikářská leads to **George's Square** (náměstí U sv. Jiří), which faces the apse of the cathedral and is named after the former Basilica of St George and its adjoining convent. The ***Convent of St George** (Klášter sv. Jiří), in the northeastern corner of the square, was founded in 937 by Prince Boleslav II and his sister Princess Mlada, who became its first abbess; rebuilt several times—including, most recently, between 1657 and 1680—it was turned into a barracks after its dissolution in 1782 and then converted in 1962–72 into a branch of the **National Gallery** containing Czech art from the medieval to Baroque periods. Since the recent reshuffle at the National Gallery, however, the medieval collections have been moved to the Convent of St Agnes (see p 117); what remains is Czech art from the 16C to 18C, as well as a few works from the famed Rudolph collection (most of which are displayed in the Prague Castle Gallery—see above). The plain white rooms arranged around the convent's simple cloister provide a perfect setting for the paintings and sculptures. Open Tues–Sun 10.00–18.00.

Baroque art at the Convent of St George

The collections of Mannerist and Baroque art begin on the first floor with works by artists of the Rudolph Circle, including an outstanding painting by Bartolomaeus Spranger of the *Risen Christ* (c 1590), which was intended for the tomb of the artist's father-in-law, the Prague goldsmith Nicholas Müller (who appears, together with other members of his family, at the bottom of the work). The 17C collections feature an especially large number of paintings by Karel Škréta, of which the most striking are the portraits, in particular of the French painter *Nicolas Poussin* (whom Škréta met in Rome in 1634–35), and an informal group portrait of the gem-carver *Dionysio Miseroni and his Family* (1653).

Among the later paintings of the 17C are the very Rubenesque *Liberation of St Andromeda* (1695) by Michael Willmann, and a number of rapid oil sketches by Jan Liška. Baroque sculpture is represented most notably by Johann Georg Bendl's *St Nicholas* of c 1670; several works by Ferdinand Brokoff, in particular two Moors of 1718–19 from the gates of the Mansion at Kounice, and a statue of *St Ludmilla* (c 1730); and Matthias Braun's hysterically posed *St Jude Thaddeus* (1712), originally forming part of an altarpiece from the now-demolished Church of Our Lady in the Old Town, and his statue of *Jupiter* (c 1715). On loan from the Carmelite Church of Our Lady of Victory in the Little Quarter (see p 132) is a painting of the *Dream of the Prophet Elijah* (1724) by Petr Brandl, one of the most successful and prolific Bohemian artists of the early 18C: in addition to this and numerous other religious works by him, the gallery has an extensive collection of his portraits, including two self-portraits dating from 1697 and 1725.

A more remarkable portraitist than Bendl was Jan Kupecký, who is represented here by two of his greatest works, a seated portrait of the ostentatiously dressed miniaturist Karl Bruni and a portrait of *The Artist with his Wife*: the latter, a work of uncompromising realism, was painted as a token of reconciliation with his wife, whom he had found to be unfaithful and whom he portrayed here in the guise of a penitent. Among the other 18C works are Václav Reiner's *Orpheus with Animals in a Landscape* (before 1720), Antonín Kern's *St John on Pathmos* (1737), and a cycle of paintings by Norbert Grund, including *Gallant Scene with a Lady on a Swing* (c 1760).

The ★**Basilica of St George** (Basilika sv. Jiří), attached to the southern side of the convent, is the oldest church in the citadel, having been founded in 905. Transformed into a three-aisled structure in 973, it was rebuilt following a fire in 1142, and then again in 1657–80; restoration campaigns undertaken in 1897–1907 and 1959–62 brought back many of the building's 10C–12C features, making the church one of the best-preserved Romanesque structures in Bohemia.

The main Baroque survival is the vivid ochre west façade (facing George's Square) and the adjoining **Chapel of St John of Nepomuk** (sv. Jan Nepomucký), which was built by František Kaňka and the Dientzenhofer brothers in 1718–22, and is adorned on the outside with a statue of the saint by Ferdinand Brokoff. The south portal of the basilica, facing Jiřská, is an early-16C coffered Classical structure by Benedikt Ried incorporating in the tympanum a late-Gothic relief of *St George and the Dragon*, the original of which is in the National Gallery. The principal Romanesque features of the basilica's exterior are the twin white towers rising up at the eastern end of the church, the northern one being currently under renovation.

The cold and heavily restored interior, now deconsecrated, retains original Romanesque arcades in the nave, at the end of which, in front of the raised choir, stand the tombs of Prince Boleslav II (encased by a Baroque grille of 1730), and Prince Vratislav I (in painted wood), the founder of the church. In between the two flights of the Baroque staircase that leads up to the choir is the entrance to the remarkable **crypt** of 1142, featuring columns with cubic capitals, and a particularly grim and realistic sculpture of a decomposing female corpse (made in 1726). The vault of the choir has scant fragments of wall-paintings of c 1200 representing the Celestial Jerusalem; fragments of 16C painting decorate the vault of the adjoining **Chapel of St Ludmila**, which was added in the late 14C and houses the tomb (from Petr Parléř's workshop) of the murdered St Ludmila, one of Bohemia's patron saints.

The Eastern Citadel

Jiřská or George's Street, which runs due east of the basilica and slowly descends through the tapering eastern half of the citadel, is the main and oldest street of the complex, and is lined with a number of Renaissance and Baroque buildings. Before reaching the finest of these, you should take the first turning to the left to visit the celebrated ★**Golden Lane** (Zlatá ulička). This row of tiny houses dating from the end of the 16C runs directly underneath the northeastern ramparts of the citadel, between the White Tower and the Daliborka Tower, both of which formed part of the new fortifications designed by Benedikt Ried for Vladislav the Jagiellon. The name of the lane is sometimes romantically connected with the alchemists at Rudolph's court, though in fact it derives from the goldsmiths who once lived here alongside the castle's guards. In the 18C and 19C the dwellings here were inhabited by the very poor, and it was only after 1960 that they were to receive their cheerfully coloured doll's-house appearance and become tiny shops selling artefacts for the thousands of tourists who daily throng this area (separate ticket required).

The **White Tower** (Bílá Věž), at the western end of the lane, served after 1584 as a prison, among its most famous inmates being the English alchemist Edward Kelley and the leaders of the anti-Habsburg uprising of 1618. It now contains a small display of armour, weapons and torture instruments.

Residents of Golden Lane

In the summer of 1916, Kafka, looking for some quiet place to write, went on a flat-hunt with his favourite sister Ottla, and asked 'just for fun' if there was any place available in the lane; to their surprise they were able to rent from November the house at No. 22, which they kept for nearly a year, Kafka reputedly drawing inspiration here for his novel, *The Castle*.

The lane is also associated with the Nobel Prize-winning poet Jaroslav Seifert, who lived in a house (now gone) between the eastern end of the lane and the Daliborka Tower in the late 1920s and early 1930s, writing here his two collections of poems, *Eight Days* and *Bathed in Light*. The latter tower, another former prison, is named after the first person to be incarcerated here, Knight Dalibor of Kozojedy, whose life was to inspire Bedřich Smetana in his opera *Dalibor* (1868); a later prisoner was the aristocratic eccentric Count Špork, the founder of the hospital and spa at Kuks in eastern Bohemia.

Golden Lane exits at the Daliborka Tower, which can be visited. In the courtyard around the corner is the former Palace of the Burgrave of Prague Castle (No. 4), which was built in 1541 by Giovanni Ventura and adapted in the early 1960s to serve as the House of Czechoslovak Children; today, it maintains its association with children by housing the deeply disappointing **Toy Museum** (Muzeum hraček), an unimaginative display of objects such as toy robots, cars, and even Barbie dolls. (Not even the most undemanding of today's children could possibly enjoy this.) Open Tues–Sun 09.30–17.30.

Marginally more interesting (at least for its setting) is the hotchpotch of drably arranged objects making up the **Historical Museum** (separate ticket required), on the other side of the street. This documents the history of Bohemia from the arrival of the Slavs up to 1848–49, and occupies the **Lobkowicz Palace** (Lobkovický palác), which was rebuilt in 1651–68 to the designs of the Italian architect Anselmo Lurago, and retains several 17C and 18C ceilings, including, in Room 19, a heavily stuccoed 17C ceiling incorporating a clumsy if amusing painted panel of the *Triumph of Caesar*. The exhibition actually begins on the second floor, before moving down to the first, where you should not miss the wonderful display celebrating the 50th anniversary (in 2003) of the **Sports Museum** (Tyršovo muzeum tělesné výchovy), which was formerly housed in the Michna Palace on Újezd (see p 132). At the time of writing the administrators had not yet found a new permanent home for the museum, but it seems that part of it will be located here in the Lobkowicz Palace, and another part in the National Museum on Wenceslas Square (see p 163). The display consists of a ramshackle but fascinating collection of old bicycles, gymnastics equipment, sports trophies, photographs and other objects relating to the history of sport in Prague. As in the Historical Museum, the labelling is in Czech only, but this hardly detracts from one's enjoyment of the place. Open Tues–Sun 09.00–17.00.

A little below the palace Jiřská reaches the citadel's eastern gate, on the other side of which you will come out at the top of the Old Castle Steps (Staré zámecké schody; see above).

Old Royal Palace and Gardens

Make your way back to George's Square and bear left, passing to your left immediately on re-entering the square the **Church of All Saints** (Všech svatých), which was rebuilt after a fire at the end of the 16C and attached after 1755 to the adjoining Theresian Convent for Noblewomen. Its furnishings are mainly 17C and 18C, and include a wooden tomb on the north wall containing the remains of St Procopius.

On the western side of the Church of All Saints is the ****Old Royal Palace** (Starý královský palác), which has parts dating back to the 12C but owes its present appearance largely to the rebuilding campaign undertaken by Benedikt Ried in the late 15C for Vladislav the Jagiellon.

> Occupying the site of the 9C palace of the Princes of Bohemia, it served from the 13C to the 16C as the palace of the Kings of Bohemia. After the Habsburgs moved their quarters to the western end of the citadel and up to the end of the 18C the building functioned as the central offices of the Bohemian state. Thereafter it was neglected until 1924, when it was thoroughly restored and taken over for governmental purposes; its main rooms, which have only been open to the public since the 1960s, are still the scene of the occasional important political assembly.

The palace is entered from the castle's Third Courtyard, and as you make your way there from the Church of All Saints you will pass to your left a parapet overlooking the palace courtyard, above which rises the **Vladislav Hall**, adorned on the outside by elegant Renaissance windows that give no hint of the late-Gothic fantasies to be found within. When you eventually enter the hall after crossing a dark and austere antechamber adjoining the palace's main entrance, you are confronted with what is architecturally one of the most exciting spaces to be seen in Europe. The vast hall—so vast that jousting tournaments had once been held here—was built by Benedikt Ried in 1493–1502 and is dominated by vaulting of breathtaking elaboration: the ribs, likened frequently to the intertwined branches of a forest, have largely ceased to play a structural role, but snake their way around the ceiling in an essentially decorative way, drawing the visitor into the room through their powerful movements, and creating dynamic effects that look ahead to the Baroque period. The vaulting, representing an extreme development of the late-Gothic style, contrasts markedly with the innovatory Renaissance windows, yet even when handling Classical forms, Ried often did so in a highly idiosyncratic fashion, as can be seen in his famous door at the northeastern end of the room, where a Renaissance arch is supported by twisted pillars which are almost a mockery of all that the Renaissance stood for.

The Second Defenestration

Early on the morning of 23 May 1618, a group of Protestants led by Count Thurn burst into the Chancellery (see below) determined to punish the two Catholic councillors Martinic and Slavata, who had been appointed by Ferdinand over their heads. Following a violent row, the councillors, accused of being traitors and worthless followers of the Jesuits, were thrown out of the window. They managed to grab on to the ledge, but Thurn beat their knuckles with the hilt of his sword until they fell. Surprisingly they were not killed; thanks to the unhygienic conditions then prevailing at the castle, the ditch which at that time ran below the whole complex was piled high with sewage which broke the two councillors' fall. This excremental intervention in the course of history was later attributed by Catholics to a miracle.

Before crossing to the eastern end of the hall, you should go through the door in its southwestern corner to visit the room of the **Bohemian Chancellery**, which is famous as the place where the 'Second Defenestration' took place in 1618 (see above).

After returning to the hall, walk across to its southeastern corner, where there is a door leading to a **terrace** offering a magnificent view of Prague; a helical staircase descends from here to the gardens below. Back once more in the hall, and crossing over to its northeastern corner, you will pass to your right a balcony, preceded by steps, which looks down into the Church of All Saints (see above). The extraordinary door with twisted pillars at the northeastern corner of the hall leads into the **Diet Hall**, which is covered with another late-Gothic vault of fascinating complexity. The room, built by Ried in 1500, was destroyed by fire in 1541, and reconstructed nine years later by Bonifác Wohlmut, who provided it with the Renaissance tribune once used by the Supreme Scribe.

Returning to the Vladislav Hall, and turning right, you will come immediately to a Renaissance double portal. Through the arch on the left is a spiral staircase climbing up to the rooms of the **New Land Rolls**, where there is a ceiling decorated with the heraldic shields of the clerks of the Land Rolls; the right-hand arch leads directly to the **Riders' Staircase**, which horses had once climbed on their way to joust in the Vladislav Hall. Built by Ried c 1500, it is vaulted in a way that almost surpasses in complexity this architect's achievement in the Vladislav Hall, with ribs that intersect, interrupt and are suddenly truncated, the overall effect being one of suspended movement, a sense of playful abandon controlled by a rigorous geometrical discipline that would have impressed the Baroque architect Borromini.

Walking down the Riders' Staircase, you reach the palace's northern door, where you can either leave the building or else continue your visit by going first to the ground-floor rooms of Charles IV's palace, and then to the gloomy cellar below, a survival of the 12C palace of Prince Soběslav I; these Romanesque and Gothic chambers are largely bare, but there are copies of some of Parléř's triforium sculptures from St Vitus's Cathedral in the large **Charles Hall** (currently removed for renovation).

After walking back to the western end of the palace, you should take a closer look at the southern half of the Third Courtyard, in the middle of which stands the famous bronze statue of *St George and the Dragon* by the brothers George and Martin of Kolozsvar (the original is in the Lapidarium of the National Museum— see p 210). Between 1928 and 1932 the whole courtyard, which at one time was slightly sloping, was relaid and straightened by Jože Plečnik, who also designed for it a granite monolith commemorating the dead of the First World War.

At the same time Plečnik pierced the eastern end of the Municipal Building on the southern side of the courtyard with a portal and ingenious staircase leading down to gardens that had originally been laid out in the late 17C over the notorious ditch into which the two councillors had been thrown in 1618. The gardens, commanding a magnificent panorama of Prague, were also relaid by Plečnik, who divided them into the **Rampart Garden** and the **Paradise Garden**, thus breaking up the monotony of the original formal plan. One of the more welcome recent changes to the castle has been the opening of these gardens to visitors, who might well find them a refreshingly quiet place to get away from the crowds. A beautiful walk can be made from here all the way down to Valdštejnská, via the so-called Gardens Below Prague Castle (see p 127); fit readers could attempt the hike in the opposite direction. From the Paradise Garden, where Plečnik placed a 40-ton granite basin on two small blocks, there is also a monumental staircase leading back to Hradčany Square. Open April–Sept Tues–Sun 10.00–18.00.

North of the Citadel

From the Third Courtyard make your way back to the Second Courtyard, which you should leave through the arch on its northern side (see map, p 141). This will take you to the **Powder Bridge** (Prašný most), which spans the so-called **Stag Moat** (Jelení příkop), where red deer were kept from the 16C to 18C. After crossing the bridge and continuing to walk north, you will pass on the left an elegantly simple building designed by Jean-Baptiste Mathey in 1694 as the **Royal Riding School** (Jízdárna), and then restored by Pavel Janák in 1948–54; it is now used for temporary exhibitions (open 10.00–18.00; separate ticket required). On the other side of the path are the gates to the beautifully maintained and azalea-laden **Royal Gardens** (Královská zahrada), which have been reopened to the public following years of closure during the Communist period.

Walking east inside the gardens you will come shortly to the much-restored **Ball-Game Court** (Míčovna), an harmonious Renaissance structure built by Bonifác Wohlmut and Ulrico Avostalis in 1565–69, and covered all over with Renaissance sgrafitto work and, for the time being, scaffolding; the interior is used for concerts and art exhibitions.

More impressive still is the ***Summer Palace** (Letohrádek královny Anny) at the gardens' eastern end, which touched the heart of Chateaubriand on his visit to Prague in 1833: 'Not far from the shapeless mass [of the Hrad]', wrote the famous French author and politician, 'there stands against the sky a pretty building decked with one of the graceful porticoes of the cinquecento: this architecture has the drawback of being out of harmony with the climate. If at least one could, during the Bohemian winter, put these Italian palaces in the hot-house, with the palm trees? I was almost preoccupied with the thought of the cold which they must feel at night.'

Popularly known as the Belvedere, the Summer Palace is indeed one of the purest examples in Central Europe of the Italian Renaissance style, the proportions of its arcaded lower level strongly recalling the architecture of Brunelleschi. Begun in 1537 to a design by Paolo della Stella (who executed as well the exquisite mythological and ornamental reliefs on the arcade), it was completed in 1552–69 by Bonifác Wohlmut, who provided it with the one feature that reveals it as a work situated in Central Europe rather than Italy—the curious copper roof shaped like the inverted hull of a ship. The interior, remodelled in the mid-19C, was restored after the Second World War by Pavel Janák, and again in recent years (open May–Oct Tues–Sun 10.00–18.00). The tiny Renaissance garden on its western side contains a celebrated bronze fountain known as the **Singing Fountain** (Zpívající fontána) on account of the sounds made by the water dropping from its two basins: the finely detailed work was designed in 1563 by Francesco Terzio.

The Castle District (Hradčany)

Return to the castle's Second Courtyard, and from there make your way back to Hradčany Square to begin a tour of the district that grew up to the west of the castle's walls. Made a township in 1320, and enlarged 40 years later by the construction of the Hunger Wall (see p 137), after 1541 this area became the scene of intensive rebuilding work; the place was raised to the status of royal town in 1598, and remained as such until the creation of a unified Prague in 1784.

The district covers a relatively small area, but is crowded with important monuments, beginning with those on **Hradčany Square** (Hradčanské náměstí) itself (see map, p 141). This sloping, wedge-shaped square, lined with imposing palaces built by the Catholic aristocracy, features at its centre a Marian column of 1726 ringed by eight statues of saints by Ferdinand Brokoff. Adjacent to the western façade of the castle is the recently restored **Archbishop's Palace** (Arcibiskupský palác; No. 16), which dates back to a building of Wohlmut's of 1562, but was rebuilt by Jean-Baptiste Mathey at the end of the 17C and given an Italianate Baroque façade, with a crowning pediment and statuary, in 1763–65. The palace is the seat of the Archbishop of Prague, and is closed to the public.

Šternberg Palace

On the left-hand side of the palace a well-signposted alleyway descends to the *Šternberg Palace (Šternberský palác, No. 15), a gloomy but impressive structure that is completely hidden from the square. Built between 1698 and 1707 by Giovanni Alliprandi and Jan Santini-Aichel, the palace is particularly remarkable for its courtyard, which is dominated on its western side by a large oval pavilion. However, the building is visited less for its architecture than for its paintings, for it houses the pre-modern Foreign School holdings of the **National Gallery** (the modern ones have now been transferred to the Trade Fair Palace in Holešovice; see p 203). Open Tues–Sun 10.00–18.00. During your tour of the gallery you can take a break at the covenient café in the courtyard.

The rooms of the Šternberg Palace, featuring a number of fine stuccoed and painted ceilings of the early 18C, make an elegant setting for the Old Master Foreign School paintings (housed here since 1945). The main staircase adjoining the ticket-office leads up to the first and second floors where the bulk of the collection is shown.

On the first floor are the Italian 14C to 16C paintings, which include works by Nardo di Cione and Bernardo Daddi and an expressive *Lamentation* by **Lorenzo di Monaco**; the 15C is represented only by four works, the finest of which are by **Benozzo Gozzoli** and **Pasqualino Veneto**, while the 16C section contains good portraits by **Lotto** and **Bronzino**, and the so-called *Madonna of the Veil*, a Holy Family group painted c 1519 by **Sebastiano del Piombo**.

Of the Netherlandish holdings of the 15C and 16C, **Jan Gossaert**'s *St Luke Drawing the Virgin and Child* (1513–16) and **Pieter Brueghel the Elder**'s *Haymaking* (1565) stand out; the former was hung on the main altar of St Vitus's Cathedral from 1618 up to the end of the 19C, while the latter formed part of a famous series of panels of the months painted for the artist's Antwerp friend Nicolaes Jonghelinck (the other surviving panels from this series are in the Kunsthistorisches Institut in Vienna). The side rooms house an interesting collection of Slavonic icons.

The second floor begins with the small and unimpressive holdings of 17C and 18C French art, featuring works by Bourdon, Charles le Brun, Boucher and Mignard. The best of the paintings—a dramatically coloured *Suicide of Lucretia* (1625/6) by **Simon Vouet**—was painted in Rome under the influence of Caravaggio and is thus displayed in the rooms devoted to the 17C–18C Italian School.

The 17C and 18C Italian paintings include Domenico Fetti's *Christ on the Mount of Olives*, Magnasco's *The Penitent Mary Magdalene in a Landscape*, Piazetta's *St Joseph and Child*, an enormous view of London by Canaletto, a head of an old man by G.D. Tiepolo (erroneously attributed to his father Giambattista), and small oils by Pittoni and Sebastiano Ricci. Also included in the Italian section are the few Spanish works in the gallery—a *St Jerome* by Ribera, El Greco's *Praying Christ*, and an indifferent portrait by Goya of *Don Miguel de Lardizabal* (1815).

Among the 17C Flemish paintings are a Van Dyck of *St Bruno* (1615) and several works by **Rubens**, including a *Portrait of the Marchese Ambrogio Spinola*, and two large canvases, one of *St Augustine* and the other of *The Martyrdom of St Thomas*, which the artist painted between 1637 and 1639 for the Augustinian Church of St Thomas in the Little Quarter.

The Dutch 17C holdings are extensive and feature genre scenes by Dou, Ter Borch, Metsu and David Teniers, still-lifes by Pieter Claesz and Willem Kalf, and landscapes by Jan van Goyen, Salamon Ruisdael and Aert von der Meer; the two outstanding works in this section are **Rembrandt**'s *Scholar in his Study* of 1634, and the half-length portrait by **Frans Hals** of *Jasper Schade van Westrum* (c 1645).

Returning to the courtyard, you should enter the ground-floor section where the true quality of the gallery is felt, beginning with an excellent group of German 15C–16C paintings. These include a massive altarpiece by Hans Raphon comprising 13 Passion scenes (c 1499); **Hans Schücklin**'s *Beheading of St Barbara* (1470); monochrome fragments of an altarpiece of 1509 by **Hans Holbein the Elder**, and a portrait by his son of *Elizabeth Vaux*; **Altdorfer**'s *Martyrdom of St Florian*; **Baldung Grien**'s *Decapitation of St Dorothy* (1516); and a variety of works by **Lucas Cranach the Elder**, most notably a delightful *Adam and Eve* of 1537, a portrait entitled *The Old Fool* of c 1530, and fragments from an altarpiece in St Vitus's Cathedral which was taken down by Protestants in 1619 (the main survival is a panel of the Assumption surrounded by angels and saints). Especially powerful are two large panels by **Hans Süss** of Kulmbach that originally decorated the organ loft of the Church of Our Lady of the Snows in the New Town (see p 172); they are vigorous and near-life-sized representations of the Emperor Henry II and the Empress Kunegunda.

Süss was an artist greatly influenced by **Albrecht Dürer**, who is represented here by one of his most famous works, *The Feast of the Rosary*. Painted in Venice in 1506 for the church of San Bartolomeo (the church of Venice's merchant colony), this work shows the great influence on the artist of the brilliant colouring of Venetian painters such as Giovanni Bellini; in turn, the painting made an enormous impact on the Venetian public, and indeed was their first main contact with contemporary German art. Among the many contemporary personalities that Dürer vividly portrayed on either side of the enthroned Virgin are Pope Julius II, Emperor Maximilian I, Domenico Grimani, Jakob Fugger and

Hieronymus of Augsburg; the artist himself, a man not known for his modesty, also included himself among this distinguished company, standing under a tree and holding his signature. The painting was acquired by Rudolph II in 1606, and is the most important of his pictures to have remained in Prague.

Leaving the gallery, proceed to the southern side of Hradčany Square, where, at No. 2, you will find the **Schwarzenberg Palace** (Schwarzenberský palác). This large gabled structure, built in 1543–63, is one of the finest examples in Prague of Bohemian Renaissance architecture, and is covered with restored sgraffito decorations, including on its wide projecting cornice. Until recently the building housed the Military Museum, but this has now closed, and when renovation is complete in 2007 the National Gallery plans to show its permanent collection of Old Masters here.

From the square, walk north along **Kanovnická**. At the end of this street you will come to the **Church of St John of Nepomuk** (sv. Jana Nepomuckého), which was built by K.I. Dientzenhofer in 1720–28 and is the first-known church by this architect; its newly repainted exterior is unremarkable, but the Greek Cross interior, with ceiling paintings of the life of the saint by Václav Reiner (1728), is richly decorated and stuccoed, and full of movement.

Turning right at the church and then immediately left, you will come to the top of what is perhaps the most picturesque of the Hradčany's streets, ***Nový Svět** or 'New World', which gives an idea of how Golden Lane (see p 149) might have looked before the onset of tourism. This narrow cobbled street, originating in a path leading from Prague to Střešovice, was lined at the end of the 16C with a number of modest houses; the latter, crumbling away over the centuries, came to be occupied by the very poor, but have now become some of Prague's most exclusive addresses. At No. 1, on the left-hand side, is the house that belonged first to the astronomer Tycho Brahe and then, after 1600, to his successor as court astronomer, Johannes Kepler, the two men being commemorated by a plaque. Next door, at No. 3, is the *U Zlaté Hrušky* restaurant (see p 29), which cheerfully tempts patrons inside with a choice of menus: 'Specialities from the Czech duck' and 'For the guests who are not able to eat a Czech duck'. Further down the same side of the street, at No. 25, is a memorial plaque by Otakar Španiel commemorating the house where the violinist František Ondříček was born in 1857.

Nový Svět ends at a vast brick wall. Turn left just before it into Černínská where, at No. 5, you will pass the *Gambra* art gallery run by the renowned Czech animator, Jan Švankmajer, who lives in the house next door.

Černínská climbs gently to the quiet and sloping **Loreto Square** (Loretánské náměstí), which was a major source of inspiration early in the 20C to the bizarre and idiosyncratic painter Jan Zrzavý, who described it as one of Prague's 'overpowering' places: 'This is the home of the poor', he continued, 'a nook inhabited by the people deserted in this world, so simple and primitive that even a child could paint it. How well I lived in this area, nowhere else in Prague did I ever feel so good.' Not only did Zrzavý paint the square repeatedly, but also conceived here many of his most famous works, including *Obsession (Lovers)*, which now hangs in the Trade Fair Palace at Holešovice (see p 203).

At the narrow northern end of the square stands the former **Capuchin Church of Our Lady of Angels** (Panny Marie Andělské), the monastery of which is the oldest Capuchin institution in Bohemia and was founded in 1600;

the mid-17C church is very plain in its architecture and decoration, in accordance with the ideals of this order, but is worth visiting during the Christmas period to see the famous crib that is assembled here. Open only for services, Mon–Sat 18.00, Sun 08.30.

Rising above a terrace, and occupying the whole western side of the square, is the vast **Černín Palace** (Černínský palác), which was designed by Francesco Caratti in 1669 for Humprecht Jan Černín of Chudenice, the imperial ambassador to Venice. Domenico Rossi, Giovanni Alliprandi and František Kaňka were among the later architects to play a part in the construction of the palace, which had fallen seriously into disrepair by the beginning of the 19C. The American diplomat and future author of *Tales from the Alhambra*, Washington Irving, saw the palace in 1822 and found there a scene of desolation even greater than that which he would discover in the Alhambra several years later. Apparently deserted by its owners, the main portal was boarded up, and there were rags and old clothes hanging out to dry from a main façade whose broken windows were patched up with paper; a side door led into a courtyard taken over by cackling geese, ruined statuary, and impoverished old women washing and drawing water from a well.

In 1928–34 the whole palace was extensively restored and remodelled by Pavel Janák. However, the main façade overlooking the Loreto Square remains, in its overall conception if not in its detailing, essentially as Caratti planned it, and is not only one of the most monumental façades in Prague, but also the first truly Baroque structure in the city, being articulated along the whole of its great length (150m) by a giant order of Corinthian columns. Since 1918 the building has served as the Ministry of Foreign Affairs, and in 1948 was the scene of a notorious incident when the last non-Communist member of the government, Jan Masaryk (the son of Czechoslovakia's first president), experienced the peculiarly Czech fate of falling out of the window. Though the official verdict was suicide, the incident became the subject of intense speculation.

Sanctuary of Our Lady of Loreto

Facing the Černín Palace on the eastern side of the square is the *****Sanctuary of Our Lady of Loreto** (Loreta), an important place of pilgrimage as well as one of the Hradčany's main tourist attractions. The sanctuary dates back to 1626 when Benigna Kateřina of Lobkowicz, anxious to revive the Marian cult, commissioned a replica of the Santa Casa, or Virgin's House, at the Italian town of Loreto, a house that, according to a 15C tradition, had been transported there miraculously from the Holy Land; at least 50 other copies of this house have been made, but the one in Prague remains the most famous. The Virgin's House is encased in a Baroque complex, the main, western façade of which was begun by Christoph Dientzenhofer in 1716 and completed by his son Kilian Ignaz in 1722; in front of it is a balustrade decorated with statues of cherubs. The elegant tripartite façade has a frontispiece crowned by a tall tower enclosing an elaborate carillon of 1694, which plays various melodies by means of a keyboard, including— at the stroke of every hour—the Marian hymn, *We Greet Thee a Thousand Times*.

After passing through the main portal you come to the cloisters, in the middle of which stands the **Virgin's House**, built by Giovanni Battista Orsi in 1626–31 and shrouded in 1664 with rich stucco decoration featuring Old Testament figures and scenes from the Life of the Virgin. The simple, barrel-vaulted interior in unfaced brick contains a polychrome figure of the Virgin and Child, set in a striking silver niche. Each year crowds of Catholic pilgrims come to pray at this holy shrine. Open Tues–Sun 09.00–12.15, 13.00–16.30.

The cloisters themselves date back to 1661 but were raised one storey by K.I. Dientzenhofer in the 1740s. They are surrounded by small and elaborately decorated 18C chapels containing wooden altars and confessionals; the corner chapel to the right of the main entrance contains an extraordinary sculpture of the bearded St Wilgefortis, the patron saint of unhappily married women. Several other women saints are honoured inside the **Church of the Nativity** (1734), off the eastern side of the cloisters. The sumptuously gilded interior has ceiling paintings by, among others, Václav Reiner.

Having walked around the cloisters in a clockwise direction you complete your tour of the sanctuary by climbing up to a room off the cloister's western side, where you will find—displayed under a modern ceiling hung with glass decoration in questionable taste—a **treasury** comprising chalices, monstrances and other liturgical objects from the 16C to the 18C. Among these is the famous Diamond Monstrance (known also as 'the Prague Sun'), which was designed by the great Viennese architect Johann Bernard Fischer von Erlach and executed in 1699 by Viennese court jewellers. A gift from Ludmila Eva Franziska of Kolovrat (who donated to the sanctuary her entire estate), it incorporates within its 12kg of silver gilt 6222 out of the 6500 diamonds that had been used for Ludmila's wedding dress (the rest comprised the craftsmen's fee). One of the more delightful touches of this spectacular piece of fantasy is the tiny enamel dove floating serenely within the explosion of rays.

At the foot of the Sanctuary's main entrance is a flight of steps leading up to the southern end of Loreto Square. Directly facing you, at No. 1, is a Renaissance building with a splendid façade whose ground floor is occupied by one of Prague's best traditional ale-houses—*U Černého vola* (see p 35), where you can refresh your senses with a pint of the excellent Velkopopovický kozel. Reasonable lunches are served at the nearby *U Ševce Matouše* restaurant (see p 29), situated under the arcades further along this side of the square.

Strahov Monastery

Beyond the arcades you will come almost immediately to **Pohořelec**, a square that has its origins in a suburb of the Hradčany founded in 1375; it is lined today with 17C and 18C buildings that, after long years of grime and decay, now sparkle in their coats of pastel paint. Climbing up the dark and narrow passage through the house at No. 8 (on the southern side of the square) will lead you into the peaceful courtyard of the ***Strahov Monastery** (Strahovský klášter); alternatively you could reach this courtyard by walking to the southwestern corner of the square, and then turning left, entering the monastery through its elegant gate of 1742, and passing on your left the early-17C Church of St Roch (now a private art gallery).

The former Premonstratensian Monastery of Strahov was founded by Vladislav II in 1140 at the instigation of the Bishop of Olomouc, who had first come into contact with the Premonstratensian Order on a visit to Palestine. The monastery, endowed with a formidable library, soon became one of the great centres of learning in Bohemia, and many of the leading personages of the day were educated here. Devastated and plundered by the Swedes in 1648, the place prospered once again after the Treaty of Westphalia, and acquired so many more books that in 1671 Giovanni Domenico Orsi began building a new library hall, known today as the Theological Hall. Between 1682 and 1689 the rest of the monastery was remodelled and extended by Jean-Baptiste Mathey, and towards the end of the following century a further library hall, the Philosophical Hall, was commissioned from Ignác Jan Palliardi by the enlightened abbot Václav Mayer (1734–1800). Mayer was also responsible for the founding of the abbey's Cabinet of Curiosities, and it was during his abbacy that the man known as the 'patriarch of Slavic philology', Josef Dobrovský , used to stay here. In deference to the monastery's literary traditions, a Museum of Czech Literature was established in the monastery buildings in 1953. Archaeological investigations carried out here during the same decade uncovered extensive remains of the 12C monastery. Since 1989 the place has become occupied again by monks (there are currently 32 of them), and they have made the complex more commercially viable than it was during the Communist period: the monastery's brewing traditions have been revived, two of its buildings have been profitably leased out, and the place's tourist potential has been exploited to the full.

On the southern side of the courtyard is the functioning **Monastery Church of Our Lady** (Nanebevzetí Panny Marie), which retains its 12C Romanesque basilica plan despite being remodelled in the early 17C and again in the middle of the following century; the mid-18C interior, visible through the grille, has a ceiling decorated with stucco cartouches by Palliardi, and an organ on which Mozart played.

The finest of the Baroque additions to the monastery are its two library halls (open 09.00–12.00, 13.00–17.00), the entrance to which is adjacent to the church's west façade. The first and grander of the two, the **Philosophical Hall**, was built at the end of the 18C around richly gilded and carved walnut furnishings brought here from the dissolved Premonstratensian monastery at Louka in Southern Moravia. In 1794 one of the greatest fresco painters of Central Europe, the Austrian Franz Maulbertsch, covered the entire vault of this hall with a superb ceiling-painting representing the modest theme of *The Struggle of Mankind to Know True Wisdom*. Just outside the hall are glass cabinets displaying some of the natural-history 'curiosities' (including a pair of whales' penises) amassed by Abbot Mayer and others.

The **Theological Hall** has kept its original wooden shelving and is adorned in its centre with 17C and 18C globes as well as tables displaying a select few of the library's unique collection of illuminated manuscripts and incunabula, among which is the Strahov New Testament, an Ottonian work of the 9C–10C constituting one of the oldest written documents surviving in the Czech Republic (displayed just outside the hall); the magnificent ceiling is decorated with late-17C stucco cartouches by Silvestro Carlone framing frescoes by Siard Nosecký also celebrating human knowledge.

The once rambling and delightfully chaotic **Museum of Czech Literature** (Památník národního písemnictví), of interest largely to Czech speakers, has now been streamlined and relegated to some ground-floor rooms off the church's adjoining cloisters (open 10.00–17.00). Proceed instead to the upper floor of the cloisters to see the small but worthwhile **Strahov Art Gallery**, which features some of the works of art acquired by the monks over the centuries and now returned to them after being confiscated by the Communists (a few of these works were hung until 1989 in the Šternberg Palace; see above). Printed hand-outs in English are available to help you navigate your way around the collection, which ranges from an excellent small group of medieval paintings—including the chubbily featured mid-14C *Strahov Madonna*, and some marvellously realistic late-15C works attributed to the Master of Litoměřice—to a number of fine Baroque and Rococo oils by Skřeta (*Ecstasy of St Caetano*, 1665), Brandl, Sebastiano Ricci (*St Francis Listening to the Music of the Heavenly Choirs*, c 1700), Antonín Kern (*St Augustine*, c 1793) and Franz Maulbertsch (*The Spiritual Development of Mankind*, 1793); in between are some striking works of the Rudolphine period, notably Spranger's *Resurrection of Christ* (c 1576), Hans von Aachen's portrait of Rudolph II (1604–12) and, more interesting still, Dirck de Quade van Ravesteyn's *Allegory of the Reign of Rudolph II* (1603), a good example of the erotic use of allegorical figures. Open Tues–Sun 09.00–17.00.

Before leaving the monastery grounds you could pay a visit to its most curious attraction—the **Museum of Miniatures** (Muzeum miniatur), situated just off the main courtyard by the steps leading down to Pohořelec. On display here is a collection of works so tiny that you can only view them through microscopes and magnifying glasses. These truly weird and fascinating exhibits, which include a portrait of Anton Chekhov on a poppyseed, a train on a strand of hair, and a camel caravan in the eye of a needle, were all painstakingly created by the Russian artist Anatoly Konenko, who is in the *Guinness Book of Records* for producing the world's smallest book. Open daily 09.00–17.00.

A gate through the monastery's eastern wall brings you out into the extensive parkland covering the Petřín Hill; going right, an enjoyable short walk, with beautiful views, can be made to the Petřín Tower at the top of the hill (see p 136); going left, the path joins Úvoz (see p 135), followed by Nerudova, leading you down to the Little Quarter Square (Malostranské náměstí).

4 The New Town (Nové Mĕsto)

The New Town, which was founded by Charles IV in 1348, lies to the south and east of the Old Town. Formed by the construction of a great line of outer fortifications stretching from the foot of the Vyšehrad hill in the south all the way to the Vltava in the north, it constituted one of the most ambitious examples of town planning in 14C Europe. The largest of the four original townships of Prague, it was to begin as the main home of the city's craftsmen and poor, and later to emerge as the commercial, administrative and social centre of Prague. The medieval street plan has been largely retained to this day, but rapid urban

NOVÉ MĚSTO

NORTH

200 metres

········· Route of Walk
○ Monument
---Ⓜ--- Metro line & Station

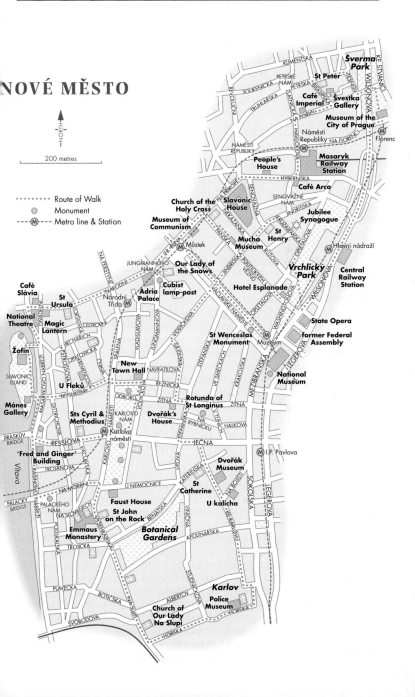

development from the late 19C onwards led to the pulling down of the fortifications in 1875, and the demolition of most of the surviving old houses to make way for large apartment blocks and imposing civic buildings. There are a number of medieval churches to be seen in the district, and numerous Baroque monuments; but the appeal of the New Town to the sightseer lies essentially in its great range of exciting monuments from the late 19C and early 20C. Nové Město is also the city's chief shopping district, with a plethora of shops, boutiques and department stores, mainly concentrated around Wenceslas Square and the showpiece streets of Národní and Na příkopě.

Wenceslas Square

First-time visitors to Prague are sometimes surprised when they finally see the legendary ★**Wenceslas Square** (Václavské náměstí), expecting perhaps a medieval space surrounded by picturesque Gothic buildings with crumbling façades of the kind so frequently encountered in Central Europe. In fact, Wenceslas Square couldn't be more different. Tall buildings dating from the late 19C onwards line the whole of its 750m-length, lending it the appearance of some grand Parisian boulevard, and along the middle of this thoroughfare runs a line of flower-beds laid out in the 1980s, which lead up to the vast National Museum building at the square's upper end. Going in the opposite direction, the square slopes gently down to a crowded pedestrianised area that marks the boundary of the Old Town.

Wenceslas Square is the heart of the Nové Město, and indeed the bustling centre of the city in general, but its present-day character belies its glorious history, the whole place having something of the tackiness and seediness of London's Leicester Square or Berlin's Kurfürstendamm. Shopping arcades, hotels, cinemas, bars and restaurants with a somewhat dated look surround the square, and at night the place teems with drunken young men heading off to the many strip clubs and 'tourist discos' in the area; pickpockets are a constant problem, and muggings have greatly increased here since the 'Revolution', but the level of street crime is still low by the standards of many Western cities.

Originally a place where horse markets were held, Wenceslas Square was known as the Horse Market (Koňský trh) up to as late as 1848, when it acquired its present name. The principal thoroughfare of Prague, since 1848 the square has also been the stage for some of the key moments in Czech history. A national mass held here in 1848 heralded the revolutionary disturbances of that year, while in 1918 crowds gathered here to celebrate the downfall of the Habsburgs.

On 25 February 1948, a popular demonstration in support of the Communist Party of Czechoslovakia took place in the square, and on 16 January 1969 the student **Jan Palach** set fire to himself near here to draw world attention to the plight of the Czech people. The square also played a major role in the great events of November 1989, beginning on the 17th of that month, when a group of students, officially commemorating the 50th anniversary of a Czech student's murder by the Nazis, made their way here from Prague's second district, their numbers greatly swollen in the course of the journey. Greeted by riot police, they burst into chants of 'Freedom' and began singing the Czech version of 'We Shall Overcome', but the police reaction was brutal, and one person was killed and many more injured. This was to spark the whole country into action, and over the next few days crowds gathered in their thousands at the square, chanting 'Freedom', 'Resign' and 'Now is the time'; the statue of Wenceslas was papered with posters and protest leaflets, and in front of it flowers and candles were placed in commemoration of Jan Palach. To the utter disbelief of the crowd, on 24 November, Alexander Dubček, followed by Václav Havel, appeared on the balcony of the Socialist Party publishing house to proclaim the imminent success of the **'Velvet Revolution'**.

National Museum

Rising on ramps at the very top of the square, and dominating the whole vista, is the vast National Museum (Národní muzeum), a pompous neo-Renaissance building, separated from the square by a dual carriageway. Open May–Sept 10.00–18.00; Oct–April 09.00–17.00.

The National Museum was founded in 1818 by a group of Czech intellectuals headed by the botanist, geologist and palaeontologist Count Kašpar Šternberg and including Josef Dobrovský, the pioneer of modern Slavonic studies. Thanks largely to the particular interests of Šternberg, the emphasis of the collections was on science, but the museum was greatly broadened in its scope from the 1830s onwards, when it became the increasing focus of Czech cultural life and national endeavours; a very important role in developing the scope of the museum was played by the celebrated historian František Palacký, who became the museum's secretary in 1841, and envisaged a place that would reflect every aspect of his country. The involvement of the institution in nationalist political movements, culminating in the insurrections of 1848–49, inspired a growing hostility towards the place on the part of the Austrian authorities, yet the museum was soon to occupy one of the most prominent sites in Prague. The collections were housed at first in the refectory of the Minorite monastery attached to the Church of St James, but the demolition of the New Town fortifications in 1875 and the consequent removal of the Horse Gate led to a site becoming available at the top of Wenceslas Square. The opportunity to use a site with such patriotic associations was immediately seized by the museum authorities, and in 1883–84 a competition was held for the design of the museum building to be erected here. The competition was won by Josef Schulz, and work on the structure was completed in 1890; its extensive sculptural embellishment involved most of the prominent academic sculptors of the day.

The main façade of the museum features a tall rusticated basement supporting a giant order of Corinthian columns, in the middle of which is a pedimented frontispiece crowned by a gilded dome. The sculptural decoration, like the architecture itself, is very conventional and includes, at the top of the double ramp that climbs up to the main entrance, a dull group by Anton Wagner representing *Bohemia between the Rivers Labe and Vltava*.

The principal component of the dauntingly large, red-marbled interior is the **Pantheon**, a room decorated all over with ambitious historical and allegorical murals by Václav Brožík, František Ženíšek and Vojtěch Hynais; in the centre of the room are six statues and 42 busts—mainly executed between 1898 and

1901—of distinguished Czechs from the 14C onwards, the work of Antonín Popp, Antonín Procházka, Josef Myslbek, Ladislav Šaloun, Jan Štursa, Karel Dvořák and others.

The National Museum's collections have now been shared out between various buildings throughout Prague, those on show here being devoted to geology, archaeology, prehistory and coins and medals (all of which are to be found on the first floor), as well as to zoology, palaeontology and anthropology (on the second floor). The display is gloomy and unimaginative, and the layman might well agree with the writer Stephen Brook's assessment (voiced in his book, *The Double Eagle* ...) that the main emotion that the museum inspires is a sense of awe at the sight 'of so many display cases exclusively devoted to the cockroach'.

Walking down Wenceslas Square from the National Museum, the first monument you come to, in the middle of the thoroughfare, is the ✳**St Wenceslas Monument**, Josef Myslbek's masterpiece, comprising an equestrian statue of Wenceslas surrounded by four other patron saints of Bohemia—Sts Ludmila, Procopius, Adalbert and Agnes. Originally conceived in 1887, the work was to occupy much of Myslbek's life up to his death in 1922; in the course of the monument's long gestation, the artist's vision of the saint significantly changed, so that the initial romantic representation of a spiritual and temporal leader of the Slavic people became transformed into a sturdy, tightly modelled portrayal of a man embodying the power and authority of the Czech state.

The buildings at this end of the square are modern and of little architectural interest, and there is no longer even the gastronomical attraction of the once wonderfully well-stocked House of Food (at No. 59), which has been turned into a McDonald's. Further down the square on the right-hand side, at No. 45, is the Jalta Hotel, another building of the 1950s, this one exemplifying the drab uniformity of so much Czech architecture of that period.

The street on the opposite side of the square to the hotel is Ve Smečkách, home to one of the Czech Republic's better-known small theatres, the **Činoherní Klub** (No. 26); emerging to prominence in the 1960s, this theatre has maintained its reputation through its long association with Jiří Menzel, who is best-known outside the Czech Republic as a leading protagonist of Czech New Wave cinema.

The next street off the left-hand side of the square is **Štěpánská**, at the entrance to which is the Supich Building, centred around a tall, imposing rotunda; this building, with its entrance at No. 40 Václavské náměstí, was erected by Matěj Blecha in 1912–16, and was originally the headquarters of the Moravian Bank (now Interbanka). Adjoining it on Štěpánská is the **Lucerna Palace** (entrances also on Václavské náměstí and Vodičkova), an ugly block of 1907–10 featuring a shopping arcade, cinema, sleazy restaurant (*Černý kůň*) and, in the basement, a large hall (Velký sál) used for concerts and dances; the arcade also contains an amusing parody of the Wenceslas Monument (see above) by David Černý, which shows the hapless Czech saint upside down. Václav Havel's grandfather, also called Václav, was one of the architects and owners of the Lucerna Palace, and the family later merged this establishment with their restaurant at Barrandov to form the lucrative Barrandov-Lucerna Enterprises.

Continuing to walk down Wenceslas Square, the next building on the left-hand side after the former Moravian Bank is the **Melantrich Building** (see p 163) at No. 36, the headquarters of the Melantrich Publishing House and the editorial offices of the former Socialist Party newspaper *Svobodné slovo* ('Free Word'). The adjoining Wiehl House at No. 34 is a gabled structure in Bohemian-Renaissance style designed by Antonín Wiehl in 1896 and covered with restored sgraffito decorations by Mikoláš Aleš. Facing this, on the other side of the square (at No. 25/27), is a far more remarkable turn-of-the-20th-century building, the **Grand Hotel Evropa** (see p 19). Built in 1903–06 by Bedřich Bendelmayer and Alois Dryák, it features a beautifully ornamented façade crowned by a large ceramic lunette (currently under renovation); but its great joy is its perfectly preserved interior, above all that of its bar and restaurant, both boasting stained-glass windows and elegant panelling, and its café, which has an impressive circular gallery and many of the original fixtures and fittings.

Further down on this same side, at No. 19, is a neo-Baroque building of 1895–96, now housing the Polish Institute but originally the Prague headquarters of the Trieste-based insurance company, **Assecurazioni generali**. This is famous as the place where the 24-year-old **Franz Kafka** began his first job, in October 1907; a medical certificate attesting to 'nervousness and cardiac excitability' allowed him to leave the company the following year, but he continued a career in insurance by joining in July 1908 the Workmen's Accident Insurance Company, where he was to remain for the rest of his life.

Most of the square's remaining buildings of architectural interest are to be found on the left-hand side, beginning with No. 28, the Alfa Building, a large Functionalist apartment block with shops and a cinema, designed by Ludvík Kysela in the late 1920s and featuring shop-windows of Cubist inspiration. The adjoining Hotel Adria (see p 18) at No. 26 is housed in the oldest surviving building on the square, dating back to the late 18C; just beyond it, at No. 22 (set back from the street), is a hotel of radically different character, the Hotel Juliš, a Functionalist work of 1931–32 by Pavel Janák. Further down, at No. 12, is the Peterka House, an Art Nouveau former bank built by Jan Kotěra between 1898 and 1910, when greatly under the influence of the Viennese architect Otto Wagner; the façade is adorned with stucco decorations by, among others, Stanislav Sucharda. A few doors further down you will reach, at No. 6, the recently restored **Bát'a Department Store**, built by Ludvík Kysela in 1926–28 for the visionary shoe-manufacturer Tomáš Bát'a, and still a good place to buy shoes.

Bát'a shoes

The shoe empire of Tomáš Bát'a (1876–1932) was initiated in 1894 with the founding of a factory in the Moravian town of Zlín. After prospering from the provision of army boots during the First World War, Bát'a went on to become an internationally known name, with outlets all over Europe; by the time of his death in a plane crash in 1932, Bát'a was employing 16,000 people to produce 150,000 shoes a day. The success of the company went hand in hand with the founder's avant-garde approach to both shoe-manufacture and architecture. Not only did he turn Zlín into a model city for his workers, but he also commissioned the most revolutionary architects of his day to build stores that would display his goods with a startling modernity in keeping with the company's progressive spirit.

The Bát'a store on Wenceslas Square, a Functionalist building of striking simplicity, comprises a reinforced-concrete frame with a minimum number of corridors in the sales areas, and some of the earliest bands of continuous glazing uninterrupted by architectural supports to be seen in Europe. Restoration work carried out in 1990–92 removed later unattractive additions but also substituted the original tubular steel furniture and fittings with some half-hearted modern imitations; the place is at its best at night, when it turns into a glowing apparition dominated by the neon sign promoting the name of Báťa. The store's architect, Ludvík Kysela, was also responsible for the adjoining and slightly fussier Lindt Department Store at No. 4, which was built two years earlier and was indeed one of the first examples of Functionalism in Prague.

Immediately north of here the square broadens to form a large pedestrian area featuring the Můstek metro station and extending into the adjacent boulevards of 28. října and Na příkopě. The last building on the right-hand side (at No. 1) is the **Koruna Palace**, a fine Art Nouveau structure of 1910–14 by Antonín Pfeiffer, with a futuristic corner tower and decorative detailing that looks ahead to the Art Deco period.

The northern and eastern New Town

The southern façade of the Koruna Palace overlooks the busy pedestrian thoroughfare of ***Na příkopě**, which is lined with banks, bookshops and department stores, including the British stores Marks & Spencer, Mothercare and Next. Turning into this boulevard from Wenceslas Square you will pass immediately to your left, at No. 1, one of the better examples of recent architecture in Prague: built by Jan Šrámek and Alena Šrámková in 1974–83, it is crowned by a glass-and-steel gable incorporating the clock of the department store that once stood here; underneath it is an entrance to the Můstek metro station. Also to your left, at No. 3, is the former Wiener Bankverein, which was built by Josef Zasche in 1906–08 and is faced with polished granite. Prague's oldest department store, known originally as Haas, is on the opposite side of the street at No. 4, and was built in a North Italian Renaissance style by the Danish architect Theophil Hansen in 1869–71.

The oldest surviving building on the street, and one of the most elegant Baroque palaces in the New Town, is further down on the right-hand side at No. 10. This, the **Sylva-Taroucca Palace** (1743–51), was built for Prince Ottavio Piccolomini by Kilian Ignaz Dientzenhofer with the assistance of Anselmo Lurago, and is a pedimented structure with a rusticated basement and a main floor articulated by giant order pilasters; the attic is decorated with sculptures of mythological figures and vases by Ignác František Platzer, who was also responsible for the putti and vases on the balustrade of the staircase inside.

The staircase leads up to one of Prague's newest attractions—the **Museum of Communism**, a tongue-in-cheek exhibition that pays ironic homage to the dark days of Communist Czechoslovakia (1948–89). It is the brainchild of American ex-pat businessman Glen Spicker, who spent several months trawling flea markets and junk shops in Prague to amass over a thousand items of memorabilia, ranging from clunky typewriters and anti-imperialist cartoons, to chemical-warfare-protection suits and busts of Marx and Lenin. This chaotic assemblage of objects is put together in what is billed as a three-act tragedy—'dream, reality and nightmare', the first being the utopian vision of communism, the second being the drudgery of daily life in Communist Czechoslovakia, and the third being the nightmare of a police state founded on brutality and repression.

A stylised 'Socialist Realist' poster by the ticket office sets the general tone of what's to come: it shows a group of defiant proletarian women gazing into the future, with the added caption: 'Like their sisters in the West, they too would have burnt their bras—if there had been any in the shops.' The display, with texts contributed by a retired Charles University professor, unashamedly celebrates the triumph of capitalism over communism and is clearly packaged for a naïve tourist market, repeating the time-worn platitudes of empty shops, queues and bureaucracy, without even attempting to explore the complex issues and ethical choices that Czechs faced under communism, or indeed their attitude towards the period now. You are led through a classroom draped with Soviet and Czechoslovak flags and Cyrillic writing on the blackboard, followed by a replica of a grocery shop selling one type of tinned meat, and finally a police interrogation cell, complete with bright lamp and other instruments of coercion. More instructive than any of these exhibits is the video show, with original archive footage from the events of 1968 and 1989. Open 09.00–21.00.

On the 1930s' bank at No. 14 Na příkopě, a bust and plaque record the site of the house where the writer Božena Němcová died in 1862. Facing this, across the narrow Panská, is the **Church of the Holy Cross** (sv. Kříže), a massively built neo-Classical structure designed by Georg Fischer in 1816.

A short detour can be made down Panská to see the **Mucha Museum** at No. 7, which opened in 1998 in the late-19C Kaunitz Palace (Kaunický palác).

Alfons Mucha

Born in 1860 in the Moravian town of Ivancice, Mucha showed a prodigiously early talent for draughtsmanship that none the less failed to get him accepted into the Prague Academy of Fine Arts. Apprenticed later as a theatrical scene painter in Vienna, he stayed there until the burning down of the Ring Theatre in 1880, soon after which he attracted the attention of the Moravian landowner Count Khuen von Belasi, who arranged for Mucha to continue his artistic training in Munich and then in Paris. Settling in Paris, he embarked on a varied artistic career that included oil painting, jewellery and furniture design. However, his popular reputation was established above all with his sinuously decorative poster designs, the fame of which was due initially to a chance commission from the actress Sarah Bernhardt, who thereafter contracted him to produce posters for all her theatrical work. After Mucha's return to Bohemia in 1910 he devoted much of his energy to a huge cycle of patriotic canvases known as the *Slav Epic* and now displayed in the Moravian town of Moravský Krumlov. He died in 1939, at a time when his Art Nouveau whimsicality and overblown historicism must have seemed ridiculously old-fashioned.

Though Mucha's popular appeal has been almost continuous since his death (his richly decorative posters were to have a special resonance during the 1960s), his critical reputation declined considerably, and only began to revive with a large retrospective of his work held in the Grand Palais in Paris in 1980.

Unfortunately, this museum is likely to come as something of a disappointment to serious Mucha fans, as it seems essentially aimed at promoting the *ersatz* Art Nouveau spirit currently sweeping through Prague. Mucha lived in a world of decorative exuberance (one need only look at photographs of the still-intact Mucha family home at No. 6 Hradčanské náměstí to be aware of this), but the small suite of sparsely hung rooms constituting his museum gives barely any hint of such a world. Apart from a large collection of his much-reproduced posters (the main reason for visiting the place), there are examples of his decorative designs, including stamps and banknotes, a handful of mediocre oil paintings, a group of pastels and figurative drawings, and some amusing photographs taken by the artist of his friend and colleague, Paul Gauguin. A significantly large amount of space is taken up by a shop selling Mucha-inspired merchandise. There is also a video show in English which documents Mucha's life and work, including the genesis of the *Slav Epic*. Open daily 10.00–18.00.

Returning to Na příkopě and continuing northeast, you will pass at No. 18 the former Provincial Bank (now offices of the national tourist agency Čedok), an Art Nouveau building of 1911–12 by Osvald Polívka, attractively decorated on the outside with mosaics by Jan Preisler and sculptures by Ladislav Šaloun. The building is connected, via a delightful covered passageway across Nekázanka, to the former Savings Bank (now the Živnostenská bank) at No. 20. This is another collaborative effort by Polívka and Šaloun, built in 1894–96 in a Czech-Renaissance style and incorporating a Baroque portal from a palace of 1757; the entrance vestibule is covered with wall-paintings of 1896 by Max Švabinský. The late-18C palace at No. 22 was converted in 1945 into the **Slavonic House** (Slovanský dům), a cultural centre with a restaurant that soon became a gastronomic mecca to the city's Spanish community, fondly remembered by Teresa Pàmies in her nostalgic book, *Praga* (1987). Nowadays, the Slovanský dům houses a surprisingly modern shopping arcade filled with expensive boutiques. Be sure to go through to the verdant inner courtyard, where there are more shops, a multiplex cinema, and several popular restaurants and lunch bars, including the minimalist *Millhouse Sushi* and the lively *Kogo* pizzeria (see p 28).

Next to the Slavonic House, at No. 24, is the Czech National Bank (Česká Národní Banka), which was put up in 1929–38 on a site that was occupied in the 19C by two hotels, The Blue Star and The Black Horse; a number of distinguished people were guests at these hotels, including the Russian anarchist Mikhail Bakunin, and the composers Chopin (to whom there is a plaque) and Liszt. Across the street, on a site occupied by the grim 1930s' administrative building at No. 33 (now the KB bank), there once stood Prague's most elegant café, the *Café Français*, where Liszt was frequently to be seen.

Na příkopě comes to an end at the Powder Gate and náměstí Republiky (see 87), where you should turn right into **Hybernská**, a narrow but busy street lined with 18C and 19C buildings, some in a decrepit condition, though many others have been restored. The first building to your right, at No. 20, was formerly a hotel where Tchaikovsky stayed in 1888 when he came to conduct the Prague première of his opera *Eugene Onegin*. Further down on the right-hand side, at No. 10, is the former **Hotel Central** (now a theatre), a narrow-fronted but lavishly ornamented Art Nouveau structure built by Bedřich Bendelmayer and Alois Dryák in 1899–1902.

On the other side of the street, the late-18C Sweerts-Špork Palace (Nos 3/5) is followed by the beautiful and recently restored **People's House** (Lidový dům), which was designed by Carlo Lurago after 1651 and given a new façade at the end of the 18C. This building, which once housed a Lenin Museum, played an important part in the history of the Czech Communist Party, and was the scene in 1912 of the 16th All-Russian Conference of the Social Democratic Party of Russia (the so-called Prague Conference), chaired by Lenin. In 1920, after the building had been forcibly occupied by the moderate faction of the Social Democratic Party (Mensheviks), the radical left-wing leadership (Bolsheviks) declared a general strike, during which there were violent clashes between workers and police on Hybernská; this conflict led to the formation in 1921 of the Communist Party of Czechoslovakia. The political traditions of the building have remained, and it is now the headquarters of the Czech Social Democratic Party (former communists), which stormed to victory in the 1998 and 2002 parliamentary elections.

Further down the street Hybernská reaches an intersection formed by Havlíčkova to the north and Dlážděná to the south; at No. 15, on the corner of these two streets, is the **Café Arco** (see p 32), latterly a downmarket and unremarkable-looking establishment, but at one time one of Prague's famed literary meeting-places. Its elegant interior was designed by Jan Kotěra and decorated with paintings by František Kysela.

> ## Café Arco
>
> The Café Arco on Hybernská came into being at the end of the 19C when the headwaiter of a staid café bearing the same name but in a far more fashionable part of town quarrelled with his employer and spitefully opened his own Café Arco in the rather less salubrious neighbourhood of Prague Central Railway Station. This new establishment, which was to reach the height of its notoriety in the years immediately preceding the First World War, soon attracted most of Prague's artistic and literary élite. Its regulars, who came to be known as the 'Arconauts', included a large proportion of German-Jewish writers, most notably Franz Werfel, Max Brod, Franz Kafka and Egon Erwin Kisch. The writer Karl Kraus, believing that this Jewish group at the Café Arco represented a cabal that besmirched the purity of the German language, penned a violent attack on the café, writing of the place the untranslatable line: 'Es werfelt und brodet und kafkat und kischt'.

The **Masaryk Railway Station** (Masarykovo nádraží), at the corner of Hybernská and Havlíčkova, proudly arose as Prague's first railway station in 1845, but construction of the far grander Hlavní nádraží (see p 171) saw its status greatly reduced. The building, which has a main hall covered with an interesting roof in iron, wood and glass, could certainly do with a major facelift. It also attracts numerous loiterers and other seedy types, and is definitely best avoided at night.

Walk to the northern end of Havlíčkova and turn right into Na poříčí, where you could stop for refreshments at the *Café Imperial* (see p 32), a spacious early-20C establishment decorated with a mass of ceramic tiles. Across the street, at No. 24, is the former **Legio Bank** (Legiobanka; now the ČSOB), an extraordinary structure of Cubist inspiration built by Josef Gočár in 1922–25. In this highly sculptural building, featuring a heavy, projecting attic and a giant order of cubic columns crossed by deeply cut bands, Gočár enjoyed a most successful collaboration with the sculptors Jan Štursa and Otto Gutfreund; above the main entrance Jan Štursa placed four enormous consoles of workers (1922–23) to support a long frieze by Gutfreund (*The Return of the Legionaries*, 1921), a work of great stateliness and power, which is considered by many to be one of the landmarks of 20C Czech sculpture.

Further along the street, at No. 40, is the Hotel Axa, a Constructivist building of 1935. Just before it, you should cross the street and head north along the short Biskupská, which was where the Merchants' Court of Poříčí's German community was situated up to 1235. A very worthwhile detour can be made from here to one of Prague's best commercial galleries—the ***Jiří Švestka Gallery**—situated in former factory premises at No. 6 Biskupský dvůr.

Established in 1995, the Švestka concentrates primarily on contemporary and modern art, and is keen to promote the work of young Czech artists. Indeed, as the only Czech gallery currently attending international art fairs, it is effectively the only route to international recognition available to such artists. It is also one of the few venues in Prague, certainly the only commercial venue, that actually presents artists of international note to the Czech audience. In recent years there have been shows by, among others, Dan Graham (American designer of the Hayward Gallery extension in London), Siah Armajani, Swedish video artist Ann-Sofi Siden, and Mark Wallinger of Brit Art fame.

One room within the gallery space is dedicated to works amassed by the most famous Czech collector, Vincenc Kramář, whose estate the gallery represents. Kramář was collecting in the early half of the 20C, and is credited with having recognised the talent of Picasso well before the rest of the art world. The majority of the collection now hangs in the National Gallery (see p 203), but what remains with the family (including Picasso prints, sculptures by Gutfreund, and Kupka paintings) is shown here in the Kramář room on a rotation basis. There is also a comprehensive English-language art bookshop on the premises and a useful website (www.jirisvestka.com) for programme information. Open Tues–Fri 12.00–18.00, Sat 11.00–18.00.

Returning to Biskupská and turning right, you will soon reach the late-Gothic tower belonging to the former German church of **St Peter na Poříčí** (sv. Petra na Poříčí). This building, just to the north of the tower, is a triple-aisled structure that dates back to the mid-12C and was originally the parish church of the German Poříčí district; in 1235 the church and surrounding area fell into the hands of the Knights of the Cross. Fragments of the original Romanesque church survive in the west façade and south wall of the nave, but the rest of the building was much altered over the centuries, and was subject to neo-Gothic remodelling by Josef Mocker in the 1870s. Open only for services, Tues–Thur 18.30, Sun 10.30.

Running behind the church is Petrská: walking east along this street and then taking the first turning to the right you will rejoin Na poříčí at the point where it disappears under the noisy Wilsonova flyover, which marks the eastern boundary of the New Town. On the other side of the flyover is the tiny and unpromisingly situated **Šverma Park** (Švermovy sady), which was founded in 1875 on the site of the recently demolished New Town fortifications. On this park's southern side, adjoining today an unappealing area occupied by tacky market stalls, stands a grand neo-Renaissance mansion built by Antonín Balšánek in 1896–98 to house the newly formed **Museum of the City of Prague** (Muzeum hlavního

města Prahy). The ground floor of this slightly run-down museum displays artefacts and works of art from the 6C onwards relating to the early history of
Prague, including Slavonic pots, fragments of 13C frescoes, old Bohemian glass,
and Renaissance and Baroque furnishings. The highlight, though, is found on
the second floor, reached by a grand oval staircase: an enormous and fantastically detailed paper model of Prague made between 1826 and 1834. Here, too,
you will find the original painted calendar executed by Josef Mánes in 1865 for
the Astronomical Clock on the Old Town Hall (see p 98). Open Tues–Sun
10.00–18.00.

Only a short distance south of the museum along Wilsonova is the magnificent
Art Nouveau *Central Station (Hlavní nádraží), but the journey is complicated
on foot and best undertaken by taking the metro from the Florenc stop on
Sokolovská (directly in front of the museum) to the following stop, Hlavní
nádraží. The metro will take you to the station's modern extension, which dates
from the 1970s and looks out onto a grotty park (Vrchlického sady). The original station (formerly named after the Emperor Francis Joseph) stands higher up,
on the busy Wilsonova bypass, and was built by Josef Fanta between 1901 and
1909. Its most exciting feature is its twin-towered façade,
comprising an ironwork central canopy and large-scale
carvings of nudes and other allegorical figures by,
among others, Stanislav Sucharda and Čeněk
Vosmík. There is a café inside the main foyer where
you can admire the decayed grandeur of the place,
now badly in need of renovation.

Further south along Wilsonova in the direction of the nearby National Museum (see p 163)
are two more buildings of note. First along is the
reconstructed late-19C Smetana Theatre, originally the main German theatre in Prague, today
used by the **State Opera** (Státní opera). Next to
it stands the ugly 1970s glass block of the
Federal Assembly, which became defunct following the 'Velvet Divorce' of 1993, and for now
houses the offices of Radio Free Europe.

*Central Station
by Josef Fanta*

At the southwestern corner of the Vrchlický
Park is another of the old luxury hotels of Prague, the Hotel Esplanade (with a
neo-Baroque gilded interior), while directly across the park from the Central
Station begins Jeruzalémská. Walking down the latter street, you will pass at
No. 5, to your right, the **Jubilee Synagogue** (Jubilejní synagoga), a neo-Moorish
building of 1908 with an extraordinarily vivid façade.

At the end of the street turn left on to Jindřišská, where you will find, to your
left, the **Church of St Henry** (sv. Jindřicha), which was founded in 1350 but
much altered in later periods and given a neo-Gothic exterior by Josef Mocker in
1879; Mocker was also responsible for the neo-Gothic remodelling of the late-
15C **belfry tower** on the other side of the street. Continuing to walk down
Jindřišská, you will soon reach its intersection with Panská and Politických
vězňů. At the corner of Panská is the Palace Hotel (see p 18), a lavishly refurbished building dating back to the turn of the century; on Politických vězňů

meanwhile, you will find at No. 20, right at the end of the street, the notorious **Petschek Palace**, a neo-Renaissance building of 1923–25 that served as the Gestapo headquarters during the last war; here numerous Czechs, including Julius Fučík, were tortured and executed. The building now houses the Ministry of Industry. Jindřišská brings you back to the lower end of Wenceslas Square.

The southern and western New Town

You can begin a tour of the southern half of the New Town from the bottom end of Wenceslas Square, where you should turn left into the quiet **Jungmann Square** (Jungmannovo náměstí), which runs parallel to the pedestrian thoroughfare of 28. října. The square epitomises the city's architectural richness, featuring as it does the back façade of the pioneering Bát'a Building (see above), a gabled late-14C Gothic gateway, and—as its centrepiece—a beautiful and highly eccentric **Cubist lamppost** of 1913; this last monument, reattributed to the minor architect Emil Králíček (but previously thought to be by the much better-known Vlatislav Hofman), is a work of great originality anticipating by many years Brancusi's *Endless Column*. The Gothic gateway at the square's southeastern corner opens out on to a courtyard leading to the former **Carmelite Church of Our Lady of the Snows** (Panny Marie Sněžné).

Lamp-post in Jungmann Square

Founded by Emperor Charles IV in 1347 on the occasion of his coronation as King of Bohemia, the church of Our Lady of the Snows was intended to be a vast triple-aisled structure that would have extended right into the present Jungmann Square. However, work on the building was interrupted during the Hussite wars, in which this church played an important role. The radical Hussite speaker Jan Želivský preached here between 1419 and 1422, and it was from here that on 30 July 1419 a procession set out to the New Town Hall to carry out the 'First Defenestration' in Prague. Želivský was buried in the church in 1422, but the building was later left to decay and its steeple demolished. The abandoned church and convent came in 1603 into the hands of the Franciscans, who embarked on a campaign of restoration and rebuilding.

On entering the church you are immediately struck by its great height and size, though in fact what you are seeing constitutes only the chancel of the triple-aisled structure originally conceived. The furnishings are Baroque, and include an imposing high altar decked out in black and gold, but the building has otherwise a completely Gothic look despite the fact that the net-vaulting and much of the masonry dates back only to the time of the Franciscan restoration. The former monastery gardens (Františkánská zahrada) on the south side of the building were relaid in the 1950s and form today a pleasant public park, shaded by trees.

At its western end Jungmann Square leads to the busy junction of 28. října, Jungmannova and Národní. The Functionalist corner building at the end of 28. října (No. 1), a mass of concrete and glass, was built as a department store in 1927–31, and is today occupied by the ČSOB bank. Further down

Jungmannova, at No. 30, stands one of the earliest Modernist buildings in Prague, the **Urbánek Publishing House** (1912–13), a structure of great geometrical purity that reveals the architect Jan Kotěra's debt to his master Otto Wagner; the grid of brickwork squares is encased within a deep rectangular frame and topped by a large triangular gable. Built for the music and arts publisher Mojmír Urbánek, it was intended to house apartments, offices, a small concert hall (the Mozarteum) and, on the ground floor (flanked by caryatid figures by Jan Štursa), an art gallery. This gallery, the Havel Gallery, was an important if brief-lived centre of the avant-garde, and organised as its inaugural show an exhibition of Futurist art that divided the Prague Cubists.

The corner of Jungmannova and Národní is taken up by the bizarre and colossal **Adria Palace**, a heavily ornamented structure built by Pavel Janák and Josef Zasche in 1923–25, and featuring an attic level made up of square, crenellated towers that give the whole building the look of some futuristic urban fortress; the sculptural decoration on the façades was carried out by Jan Štursa, Otto Gutfreund and Karel Dvořák. This fantastical building appropriately hosted for many years the theatrical spectacle known as the Magic Lantern, which has now transferred to a specially built venue next to the National Theatre (see below).

The Magic Lantern

The Magic Lantern was created for the Brussels World Exhibition of 1958 by Alfréd Radok, who, together with the brilliant stage designer Josef Svoboda and up-and-coming talents such as the film director Miloš Forman, devised a brilliant illusionistic spectacle involving stage-sets, actors and film. Such was its success in Brussels, where it did much to draw world attention to the cultural life of Czechoslovakia, that it was decided afterwards to turn it into a permanent cultural institution in Prague. However, Radok and his collaborators were soon to fall victims to the political situation of the time, and were ousted and replaced by lesser talents.

Performances of the Magic Lantern were still taking place here in November 1989, when its theatre became the meeting-place of the newly formed Civic Forum, which in a matter of days succeeded in ousting the Communist government of Czechoslovakia and later hoisting Havel to the presidency of the country. The only foreigner present for most of the meetings was the Englishman Timothy Garton Ash, who wrote that for nearly two weeks he was 'privileged to watch history being made inside the Magic Lantern'.

*Národní avenue is Prague's most important thoroughfare; it is vibrant with cars and people, and lined along its whole length with department stores and monumental civic buildings. As you walk down it in the direction of the Vltava, the first major building you pass to your right is the **Platýs House** at No. 37, which was rebuilt and enlarged after 1813 and turned into the first tenement building in Prague; the main wing contains a hall where concerts were once held, one of the musicians who performed here being Liszt in 1840 and 1846 (a marble bust of the composer has been placed to the right of the building's back entrance); the courtyard is now filled with shops and a café. On the other side of the street, at No. 26 (at the junction with Spálená), is one of Prague's biggest department stores, a light structure in glass and aluminium built in the 1970s by the Liberec architectural firm SIAL 02. During the Communist period it was called Máj, in reference to the International Labour Day (1 May), but since 1996 it has been taken over by Tesco. In the small square behind the store is an open-air market selling fruit and vegetables.

At the junction with Spálená's northern continuation, Na Perštýně, there stood until 1950 one of Prague's most celebrated artistic and literary cafés of old, the *Café Union*: situated in a late-18C palace (demolished in 1950; now the Česká Spořitelna, No. 29), this experienced its heyday in the first two decades of the 20C, when its series of small interconnected rooms were individually appropriated by the city's various literary and intellectual coteries, such as Tomáš Masaryk and his university colleagues, Hašek and his drinking pals, and all the leading Czech Cubists from Janák to Kubista (who were able to benefit from the café's large collection of specialist art books and magazines).

Continuing to walk west, you will pass almost immediately on the left-hand side, at No. 20, the **Reduta** (see p 37), a famous and tourist-loved jazz club, which has photographs and a plaque recording its most recent moment of glory: the visit in 1994 of President Clinton, who played his saxophone here before a global audience. The bronze memorial at No. 16 marks the spot where peaceful protesters were attacked and brutally beaten by the Czechoslovak riot police on 17 November 1989 during one of the largest street demonstrations leading up to the 'Velvet Revolution'.

Just after crossing Voršiliská you will come to the late-17C former **Convent Church of St Ursula** (sv. Voršily), which was designed by Marcantonio Canevalle. Facing this on the other side of Národní avenue are two remarkable and adjoining Art Nouveau buildings, both designed by Osvald Polívka. The first of these, at No. 9, is the former Topič Publishing House (Topičův dům), a richly stuccoed building of 1910 which is now used by the Raffeisenbank; the second building, at No. 7, is the former headquarters of Praha Assurance (pojišt'ovna Praha) (1905–07) and, though a less-decorative structure than its neighbour, has superlative reliefs on its façade by Ladislav Šaloun. Much of the remaining right-hand side of the street is taken up by the Czech Academy of Sciences (Akademie věd České republiky), a grimly impressive neo-Renaissance structure built by Vojtěch Ullmann in 1858–61 as the headquarters of a bank. The last building on the right, at No. 1, is the famous **Café Slavia** (see p 33), a popular tourist haunt, which is also one of the oldest of Prague's surviving literary cafés.

Café Slavia

The German poet Rainer Maria Rilke was one of the many artists and writers who frequented the *Café Slavia* in the early years of the 20C, and he used the place as the setting of his evocative short stories, *Tales of Prague*. A later habitué was the poet Jaroslav Seifert, who was one of the stalwarts of Prague's coffee-house culture from the 1920s right up to the 1960s; he evoked the place in his *Slavia Poems*, in which he dreamt up imaginary encounters with the likes of Apollinaire. Another, more recent writer to feature the café in his works is Michal Ajvaz (born 1949), whose short story *The Past* (1991) opens with the words, 'I'm sitting at the Slavia, people-watching.'

From the 1960s onwards the place held regular jazz concerts, which used to attract many of the city's political dissidents, including Václav Havel, who protested vigorously when the café closed down in 1991 for restoration that was endlessly protracted as a result of a leasing dispute between a group of Boston investors and the next-door film school. When the latter eventually won, and the café reopened in January 1998, Havel was reported in the world press as saying that a national institution had been saved.

The two end buildings on the left-hand side of the street are the **New National Theatre** (Nová scéna) at No. 4 and the National Theatre at No. 2. The former, one of the boldest examples of recent Czech architecture, was built in 1977–83 by Karel Prager. It is arranged around a small square and comprises three shaped blocks coated in glass, the one facing the street resembling a translucent honeycomb, and southern one being the new home of the Magic Lantern (see p 173). The building is used almost exclusively for drama productions organised by the National Theatre Company. For programme information and bookings, ask at the tourist information centre inside the foyer; the box office is open Mon–Fri 10.00–20.00, Sat, Sun 15.00–18.00.

National Theatre

As a result of recent privatisation, Prague opera is now divided between the State Opera (see p 171) and the National Opera, the latter having as its premises the superb ****National Theatre** (Národní divadlo), one of the great landmarks of Prague and by far the most eloquent architectural expression of Czech nationalist aspirations in the late 19C.

In 1845 a group of prominent Czech patriots, including František Palacký, Josef Jungmann, Josef Kajetán Tyl and Jan Evangelista Purkyně, sent a petition to Emperor Ferdinand V asking for permission to build an independent Czech theatre in Prague. The proposal was also supported by the writers Jan Neruda, Vítězslav Hálek and Karel Havlíček Borovský, the last making the practical suggestion that the money for the building should be raised through voluntary contributions. A fund-raising campaign with the slogan 'the Nation for Itself' was subsequently begun, but it was not until 1868 that the foundation stone of the building was laid. The architect chosen was Josef Zítek, who was supervising the final details of his work in 1881 when a fire broke out, destroying the auditorium and much of the building's decorations. Within the remarkably short space of six weeks enough money had been raised to rebuild the theatre, a task that was given to Josef Schulz. The theatre was finally opened on 18 November 1883 with a production of Bedřich Smetana's opera *Libuše*.

The painters and sculptors involved in the decoration of the building include almost all the leading Czech artists of the late 19C, a generation that is in fact referred to as 'The National Theatre Generation'; among these artists were the sculptors Josef Myslbek, Bohuslav Schnirch and Anton Wagner, and the painters Mikoláš Aleš, Václav Brožík, Vojtěch Hynais and František Ženíšek. In 1977–83 the building was extensively restored by Karel Prager, and can be appreciated today at its resplendent best.

The grand exterior of the building, which has echoes of the Vienna Opera House and rather more distant ones of Renaissance Italy, is crowned by a Palladian-style roof highlighted by gilding. Some of the finest **statuary** of the main façade is concentrated on the attic level where there is a row of statues of *Apollo* and the

Muses by Bohuslav Schnirch, who also modelled the flanking bronze chariot groups; on the side façade overlooking the Masaryk Embankment is a portal decorated with reclining figures of *Opera* and *Drama* by Josef Myslbek.

A bronze figure by Myslbek representing *Music* presides over the profusely embellished main foyer (open 45 minutes before performances), where there are allegorical ceiling paintings by Ženíšek, 14 lunette paintings by Aleš of scenes from Smetana's symphonic poem, *My Country* (*Má Vlast*), and a gallery of bronze busts by different artists of the leading figures in the history of Czech theatre and opera. Of the many other decorations in the building, special mention must be made of the works of Vojtěch Hynais. He decorated the stairs leading up to the **presidential box** with an allegorical frieze, painted vivid representations of the Four Seasons for the ladies' boudoir of the presidential box (note, in particular, the female figure floating over a snow-covered landscape), and provided the stage with its superlative and celebrated **back-cloth**; the latter, portraying the unpromising theme of *The Origin of the National Theatre*, is full of references to Raphael and Renaissance painting and yet is saved from the absurder excesses of academic art through the sheer energy of the composition and execution. The auditorium is best appreciated during performances—ballet and opera, presenting less of a language problem to non-Czechs, feature regularly in the repertoire alongside plays. On weekdays, guided tours of the auditorium can also be made by prior arrangement (call the National Theatre on ☎ 2491 4153).

Národní avenue comes to an end by the Vltava River, where you should head south down the **Masaryk Embankment** (Masarykovo nábřeží) passing alongside **Slavonic Island** (Slovanský ostrov). This island, formed by alluvial deposits in the 18C, was strengthened by container walls in 1784, and partially built upon. In 1830 a restaurant was erected in its southern half, and this soon became one of the main centres of Prague's social and political life. Concerts were held in the building—including ones given by Berlioz and Liszt—and in 1848 the place hosted the inaugural session of the Slavonic Congress. Memorial plaques commemorating both this congress and the distinguished Slovak writer Ludovít Štúr, one of its participants, are to be seen on the walls of the present cultural centre (Žofín), a large yellow building with a mediocre restaurant and excellent beer-garden at the back.

The rest of the island is taken up by a wooded public park laid out in 1931 and containing at its northern end a bronze memorial by Karel Pokorný to the writer Božena Němcová. Nearby, rowing boats are available for hire.

Straddling the narrow stretch of water between the island and the southern end of the Masaryk Embankment is the **Mánes Gallery** (Výstavní síň Mánes), the seat of the Mánes Society of Artists, which was founded in 1898 in opposition to the Czech Academy of Arts. Their present headquarters, a simple, rather run-down Functionalist building erected by Otakar Novotný in 1923–25, is curiously but picturesquely linked to a Renaissance water tower that once formed part of the Sitka Mills; the gallery puts on exhibitions by contemporary artists (open Tues–Sun 10.00–18.00); there is also a café and dance club with seating on the terrace.

The Mánes Gallery is a favourite building of Václav Havel, despite the one-time presence there of agents from the Czech Secret Service, who used to spy on him from the top of its water tower when he was living at No. 78 Rašínovo nábřeží, immediately to the south of the Masaryk Embankment. His riverside apartment, designed by his grandfather, adjoins today a controversial new building that has proved especially popular with the city's foreign tourists. Popularly known as the ***'Fred and Ginger Building'** (Tančící dům), on account of its vague resemblance to a dancing couple, it was designed in 1993–94 by the Canadian-born architect Frank Gehry, who achieved international fame following the opening in 1997 of his Guggenheim Museum in Bilbao. Although this gloriously topsy-turvy, inebriated-looking structure is intentionally at variance with its sombre neighbouring buildings, it seems perfectly in tune with the more expressionistic and fantastical side to the Central European spirit.

The interior, sadly, is rather less interesting than the exterior, and is partly occupied by the singularly unfriendly French-run café and restaurant pretentiously calling itself *La Perle de Prague* (see p 30). The restaurant, on the top floor, is none the less worth a visit simply to climb out on to its terrace, which enjoys perhaps the most overwhelmingly beautiful views in the whole city; there are occasional group visits to the building for those who do not want either to eat here or try to gain entry through their powers of persuasion (a largely futile task).

Retrace your steps towards the Mánes Gallery and then head east down Myslíkova, turning off on to the third street to the left, Křemencova, to visit at No. 11 on the left-hand side Prague's most famous beer hall, ***U Fleků** (see p 36). Open 09.00–23.00.

The origins of U Fleků go back to at least 1499 when the brewer Vít Skřemenec acquired the house that stood on the site of the present building and founded the beer-cellar and small brewery that came to be known for the next 250 years as *Na Skřemenici* (hence the name of the street). The name 'U Fleků' dates back to after 1762, when the establishment was bought by the Flekovsky family from Počenice, who, during the short time that they owned the place, became celebrated throughout Prague for the quality of their beer. The present neo-Gothic appearance of the interior is due to renovations carried out in 1898–1905. The newly restored ale-house soon became a popular literary haunt, and for years afterwards there would always be a section reserved for writers.

In the early years of the 20C the place served as the meeting-place for the literary club known as *Syrinx*, whose members included a number of future leading Czech writers and dramatists, including Karel Hugo Hilar (later to become director of the Prague National Theatre under the Republic), the playwright Jiří Mahen, and Rudolf Těsnohlídek, who wrote the story of Janáček's opera, *The Cunning Little Vixen*. Another of its members, then experiencing his first taste of Bohemian life, was the future author of *The Good Soldier Švejk*, Jaroslav Hašek, who doubtless enjoyed the rowdiness of many of their meetings, the tone of which can be judged from what one of its sculptor members once told him: 'Come here, you hairy bastard, and let me tear all those lice off you!' Later the club changed its allegiance to the *U sv. Tomáše* tavern in the Little Quarter (see p 128), but Hašek himself was soon to tire of the group, finding it not too silly but too intellectual, and having no interest in its occasional serious discussions about 'modern art'.

A picturesque old clock, hung like a tavern sign, marks the entrance to U Fleků, which still retains a number of attractively panelled rooms with wooden tables and neo-Gothic vaulting. Yet to all those who had the privilege of visiting this place before 1989, its new commercial incarnation will come as something of a disappointment. Gone are the sallow-faced regulars discussing politics in smoky rooms, their place taken by coachloads of noisy German tourists, who sing along to the stomper bands or come to gawp at the cringingly bad cabaret shows featuring semi-naked young women. The shady courtyard offers some respite from the revelries within, but even here dapper waiters will insist that you partake of a shot of *becherovka* ('because it's traditional') and then charge you handsomely for the pleasure. The very idea of food and snacks would have been an anathema to the boozy patrons of Hašek's day; now the extensive menu includes a nauseatingly pungent cheese marinaded in beer, overcooked chips and gristly sausages. At a feisty 13%, the sweet dark beer, brewed on-site, is as excellent as it ever was, though some 'insiders' claim it is watered down for the tourist market. Whatever the case, the famously frothy 'Flek' is still the best reason for coming here. You can see how it is produced by visiting the on-site **Brewery Museum** (open Mon–Sat 10.00–17.00), contained in the former malthouse, which was opened in 1999 to mark the 500th anniversary of U Fleků.

Prague's most famous beer cellar, U Fleků

The charming backstreets between Národní and Myslíkova, an area known to Prague's ex-pat community as SONA (South of the National Theatre), are filled with a whole host of cafés, pubs and clubs that might compensate for the disappointments of U Fleků. The best-known of these is the now-legendary *Globe Bookstore and Coffeehouse* (see p 32), around the corner on Pštrossova, which was founded in 1993 by a Beat Generation enthusiast from San Francisco, Scott Rodgers. Other popular haunts include *Ultramarin* on Ostrovní (see Hotel Élite, p 18), with a cosy dance club in the basement; *Velryba* on Opatovická (see p 33), a lunch bar and gallery inhabited by sweet-faced Charles University students; the arty *Jazz café č. 14* (see p 35) on the same street; and, finally, the brazen pick-up joint that is *Solidni nejistota* on Pštrossova (see p 36).

Returning to Myslíkova, turn left until you reach the lower end of Spálená, where, on turning right you will soon reach the northwestern corner of the long **Charles Square** (Karlovo náměstí), which is even larger than Wenceslas Square, but with a much more sober and less energetic character. Known as the Cattle Market until 1848, it was transformed in the middle of the 19C into a wooded public park, complete with statues to famous Czechs such as the poet Vítězslav Hálek and the botanist Benedikt Roezl; the buildings that surround the park are set back from it by wide and busy streets and have largely a stately but unremarkable 19C character.

The main building at the square's northern end is the **New Town Hall** (Novoměstská radnice), which dates back to 1367 but has kept little of its medieval structure apart from the tower of 1425–26 (which can be climbed), the cellars and the double-aisled entrance hall; the gabled façade overlooking the square is an early-20C reconstruction of the building as it appeared in the 16C. The town hall is famous as the place where on 30 July 1419 an irate mob led by the reformist preacher Jan Želivský were greeted by stones as they stood outside demanding the release of certain reformist prisoners; in anger they stormed the building, and flung the mayor and several of his councillors out of the window and onto the square, where they were torn limb from limb, thus sparking off the Hussite revolution and inaugurating a long Czech tradition of 'defenestration'. Open Tues–Sun 10.00–18.00.

Adjacent to the Town Hall, on the northeastern corner of the square, is the late-18C **Salm House** (No. 24), which marks the site of a Renaissance home (of which the portal has survived) owned in the early 18C by the leading Baroque sculptor Matthias Braun, who died here in 1738.

Cross over to the western side of the square and walk half-way down it to **Resslova**, where you turn right, heading back in the direction of the river. On the right-hand side of the street at No. 9 is a former priest's home designed in 1736 by K.I. Dientzenhofer, who was also responsible for the adjoining Church of **Sts Cyril and Methodius** (sv. Cyrila a Metoděje) to which this institution was attached. Built in 1730–36 and originally dedicated to St Charles Borromeo, this church is a tightly composed structure with symmetrically treated pedimented façades and a powerful entablature tying the whole building together; the interior (entrance on Na Zderaze) is stuccoed by Ignác Jan Palliardi and decorated with frescoes depicting the life of St Charles Borromeo. More interesting than the church itself, however, are the ***crypts** below the main entrance, for it was here, in 1942, that one of the most heroic and tragic episodes in the history of the Czech resistance took place.

The Assassination of Heydrich

In September 1941, Hitler appointed Reinhard Heydrich as *Reichsprotektor* of Bohemia and Moravia. Heydrich was perfectly suited to the task of implementing the 'Final Solution' in the Czech lands. A former naval officer who joined the SS in 1932, he later came to head the Gestapo and, following the outbreak of the Second World War, organised the *Einsatzgruppen* that systematically murdered Jews in occupied Russia. In January 1942, he chaired the infamous Wannsee Conference attended by many high-ranking Nazis, including Eichmann, at which plans for the extermination of European Jewry were discussed and finalised. Heydrich instituted what he termed a 'whip and sugar' policy in the Czech lands, encouraging the local population to work hard in return for larger food rations, and carrying our reprisals if they did not; he quickly earned himself the epithet of the 'Hangman of Prague'.

Back in London, the Czech government-in-exile, headed by President Edvard Beneš, devised a plan to assassinate Heydrich, hoping that such a spectacular show of resistance would give them more leverage over the Allies in the event of a negotiated peace settlement with Hitler. The government knew full well that Nazi revenge against the Czech population would be terrible, but nevertheless gave the go-ahead for the operation in October 1941 (for which the Czech Communist Party never forgave them). Two Czech agents—Jan Kubiš and Josef Gabčík—were chosen for the task and given special training by the British Special Operations Executive. Armed with forged papers, contact lists and Sten guns, they were parachuted into occupied Czechoslovakia on 28 December 1941.

Having made contact with the Czech partisans, Kubiš and Gabčik set up their surveillance operation in the village of Panenské Břežany near Prague, where Heydrich and his family lived. Over the next few months they studied Heydrich's daily routine, trying to determine when and where he would be most vulnerable. The spot they finally chose for the assassination was in the northern district of Holešovice, by a hairpin bend, where Heydrich's car would have to slow down in order to turn. On the morning of 27 May 1942, Gabčik, Kubiš and a third accomplice got into position and waited for their target. Heydrich's arrogance—his refusal to drive with a security escort or install armour plating on his car—worked in the assassins' favour. When his car appeared at 10.25, Gabčik ran into the road and fired at Heydrich's head, but—to his horror—the gun jammed. Rather than escape immediately, Heydrich and his driver began firing at Gabčik, which gave the unseen Kubiš enough time to throw a grenade into the car. The blast destroyed the rear of the vehicle, but, amazingly, Heydrich emerged from the wreckage, gun in hand. Seriously wounded, he ran in pursuit of Kubiš before eventually collapsing; he died in hospital from kidney failure eight days later, having been visited on his death-bed by a tearful Himmler.

Kubiš and Gabčik escaped from the scene and, along with five accomplices, took refuge in the crypt of the Sts Cyril and Methodius Church. Everything seemed to be going according to plan until a member of the Czech resistance betrayed the group's whereabouts to the Nazi authorities. On the morning of 18 June, heavily armoured SS and Gestapo units surrounded the church and for the next six hours peppered the crypt with bullets and grenades, one of which killed Kubiš. The remaining conspirators refused to give themselves up, and, when the Germans finally flooded the crypt, committed suicide with their final rounds.

The Nazi reprisals following Heydrich's assassination were swift and even more horrific than had been initially feared. An enraged Hitler ordered the death of 10,000 Czechs, many of whom were rounded up in Prague and immediately shot; but the worst fate would befall the village of Lidice (see p 217), which was razed to the ground on Hitler's orders. Of the villagers, all but 26 of the men were shot, the others being burnt alive in the village barn; the women and children, having watched their men die, were sent to the Ravensbruck and Gneisenau concentration camps, where almost all perished.

The crypts contain a fascinating and very moving potted history of the assassination and the conspirators' final stand—their story is also told in the 1977 film *Operation Daybreak*. A small shrine has been set up, where visitors, many of them war veterans, leave messages and tributes to the men who embarked on that fateful mission. Kubiš and Gabčik knew that their chances of survival were practically zero; you can see the tunnel they tried to dig in a desperate attempt to reach the city's sewers when the Germans started flooding the building. Outside, the crypt wall is still scarred with bullet holes; there is also a plaque commemorating the men, and a memorial shrouded with flowers. Crypt open Tues–Sun 09.00–16.00.

Further down the Resslova, on the left-hand side, is the **Church of St**

Wenceslas (sv. Václava), which was founded in 1170 but rebuilt at the end of the 14C, during the reign of King Wenceslas IV. The building has been much altered over the centuries though fragments of the medieval masonry are to be seen in the façade, and there survives inside a late-Gothic vault of 1586–87; the distinguished Art Nouveau sculptor František Bílek executed the pews and the altar of the *Crucifixion* (1930).

At the end of the street, head south down the Rašínovo Embankment (Rašínovo nábřeží) until you come to **Palacký Square** (Palackého náměstí). The late-19C **Palacký Bridge**, which spans the river at this point, was once crowned at its corners by large and imposing sculptural groups by Josef Myslbek representing mythical figures from Prague's early history, but these were transferred in 1945 to the park at Vyšehrad. Their absence is amply compensated for by the presence in the middle of the square of the *Palacký Monument, one of the most exciting examples of public statuary in Prague, which commemorates the great 19C Czech politician and historian, František Palacký. The work is the masterpiece of Stanislav Sucharda, assisted by the architect Alois Dryák. As with the near-contemporary Hus Monument in the Old Town Square, its gestation was a long one, being first planned in 1898 and not unveiled until 1912, by which time it was to seem rather dated and its outstanding qualities not fully appreciated; a romantic and deeply poetic work, it shows an ingenious use of different materials, the real world—including the heavy, seated figure of Palacký himself—being depicted in stone, the allegorical one in bronze, and the whole composition culminating in a magnificent, asymmetrically placed bronze group soaring above the central stone plinth.

From the square head east up Na Moráni, which will bring you back to Charles Square, at its lower end. The southern side of the square is taken up by a hospital wing of the Charles University, the large building at its western corner being romantically known as the **Faust House** (Faustův dům). This late-18C structure marks the site of a house where Edward Kelley—the English adventurer at the court of Rudolph II—carried out his alchemical experiments in the hope of producing gold; later alchemists also worked here, and in the 18C, when a chemist occupied the building, the legend was born that the imaginary Dr Faust had been another of its occupants until he was carried off through its laboratory ceiling after having sold his soul to the devil. Whether out of a sense of humour or in deference to the building's tradition, the Medical Faculty of Charles University has installed here its own pharmacy (in the courtyard).

Walking south from the Faust House down **Vyšehradská** you will soon see, picturesquely rising above a great double-ramp staircase on the left-hand side of the street, the **Church of St John on the Rock** (sv. Jana Na skalce), which was built between 1729 and 1739 and is one of the more remarkable buildings by K.I. Dientzenhofer. Extracting the maximum dramatic potential from the restricted site, the architect canted the twin towers of the west façade to create a powerful sense of movement that is continued in the interior, the nave of which comprises an octagon with concave sides. Floating above the white walls inside are ceiling frescoes depicting the *Glorification of St John of Nepomuk* (1745), while on the high altar has been placed a wooden statue of the saint by Jan Brokoff (1682), a work that served as the model for the bronze of this subject on the Charles Bridge.

On the other side of the street to the church is the former Monastery of the Slavs (Klášter Na Slovanech), popularly known as the **Emmaus Monastery**, which was founded by Charles IV in 1347 for the Croatian Benedictines. Extensively remodelled and rebuilt during the 18C and 19C, the whole complex was heavily damaged by a stray Allied bomb in 1945. Restored after the war for the use of the Czechoslovak Academy of Sciences, it was finally handed back to the Benedictines in 1990. The finest medieval survival, though heavily restored after 1960, are the frescoes of 1370–75 preserved in the vaulted monastery cloisters and representing scenes from the Old and New Testaments; these were the work of three painters, Nikolaus Wurmser, Master Theodoric and the painter known as the Master of the Emmaus Cycle. The cloisters give access to the monastery church, whose sparse, freshly renovated interior is used for concerts and contains a potted history of the monastery (in English) along the south aisle wall. The Gothic walls of the church support a daring but very elegant modern superstructure built in 1965–68 (currently under renovation) and comprising two interlaced sail-like forms soaring up into the sky. The church and cloisters are open 07.00–18.30.

Continue down the sloping Vyšehradská and bear left into Na slupi, which skirts the **University Botanical Gardens** (Botanická zahrada; open daily April–Aug 10.00–18.00; Sept–Oct and Jan–March 10.00–17.00; Nov, Dec 10.00–16.00; entrance free), an agreeable spot for an afternoon walk, where you can visit the newly-restored 1930s' greenhouses. The first church you pass on the left further down Na slupi can safely be ignored, but as the road nears Vyšehrad Hill you could take a brief look at the **Church of Our Lady Na Slupi** (Panna Maria na Slupi), a building of late-14C origin that was restored in 1858–63; a notable feature of the interior is the way the 15C vault is supported by a single pillar.

Immediately south of the church turn left into Horská and head east, passing university buildings and laboratories. The road eventually narrows to a path, with steps ascending to the large monastic complex known simply as the *****Karlov**. This former Augustinian monastery was founded by Charles IV in 1351 and has a most exciting church, the nave of which is octagonal in emulation of Charlemagne's burial chapel at Aachen.

The church was completed in 1377, but in 1575 Bonifác Wohlmut covered its nave with an astonishingly bold star-shaped vault. The furnishings and other elements of the building are additions of the Baroque period, including the steep triple-flighted staircase that leads up to the Chapel of the Holy Steps on the southern side of the church; this *Scala Santa*, up which pilgrims are meant to climb on their knees, was built in 1708–09 and is often attributed to Santini-Aichel.

A visit to the church is completed by descending into the crypt, where you will find yourself in an early-18C grotto imitating the cave in Bethlehem where Christ was born; the walls are covered with pastel-coloured stucco decorations representing Classical buildings, and giving you the impression that you have taken a wrong turning and stumbled from the Holy Land into Arcadia. Open Sun 14.00–17.00.

The fantasy of the whole experience will soon disappear as you walk from the church to the adjoining monastic buildings, where there is a museum dedicated to the now not very fascinating subject of the Czech Police Force: the **Police Museum** (Muzeum policie ČR), dating back to the 1970s, but completely changed since 1989, is today full of displays relating not to 'spies and agents' but to such pedestrian topics as traffic offences and crime prevention. The museum's prize exhibit of old—the stuffed carcass of Brek, an Alsatian hound famous for capturing an exceptionally large number of fugitives trying to escape from Communist Czechoslovakia, has now sadly gone; what remains makes for a fairly tedious experience, not helped by the absence of English labelling. Open Tues–Sun 10.00–17.00.

Heading north from the Karlov up **Ke Karlovu**, the third street that you will pass to your right is Na Bojišti, where, at No. 12, is a large beer-house (see p 36) that owes its fame to being mentioned in Jaroslav Hašek's book *The Good Soldier Švejk*. To this establishment, known as **U kalicha** (The Chalice), the congenital idiot Švejk decides to come on the day that the Sarajevo assassination is announced in Prague. He soon enters into an unwise conversation with the only client then present in the bar, a plain-clothes police-officer, and thus unwittingly embarks on his inglorious career in the Austrian army. The landlord described in the book is one Mr Palivec, a notoriously rude man whose every other word is 'arse' or 'shit'. The present-day establishment is scarcely more prepossessing than the place known to Hašek, but with the difference that it is often booked up by tour groups. It exploits to the full its Hašek connections, with representations of people from the book covering the walls of its large dining-room, and numerous Švejk souvenirs being sold in its vestibule. The usual drab Czech dishes it serves are given exotic 'Švejkian' names such as 'Mrs Müller's dumplings' or 'Mr Palivec's skewer' and, as in the equally tourist-savvy *U Fleků* (see p 36), the conspicuous and overbearing waiters will seek to dismantle your resistance with a 'free *becherovka* aperitif'.

Returning to Ke Karlovu and continuing north, you will come almost immediately to the elegant summer pavilion built by K.I. Dientzenhofer in 1715–20 (No. 20, on the right-hand side), which is generally known as the ***Villa America** on account of a hotel which existed nearby. This jewel-like building, painted outside a vivid red, is set in a small garden adorned with sculptures from the workshop of Matthias Braun; the main room on the first floor, used for chamber concerts, is covered with a delightful illusionistic ceiling painting (c 1730) by Johann Ferdinand Schor. Since 1934 the building has housed the **Dvořák Museum** (Muzeum Antonína Dvořáka); the composer lived in the vicinity (see below) and his Bösendorfer piano and other personal belongings are exhibited here. More interesting than the display, however, is the building itself, which you can admire to the mellifluous strains of Dvořák's music. Open Tues–Sun 10.00–17.00.

On the other side of the street is a small and rather neglected wooded park, off which stands the former Augustinian **Church of St Catherine** (sv. Kateřiny). This building and its adjoining convent were founded by Charles IV in 1354 as a votive offering for his victory at the battle of San Felice in Italy. Destroyed by the Hussites in 1420, the church was rebuilt in 1518–22, and then again by K.I. Dientzenhofer and František Kaňka in 1737–41. The one survival of the medieval church is its enormously tall tower, which, thanks to its octagonal upper floors, is sometimes known as 'the Minaret of Prague'. The magnificent Baroque interior, with ceiling frescoes by Václav Reiner, is currently undergoing extensive renovation.

At its northern end Ke Karlovu emerges at the wide and busy Ječná. Turning left, you could stop for refreshments at the *Pivovarský dům* (see p 36), situated at the corner of Lipová, which was awarded the Best Czech Pub Brewery prize in 2002 in recognition of its fine dark and light beers, brewed on site. Alternatively, proceed down the street facing this establishment—**Štěpánská**, turning right just after the church into Na Rybníčku. Standing in a tiny park on this street is the much-restored and altered **Rotunda of St Longinus** (rotunda sv. Longina), which dates back to the beginning of the 12C and is the smallest of Prague's Romanesque rotundas. Further north Štěpánská joins **Žitná**, another busy thoroughfare, where, if you turn left, you will find on the left-hand side, at No. 14, the dilapidated building where the composer Antonín Dvořák lived from 1877 up to his death in 1901; he stayed at first in a now-ruinous house in the courtyard, but later moved to a more salubrious location at the front of the building (where a plaque to him has been placed high up on the façade). On the opposite side of the street begins Školská, where at No. 16 you will find a plaque recording the house where the writer Jaroslav Hašek was born on 30 April 1883; ironically for the birthplace of the future *enfant terrible*, the house belonged at that time to a respected advocate and Prague alderman, Dr Jakub Škarda, a family relative. Continue to the end of Školská and turn right into Vodičkova, which will bring you back to Wenceslas Square.

5 Southern Prague

Vyšehrad

Below the southern end of the New Town is a great wooded outcrop of rock rising directly and steeply above the Vltava River and supporting the **citadel of Vyšehrad** ('The Castle on the Heights'), the history of which is tied to the mythical origins of Prague.

According to legend, the castle at Vyšehrad was the home of Princess Libuše, who foresaw from this site the future glories of Prague, and married here the ploughman founder of the Přemyslid dynasty. The truth, however, is that this was not the first seat of the Czech princes, being preceded both by Prague Castle and Levý Hradec. Founded probably in the early 10C, it briefly became the seat of Boleslav II. In the late 11C the Přemyslid princes once again abandoned Prague Castle in favour of Vyšehrad, and in 1070 founded a Collegiate Chapter here. The latter, headed by a dean whose role came to be analogous to that of Chancellor of Bohemia, was to remain here for centuries, but the princes themselves returned permanently to Prague Castle in 1140. The importance of Vyšehrad declined, though it was to be renewed once more during the reign of Charles IV, who rebuilt the royal palace, erected new fortifications, and established the castle as the starting-point of Czech coro-

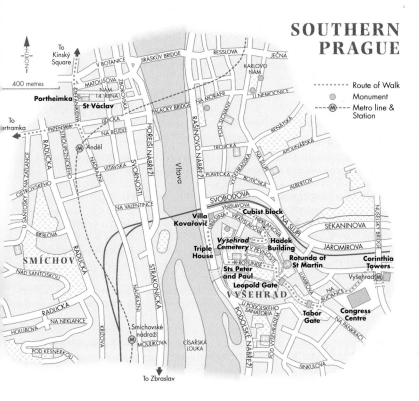

SOUTHERN PRAGUE

- - - - - - - - Route of Walk
⊙ Monument
- - -Ⓜ- - - Metro line & Station

nation processions. In 1420, during the Hussite Wars, almost all the buildings on Vyšehrad were destroyed, and in their place a small town of craftsmen and tradesmen emerged. This town, known as the Town of Mount Vyšehrad, was destroyed in the mid-17C to make way for a Baroque fortress, which was to be abolished in 1866, just under 20 years before Vyšehrad was incorporated into the city of Prague.

Vyšehrad's mythical early history, its nationalist associations and, not least, the romantic beauty of its site, combined to make the place a great source of inspiration to 19C artists, writers and musicians, and not only to those of Czech blood, but also to a number of Germans as well. The German works referring to the rock and its history include Conradin Kreutzer's opera *Libussa*, Mendelssohn's sonata, *Libussa's Prophecy*, K.E. Ebert's poem, *Vision from the Vyšehrad* and Grillparzer's drama, *Libussa*. Mikoláš Aleš, J. Döbler, Karel Postl, E.G. Buquoy and K. Pluth were among the many Czech painters to feature the place in their works, while their compatriot Julius Zeyer wrote an enormously popular series of poems entitled *Vyšehrad* (1879–80). But the Czech who did most to establish the place and its legends in the national consciousness was Bedřich Smetana, whose opera *Libuše* (with a libretto by Josef Wenzig) was chosen appropriately for the inauguration of the Prague

National Theatre in 1883. At the height of all this romantic adulation of Vyšehrad, two deans proposed to convert the original parish cemetery of the Collegiate Chapter into a national cemetery, a scheme that took root in the 1880s and culminated in the building between 1889 and 1893 of a great pantheon of celebrated Czechs—the Slavín. The rest of the citadel was laid out in 1927 as a public park.

• **Getting there** The easiest way to reach Vyšehrad from the centre of Prague is to take the metro to Vyšehrad station, where you will find yourself on the southern side of a massive road bridge that connects the hill with the New Town and the district of Vinohrady.

With its fantastic river views and secluded parkland, the Vyšehrad citadel is an ideal place to escape the noise and fumes of the city centre. The whole complex can easily be visited during an afternoon, especially as the volume of tourist traffic here is comparatively small: you won't find yourself having to queue or join a compulsory guided tour to get into any of the sites. On the eastern side of Vyšehrad station stands one of Prague's luxury hotels, the bland, American-style Corinthia Towers (opened in 1989), which overlooks a large prison, the courtyard of which had to be roofed over so that the hotel guests would not be offended by the sight of exercising prisoners. Across the busy dual carriageway is the similarly characterless Congress Centre (Kongresové centrum)—formerly known as the Palace of Culture and once used for Communist Party conventions—which nonetheless sports a wide terrace with extensive views to the north, a panorama dominated by the Karlov church (see p 182).

Walking west along this terrace you will come to Na Bučance, a quiet street that will take you to the eastern entrance of the Vyšehrad citadel in a few minutes. Enter through the mid-17C **Tábor Gate** (Táborská brána), and, after passing to your right the scant ruins of part of the 14C fortifications erected by Charles IV, you will reach the monumental **Leopold Gate** (Leopoldova brána), the most impressive survival of the 17C citadel. Built before 1678 by Carlo Lurago, the gate is protected by a deep ditch, which was once spanned by a drawbridge; between the two gates is a small **tourist information centre** selling maps and guides. Further along the road, you will see to your right the oldest surviving structure in Vyšehrad, the **Rotunda of St Martin** (Rotunda sv. Martina), beautifully shaded by trees. This is the earliest of Prague's Romanesque rotundas, dating back to the late 11C, though heavily restored in 1878–80; it is also the only one to have kept its original shape (open only for services).

Walking west from here along the lane called K rotundě, you will pass to your left the late-18C former **Deanery** (Staré děkanství), which was built on the site of the Romanesque basilica of St Lawrence; the foundations of this church, destroyed by the Hussites in 1421, can be seen at the back of the building, while inside is a small display relating to the history of the Vyšehrad. To enter, you should ask for the key at the café on Soběslavova (next left).

Rotunda of St Martin

Further west on the right-hand side of the road is the ***Church of Sts Peter and Paul** (sv. Petra a Pavla), which, though founded by Vratislav II in 1070 in conjunction with the Collegiate Chapter, owes its present appearance to neo-Gothic remodelling by Josef Mocker between 1885 and 1903. The church's twin stone towers constitute one of Prague's picture-postcard landmarks, though the interior, with its exuberant early-20C painted decoration, is also impressive. Open Wed–Thur, Sat–Mon 09.00–12.00, 13.00–17.00, Fri 09.00–12.00.

The restaurant opposite the church, with seating outside in summer, is a convenient place to stop for lunch before proceeding to the ***Vyšehrad Cemetery**, the entrance to which is beside the church's western façade. Open daily May–Sept 08.00–19.00; March, April, Oct 08.00–18.00; Nov–Feb 09.00–16.00.

In the late 19C it was decided to convert the former parish cemetery into the resting-place of great and famous Czechs, but apart from its historical and sentimental interest the cemetery constitutes a major **gallery of sculpture**: many of the tombs were executed by leading sculptors who themselves lie buried here, such as Josef Myslbek, Otakar Španiel and Bohumil Kafka; in 1887 the grounds were encircled with a beautiful neo-Renaissance arcade designed by Antonín Wiehl.

The **plan** by the entrance will direct you to the tombs found in the main section of the cemetery, which include those of the artists Mikoláš Aleš, Antonín Chitussi, Julius Mařák, Karel Purkyně and Václav Levý; the musicians Antonín Dvořák, Bedřich Smetana, František Ondříček, Josef Slavík and Zdeněk Fibich; the scientists Jan Purkyně and Josef Heyrovský; and the writers Karel Čapek, Karel Mácha, Jan Neruda, Vítězslav Nezval and Božena Němcová. Particularly touching is the grave of Němcová, who was treated better in death than she was in life (she died neglected and poverty-stricken), and given a tombstone carved with scenes from her best-known work, *The Grandmother*.

A special part of the cemetery (on the eastern side) is taken up by the Pantheon or **Slavín**, a raised structure preceded by steps and dominated by statues representing the *Rejoicing Homeland* and the *Mourning Homeland*, which was designed by Wiehl in 1889–93. Over 50 people have been buried here to date, including the artists Vojtěch Hynais, Ladislav Šaloun, Jan Lauda, Alfons Mucha, Jan Štursa and Václav Špála; the architects Josef Gočár, Kamil Hilbert and Jaroslav Fragner; the writers Julius Zeyer, Josef Hora and Jaroslav Vrchlický; the musicians Jan Kubelík, Jan Heřman and Zdeněk Otava; and the actors Zdeněk Štěpánek and Eduard Kohout.

To the south of the church is a shady **park** (Vyšehradské sady) entered through a Baroque gate taken from a 17C armoury; standing forlorn and neglected in the middle of this area are Josef Myslbek's large sculptural groups of mythical Czech figures such as *Libuše and Přemysl* (the couple nearest the church),

Vyšehrad Cemetery

which once proudly stood on the corners of the Palacký Bridge in the New Town. The most enjoyable feature of the park is the dramatic view down to the Vltava from the western ramparts, from where you will also see, clinging to the rockface (above the Vyšehrad tunnel), the ruins of a medieval watch-tower, which in the 19C was given the romantic name of Libuše's Baths.

After leaving the park turn right down K rotundě, and then immediately left, skirting the eastern wall of the cemetery. You will soon reach the citadel's 19C northern gate (Cihelná brána), inside which is the entrance to a series of subterranean passageways culminating in a medieval hall used for storage (tours on the hour, 10.00–17.00). From the gate you begin the sharp descent to the heavily built area comprising the former outer bailey of the castle.

Most of the buildings are apartment blocks of the 19C and 20C, and at the bottom of the first street to the right, Přemyslova, you will find, at the corner with Neklanova (No. 30), a tall, angular and exceedingly graceful building articulated by prismatic forms (now with a restaurant on the ground floor). Known as the Hodek, this remarkable edifice (1911–13) is the earliest and largest of three **Cubist buildings** erected by Josef Chochol at the foot of the Vyšehrad. Turning left at Neklanova and walking around the hill in an anti-clockwise direction you will pass, at No. 2, another fine apartment block, designed by Chochol's contemporary Antonín Belada. Vnislavova merges with Libušina, on which stands, at No. 3, the Villa Kovařovič, a building by Chochol of 1912–13 intended for single-family occupancy and featuring a beautiful façade built up of diamond shapes. At its southern end the short Libušina joins Rašínovo nábřeží (the former Engels Embankment), where, on turning left, you will shortly find on the left-hand side of the street, at Nos 6–8, the third of Chochol's buildings in the area: a house intended for three families ('Rodinný trojdům'), also dating from 1912–13, with a mansard roof and central gable.

Smíchov

Prague's western district of Smíchov is a curious blend of old and new: a traditionally working-class area filled with antiquated factories and crumbling 19C tenements, it has in recent years acquired a high-tech shopping mall, multiplex cinema and modern office blocks that seem almost incongruous in the bleak urban landscape. Industrialisation has left another legacy in the form of pollution, which is still a problem, not least in the vicinity of the Staropramen brewery where one of the city's trademark beers is produced. There are several places of interest, though, all of which are located to the north and west of **Smíchov station** (Smíchovské nádraží). Modernised and enlarged after the Second World War, this is one of the oldest of Prague's main railway stations, founded in the 1860s. One metro stop from here is Anděl, a temple of Soviet kitsch formerly known as Moskevská (there is an identical station in Moscow called Prashkaya or Prague Station). Anděl might have lost its Russian name but it has kept its utopian murals of Soviet workers marching into a future in which thrusting tower blocks rise up alongside St Basil's Cathedral.

Leave Anděl station by the Stroupežnického exit and head north to the junction with Plzeňská. Walk west along this busy street for about 1km, eventually turning left onto Mozartova, which rises up through a wooded park. At the upper end of the street (No. 169) is the main tourist attraction of Smíchov—the **Bertramka**. This modest and recently restored 18C villa, with a wooden gallery and a quiet, bosky garden, was the home in the late 18C of the composer František Xaver Dušek and his wife Josefa, a famous singer. They were close friends of Mozart, who stayed with them on his visits to Prague in 1786, 1787 and 1791. The house has now been done up as a delightful small *Mozart Museum, with appropriate 18C furnishings, unobtrusive background music, and several mementoes of the composer's stay in Prague: these include a piano and harpsichord on which he allegedly played, and a curious German painting of c 1800 showing the interior of a former beer-cellar near the Powder Gate (see p 87), and bearing the inscription: 'This is where Mozart ate, drank and composed *Don Giovanni* in 1787.' Casanova, who was also staying in Prague at the time, later claimed responsibility for forcing Mozart to write this opera; whether it was indeed finished here at the Bertramka, as the museum brochures like to claim, is unknown. In any case, summer recitals of Mozart's music are held at the house, and are usually well worth attending. Open Tues–Sun 09.30–18.00.

Return all the way back along Plzeňská and turn left (north) into the busy shopping street of Štefánikova, where you will shortly pass to your right the dark neo-Renaissance **Church of St Václav**, designed by Antonín Barvitius in 1881–85. In the garden on its northern side is the **Portheimka**, a small summer villa built by K.I. Dientzenhofer for his family, with a first-floor room covered with a ceiling painting by Václav Reiner; the ground floor of this toy-like building is today occupied by the pleasant *Café Apostrof* (see p 33), a good place to stop for coffee.

Further north, Štefánikova emerges onto **Kinský Square** (náměstí Kinských), which, until only a few years ago, was named náměstí Sovětských tankistů in honour of the Red Army, and had at its centre a plinth (now a fountain) supporting one of the first Soviet tanks to reach Prague in May 1945.

Černý's Tank

The presence here of this Soviet tank after 1989 was the subject of much controversy, but suggestions that it should be removed were turned down on the grounds that it was one of the more familiar of Prague's landmarks, as well as being a popular meeting-place. As a compromise solution, a 'Situationist artist' called David Černý gave the tank a more friendly and human aspect by painting it a vivid pink early in 1991; but this 'unlawful' artistic act led to protests from the Soviet Embassy, with whom the new non-communist government was then engaged in sensitive negotiations about the removal of the Soviet military presence from Czechoslovak territory. The paint was subsequently removed, and Černý was arrested; protests then followed, the paint was reapplied (this time by a group of MPs using their parliamentary immunity), and Černý released. The tank remained pink for a while before being removed for good.

On the western side of the square is the entrance to the **Kinský Gardens** (Kinského zahrada), which form part of a vast area of parkland stretching up Petřín Hill and into the Little Quarter. Turning left immediately on entering the gardens and following the path parallel to Holečkova, you will reach the early 19C **Kinský Villa** (Letohrádek Kinských), which is due to reopen in 2004 to house the ethnographic and other collections of the National Museum.

Zbraslav

South of Smíchov extends a sprawling area of suburbs with little architectural or scenic interest until you reach the outlying district of Zbraslav, 12km from the centre of Prague, which was not incorporated into the city until 1974. The beauty of Zbraslav lies essentially in the wooded riverside parkland attached to its former ***Cistercian Monastery**, which continues to be a popular destination for weekend excursions, being accessible in the summer months by a pleasure boat departing from below the Palacký Bridge: it was on a boat outing to Zbraslav organised by the Mánes Association of Artists in 1926 that Kafka's former mistress, Milena Jesenská, met and fell in love with the man who was to become her first husband, the architect Jaromír Krejcar.

• **Getting there** Unfortunately, boat services to Zbraslav have been erratic in recent years (visit www.paroplavba.cz or ☎ 224 931 013 for current schedules), so your safest bet is to catch bus No. 129, 241, 243, 255 or 360 from the Smíchov station (see p 188), getting off at the Zbraslavske náměstí stop. The journey takes about 20 minutes.

The monastery, founded in 1292 on the site of a royal hunting-lodge, was entirely rebuilt in the early 18C, first under the direction of Jan Santini-Aichel (from about 1700) and later under that of František Kaňka (from 1724–32). The elegant buildings, with their whitewashed rooms and large ceiling paintings by Václav Reiner and Franz Palko, once made a most beautiful and restful setting for the National Gallery's remarkable Czech sculptures of the 19C and 20C, many of which are now in the Trade Fair Palace at Holešovice (see p 203), and many others in storage while awaiting the possible setting up of a museum of 19C Czech sculpture. A scattering of sculptures can still be seen in the monastery garden, but the building itself was reopened in October 1998 to show off the National Gallery's extensive and outstanding **Collection of Asian art**, which contains some 12,000 pieces that had not been seen by the general public for 46 years. Open Tues–Sun 10.00–18.00.

The relative remoteness of Zbraslav should not deter anyone from visiting the Asian museum, which is surely one of the finest of its kind in Europe, not simply for the high quality of the exhibits but also for the sensational nature of the actual display. Information panels of exemplary clarity and informativeness in both Czech and English guide you through a museum that can also be enjoyed as a purely aesthetic and, at times, theatrical experience: imaginative lighting, and coloured timbers arranged to suggest bridges, temples, tea-rooms and so on, convey an oriental context and atmosphere with the most stunningly simple of means.

The **ground floor** rooms are taken up almost entirely by the Japanese holdings, which range mainly from the 16C–19C, and feature superlative examples of laquerwork, enamelling, sword hilts, porcelain, metalwork and Buddhist sculptures, as well a regularly changing selection of screens, prints and painted scrolls. But the museum's greatest strength are the Chinese works on the **second floor**, which were largely amassed by Czech archaeologists and collectors travelling in China between the wars. These objects had an enormous influence on leading Czech artists of those years such as Emil Filla and Ludvík Kuba, who is represented here by a self-portrait in front of Chinese porcelain. The Chinese holdings, dating from the Bronze Age right up to the 19C, comprise works in a great variety of media (with even some wonderful fragments of 6C AD wall painting), and reveal the extraordinary degree of naturalism attained by Chinese artists during Europe's Dark Ages; for instance, in the funerary ceramics of animals and other figures from the Six and Tang dynasties. A highpoint of the collection is the darkened room showing a series of 11C–14C Buddhas against a dark-blue ramp, which gives the viewer a strong sense of being inside in a cave temple. Moving on from the Chinese collection to the relatively small holdings of Islamic and South-East Asian art comes inevitably as a slight disappointment, but there is the consolation of a large and dramatically lit group of painted Tibetan scrolls from the 18C.

6 Eastern Prague

Vinohrady

East of Wenceslas Square extends the district of Vinohrady, a large grid of long, straight streets lined with turn-of-the-last-century apartment blocks and offices, some with a decayed splendour. Up until the Second World War this was the epicentre of bourgeois Prague, subsequently left to stagnate during 40 years of communism: investment in this hub of 'reactionary values' was hardly on the planners' list of priorities. Since 1989, though, life has been slowly returning to the district, which is now a firm favourite among the city's ex-pat community and young middle-class Czechs. Certainly, when one considers the cleaner air, affordable rents, and discreetly charming bars and cafés, Vinohrady is a very desirable place to live. As far as sightseeing goes, the places of specific interest are widely scattered, as throughout eastern Prague, making a walking tour practicable only to the most dedicated tourist. The district's main civic buildings are centred around the large **náměstí Míru**, which lies one metro stop away from the southern end of Wenceslas Square.

The middle of náměstí Míru is occupied by the brick neo-Gothic **Church of St Ludmila** (sv. Ludmily), which was built by Josef Mocker in 1888–93 and has a west tympanum decorated with a relief by Josef Myslbek of *Christ with Sts Wenceslas and Ludmila*. The northern side of the square is dominated by the grand façade of the recently restored Vinohrady Theatre (divadlo Na vinohradech), a neo-Baroque building with Art Nouveau elements, built in 1903–06 and crowned by winged allegorical groups.

One of the best pizza parlours in town—*Pizzeria Grosseto* (see p 31)—is found the southeast corner of the square, by the junction with Francouszká, while two excellent cafés, both with a relaxed and friendly atmosphere, are situated on streets running off the square: *Medúza* (see p 33) on Belgická, and *Dobra Trafiká* (see p 33) on Korunní; the latter is easily missed as it occupies the back rooms of a tobacconist's shop.

East off náměstí Míru runs one of Vinohrady's longest streets—Slezská, where, on the left-hand side at No. 7, is an interesting red-brick building by Josef Gočár, built in 1924–26 as an agricultural college. Nearby, at the corner of

Blanická and Vinohradská (No. 38), stands the former School of Commerce, which is decorated around its entrance by four sculptural groups of workers by Karel Dvořák (1925), a very lively example of so-called Objective Realism.

Further east down Vinohradská, adjoining the Jiřího z Poděbrad metro station (one stop from náměstí Míru), is one of the greatest and most original monuments erected in Czechoslovakia between the wars. This, the *Church of the Sacred Heart (Nejsvětějšího Srdce Páně), was built by Jože Plečnik in 1929–33, and looms massively over the bleak gardens that have been laid out in the middle of George of Poděbrady Square (náměstí Jiřího z Poděbrad). Inspired by a combination of an early-Christian basilica and an Egyptian temple, it handles its eclectic borrowings with a boldness that is uncompromisingly modern. Its glazed-brick exterior, studded all over with what seem to be overblown *guttae*, has walls that project diagonally near the top to form a massive cornice; a great pedimented clock tower, as wide as the building itself, rises high above the east end of the building and supports an enormous clock, glass-fronted on both sides and resembling a rose window.

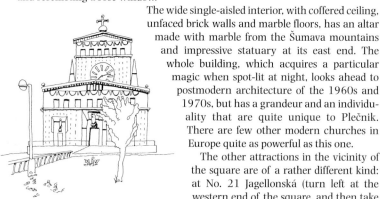

The wide single-aisled interior, with coffered ceiling, unfaced brick walls and marble floors, has an altar made with marble from the Šumava mountains and impressive statuary at its east end. The whole building, which acquires a particular magic when spot-lit at night, looks ahead to postmodern architecture of the 1960s and 1970s, but has a grandeur and an individuality that are quite unique to Plečnik. There are few other modern churches in Europe quite as powerful as this one.

The other attractions in the vicinity of the square are of a rather different kind: at No. 21 Jagellonská (turn left at the western end of the square, and then take the first turning to the right) is Prague's longest-established game restaurant—

Church of the Sacred Heart

the *Myslivna* (see p 31), a place serving good food in intimate surroundings that have yet to be taken over by tourists, while on nearby Orlická you could brave the devilish cocktails served at *Hapu* (see p 36), one of Vinohrady's homeliest underground bars. Just to the north of the *Myslivna*, in the Mahler Park (Mahlerovy sady), soars the futuristic Žižkov Television Tower, which is described below.

At its bleak, easternmost end, Vinohradská passes next to three of Prague's largest cemeteries. Beyond the Flora metro station the street skirts the southern side of the **Olšany Cemetery** (Olšanské hřbitovy), which was founded during the big plague in 1680, and soon became the main burial place serving the communities on the right bank of the Vltava; the main entrance gates are on náměstí Jiřího z Lobkovic. Some of the famous Czechs who are buried here include the writers Josef Jungmann and Jan Kollár; the philosopher Bernard Bolzano; the architects Antonín Barvitius and Josef Fanta; the sculptors Josef Max, Bohuslav Schnirch and Josef Mařatka; and the painters Josef Mánes, Josef Navrátil and Antonín Slavícek. The tombs are adorned with works by many of the leading

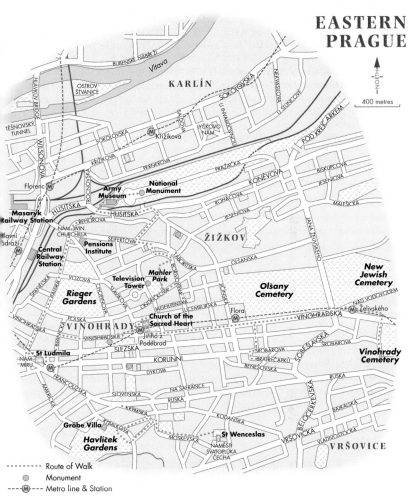

EASTERN PRAGUE

400 metres

Vltava

KARLÍN

OSTROV
ŠTVANICE

BUBENSKÉ NÁBŘEŽÍ

HLÁVKŮV BRIDGE

TĚŠNOVSKÝ
TUNNEL

WILSONOVA

SOKOLOVSKÁ

SOKOLOVSKÁ

Křižíkova

LYČKOVO
NÁM.

U INVALIDOVNY

NEKVASILOVA

ŠALDOVA

SLUNCOVÉ

POD KREJCÁRKEM

Florenc

KŘIŽÍKOVA

PERNEROVA

PRAŽAČKA

BISKUPCOVA

JESENIOVA

HUSITSKÁ

TROCNOVSKÁ

**Army
Museum**

**National
Monument**

KONĚVOVA

ROHÁČOVA

MALEŠICKÁ

**Masaryk
Railway Station**

ŘEHOŘOVA

HUSITSKÁ

JESENIOVA

JÁNA ŽELIVSKÉHO

Hlavní
nádraží

NÁM. WIN.
CHURCHILLA

SEIFERTOVA

ŽIŽKOV

**Central
Railway
Station**

**Pensions
Institute**

TÁBORITSKÁ

OLŠANSKÁ

**New
Jewish
Cemetery**

VOZOVÁ

**Television
Tower**

**Mahler
Park**

BOŘIVOJOVA

ONDŘÍČKOVA

JAGELLONSKÁ

LUCEMBURSKÁ

**Olšany
Cemetery**

NAD VODOVODEM

ŠPÁLELSKÁ

**Rieger
Gardens**

CHOPINOVA

SLAVÍKOVA

Flora

Želivského

VINOHRADSKÁ

POLSKÁ

**Church of the
Sacred Heart**

VINOHRADSKÁ

SOBĚSLAVSKÁ

ŠROBÁROVA

**Vinohrady
Cemetery**

VINOHRADY

VINOHRADSKÁ

Jiřího z
Poděbrad

SLEZSKÁ

KORUNNÍ

ŠROBÁROVA

BRATŘÍ ČAPKŮ

RUSKÁ

St Ludmila

NÁM.
MÍRU

DYKOVA

BENEŠOVSKÁ

FRANCOUZSKÁ

SLOVENSKÁ

RUSKÁ

BĚLOCERKEVSKÁ

RUSKÁ

BAJKALSKÁ

AMERICKÁ

NA ŠAFRÁNCE

KRYMSKÁ

KODAŇSKÁ

Gröbe Villa

RYBALKOVA

MOSKEVSKÁ

VRŠOVICKÁ

VLADIVOSTOCKÁ

**Havlíček
Gardens**

St Wenceslas

NÁMĚSTÍ
SVATOPLUKA
ČECHA

VRŠOVICE

········· Route of Walk

○ Monument

---Ⓜ--- Metro line & Station

Czech sculptors, including Myslbek, Mařatka, Max, Bílek and Kafka, but perhaps
the most endearing is that of the illustrator to Švejk, Josef Lada, who is commemorated by a tomb shaped like a bird's house. Still one of the most honoured
occupants of the cemetery is the student **Jan Palach**, whose tomb (to the east of
the main entrance) is usually shrouded with flowers and candles; his body was
placed here immediately after his dramatic death in 1969 (see p 162), but then
removed to his country village in 1974 when the Communist authorities grew
concerned about the vigils that would take place by the grave; Palach's remains
were eventually brought back here in November 1990.

Immediately to the east of this cemetery is the **New Jewish Cemetery**
(Židovské hřbitovy), the entrance to which is adjacent to the Želivského metro

station: arrows here will direct you to its most visited tombstone, that of the writer **Franz Kafka**, who is buried here alongside his parents; the monument is a symbolic Cubist crystal designed in 1924 by Leopold Ehrmann. Slightly further east Vinohradská skirts the northern side of the **Vinohrady Cemetery** (Vinohradské hřbitovy), which was founded in 1885 and has in its centre the neo-Gothic chapel of St Wenceslas. One of the greatest Czech painters of the turn of the last century, Jakub Schikaneder, is buried here, as is the most influential and original Czech sculptor of the 20C, Otto Gutfreund, who drowned in 1926 and is commemorated here by a bust by his close friend Karel Dvořák. In the Functionalist crematorium to the east of the cemetery lie the ashes of the journalist and writer Egon Erwin Kisch.

- **Admission** Olšany and Vinohrady Cemeteries open daily 08.00–19.00 (summer) and 08.00–17.00 (winter). New Jewish Cemetery open Sun–Thur 09.00–17.00, Fri 09.00–14.00.

Due south of the Olšany Cemetery is a quiet residential street lined with grand suburban villas and named Bratří Čapků after the brothers Josef and Karel Čapek who spent much of their later life in the ochre-coloured building at No. 30, built in 1923–24. Further south begins the district of **Vršovice**, where you will find, standing on náměstí Svatopluka Čecha, the Constructivist **Church of St Wenceslas** (sv. Václav), which was built by Josef Gočár in 1929–30 and is dominated by a tall tower, now turned a dirty grey on the outside. This narrow building clings to the slope of a verdant hill, and is built on different levels that lead up to the apse, a delicate and luminous structure largely composed of stained glass. On a hill to the west of the church are the pleasant **Havlíček Gardens** (Havlíčkovy sady), commanding good views of southern Prague, and featuring at their northern end the late-19C **Gröbe Villa** (Gröbovka), a large villa of Italian Renaissance inspiration, designed by Antonín Barvitius. You could finish your tour with a well-earned rest at one of Vinohrady's newest cafés—*Shakespeare and Sons* on Krymská (see p 36), a ground-floor room filled, appropriately, with bookish young Czechs.

Žižkov

North of Vinohrady is the ramshackle and slightly seedy district of Žižkov, a traditional working-class area with a long history of revolutionary activity that once earned it the nickname of 'Red Prague'. It also has strong associations with poetry, being the birthplace both of the German poet Rainer Maria Rilke and of the Nobel Prize-winning poet Jaroslav Seifert, who was born here in 1901 and was recently honoured when the name of the district's main street was changed from Kalininova to Seifertova. Seifert once referred to this place where he had spent both his childhood and adolescence as 'my beautiful and adored Žižkov', though this is not a reaction usually shared by most casual visitors here, the majority of whom come simply to climb up to the monument of Jan Žižka. The traditional approach to this monument from the centre of Prague is to walk from the Powder Gate to the eastern end of Hybernská, and then turn left on to Husitská. Coming instead from Vinohrady's náměstí Míru, you should walk north along Italská, skirting the western side of the **Rieger Gardens** (Riegrovy sady), a late-19C space with fine views and, in its southwestern corner, a monument to the 19C politician František Rieger by Josef Myslbek. At the northern end of Italská you will reach Seifertova, a junction marked by the náměstí Winstona Churchilla, on which stands one of the pioneering examples of Functionalist architecture of the 1930s, the former **Pensions Institute** (Dům Odborových svazů). This vast structure, comprising two great rectangular blocks arranged in cross formation, was described by the architect Martin Shand as 'the white cathedral of Prague', but now is a depressing grey and, for all its originality in the context of 1930s' architecture, is a foretaste of the worst architecture of the post-war period.

After crossing Seifertova and continuing north along Řehořova, you will come to Husitská: off its western end, by the rail bridge, begins U památníku, which climbs up the wooded hill to the Jan Žižka monument, passing to the right a grey block containing the post-1914 holdings of the **Army Museum** (Armádní muzeum): a forlorn tank guards the entrance to the building, while inside are permanent exhibitions on the Czech resistance during the two world wars, and the history of the Czech army during the inter-war period. Open April–Oct Tues–Sun 09.30–18.00; Nov–March Tues–Sat 09.30–17.00.

Some knowledge of an earlier period in Bohemia's military history is needed to appreciate fully the monument to Jan Žižka, the Hussite hero, at the top of the hill.

Jan Žižka and the National Monument

After the burning at the stake of Jan Hus in 1415, the Hussites came to be divided into two main camps, moderate and radical, the former (known usually as the Utraquists) being drawn mainly from the Bohemian nobility and the more conservative nationalists. The more popularly based radical wing of the Hussites went far further in their views than the Utraquists, maintaining that the Holy Bible was the sole authority in all matters of religious belief, and rejecting the doctrine of the existence of Purgatory, all the Sacraments with the exception of baptism and communion, and many other teachings of the Church. The radicals enjoyed the leadership of one of Bohemia's greatest military commanders, Jan Žižka, a man whose early background is little known other than that he came from a family of the lesser nobility in Southern Bohemia, and had held a post at the court of Queen Sophia; he and his followers, the Taborites, were to establish as their principal base a stronghold in Southern Bohemia, which they named Tábor after the Biblical hill where Christ had been transfigured.

The widespread unrest resulting from Hus's death came to a head in the summer of 1419 with Taborites from all over the country gathering at Tábor, and Utraquists storming into Prague's New Town Hall to perpetrate the first 'defenestration' (see p 47). The news of what had happened at the Town Hall had the immediate effect of making King Wenceslas IV so annoyed that he died of apoplexy; as he was heirless, this in turn led to the thorny problem of succession. The principal claimant to the throne was his brother Sigismund, a man widely hated in Bohemia, particularly after his treacherous behaviour towards Jan Hus at Constance (see p 109); his only supporters were the Roman Catholics, most of whom belonged to the country's German communities. In the absence of a king, Queen Sophia was appointed Regentess of the country, but shortly afterwards a Papal Bull was issued proclaiming a crusade against the heretics of Bohemia.

By June 1420, Sigismund, at the head of crusading forces drawn from almost every European country, reached the outskirts of Prague where, on 14 July, he was defeated in battle by Jan Žižka, whose forces knelt upon the field of victory and intoned the *Te Deum*. Before fleeing to Moravia, Sigismund had himself crowned in Prague's St Vitus's Cathedral, but the ceremony was such a hurried affair that his opponents considered it to be invalid. It was in any case to be a further 16 years before he would be able to take possession of his kingdom, following the crushing defeat at the Battle of Lipany near Kolín of the Taborite forces led by Prokop, who had succeeded Jan Žižka after the latter had died of plague in 1424.

In 1877 the suburb of Prague where Žižka's victory against Sigismund had taken place was renamed Žižkov; and, early the next century, when patriotic monuments on a vast scale were at the height of their fashion in Bohemia, plans were made to build here a giant concrete figure of Žižka, containing a staircase leading up to an observation platform inside the warrior's head. This idea was later dropped, and in 1913 a public competition was held to find another design with which to commemorate the great hero. Many of the country's leading artists and architects participated, including several prominent 'Cubists', who were anxious to respond to the challenge of reconciling Cubist architecture with figural sculpture. 'It's a long time since I have seen such a distressing sight as this exhibition of draft projects for a Žižka monument', was how the poet František Procházka (an outspoken opponent of Cubism) judged these various efforts, among which was a sensational collaborative design by the architect Pavel Janák and the sculptor Otto Gutfreund. Two further competitions had to be held—in 1923 and 1925—before the decision was made to adopt a rather conservative scheme by the architect Jan Zázvorka and the sculptor Bohumil Kafka.

The monument, known officially as the ***National Monument**, partly comprises a granite-faced building dating back to 1929–30, adorned inside with mosaics by Max Švabinský and Jakub Obrovský, and relief carvings by Karel Pokorný. This building was enlarged and adapted after the Second World War to contain the Grave of an Unknown Soldier from Dukla, together with the tombs of prominent Communists such as Klement Gottwald, Antonín Zápotocký and Ludvík Svoboda. Gottwald himself was originally embalmed Lenin-style, which involved the construction of a refrigerated morgue as well as elaborate apparatus both to control carefully the monument's temperature and to raise the mummy up and down from casket to slab. Unfortunately, Gottwald's corpse, heavily pickled in alcohol even before he died, disintegrated at a rate that defeated the finest scientific attempts to preserve it; damaged further by fire in 1963, it was finally cremated. In 1990 the remains of both Gottwald and his fellow Communists were offered back to their next-of-kin (Gottwald's ashes, refused by his family, were placed in a mass grave in the Olšany Cemetery—see p 192). Since then the building has been closed pending a decision about its final fate.

In front of the building rises the monument's great focal-point—Bohumil Kafka's enormous equestrian bronze statue of Žižka, which is certainly impressive from a great distance, but is largely of interest for featuring in *The Guinness Book of Records* as the world's largest sculpture.

The greatest reward of a walk up to the monument is the magnificent panorama of Prague to be had from here, a panorama that used to inspire the young Jaroslav Seifert, who was later to write some of the finest poetry ever dedicated to the city.

Equally fine views are to be had from the eighth floor of the Žižkov Television Tower, situated in the southern part of the district. To get there, return to the rail bridge and continue east along Husitská. In the narrow cul-de-sac (U božich bojovníků) off this street to the left, you could stop for refreshments at the wonderfully weird *U vystřelenýho oka* ('the shot-out eye'; see p 37), a tatty pub named in honour of Jan Žižka and situated at the foot of the hill on which his monument stands. From here, head south towards the Mahler Park (Mahlerovy sady) to see, at close quarters, the **Žižkov Television Tower**, a vast (216m) futuristic mass of polished steel, rivalled only by its sister monument on Berlin's Alexanderplatz. Begun in the 1970s, but not completed until 1990, the tower was initially conceived as a means of jamming 'imperialist' radio stations such as Voice of America, Radio Free Europe or the BBC; its construction also involved the demolition of a Jewish cemetery on the square, much to the anger of local residents. In the 1990s, the somewhat drab appearance of the tower was enlivened by the controversial artist David Černý, who added the strange giant babies that now crawl up the exterior. Take the lift up to the fifth-floor café for a fantastic panorama of Prague, or continue up to the observation platform on the eighth floor, for more of the same.

7 Western Prague

- **Getting there**   The best way to get to the places described in this chapter is by No. 8 tram from the Hradčanská metro station.

Střešovice

Střešovice, which lies immediately to the west of the Hradčany, is traditionally the most luxurious of Prague's suburbs, and is a quiet area of attractive modern villas, spaciously laid out. The district had sinister connotations for Prague's Jewish community during the Second World War, for it was in one of these villas, confiscated from a wealthy Jew, that the Central Office for Jewish Emigration was situated. This office was directly subordinate to the Gestapo and was responsible for the organisation of the notorious 'transports' to the ghetto at Terezín and elsewhere: accounts of the compulsory visits to Střešovice are included in Jiří Weil's disturbing novel, *Life with a Star* (1964), which was based on the author's war-time experiences.

Examples of the sort of tram used by Weil's protagonist can be seen in the enjoyable **City Transport Museum** (Muzeum městské hromadné dopravy) at Patočkova 4, which has shiningly maintained examples of every type of city tram and trolley-bus that ever ran through the streets of Prague. (Open

WESTERN PRAGUE

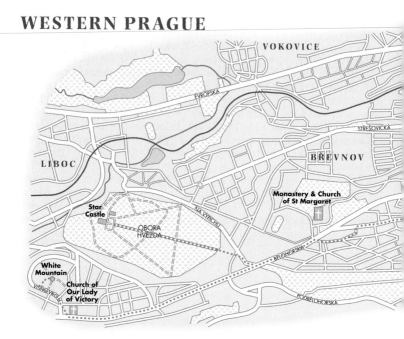

April–Oct Sat, Sun 09.00–17.00.) West of the museum extends the large area of Střešovice known as the **Ořechovka Villa Quarter**, which was planned in 1920–23 on the model of England's 'garden suburbs'. In the course of the 1920s this quarter was greatly expanded and, between 1929 and 1931, there was built on its outer southern limits (at No. 14 Nad hradním vodojemem) by far the most distinguished of Střešovice's villas, the **Maison Müller**. This cube-like structure, with large expanses of bare masonry discreetly pierced by small, irregularly placed openings, is the work of the revolutionary Moravian-born architect Adolf Loos (assisted by Josef Fanta), and is the only one of his buildings to be seen in the Czech Republic; the interior, characterised by its every space being of different height and shape, can be visited by guided tour (Tues, Thur, Sat, Sun 10.00, 12.00, 14.00, 16.00; prior booking only).

Břevnov

The district of Břevnov, which extends to the south of Střešovice and to the west of Petřín Hill, begins at its eastern end with the largest sports stadium in the world, the **Strahov Stadium** (Strahovský stadión). Designed by Alois Dryák in 1926 for a seating capacity of over 200,000, this ungainly complex looks like some stranded folly of megalomaniac scale. During Communist times it would come to life every five years with a mass synchronised gymnastics display known

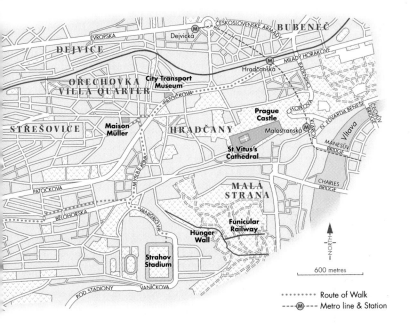

········ Route of Walk

---Ⓜ--- Metro line & Station

as the Spartakiáda; this tradition has now been revived by the Sokol ('falcon') organisation, which the Communist authorities had banned. The stadium is also used as a concert venue, with special buses put on for large gigs.

The No. 8 tram route follows the long **Bělohorská**, which runs west of here, passing through an area of large housing estates, including one of 600 apartments dating from the late 1930s.

Eventually the street turns into a wide thoroughfare which is bordered on its northern side by the beautiful parkland, including a lake obscured by willows, that surrounds the ***Monastery and Church of St Margaret** (sv. Markéty). Though recently restored, and reclaimed by monks, this unfairly neglected place, with its isolated situation in a generally grey Prague suburb, may induce a sense of great pathos, particularly in those who come here in the knowledge that they are visiting the oldest monastery in Bohemia and one of Prague's finer Baroque complexes.

Founded for the Benedictine Order in 993 by Boleslav II and the Prague bishop, St Adalbert, the monastery and church were completely rebuilt by Christoph and Kilian Ignaz Dientzenhofer in the early 18C. The monastic buildings, with fine ceiling frescoes of 1727, are not open to the public. But the interest of the complex lies essentially in its church, which was built by Christoph Dientzenhofer between 1700 and 1715, and has a powerful and tightly composed exterior with a giant order of pilasters and columns running around its whole length, and a dynamic attic level of gables crowned by undulant pediments.

The single-aisled interior is composed of a series of intersecting transverse ovals, with giant piers projecting diagonally into the nave as in Christoph Dientzenhofer's comparably majestic Church of St Nicholas in the Little Quarter. *Trompe l'oeil* altars line the walls of the nave, while on the ceiling are frescoes depicting the founding of the monastery by St Adalbert. The crypt is that of the original Romanesque building of the late 10C and contains several monks' tombs and skeletons. Within the orchard garden behind the church is a Baroque pavilion surrounding a well where St Adalbert is said to have met Boleslav II at the time of the monastery's foundation.

The church and crypt can be visited on an excellent guided tour (Sat, Sun 10.00, 14.00, 16.00) conducted in Czech by the enthusiastic local priest; tours in English must be booked in advance.

Continue along Bělohorská on tram Nos 8 or 22, getting off at the Vypich stop, to reach the main gates of a lush English-style **park** (obora Hvězda), which was laid out in 1797 on a game reserve founded by Ferdinand I in 1530. Within the park long alleys of trees lead to the remarkable Renaissance building known as the **Star Castle** (letohrádek Hvězda). This star-shaped structure of 1555–58 was built by Hans Tirol and Bonifác Wohlmut as a hunting-lodge for the Archduke Ferdinand, and later became the residence of the latter's future wife, Philippine Welser. The exterior, restored by Pavel Janák after the Second World War, is rather austere, but the interior features on its ground floor outstanding stucco decorations of mythological scenes and grotesques by Italian artists. The building, which was turned into a powder-magazine after the 16C, houses on its first floor a **Museum of Czech Literature**, of interest largely to Czech speakers, with chamber concerts being held upstairs. In the basement is a large, albeit not very informative, model of the Battle of the White Mountain. Open Tues–Sat 09.00–16.00, Sun 10.00–17.00.

The limestone hill where the Battle of the **White Mountain** (Bílá Hora) took place is situated at the westernmost end of Břevnov. It was one of the most famous and tragic battles in the history of Bohemia: on 8 November 1620, the Protestant army led by Count Matthias von Thurn was defeated by the Habsburg troops under Maximillian of Bavaria; Elector Frederick of the Palatinate, who had been elected King of Bohemia by the Protestants the previous year, was forced to flee (hence his nickname 'The Winter King'), and Bohemia was not to regain its independence until after the First World War. There is nothing to see at the site itself, but at the foot of the hill you could visit the early-18C **Church of Our Lady of Victory** (Panny Marie Vítězné), which was built to commemorate the Habsburgs' success; the interior has ceiling paintings by, among others, Václav Reiner. The church is conveniently situated near the terminus of the No. 8 and 22 trams; to get to the battle site from here, walk up Nad Višňovkou.

8 Northern Prague

Letná

Above the Vltava immediately to the northeast of the Little Quarter extends the large **Letná Park** (Letenské sady), which was laid out after 1858. Occupying an excellent vantage point at its western end, with beautiful views across the river to the Old Town, is the **Hanava Pavilion** (Hanavský pavilon), an exuberantly eclectic structure mingling the neo-Baroque with tentative Art Nouveau forms. Built by Otto Prieser for Prague's Jubilee Industrial Exhibition of 1891, it was admired in its time (and later by Le Corbusier) for its innovative use of cast iron—a material promoted in Bohemia by the man who commissioned the building, Count William of Hanava, the owner of ironworks at Komárov near Hořovice.

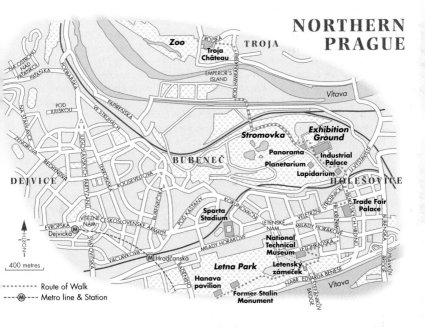

The building proved so popular with those who attended the exhibition that it was rebuilt in its present location seven years later; now brightly restored, it functions as an elegant café and restaurant (see p 31).

Nowadays, strolling through the peaceful tree-lined alleys of the Letna Park it is hard to imagine that that the place was once the scene of mass civic demonstrations. During the Communist period it was the venue for the annual May Day parades, when thousands would cheerily march along Milady Horákové to the north, observed by Party leaders from a giant stage set up in front of the Sparta stadium. But the Communists' predilection for large-scale public events would eventually backfire in spectacular fashion: in 1989, one million people gathered in Letná to demand democracy and the end of the regime, in what was the largest mass protest leading up to the 'Velvet Revolution'.

Letná is also the place where, until 1962, there stood the most hated monument in Prague: a massive statue of Stalin on a granite plinth. The spot, further east in the park, is now marked by a giant red **metronome** designed by David Černý in 1991, the same year that this notorious 'Situationist artist' was arrested for painting the Soviet tank memorial in Smíchov (see p 189).

The Stalin Monument

The competition held in 1953 to erect a Stalin monument was won by a team that included Otakar Švec, who ingeniously overcame the problem of spectators having to look up at Stalin's backside by placing behind his figure lines of Czech and Soviet workers (hence the monument's nickname of 'the queue'). Six hundred men spent 500 days erecting the colossus, which weighed in at 14,000 tons and attained a height of 30m. By the time it was finally completed in 1955, Švec had committed suicide, and Stalin's reputation was on the verge of collapsing. Krushchev's speech of 1956 denouncing Stalin's personality cult led the embarrassed Czech Communists to encase the monument in scaffolding which remained in place until 1962, when demolition by a series of small detonations became the only solution (a single explosion would have done away with most of the hill and the bridge below). In his novel *The Miracle Game* (1972), Josef Škvorecký described the monument's surviving base as looking 'like the dark side of a Mayan pyramid, with wide granite steps on either side leading to an empty platform on top'. The bunkers below, used intermittently since 1962 to store potatoes and hold unofficial parties, are now abandoned.

At the opposite end of the park to the Hanava Pavilion is the similarly well-located **Letenský zámeček**, a manor house now containing two French restaurants—the *Brasserie Ullman* on the ground floor, and the more stylish *Belcredi* upstairs (see p 31). There is also a huge and popular beer-garden, with wooden tables shaded by trees, and fantastic river views.

Holešovice

To the east and north of the Letenský zámeček extends the district of Holešovice, which was annexed in 1869 to the village of Bubeneč, and incorporated into Prague in 1884; the place today is now experiencing new life thanks to its popularity with the city's expatriate communities, and the recent opening of its extraordinary Gallery of Modern Art (see below). A grim Functionalist block on Kostelní, immediately behind the Letenský zámeček, houses the surprisingly good *National Technical Museum* (Národní technické muzeum), which includes among its extensive collections sections devoted to astronomy, horology, photography and telecommunications. Of particular interest to children is the guided tour of a reconstructed coal-mine in the basement; also entertaining is the section labelled in English 'the Centre for Noise Ecology', where you can play around with numerous objects for making and recording sounds. But, above all, you should visit the Hall of Transport at the back of the building, a tall space crammed to capacity with every conceivable form of transport from the early 19C onwards; the exhibits are arranged in three superimposed galleries around the hall and also in the centre of the room, where old bi-planes and even a hot-air balloon hover above a traffic-jam of old cars and trains, including the luxury train carriage in which Emperor Francis Joseph travelled in 1891. Open Tues–Sun 09.00–17.00.

The Trade Fair Palace

A grid of streets lined with blackened apartment blocks of the 19C and 20C begins behind the museum. Head east on Letohradská, and at the end of this street turn left on to Františka Křížka, which crosses the busy shopping street of Milady Horákové and comes to an end at the wide Veletržní. Turn right and proceed to the junction with Dukelských hrdinů, on which stands the enormous former **Trade Fair Palace** (Veletržní palác), the first Functionalist building of its scale in Europe, now stunningly adapted to house the modern holdings of the National Gallery.

The enormous success of the Prague Jubilee Industrial Exhibition of 1891, and of its more modest 1908 sequel (the Chamber of Commerce Exhibition), highlighted the need among Czech politicians and businessmen for an annual trade fair at the heart of what had by now become the Habsburg Empire's most industrial region. However, it was not until the creation of Czechoslovakia that a Prague Trade Fair Committee was finally established. In 1924, in a competition held to design a Trade Fair Palace (for which six architects were invited to submit plans), first prize was awarded to Oldřich Tyl, a graduate of the Prague Technical University, and third prize to Josef Fuchs, a pupil of the idiosyncratic Classical architect Jože Plečnik. In the end Tyl and Fuchs combined their talents to produce the project that was eventually carried out, following a second competition held in 1925. The building, erected between 1926 and 1928, was designed to hold 10,000 visitors and 4000 exhibitors: in addition to its administrative offices, corridors with 'shop bays', and a Great Hall (the latter reserved for heavy machinery), the palace featured an elegant restaurant, a 600-seat cinema, a post office and a telephone exchange; it was also the first building in Prague to be centrally heated from a remote source, in this case from the Holešovice Power Plant.

Among the first visitors to see the completed building was the Swiss architect Le Corbusier, who, despite a number of criticisms, was excited to find vindicated his belief in applying Functionalism on a vast scale: 'Seeing a building quite as large as this one,' he wrote, 'quite unique in its category, I can imagine what my United Nations Palace, which exists only on paper, would look like, and what my even bigger Centrosaiuz building in Moscow is going to look like ... Seeing the Trade Fair Palace, I understood how to make large buildings, having so far built only relatively small houses on a low budget.'

Bizarrely, for a building of such bold modernity, the official opening of the palace—which took place on 21 September 1928, two weeks before Le Corbusier's visit—was marked by an exhibition of the monumental but highly reactionary canvases constituting Alfons Mucha's **Slav Epic** of 1911–28 (now in the castle of Moravský Krumlov in Southern Moravia). The celebrated Art Nouveau artist had himself proposed the idea, having probably been excited by the newspaper reports of the enormous dimensions of the Great Hall. The clash between the daringly simple, light and futuristic setting of the palace and the fussily detailed historical bombast of Mucha's paintings was none the less glossed over in the exhibition's pre-publicity, which stressed instead that with these works on the walls, 'the monumental hall of the Trade Fair Palace will be transformed into an exquisite temple dedicated to the Slavic spirit, love and enthusiasm, where the individual images will be symbolical steps in the historical journey of the Slavs toward the final victory of the Slavic race.'

The Trade Fair Palace maintained its original function until 1951, when the Prague Trade Fair was closed down and its activities transferred to Brno. Subsequently the palace was used by several state-run foreign-trade companies, who treated the building with scant respect either for the architecture or for the safety of their employees. In 1974, some varnish-soaked overalls in a makeshift painting workshop self-ignited and set fire to the building. After four years of deliberating about what to do with the charred surviving structure, the stubborn persistence of one-time law student, political prisoner and minor employee of the National Gallery, Vratislav Vaňousek, finally persuaded the Czech Government to let the building be used to display the National Gallery's modern holdings. The reconstruction of the building, entrusted to the Liberec architectural firm of SIAL, was finally begun in 1985 and not completed until 1994, nine years after Vaňousek's death. The gallery opened its doors to the public early in 1997.

With the opening of the **National Gallery's Collection of Modern Art** in the Trade Fair Palace, Prague has gained not only an attraction rivalling any of its older monuments, but also one of Europe's most exciting new galleries. As yet attracting a relatively small stream of tourists, this spacious and peaceful gallery is worth a visit as much for the architecture as for the collections: the building shows that Functionalism in its early stages was far from being the drab and pedestrian style that it so often became in the hands of its later imitators. The vitality, originality and exhilarating freshness of the building is exemplified above all in the pristinely white **atrium**, which offers an architectural thrill as intense as the Vladislav Hall in the Hradčany. This luminous sky-lit hall, situated at the northern end of the palace, near the entrance to the collections proper, is surrounded by balconied galleries that, on one side, form an inwardly sloping wall of railings reminiscent of the hull of some futuristic ocean liner of *Titanic* proportions. Although the galleries themselves are lined with lively modern sculptures and applied art, the hall itself has sensibly been left bare, allowing visitors to catch their breath before taking the lift to the permanent collections on the upper floors. Open Tues–Sun 10.00–18.00.

• **Tickets** to the collections are available from the main foyer (next to the atrium). Due to the sheer volume of exhibits, you may purchase tickets for a single floor, two floors, or even four floors, depending on how much time and energy you have, though to visit all the exhibitions would take a whole day at the very least.

The gallery's permanent exhibitions are: Art from 1930 to the present day (second floor); Czech art 1900–30, and mid-19C to early-20C French art (third floor); 19C century art (fourth floor). The first floor currently has a fine collection of 20C foreign art, but this may be moved in future. Temporary exhibitions, for which separate tickets are required, are held on the ground and fifth floors.

The well-stocked gallery bookshop sells catalogues to the exhibitions as well as albums and postcards; there is also a spacious café (to the left of the main entrance) and modest restaurant for quick snacks (through the doors at the far end of the foyer).

Modern Art at the Trade Fair Palace

Third floor Inevitably, in view of how little is known about Czech art outside the Czech Republic, most foreign visitors head directly for the third floor, where the gallery's celebrated collection of French art from the Impressionists to the Cubists is found. This is preceded, however, by a larger and equally fascinating collection of **early-20C Czech painting**, which covers all the leading artists of the period. Perhaps the greatest influence on this generation was the Norwegian Edvard Munch, whose retrospective held in 1905 in Prague's Mánes Gallery led to the formation of the Osma ('The Eight') art movement, its members being, among others, **Václav Špála**, **Emil Filla** and **Bohumil Kubišta**. Works such as Špála's fiery *Self-Portrait with Palette* (1908), Filla's spiritually tormented *Reader of Dostoyevsky* (1907) and Kubišta's sinisterly green *Cardplayers* (1909) are pure homages to the Norwegian artist. These three painters, together with **Otakar Kubín**, **Antonín Procházka** and **Josef Čapek**, later embraced no less wholeheartedly the Cubist works of Picasso and Braque: many of their Cubist paintings would be virtually indistinguishable from the art of their French peers were it not for the occasional Czech lettering and landscapes, as in, for instance, Kubišta's *Quarry in Braník* (1910–11) and Filla's *Still Life with Art Monthly* (1914).

A far more idiosyncratic painter than any of these was the deeply spiritual artist **Jan Zrzavý**, some of whose early works, such as *The Anti-Christ* (1909), display a powerfully expressive use of colour and brushstroke. At the same time he began developing a completely different style characterised by strange doll-like figures and an almost naively simple handling of paint and composition: one of the earliest such paintings was his *Valley of Sorrow* (1908), which he later described as being imbued with all his sense of 'sadness and hopelessness'.

But the most original and truly outstanding Czech painter of these years was **František Kupka**, whose works on show here reveal his development from a Fauve-like manner in, for instance, his *Cabaret Actress* (1909–10), to the pioneering abstract compositions of 1911 onwards, such as the fluently lyrical blue and red *Fugue in Two Colours* (1912). A sensational transitional work—and one that first reveals the influence of music on his art—is *Piano Keys–Lake* (1909), in which reflections on water are effortlessly transformed into the keys of a piano. With his creation of pure abstraction two years later, Kupka experimented with what he called 'cosmic architecture', which is demonstrated here in a series of ambitious canvases begun in 1911–13 and reworked at the beginning of the 1920s, some of which resemble coloured and fractured organ pipes, such as his *Perpendicular and Transverse Surfaces* (1913–23) or *Colour Planes, Winter Recollection* (1913–23). A literal climax to his art is reached in the magnificent *Story about Pistils and Stamens, 1* (1920), which has been described as a 'depiction of a cosmic sexual act'. From the 1930s onwards, his art becomes more academic and rigorously geometric, in particular in his *Abstract Painting*

(1930), which comprises a white canvas marked with one vertical and two horizontal black lines: not even Mondrian could match such minimalism.

The early 20C Czech paintings are interspersed with applied art and a vast collection of sculptures by **Otto Gutfreund**, who dominated Czech 20C sculpture in the same way that Myslbek had presided over the preceding century. Gutfreund began his career in a Cubist vein (for instance, the bronze *Head of Viki*, 1912–13, and *Anxiety*, 1911–12), and later went on to develop a very realistic yet highly personal style devoted to the portrayal of the everyday world. These latter works, characterised by their simple, stately forms and complete lack of sentimentality, as in the bronze *Family* (1925), often made use of colour, for instance, in the terracotta *Self-portrait* (1919) and the groups *Industry* and *Commerce* (both 1923) in wood and plaster respectively. They represent a truly Czech style of sculpture and their so-called Objective Realism was to be emulated

by numerous other artists such as **Karel Pokorný** in *Earth* (1925), **Josef Jiřikovský** in *Woman Combing her Hair* (1923), **Jan Lauda** in *The Potter* (1923), **Bedřich Štefan** in *Girl with Absinthe* (1924), **Karel Dvořák** in *Friends* (1924), and **Otakar Švec** in *The Motorcyclist* (1924), the last work being situated by the entrance.

Many of the works comprising the **collection of French art** were amassed by **Vincenc Kramář**, the enlightened director of the National Gallery during the 1920s, who 'donated' his collection to the gallery in 1960 (in fact, he had been forced to do so by the Communist authorities), a few months before his death at the age of 83. Among the artists represented are **Delacroix** (*Jaguar Attacking a Horseman*, 1855), **Pissarro** (an excellent view of Pontoise, before 1870), **Renoir** (*The Lovers*, 1875), **Monet** (*Ladies among Flowers*, 1875), **Degas** (*Portrait of Lorenzo Pagans*, 1882), **Van Gogh** (*Green Wheat*, 1889–90), Sisley, **Cézanne** (*House in Aix*, 1885–87, and a superlative portrait of the Pontoise doctor, patron and friend to the Impressionists, Joachim Gasquet, 1896–97), **Gauguin** (the famous Pont-Aven parody of Courbet, *Good-day Mr Gauguin*, 1889), **Rodin** (three bronze busts, and a bronze maquette of his Balzac monument), **Toulouse-Lautrec** (*Moulin-Rouge*, 1892), **Le Douanier Rousseau** (this artist's only known self-portrait, 1890), Seurat, Matisse, Bonnard, Chagall, Utrillo and Dufy.

A work by Otto Gutfreund

Kramář's greatest contribution to the arts in Czechoslovakia was his early championing of Cubism, buying in Paris in the first and second decades of the 20C works that would profoundly influence a whole generation of avant-garde Czech artists and architects. Thanks to Kramář, the National Gallery has a collection unrivalled in Central Europe of the works of Picasso and Braque. The **Picassos** (which, due to the chronological arrangement of the collections are spread out over the first three floors), include two paintings belonging to his so-called Negro Period (a *Self-Portrait* of 1907 and a *Female Head* of the same year), a large group of 'analytical Cubist' works of 1910 and 1911, and some 'synthetic Cubist' works of 1912 and 1913; there are also later purchases such as his monumental *Standing Nude* of 1921, as well as works on loan from other museums, such as *The Rape of the Sabine Women* (1962; Museum of Fine Arts in Boston). The paintings by **Braque** trace his career from the analytical Cubist period of 1910–11—when his works were virtually identical to Picasso's of these years—to the development of his very lyrical and painterly still-lifes of the 1920s. Among the other Cubist paintings are some early works by Derain, most notably a view of Cadaqués of 1910; Derain's later manner is represented by a sturdy and very Classical *Seated Woman* of 1920.

Fourth floor The fourth floor is devoted almost exclusively to **19C Czech painting** and comprises works which, though for the most part mediocre, provide valuable insight into the subject-matter that has always preoccupied Czech nationalists. It begins with the more important Czech artists of the early 19C, including the painter of romantic Gothic interiors, Ludvík Kohl, the portraitist Antonín Machek, the mythological painter František Tkadlík, and the landscapists August Piepenhagen and Karel Postl, the latter being the first professor of landscape painting at the Prague Academy. Two other major names are **Josef Navrátil**—the author of a stunningly simple and realistic series of still-lifes—and **Antonín Mánes**, who is represented here by a number of romantic landscapes imbued with nationalist sentiment, most notably his view of the ruins of Kokořín Castle (1839). Two of Mánes's sons were painters, the most famous being the elder one, Josef, whose work dominates Czech 19C art. The paintings of his that are on show here reveal his extraordinary range, from such academic canvases as *Petrarch and Laura* (1845–46) to a series of remarkably fresh landscapes painted in the 1850s and 1860s (for instance *View of Gmunden* and *Mountain Hut*); among his other works here are lively portraits of *Luisa Bělská* (1857) and *Anna Václavíková* (1862), detailed drawings of national folk costumes, a pair of mysteriously lit nudes (*Dawn* and *Evening*, 1857), and two large-scale oil studies for banners (one for the Říp Association at Roudnice, 1863–64, and the other for the Smíchov Luke's Choir, 1868).

Of Mánes's younger contemporaries, the only one to achieve an international reputation was **Jaroslav Čermák**, who specialised in ambitious scenes of Czech history, such as *The Hussites Defending the Pass* (1857). Čermák, a Byronic figure with the painterly pretensions of a Delacroix, became an active witness to history by going off to record the war between Turkey and Montenegro, the subject of several scenes here, including *Captives* (1870). Academic landscapists of this period include Bedřich Havránek, Alois Bubák, and Adolf Kosárek, while one of the finest of the genre painters was **Soběslav Pinkas**, who did numerous scenes of Prague life, such as *Children on Kampa Island* (1854).

From the 1850s onwards an increasing number of Czech artists spent long periods in France, including Pinkas himself, **Viktor Barvitius**, **Karel Purkyně**, and **Antonín Chitussi**. Barvitius was the author of the delightfully detailed and atmospherically lit genre scene, *Thursday in Stromovka Park* (1865); Purkyně meanwhile was an artist who fell strongly under the influence of Courbet, as can be seen in his powerful portrait of *Jech the Blacksmith* (1860) and in the boldly painted still-lifes *The Snow Owl* (1862) and *Onions and Partridges* (1862). Chitussi painted many landscapes while staying in and around Paris, and on his return to Czechoslovakia did numerous Barbizon-inspired scenes in the region where he was born—the Czech Moravian Highlands.

Towards the end of the 19C many of the leading Czech artists were engaged in the decoration of the Prague National Theatre, including the landscapist Julius

Mařák, and the specialists in allegorical and Classical scenes involving female nudes, Vojtech Hynais and František Ženíšek. The most important of the artists of the so-called National Theatre Generation was the prolific **Mikoláš Aleš**, who did drawings and decorative designs as well as historical canvases, two examples of which can be seen here: *The Meeting of George of Poděbrady with Matthias Corvinus* (1877) and *At the Grave of a Fighter of the Lord* (1877), a bleak snow-covered landscape featuring a lone rider on horseback in front of the tomb of one of his comrades.

The turn-of-the-last-century Czech artist best known outside the Czech Republic, **Alfons Mucha**, is represented here only by *Gismonde* (1894), though more of his work can be seen in the decorative arts section. In compensation there is a superb group of paintings by **Jakub Schikaneder**, ranging from beautifully melancholic works such as *All Souls Say* (1888) and *Sorrowful Homecoming* (1886), to the large, suggestive and almost monochromatic city scenes of the first and second decades of the 20C, including *Evening Interior* (1909–10) and *Embankment* (1916–18).

An almost Scandinavian degree of introspection is evident in the penumbral landscapes of **Antonín Hudeček**, which feature the small lake at Okoř (20km northwest of Prague off the Kralupy road), where the artist Julius Mařák had a small painting school: especially haunting is the work entitled *Evening Silence* (1900), in which a woman with her back to the spectator stares down towards the fading light of the distant lake. Another lake, the imaginary Black Lake, is an obsessive motif in the works of Hudeček's contemporary **Jan Preisler**, an artist of strong Symbolist orientation whose paintings betray the influence of Puvis de Chavannes and Gauguin. The third outstanding painter of this generation is **Antonín Slavícek**, who created landscapes and cityscapes of extraordinary emotional intensity and pictorial expressiveness, including a number of rain-swept views of Prague and its surroundings.

Second floor Much of the space on the second floor, covering **art from 1930 to the present day**, is taken up with the delicate dream-like Surrealism of painters who came to the fore in the 1920s such as **Toyen**, **Jindřich Štyrský** and **Josef Šíma**. More arresting and memorable examples of the influence of Surrealism are the 1930s' assemblages of **Zdeněk Rykr** and **Ladislav Zívr**: Rykr used glass boxes in which he assembled a mixture of treated paper and unorthodox (and often ephemeral) materials such as pebbles, paper, cotton wool, wood and silver foil (as in his Orient series of 1935); Zívr also improvised from random materials but in a more three-dimensional and morbid way, as in his *Heart Incognito* (1936), in which a heart-like object is trapped in netting above a black vase. But the prize for originality must be awarded to the kinetic light sculptures of **Zdeněk Pešánek**, whose principle work on this floor is the *Recumbent Torso* that formed part of a fountain exhibited at the World Exhibition of Art and Technology in Paris in 1937: this luminous, welded blend of plastic, glass, neon and lightbulbs is like an avant-garde response to the Venus de Milo. Sadly, the Second World War intervened before the artist was able, as he intended, to reassemble the whole fountain on a site in between Prague's Rudolfinum and the Vltava.

Surrealism continued to dominate the work of the avant-garde (and often censored) Czech artists of the 1940s and afterwards, such as **Mikuláš Medek**. But the works on the second floor that have perhaps the greatest appeal today are the haunting urban landscapes of **Jan Smetana**, such as *Last Stop* (1944), **František Gross**'s ironically titled *Garden of Eden* (1943) and, above all, the works of **Kamil Lhoták**, which are a perfect blend of realism, poetry, colouristic subtlety and arresting imagery, notably the *Officer's Mess in Paris* (1947), *Baseball Player* (1947) and *Meteorological Station after a Storm*.

The gallery's modern-art section has been expanded in recent years to take the story right up to the 1990s, but the sheer quantity of exhibits on show can overwhelm the visitor. There is an amusing collection of Socialist Realist art, including edifying images of 'heroic' proletarians and models of limousines used by party apparatchiks, as well as examples of the roughly contemporaneous *Art Informel*, Europe's answer to Abstract Expressionism. Brief tribute is paid to Czech performance art of the 1960s, which is followed by some of the Surrealistic photomontages for which **Jiří Kolář** is famous. Finally, you are shown works, of varying quality, by 'underground' artists active in Czechoslovakia during the 1980s, some of whom went on to higher and greater things after the 'Velvet Revolution'.

First floor The foreign-school holdings on the first floor are particularly notable for their fine **German and Austrian works** dating mainly from the first three decades of the 20C. Among the former are Max Ernst's *Life in a House* (1919), a *Still-Life with Flowers and an Envelope* (1922) by Corinth, Expressionist canvases by Schmidt-Rottluff and Pechstein, and a disturbing work by the undeservedly little-known Max Oppenheimer, entitled *The Operation*, which shows an hysterical group of hands and scalpels. The Austrian holdings are dominated by superb paintings by Schiele, Klimt and Kokoschka. **Schiele** is represented by a small townscape of 1911 (a view of Česky Krumlov, the birthplace of Schiele's mother) and a haunting tall canvas of a monk and a woman, entitled *Pregnant Woman and Death* (1911). **Klimt**'s *The Virgin* (1913) is a large decorative composition in vivid blues and purples, showing an entwined group of female nudes; there is also one landscape (*Castle with a Moat*, 1909) and an armchair he designed for the Primavesi Villa (1905). **Kokoschka** lived in Prague in 1934–35, and there are several works by him from this period, of which pride of place must go to three large and expressively painted views of Prague from the river, constituting possibly the finest landscapes ever made of this city. Don't miss, also, his delightfully amusing *Red Eggs* (1939), which looks like something straight out of *Alice's Adventures in Wonderland*.

The Russians Repin, Mikhail Nesterov and Aristarkh Lentulov, the Italians Severini, Guttoso and Carlo Carrà, the Spaniards Oscar Dominguez, Miró and Tàpies, and the Pole Tadeusz Kantor, are among the other foreign artists whose works are owned by the National Gallery. But the artist whose work was of most relevance to the development of early-20C Czech art was **Edvard Munch**, who is represented here by only two works, the best being a highly atmospheric painting of a group of women dancing on a shore by moonlight (1900).

Dukelských hrdinů leads north of the gallery to the gates of the **Prague Exhibition Ground** (Výstaviště Praha), which was the main site of the Jubilee Exhibition of 1891, thereafter being used primarily for trade fairs. The large glass and ironwork structure that faces you on entering the park is the Industrial Palace (Průmyslový palác), built as the main hall of the Jubilee Exhibition by Bedřich Münzberger and František Prásil in 1891.

The adjoining pavilion houses the remarkable **Lapidarium of the National Museum** (Lapidárium Národního muzea), which features many of the originals of famous public statues and monuments in Prague that have been replaced *in situ* by copies, for instance the bronze statue of St George and the Dragon from the courtyard of Prague Castle, or the 14C tympanum from the north portal of the Týn church on the Old Town Square. The museum also has countless other Czech sculptures from the 11C–19C, the majority in storage because there is insufficient space to exhibit them. Open Tues–Fri 12.00–18.00, Sat, Sun 10.00–12.30, 13.00–18.00.

Behind and to the left of the Industrial Palace is a large cylindrical structure (currently under renovation) containing a vast **panorama** by Luděk Marold of the *Battle of Lipany* of 1434; the canvas is displayed in a darkened setting, surrounded by real earth, sticks and other objects, the whole forming a powerful illusionistic recreation of the battlefield. Elsewhere in the grounds, which are used regularly for folkloric events and an annual reconstruction of battles in the Thirty Years War, are a sports hall, funfair, swimming pool, planetarium, and a new theatre modelled on London's Globe, which puts on Shakespeare plays in summer.

A gate on the western side of the exhibition grounds leads into the large and wooded Stromovka, which was laid out as a public park in 1804 on the site of a royal hunting-ground founded by King John of Luxemburg in the early 14C. From here it is a pleasant 30-minute walk to Troja (see below) via the footbridges on Emperor's Island (Císařský ostrov).

Troja

North of Holešovice-Bubeneč, on the other side of the Vltava, is the suburban district of Troja, which was named after a large Baroque country house known generally as the ***Troja Château** (Trojský zámek).

• **Getting there** The easiest access by public transport is by bus No. 112 from the Nádraží-Holešovice metro station.

This magnificent house, brashly restored in the late 1980s and early 1990s, suffered extensive flood damage in 2002 when its beautiful grounds were completely submerged in water, though luckily the house itself escaped intact. It was built in 1679–85 for Count Šternberg, the architect being Jean-Baptiste Mathey, who introduced a French pavilion plan with projecting wings. The principal façade is its southern one, dominated by a monumental oval staircase profusely decorated with statues of gods and goddesses battling with Titans. The rooms on the upper floor boast one of the most extensive cycles of Baroque frescoes to be seen in the Czech Republic, including, in the side rooms, some amusing allegorical ceiling paintings by Francesco and Giovanni Francesco Marchetti, and illusionistic landscapes on the walls; the enormous Grand Hall is covered all over with magnificent frescoes by Abraham Godyn set in an ambitious cartoon-like framework featuring fictive architecture and tapestries, one of which is marked by the shadow cast by a Moor plunging head forwards into the room.

Aside from hosting classical concerts, the building houses a collection of 19C Czech painting belonging to the **Prague City Gallery**. Most of the leading Czech artists of this period are represented, though largely with minor works: among these artists are Viktor Barvitius, Alois Bubák, František Ženíšek, Max Švabinský, Jan Preisler, Luděk Marold and Mikoláš Aleš. Particularly numerous are the works of Jaroslav Čermák and Václav Brožík, but the highlight of the collection is undoubtedly a group of eerily atmospheric city scenes by Jakub Schikaneder, including the extraordinary *Murder in the House* (1890). Below the building's southern façade is a grand double-staircase decorated with figures of battling gods and giants, and one of the earliest examples in Bohemia of a French formal garden, its terraces adorned with eccentric ornamental vases. Open April–Oct Tues–Sun 09.00–18.00; Nov–March Sat, Sun 10.00–17.00.

Near the house is the entrance to Prague's **Zoo**, founded in 1931, which can be recommended only to those who might enjoy the experience of riding over an aviary in a chair-lift. Open daily April 09.00–17.00; May 09.00–18.00; June–Sept 09.00–19.00; Oct–March 09.00–16.00.

9 Days out from Prague

Kutná Hora

Picturesquely situated above the northern banks of the narrow and meandering Vrchlice River, Kutná Hora (pop: 20,000) is a place that had until very recently a melancholic, decayed beauty. Major restoration is now rapidly turning the town into a pedestrianised showpiece, and bringing back some of the splendour of its medieval heyday, when it was the second-most-important town in Bohemia. In 1996, the town was entered onto UNESCO's World Heritage List.

• **Getting there** Buses depart regularly to Kutná Hora on weekdays from ÚAN Florenc, but there is only one direct bus on Saturday and five on Sunday. Six direct trains go to Kutná Hora from Prague's Central Station (Hlavní nádraží), but only one of these is fast (1-hour journey time as opposed to 2 hours). The main station at Kutná Hora (Kutná Hora hlavní nádraží) is near the outlying township of Sedlec; to get from here to the centre (3km) you have either to take a No. 1 or 4 bus, or else the shuttle train service to the Kutná Hora město station. The shuttle service conveniently meets trains arriving from Prague.

The rapid development of Kutná Hora in the Middle Ages was due to the discovery here, in the late 13C, of rich silver deposits, a discovery that was soon to make the Czech monarchs among the richest in Europe. Wenceslas II invited Florentine minters to found a Royal Mint at Kutná Hora, and, by the 1380s work was begun on one of the greatest of Bohemia's cathedrals. At the end of the century the town became the favourite residence of Wenceslas IV, but it was to suffer greatly in the course of the Hussite Wars, the retreating Hungarian troops under Sigismund of Luxemburg even setting fire to the place in 1421. Kutná Hora experienced a brief renewal of prosperity during the late 15C and early 16C, when the townspeople were able to secure for the completion of their cathedral two of the most outstanding architects of the time, Matěj Rejsek and Benedikt Ried. However, by the middle of the 16C the local silver deposits were exhausted, a crisis resulting in the cathedral being left unfinished in 1558, and the town entered a long period of decline exacerbated by the Thirty Years War and a severe fire in 1771. Kutná Hora is today a district capital, with engineering works and a tobacco factory on its outskirts, but with an essentially unspoilt historical centre reflecting the town's many years of stagnation. Today new life is being given to the local economy both by renewed tourism and by a huge injection of cash from the American tobacco giant Philip Morris.

The highpoint of a tour to Kutná Hora is the ***Cathedral of St Barbara** (Chrám sv. Barbory), which is situated in a verdant southwestern corner of the town. The cathedral represents one of the most extreme developments of the late-Gothic style in Europe, and has a bizarre and exotic skyline comprising three massive tent-like forms that from a distance give the impression that some fabulous Turkish sultan has encamped here.

The building, founded in 1388, was initially conceived on the model of a French Gothic cathedral, in emulation of Petr Parléř's cathedral at nearby Kolín; by 1421, however, when work was suspended, only the eight chapels in the apse and part of the aisles had been vaulted. Work on the building was not to be resumed until 1481, first under the direction of Master Hanuš of Růže, and then, after 1489, under that of the great Matěj Rejsek, who was responsible for the vaulting of the chancel. Six years after Rejsek's death in 1506, the burghers of Kutná Hora, anxious as always to employ the most fashionable and prestigious architects of the time, called on the services of the royal architect Benedikt Ried, who had only recently completed his remarkable work for Prague Castle. The possibility that funds might run out before the massive structure originally envisaged could be finished may have encouraged Ried to change drastically the plan of the building and transform it into a three-aisled hall church, the side aisles becoming galleries, and flying buttresses being used to support sheer walls pierced with enormous, traceried windows. The vaulting of the nave was completed to his design in 1547, but just over ten years later work on the cathedral was abandoned, and the west end left as a blank wall; the present west façade is a dreary, compromise solution of the late 19C.

The fantastical character of the light and spacious interior is due largely to the extraordinary **vaulting**, comprising stiff rib patterns of exceptional complexity in the chancel and, in the nave, flowing lines of endlessly fascinating geometrical inventiveness, spreading out like tree branches from the piers before bursting out in the centre into six-petalled flowers. The furnishings of the cathedral include a pulpit of c 1560 decorated with stone reliefs of the Evangelists, 17C confessionals, and an exuberant Baroque organ. The most interesting additions to the interior are the anonymous late-15C frescoes to be found in the **Smíšek Chapel** on the southern side of the ambulatory. Jan Smíšek of Vrchoviště—a rich mine owner and Administrator of the Royal Mines—acquired this chapel in 1485 and was buried here in 1512. The decorations on the walls, executed

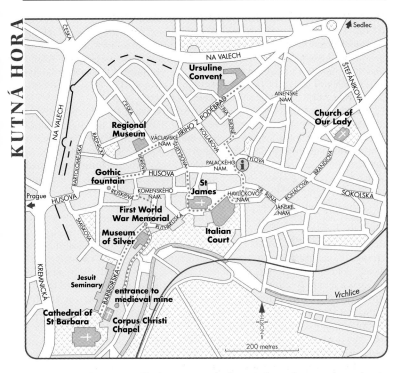

KUTNÁ HORA

c 1496, include a *trompe l'oeil* recess in which Smíšek can be seen dressed as a sacristan and preparing for a mass with the assistance of his two sons; the other scenes are the *Crucifixion, Trajan's Justice,* the *Arrival of the Queen of Sheba before Solomon,* and *Augustus with the Tiburtine Sibyl.* The figurative style of these works and their perspectival illusionism suggest a knowledge of North Italian painting of the early Renaissance. More late-15C frescoes can be seen in the adjoining chapels; even more impressive are the frescoes in the south aisle, showing the royal minters at work. Open Tues–Sun 09.00–16.00.

As you exit the cathedral through its west portal you could briefly visit the medieval Corpus Christi Chapel (open 09.00–17.00), which stands close by. The chapel is situated below a terrace affording one of the best views of Kutná Hora, with some of the town's finest buildings—including the distant church of St James (sv. Jakub)—standing huddled around the edge of a curving slope, which is covered in gardens and falls steeply down to the Vrchlice River. Across the street from the chapel is the Jesuit **seminary**, built in the 17C at a time when the cathedral once stood isolated from the rest of the town. The attractive **Barborská** runs in between the long eastern façade of this building and a Baroque balustrade adorned with statues. Further up the street, on the right-hand side (No. 28), is the **Hrádek**, a structure of 13C origin with a charming late-Gothic oriel window, originally forming part of the fortifications but later adapted as the home of the Administrator of the Mines, Jan Smíšek; it now houses the town's **Museum of Silver and Medieval Mine** (Muzeum stříbra a středověké důlni dílo), with an interesting display on the history of silver mining contained in rooms with original Gothic vaulting. The mine itself can only be visited with a guide (ask at the ticket office); you will be given a white coat, helmet and torch and led through gardens down to the entrance of the medieval mine, into which you descend to a depth of 50m. Open April, Oct Tues–Sun 09.00–17.00; July, Aug 10.00–18.00; May, June, Sept 09.00–18.00.

From the First World War Memorial just to the north of the Hrádek, a charming, cobbled lane called Ruthardská heads east towards the Church of St James (see below). Continuing instead north on Barborská, at the end of the street you will reach Komenského náměstí, where you should turn left and walk up Rejskova until you come to a remarkable 12-sided **Gothic fountain** (*kašna*), which was created in 1493–95 to provide the town with a supply of drinking-water uncontaminated by the mine workings: designed probably by Matěj Rejsek, this is an extensively rebuilt structure ringed with finials and blind ogee arcading. Head east (right) of here along Husova, past the Church of St John of Nepomuk, and take the first turning to the left (Lierova), which joins up with Radnická. Facing you, on the opposite side of the street, is the so-called **Stone House** (Kamenný dům), a late 15C structure with a much-restored gabled façade dominated by a box-shaped oriel covered all over with lively carvings; inside is a dreary **Regional Museum** charting the history of the royal mining town. Open April, Oct Tues–Sun 09.00–17.00; July, Aug 10.00–18.00; May, June, Sept 09.00–18.00. Just to the east of the museum is Václavské náměstí, where you should head south on Šultysova, a short street lined with fine 17C and 18C buildings, which leads to a Marian **plague column** of the early 18C. At the end of the street, on the left-hand side, you could stop for lunch at the *Restaurace U havířů*, a famous old beer-cellar serving standard Czech fare; alternatively, there are two more good restaurants close by: *U Bakaláře* on Husova and *Harmonia* on Vysokokostelecká.

The exceedingly narrow Vysokokostelecká, which faces the exit of Šultysova, is hemmed in by narrow houses, above which rises the impressively tall Gothic tower of the **Church of St James** (sv. Jakuba). When this triple-aisled hall church was begun in the 1330s, it was conceived on a scale comparable to that of deanery churches such as the one at Plzeň, but work was brought to a halt by the Hussite Wars, leaving even the south tower unfinished; the interior, completed at a much later date, is Gothic in structure, but entirely Baroque in its furnishings, which include a high altar of *Christ and St James* by Petr Bendl.

Leaving the church by its south portal you will find immediately to your left, on Havlíčkovo náměstí, the most important secular building in town, the former Royal Mint or ***Italian Court** (Vlasský dvůr), which was built in 1300 for the Italian minters invited to Kutná Hora by Wenceslas II; the place was enlarged and remodelled c 1400 as a residence for Wenceslas IV and, following the closure of the mint in 1727, was converted into a town hall (now municipal offices). The interior, which can be visited on a 30-minute guided tour (entrance in the courtyard), features a ground-floor room where a selection of coins is displayed, including the most famous ones to have been minted at Kutná Hora. The most important room is the early-15C **Royal Audience Hall**, which has a panelled ceiling of 1400 and two large 19C wall-paintings representing *The Election of Vladislav the Jagiellon* and *The Decree of Kutná Hora*—a decree passed by

Wenceslas IV in 1409 whereby the rights of Czechs at Prague University were greatly improved. The chapel, which Wenceslas IV founded in 1400, was completely redecorated early in the 20C. Open daily April–Sept 09.00–17.00; Oct–March 10.00–16.00.

Turn left along 28. října to reach the large **Palackého náměstí**, the town's main square, where there are a number of fine old houses as well as a rather bleak modern hotel, the Mědínek, with a restaurant that recalls the Communist era both in terms of its décor and standard of service. Inside the nearby Sankturinovský dům you will find a **tourist information centre** selling books, maps and guides, as well as a small **Museum of Alchemy**, with a laboratory in the basement and an oratory in the Gothic tower. Open April–Oct 10.00–17.00; Nov–March 10.00–15.00.

From Palackého náměstí head north on Na Sioně, which will take you to Jiřího z Poděbrad, where there stands a former **Ursuline Convent**, begun by K.I. Dientzenhofer on a pentagonal plan in 1734 and never finished.

One of the outlying residential districts to the east of the convent is **Sedlec**, which you can reach by a No. 1 or 4 bus from the town's inner ring road. The first monument you will see as you head there from the ring road is the imposing church of the former **Cistercian Abbey of Sedlec**.

> The abbey was founded in 1142, but the present church dates back to c 1300, when work was begun on a building modelled on a French cathedral, with a five-sided apse and seven radiating chapels in the chevet. This church, which was more or less complete by the 1320s, was gutted during the Hussite Wars and not rebuilt until the early 18C. The new building, designed by Jan Santini-Aichel, is a masterly example of the 'Baroque-Gothic' manner peculiar to this architect, and features vaulting which is as complex as Ried's in the cathedral of St Barbara (to which it clearly owes a debt; see p 212), but treated with dynamic, Baroque fluency.

At present, unfortunately, you can visit neither the church—which has been closed for many years for restoration—nor the adjoining monastic buildings (now a tobacco factory partly owned by Philip Morris). What you can see, however, is the incredible ***ossuary** (*kostnice*) on nearby Zámecká (just to the north of the church), which was formed initially from the bones of 30,000 people killed in a plague of 1318; the chapel to house these was remodelled in the 18C by Santini-Aichel, and again in the 19C. Open Tues–Sun April–Sept 08.00–18.00; Oct 08.00–12.00, 13.00–17.00; Nov–March 09.00–12.00, 13.00–16.00.

In 1870 the Schwarzenberg family, who had acquired the chapel following the dissolution of the monastery in 1783, commissioned one František Rint to arrange the skulls and bones in a decorative manner, a task which had first been undertaken in the early 16C by a half-blind monk. The results of Rint's endeavours, which were to occupy him and members of his family for four years, are morbidly fascinating, and include chandeliers, bones hung like Christmas paper chains, and even the coat of arms of the Schwarzenberg family.

Karlštejn

Karlštejn is a small wine-growing village lying under the shadow of one of the largest and most fantastically shaped castles in Bohemia. *Karlštejn Castle, which projects high above the steep and densely forested slopes behind the village, is by far the most popular sight near Prague, attracting daily coachloads of tourists. Open daily Jan, March, Nov, Dec 09.00–12.00, 13.00–15.00; April, Oct 09.00–12.00 and 13.00–16.00; May, June, Sept 09.00–12.00, 13.00–17.00; July, Aug 09.00–12.00, 13.00–18.00.

- **Getting there** There are nine direct trains to Karlštejn (45 minutes) each day from Prague's Central Station (Hlavní nádraží). Alternatively, you can go from the Praha Smíchov station (six direct trains on weekdays, nine at weekends). In either case, if there is no direct train you can change in Beroun (1 hour 20 minutes).

The castle was built by Charles IV in the mid-14C to house the imperial crown jewels, the Bohemian royal insignia and a large collection of relics. Designed by the great French architect, Matthew of Arras, the building was begun in 1348 and completed in the remarkably short space of seven years.

The imperial jewels were removed to Prague by Sigismund of Luxemburg in 1420, shortly before the castle was besieged for seven months by the Hussites; the jewels were eventually to end up at the Hofburg in Vienna. As for the Bohemian royal insignia, these were returned at the outbreak of the Thirty Years War to St Vitus's Cathedral, where they are now kept in a room above the Wenceslas Chapel (see p 147). Extensively rebuilt between 1575 and 1597, the castle complex later lost its importance and was in a ruinous state when, in 1887, Friedrich Schmidt and Josef Mocker embarked on a restoration campaign that was to be no less drastic than that of Viollet-le-Duc at Carcassonne.

Those coming to Karlštejn by car are not allowed to drive up to the castle from the village, and have to make the arduous ascent on foot, sharing the narrow, winding road with a queue of other tourists. Your spirits are at first maintained by the castle's extraordinarily romantic and picturesque profile, but begin to sag the more you realise that what you see is largely a medieval sham, which seems almost to have been devised for the tourist market. Gloomy, insensitively restored rooms await you, but a visit to the castle is made worthwhile by the magnificent forest views to be had from the top and, more importantly, the outstanding 14C decorations to be found within. The road from the village up to the castle is lined with souvenir shops and several eateries, the best of which are *Koruna* and *U Janů*, serving standard Czech fare at inflated prices; there is also a small **museum** (Muzeum Betlémů) in the 14C house at No. 11, with a display of 19C and 20C nativity scenes made from an astonishing variety of materials.

After passing through two gates you will find yourself in the **Burgrave's Courtyard**, beyond which to the west steps descend to a narrow stretch of battlements containing an 80m-deep well built in the 14C by mining experts from Kutná Hora. You should return to the courtyard (where the castle's ticket office is located) to begin a tour of the main part of the castle complex, which is built up on the slope to the north of here, its highest and furthest point being the Great Tower.

There are two tours on offer, but the far better tour II is, rather annoyingly, only available to those who book three days in advance (☎ 274 008 155). The majority of visitors end up taking tour I (45 minutes), which explores the **Imperial Palace**, with displays relating to the Bohemia of Charles IV as well as a diptych by Tommasso da Modena kept in what was once the imperial bedroom. Next you are allowed to peep into the **Marian Tower**, which features on its second floor the **Chapel of St Mary**, its walls covered with dark and faded murals—attributed to Nikolaus Wurmser and painted in the 1370s—representing the Apocalypse and scenes in the history of the castle's creation (including the gift from the King and Dauphin of France of two thorns from the Crown of Thorns), and Charles IV himself, who is portrayed with unflattering realism, stooped before a gilded cross. The emperor's own, private chapel was the adjoining **St Catherine's Chapel**, where he would shut himself up for hours in deep meditation, important documents being passed to him through a hole in the west wall. This tiny chapel can literally be described as jewel-like, for Charles had the walls embellished all over with gilded plaster and a dazzling array of coloured, polished stones, leaving uncovered only some murals of saints, of slightly earlier date.

A covered, wooden gallery connects the Marian Tower with the **Great Tower**, which can only be visited on tour II. Inside is the highlight of the entire castle: the remarkable *****Chapel of the Holy Cross**. Consecrated in 1360, the chapel is divided by a gilded iron screen and has a gilded ceiling set with glass stars and walls encrusted with no less than 2200 semi-precious stones as well as 128 painted wooden panels by one of the greatest Bohemian painters of the 14C, Master Theodoric. The relics were once to be found behind the panels, while the jewels and insignia were kept in a niche behind the altar, over which Tomaso da Modena's diptych was originally placed.

Lidice

Few places in Europe testify so poignantly to Nazi atrocities as Lidice, situated 20km northwest of Prague in a flat coal-mining area. The present village, a characterless grid of the post-war years, lies just to the west of the extensive memorial marking the site of the previous village, a place which the Nazis had hoped to obliterate completely from all maps but which is now, ironically, one of the most visited of Czechoslovakia's war monuments.

- **Getting there** Lidice is a short bus journey from Prague on the line from the Dejvická metro station to Kladno (30 minutes). The bus stop is on Evropská, opposite the *Hotel Diplomat*. Buses to Kladno leave every 30 to 60 minutes, but do not take the direct one (*přímý spoj*), which does not stop at Lidice. You should get off just after the bus turns off the main road.

The former village is situated in a poignantly tranquil spot, spread out over a beautiful green slope fringed with distant pines. At the higher end of the hill are the **Rose Garden of Friendship and Peace** and a large and austere arcaded memorial centred around an eternal flame. The **museum**, situated at the end of the eastern arcade, contains photographs of the murdered villagers and other sad mementoes, such as identification cards pierced by bullet-holes; in the basement, visitors are shown an old documentary film about the tragic events that took place here. Open daily April–Sept 09.00–18.00; Oct–March 09.00–16.00.

A path below the museum leads down the green slope to a haunting sculpture of the 82 Lidice children gassed by the Nazis in 1942. Further on is the mass grave of the murdered men, which adjoins a reconstructed wall of the farm where they were shot. Nearby are the foundations of the village church and school, the latter once bearing the inscription, 'School, My Happiness'.

Massacre at Lidice

The destruction of the village of Lidice on 10 June 1942 was the most notorious of the many Nazi reprisals that followed the assassination of the German Protector of Czechoslovakia, Reinhard Heydrich. Lidice appears to have been chosen for no apparent reason other than that it belonged to a coal-mining region with a strong Socialist tradition. The official Nazi explanation was that the villagers were all partisans who had supported Heydrich's assassins, though it was later to transpire that the Nazis themselves had compromised the place by hiding a large cache of weapons in a mill outside the village. On the evening of 9 June 1942, shortly after placing these weapons, members of the Gestapo and the SS surrounded Lidice, rounding up all the village men into a farmyard and taking the women and young children to the village school. In the course of the night 173 men were executed, the oldest being a man of 84, the youngest being not yet 15; another 26 men were burnt alive in a barn early the following day after returning from night-shift in the mines. The women were all sent to concentration camps, as were most of the children (the majority being eventually gassed in Poland); the more Aryan-looking children were given German names and placed in German homes. The village was razed to the ground, buried under soil and its name obliterated. The only male villager later to return was a murderer who had been in a Prague prison, and went back to Lidice one day hoping to surprise his mother and ask her forgiveness for his crime. The story of his return home has fired the imagination of several Czech writers, most notably Bohumil Hrabal in his novel, *I Served the King of England*: 'The murderer sat down, his hands hanging over his knees like two flippers, then stood up again and stumbled through that moonlit landscape like a drunk. He stopped by what looked like a post in the ground, fell down, and embraced it. It wasn't a post at all, it was what was left of a tree trunk with the stump of a single branch on it, as though it had been used as a gallows. This, said the murderer, used to be our walnut tree, this is where our garden was, and here ... he knelt down and felt around with his hands for the crumbled foundations of the house and the farm buildings.'

The decision to rebuild the village and erect a commemorative memorial to the old Lidice was taken almost immediately after the Soviet 'liberation' of Czechoslovakia in May 1945. An architectural competition was subsequently held, and the foundation stone of the new village was laid in June 1947. In the summer of 1954, the chairman of the British committee 'Lidice Shall Live' proposed to enlarge the memorial with the creation of a 'Rose Garden of Friendship and Peace'; opened in 1955, this was created from rose seedlings sent from all over the world.

Index

For churches, galleries, museums and Prague Castle, see the relevant sub-indexes.

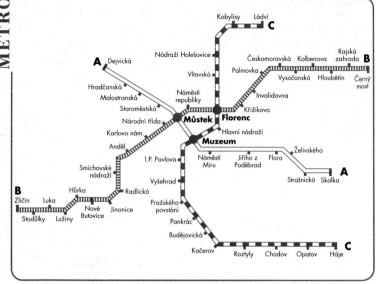